Are You
Being
Served?

Are You Being Served?

New Tools for Measuring Service Delivery

EDITED BY

Samia Amin

Jishnu Das

Markus Goldstein

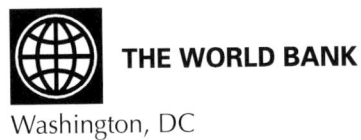

THE WORLD BANK

Washington, DC

© 2008 The International Bank for Reconstruction and Development / The World Bank
1818 H Street NW
Washington DC 20433
Telephone: 202-473-1000
Internet: www.worldbank.org
E-mail: feedback@worldbank.org

ISBN: 978-0-8213-7185-5
eISBN: 978-0-8213-7186-2
DOI: 10.1596/978-0-8213-7185-5

Cover design by: Serif Design Group, Inc.

Library of Congress Cataloging-in-Publication Data

Are you being served? : new tools for measuring service delivery / edited by Samia Amin, Jishnu Das, Markus Goldstein.
     p. ; cm.
 Includes bibliographical references and index.
  ISBN 978-0-8213-7185-5 — ISBN 978-0-8213-7186-2
 1. Medical care—Developing countries—Quality control—Measurement. 2. Health facilities—Developing countries—Quality control—Measurement. 3. School surveys—Developing countries. 4. Quality assurance—Developing countries—Measurement. I. Amin, Samia, 1980- II. Das, Jishnu. III. Goldstein, Markus P., 1970-
  [DNLM: 1. Data Collection—methods. 2. Developing Countries. 3. Health Services Research—methods. 4. Quality Assurance, Health Care—economics. 5. Quality Assurance, Health Care—methods. WA 950 A678 2007]
  RA399.D44A74 2007
  362.1—dc22
                    2007019898

Contents

Boxes

Figures

Tables

Foreword

Experience shows that increasing government spending on public services alone is not sufficient to raise standards of living and improve access to health, education, and other public services. Although significant strides have been made in expanding access to education and health services in the past decade, the quality of those services remains a serious concern. Strengthening accountability and supporting governance reforms in service delivery are thus major priorities for the World Bank and its development partners.

A wide array of instruments has been developed in an effort to measure the performance and quality of public services. However, our knowledge of how to use and customize those new tools to country circumstances and of the limited available data is still at a basic level. This knowledge poses a key challenge because many of the policy options for reducing poverty and achieving the Millennium Development Goals rely on improving the supply and quality of public services.

This volume provides an overview of a range of tools for measuring service delivery and offers valuable lessons on the opportunities and constraints practitioners face in measuring performance. The authors investigate country cases using data from a range of sources in a variety of contexts. Their experiences yield important insights on how to avoid pitfalls, what practices to improve, and how to learn the most from the data at hand. Taken together, those lessons represent an important step in strengthening accountability and governance so as to enhance service delivery. They will, we hope, lead to an important advance in our thinking.

Danny Leipziger
Vice President and Head of Network
Poverty Reduction and Economic
    Management
The World Bank

Joy Phumaphi
Vice President and Head of Network
Human Development
The World Bank

Acknowledgments

This book has benefited from the comments and guidance of Louise Cord and Elizabeth King. Aline Coudouel provided critical encouragement and helped with the initial conceptualization. Jessica Todd provided valuable comments, in addition to serving as the rapporteur for the workshop at which the chapters were discussed. The peer reviewers for the manuscript were Kenneth Leonard and Maureen Lewis. We thank them for their insightful and constructive comments. Valuable organizational, logistical, and proofreading support was provided by Sumeet Bhatti, Angeli Kirk, and Cécile Wodon. We would like to thank Robert Zimmermann for his excellent work in editing these chapters, and Stephen McGroarty, Nora Ridolfi, and Dina Towbin for their diligence and patience in producing this volume.

Are You Being Served? draws on a work program led by Markus Goldstein and financed through generous grants from the Trust Fund for Environmentally and Socially Sustainable Development, supported by Finland and Norway and the Bank-Netherlands Partnership Program.

About the Editors and Authors

Samia Amin has been working on impact evaluation and monitoring systems as a junior professional associate with the Poverty Reduction Group at the World Bank since 2006. She received a bachelor's degree in political science and French from Middlebury College, Middlebury, Vermont, and a master's degree in public policy from the John F. Kennedy School of Government, Harvard University, Cambridge, Massachusetts. She previously worked as a junior fellow at the Carnegie Endowment for International Peace, Washington, D.C., where she researched issues related to nation building and nuclear nonproliferation. Her primary interest lies in studying education policies in developing countries as a means of spurring human development.

Kathleen Beegle, senior economist with the Development Research Group, the World Bank, is currently investigating the socioeconomic and gender dimensions of HIV/AIDS in Sub-Saharan Africa. Among her studies are an analysis of the impact of gender income inequality on the spread of HIV/AIDS in Kenya and an examination of household coping strategies in Tanzania, which was based on a 13-year longitudinal survey. Other work focuses on the causes and consequences of child labor and on household dependency on food aid in Malawi. She is active on the Bank's Living Standards Measurement Study team, where she applies her expertise in the design and implementation of household surveys and the use of such surveys in poverty and policy analysis. She earned her PhD in economics at Michigan State University, East Lansing, Michigan, in 1997.

Jere Behrman received his PhD from the Massachusetts Institute of Technology, Cambridge, Massachusetts, in 1966. He is the William R. Kenan, Jr. Professor (and former chair) of Economics and a research associate (and former director) of the Population Studies Center at the University of Pennsylvania, Philadelphia, where he has been on the faculty since 1965. His research interests are empirical microeconomics, economic development, labor economics, human resources, economic demography, household behavior, and the determinants and impacts of nutrition through the use of integrated modeling-estimation approaches. He has published more than 300 professional articles and 32 books and monographs on those topics. He has been the principal or coprincipal investigator on more than 50 research projects.

Olena Bekh is an education specialist at the World Bank, which she joined following a successful professional career in higher education and research in Ukraine and elsewhere. She defended her candidate of science dissertation at Taras Shevchenko National University of Kyiv (Ukraine). Since 1989, she has been teaching and conducting research at Taras Shevchenko National University of Kyiv, the University of London, the University of North London, and Columbia University in New York City. Since 1998, she has been working in international development. She joined the Bank in 2002 and has been working in the Human Development Sector in the Ukraine country office, covering a broad spectrum of issues related to the development of human capital and social sector reform in Ukraine, including education, health among youth, and governance.

Nazmul Chaudhury is senior economist with the World Bank's South Asia Region. He is engaged in operational work and research to improve school quality, integrate impact evaluations into Bank operations, and examine conditional cash transfer programs that target excluded groups. He is also involved in research on the impact of sanitation on child health and the relationship between early childhood morbidity and cognitive development. He was previously with the Development Research Group at the Bank, where he was active in research on governance and service delivery. He was on the team for *World Development Report 2004: Making Services Work for Poor People*. A Bangladeshi national, he has a bachelor of science degree in electrical engineering, a PhD in economics, and a PhD in environmental policy.

Jishnu Das is senior economist with the Human Development and Public Services Team, Development Research Group, the World Bank, and a visiting scholar at the Center for Policy Research, New Delhi. He received his PhD in economics from Harvard University, Cambridge, Massachusetts, in 2001. Since joining the Bank, he has worked on issues related to the delivery of basic services, particularly health and education. His research focuses on the interactions between households and private and public service providers. For the past two years, he has also been working on natural disasters in the context of the earthquake that hit northern India and Pakistan in October 2005. He cofounded the Web site http://www.risepak.com/ to help coordinate relief in the aftermath of the quake.

Deon Filmer is senior economist with the Human Development and Public Services Team, Development Research Group, the World Bank. He received his PhD in economics from Brown University, Providence, Rhode Island, in 1995, after which he joined the research group at the Bank. He was a core team member of the *World Development Report 2004: Making Services Work for Poor People*. His research focuses on inequalities in education and health outcomes, education and health service delivery, and the impact evaluation of interventions and programs.

Elizabeth Frankenberg is a demographer and sociologist whose research focuses on assessing the role in adult and child health outcomes of individual, family, and community characteristics, particularly health service availability and quality. She is an associate professor of public policy studies at Duke University, Durham, North Carolina.

Jed Friedman is an economist with the Development Research Group, the World Bank. His research interests include the measurement of poverty dynamics and the interactions between poverty and health. He is currently involved in assessing the socioeconomic impact of the 2004 Indian Ocean tsunami, as well as the efficacy of the related reconstruction and aid.

Emanuela Galasso is an economist in the Poverty Group of the Development Research Group, the World Bank. She joined the Bank as a Young Economist in 2000. Her recent research has focused on assessing the effectiveness of large-scale social programs, with specific emphasis on distributional impacts. Her ongoing work centers on the use of multiyear longitudinal surveys to measure the medium-term and dynamic effects of a community-based nutrition intervention in Madagascar and an antipoverty program in Chile. She completed her master's degree and PhD in economics at Boston College, Chestnut Hill, Massachusetts, in 2000.

Markus Goldstein is a senior economist with the Poverty Reduction Group, the World Bank, where he works on poverty analysis, monitoring, and impact evaluation. His research interests include poverty measurement and development economics. His recent research involves work on HIV/AIDS, land tenure, poverty over time, risk, and intrahousehold allocation. He is the author or coauthor of a number of scholarly articles and books, including the recent book, *Beyond the Numbers: Understanding the Institutions for Monitoring Poverty Reduction Strategies*, as well as a chapter on African poverty in the book edited by Todd Moss, *African Development: Making Sense of the Issues and Actors*. He has taught at the London School of Economics; the University of Ghana, Legon; and Georgetown University, Washington, D.C.

Elizabeth King is research manager for public services at the Development Research Group, the World Bank. She was previously lead economist at the Human Development Unit in the Bank's East Asia and Pacific Region. Her main research interests have been the determinants of investment in human capital, the links among human capital, poverty, and economic development, and the impact of education reforms, such as decentralization, in developing countries. She has also examined the significance of gender differences for the development process. She has been a member of two *World Development Report* teams. She earned her PhD in economics at Yale University, New Haven, Connecticut, and has taught at the University of the Philippines; Tulane University, New Orleans; and the University of California, Los Angeles.

Peter Lanjouw, a Dutch national, is a lead economist in the Development Economics Research Group, the World Bank, and Fellow of the Tinbergen Institute, Amsterdam. He completed his PhD in economics at the London School of Economics in 1992. From September 1998 until May 2000, he was professor of economics at the Free University of Amsterdam. He has also taught at the University of Namur, Namur, Belgium, and the Foundation for the Advanced Study of International Development,

Tokyo. His research focuses on various aspects of poverty and inequality measurement, as well as on rural development issues.

Kenneth Leonard received a PhD in economics from the University of California, Berkeley, in 1997. He is assistant professor in the Department of Agricultural and Resource Economics and faculty associate at the Maryland Population Research Center, University of Maryland, College Park, Maryland. His early work focused on the role of traditional healers, particularly the related lessons for modern health care delivery. Those lessons point to the nongovernmental sector as a potentially important path for service delivery. His current research centers on the delivery of key public services, especially curative health services, in rural areas in developing countries, especially the way information about the quality of care is shared in rural communities and how households improve outcomes by choosing doctors according to illness.

Tomas Lievens is a health economist with experience in research and policy settings. His areas of interest include quantitative and qualitative analysis and policy advice in health financing, health labor markets, and health insurance. Much of his work has focused on ways to introduce financing mechanisms to assist the poor in gaining access to health services. His interest in health labor markets centers on the determinants of health worker career and performance choices. He was advisor to the minister for development cooperation of Belgium. He is presently working at the International Labour Organization and as a consultant at Oxford Policy Management, Oxford.

Magnus Lindelow is an economist in the Human Development Sector Unit, East Asia and Pacific Region, the World Bank. Before joining the Bank, he worked as an economist in the Ministry of Planning and Finance, Mozambique, and as a consultant on public expenditure and health sector issues in developing countries. He has published on a wide range of issues, including distributional analysis in the health sector, health risks and health insurance, service delivery performance, survey methodologies, human resource issues in the health sector, corruption and governance, and public expenditure analysis. He is involved in the design and management of health projects in China and is a contributing author for an ongoing World

Bank study on China's rural health sector. He holds a PhD in economics from Oxford University.

Mattias Lundberg is senior economist with the Human Development Network, the World Bank. He was one of the principal authors of the *World Development Report 2007: Development and the Next Generation*. Previously, he worked with the Development Research Group at the Bank. His research includes the impact of HIV/AIDS and other shocks on households, the delivery of primary health care and public service provision to the poor, impact evaluation and the measurement of efficiency in public services, and the relationship among trade, economic growth, and income distribution. Before coming to the Bank, he worked at the International Food Policy Research Institute, Washington, D.C., the Asian Development Bank, and private consulting companies.

Edmundo Murrugarra is senior economist with the Poverty Reduction and Development Effectiveness Group and member of the Gender Board, the World Bank. His areas of interest are human development in health and education, labor economics, and poverty. He currently leads a cross-sectoral team involved in streamlining migration issues in analytical and operational products. He previously worked on the links between poverty, health status, and health care utilization; social assistance programs; and vulnerability and poverty. He has taught at the Pontificia Universidad Católica del Perú and the Central Reserve Bank of Peru, Lima. He earned a bachelor's degree in economics from the Pontificia Universidad Católica del Perú and a master's degree and PhD in economics from the University of California, Los Angeles.

Berk Özler has been an economist at the Development Research Group, the World Bank, since 2001. He has worked on poverty and inequality measurement and focused on the possible effects of income inequality on outcomes such as crime, targeting, elite capture, and, most recently, health. His current projects include a randomized evaluation of a Social Funds Project in Tanzania and a study on the relationship between marital transitions and HIV/AIDS among adolescents and young people in Malawi. He is also designing a cash transfer experiment in Malawi to assess the impact of income and schooling on the risk of HIV among young women. He is to undertake residence at the School of International Relations and

Pacific Studies at the University of California, San Diego, in La Jolla, California, to work on those projects.

Volodymir Paniotto, doctor of sciences, is director of the Kiev International Institute of Sociology, and professor at the National University of Kyiv-Mohyla Academy. He is the vice president of the Ukrainian Marketing Association. He is also a member of the American Sociological Association; ESOMAR, the European Society for Opinion and Marketing Research; the World Association for Public Opinion Research; and the American Association for Public Opinion Research. He is a member of the editorial boards of several Russian and Ukrainian journals. He is the author of 10 books and more than 150 articles. His principal work is on research methodologies, including marketing and survey methods, data validity and reliability, mathematical sociology, poverty assessment, and interethnic relations.

Tatyana Petrenko has a master's degree in sociology. She is a senior manager at the Kiev International Institute of Sociology, where she specializes in the management of complex socioeconomic studies. Among major projects that she has led are the Ukrainian Study of Men Who Have Sex with Men, which is directed at estimating the size of HIV-risk groups in Ukraine, and the Transition from Education to Work in Ukraine, which is a youth study. She also manages research at the Open Bank of Social Data at the Kiev International Institute of Sociology.

Fadia Saadah holds a PhD in public health and is currently the sector manager for health, nutrition, and population in the East Asia and Pacific Region at the World Bank. She has extensive programmatic and research experience in health and development issues in Indonesia.

Volodymir Sarioglo was born in Moldova, is a Bulgarian national, and is a citizen of Ukraine. He attended the National Technical University Kyiv Polytechnic Institute from 1978 to 1984 and the Kyiv National University of Economics from 1999 to 2001. He has a PhD in economics sciences, with a specialty in statistics. He is currently senior scientist at the Institute for Demography and Social Research of the National Academy of Sciences of Ukraine, where he is head of the Department of Social-Demographic Statistics.

Kinnon Scott is senior economist in the Poverty Group of the Development Economics Research Group, the World Bank. She has a master's degree in public and international affairs, a master's degree in urban and regional planning, and a PhD from the Graduate School of Public and International Affairs at the University of Pittsburgh. Her research projects center on the nexus of disability and poverty in developing countries and the impact of public spending on poverty reduction over time. She also manages the World Bank's Living Standards Measurement Study, an ongoing research initiative generating policy-relevant, household-level data on developing countries. She manages two annual training courses within the World Bank on household surveys and data for social policy, and she continues to design and teach modules on social policy analysis.

Pieter Serneels is an economist at the World Bank. He has been working extensively on issues related to labor, poverty, and service delivery in low-income countries. He has held posts at the University of Oxford, the University of Copenhagen, and the International Labour Organization and has given advice to governments in developing countries. He holds a master of science degree in economics from the University of Warwick, Coventry, United Kingdom, and a PhD in economics from the University of Oxford.

Bondan Sikoki has studied demography and sociology and has extensive experience in survey data collection in Indonesia. Bondan Sikoki is the director of SurveyMETER, a nongovernmental organization located in Yogyakarta, Indonesia, that specializes in the collection and analysis of household survey data in Indonesia.

Cecep Sumantri has a master's degree in public health. He specializes in health issues, particularly the development of protocols and the fielding of physical assessments of health status in household surveys. He is a senior research associate at SurveyMETER, Yogyakarta, Indonesia.

Wayan Suriastini has a master's degree in public policy and is completing a PhD in population studies. She is the project leader of BEST, a longitudinal survey of households on Bali before and after the terrorist bombing of 2002. She is a senior research associate at SurveyMETER, Yogyakarta, Indonesia.

Duncan Thomas, an economist, works on models of household behavior that focus on investments in health and human capital in low-income settings and on household and individual responses to economic crises. He is professor of economics at Duke University, Durham, North Carolina.

Adam Wagstaff is lead economist (health) on the Human Development and Public Services Team, Development Research Group, and the Human Development Unit within the East Asia and Pacific Region, the World Bank. He holds a DPhil in economics from the University of York, United Kingdom. He was previously professor of economics at the University of Sussex, Brighton, United Kingdom. He has been an associate editor of the *Journal of Health Economics* since 1989. He has published extensively on the valuation of health, the demand for and production of health, efficiency measurement, and illicit drugs. His work has involved conceptual and empirical studies of equity, poverty, and health. His health research includes work on risks and shocks and the targeting and impacts of insurance and safety net programs.

Waly Wane holds a PhD in economics from the University of Toulouse, Toulouse, France. He joined the World Bank in August 1999 and is an economist on the Public Services Team, Development Research Group, the World Bank. His research interests include analysis of the impact of complex organizational incentive structures on the determination of outcomes, which he has applied to corruption, foreign aid, service delivery, and other topics. He has been involved in many Public Expenditure Tracking Surveys, especially in Sub-Saharan Africa, and is currently leading an effort to harmonize such surveys.

Abbreviations

DHS	Demographic and Health Surveys (program)
ECD	early childhood development
EMIS	education management information system
FISE	Fondo Inversión Social de Emergencia (Social Investment Fund, Ecuador)
IEA	International Association for the Evaluation of Educational Achievement
IFLS	Indonesia Family Life Survey
IMCI	integrated management of childhood illness (strategy)
GPS	global positioning system
ITT	intent-to-treat (effect)
LSMS	Living Standards Measurement Study (surveys)
MICS	Multiple Indicator Cluster Survey
MIS	management information system
MoH	Ministry of Health
NGO	nongovernmental organization
PETS	Public Expenditure Tracking Survey
PNFP	private not-for-profit (facility)
QSDS	Quantitative Service Delivery Survey
SAR	service availability roster
STAR	Study of the Tsunami Aftermath and Recovery
TIMSS	Trends in International Mathematics and Science Study
TOT	treatment-of-the-treated (effect)

All dollar amounts (US$) are U.S. dollars unless otherwise indicated.

1

Introduction

Why Measure Service Delivery?

Markus Goldstein

"The beginning of knowledge is the discovery of something we do not understand."

Frank Herbert

One of the cornerstones in building policies to improve welfare is the services that governments offer to citizens. In most countries, governments provide some form of basic education and health services. Governments also supply a variety of other services ranging from essential public goods such as police services to administrative services such as drivers' licenses. Taken as a whole, those services are critical for economic growth and the reduction of poverty.

Although we have an array of tools and techniques to measure ultimate welfare outcomes, our tools for measuring the services aimed at improving these outcomes are less well developed. This book explores some of those tools, their uses, and the way they are implemented in practice. Through those lessons, we may expand our understanding of welfare outcomes and

The author wishes to thank Samia Amin, Louise Cord, Elizabeth King, Kenneth Leonard, and Maureen Lewis for valuable comments and Deon Filmer and Shanta Devarajan for useful conversations.

the processes of accountability, governance, and service delivery that help produce these outcomes.

There is a temptation to view the relationships between welfare outcomes and these processes simplistically: if more money is spent on basic services, welfare outcomes will improve. However, this view flies in the face of the empirical fact that there is a weak correlation between spending and outcomes. See, for example, figure 1.1, which is taken from *World Development Report 2004* (World Bank 2003). The charts in figure 1.1 show the relationship between spending and selected health and education outcomes across a large number of countries. Because national wealth might affect those welfare indicators through mechanisms other than government spending, the charts use a measure of expenditure that captures the difference between actual spending in a country and what might be expected, on average, for a country at the same level of gross domestic product. We may see that, even if we account for national income, there is a weak association between spending and outcomes.

Unfortunately, this association robs us of the easy solution of simply spending more money to improve welfare. Instead, we need to understand the process by which funds are transformed into outcomes. Many factors intervene between the input of spending and the outcome of individual welfare, including the functioning and failure of markets, the composition of spending (for example, for tertiary versus primary education or health), corruption, and the effectiveness of service delivery. There is a significant and growing literature showing that understanding some of those intervening factors would help us work out a great deal about how service delivery institutions affect outcomes. For instance, Lewis (2006) provides cross-country evidence on the correlation between governance and health outcomes, while Wane (chapter 8 in this volume) shows that, once leakages are accounted for, there is, indeed, a positive relationship between central government spending and health outcomes in Chad. Broader discussions, such as Filmer, Hammer, and Pritchett (2000) and *World Development Report 2004*, look at the multiple ways in which those intervening factors may shape the relationship between inputs and welfare outcomes.

This volume focuses on one key aspect of the process of transforming inputs into outcomes: the process of service delivery. The key question here is: are citizens being served? Asking this question in the context of the benchmarking of public services raises a host of other questions. Are we

FIGURE 1.1   Association between Outcomes and
Public Spending

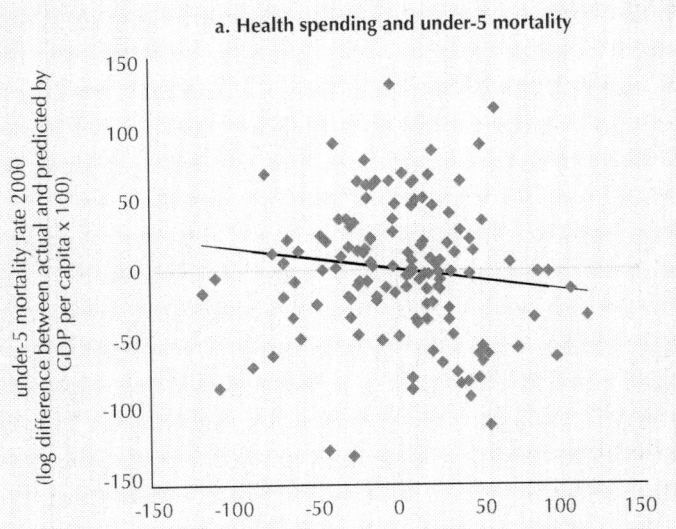

a. Health spending and under-5 mortality

under-5 mortality rate 2000
(log difference between actual and predicted by
GDP per capita x 100)

per capita public spending: health 1990s average
(log difference between actual and predicted by GDP per capita X 100)

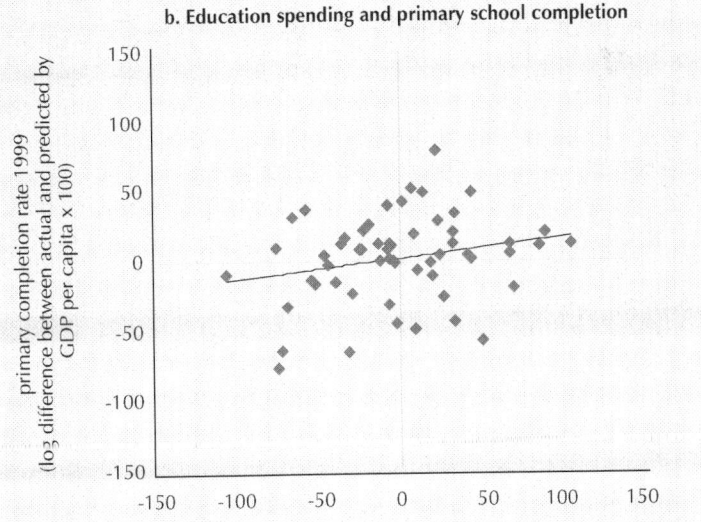

b. Education spending and primary school completion

primary completion rate 1999
(log difference between actual and predicted by
GDP per capita x 100)

per child public spending: education 1990s average
(log difference between actual and predicted by GDP per capita X 100)

Source: World Bank 2003.

talking about quality, efficiency, or another dimension? Should we gather data from clients, providers, surveys, or administrative records? For what purposes should such data be used?

This book offers a starting point for answering these questions. Building on the authors' experiences in a wide range of settings, the chapters provide not only an overview of service delivery measurement tools and what they may be used for, but also lessons about what works and what does not work in practice. Those discussions reveal a process that is rarely easy, but one that may provide powerful inputs for making effective policy.

The general state of knowledge is less developed on measuring service delivery than on household surveys. For example, for household surveys, someone interested in designing a survey may refer to the volumes edited by Grosh and Glewwe (2000), who offer a chapter-by-chapter discussion of potential modules and methodological issues. No such reference exists for measuring service delivery; it may even be argued that not enough consistent and comprehensive attempts have been made to warrant a definitive guide. One might also argue that the tools for measuring service delivery—ranging from the use of routine administrative data to the presentation of case studies to doctors for comment to gauge the ability of the doctors—are so diverse that analyzing them all in one definitive volume would be impossible.

Instead, we seek in this volume to bring together a set of lessons arising from the application of some of the various tools, and we have asked people who have engaged with these tools to report on their experiences, on what has worked well and what has not, and on what the data may be used for. In terms of overall success, the experience of the authors is mixed; every author has indicated the difficulty of collecting those types of data. Indeed, during the authors workshop held as part of the preparations for this volume, one author regaled us with tales of chasing peanut vendors outside a ministry to track down missing records because the records were being recycled as food wrappers. However, there remains a selection bias in this volume: we do not observe complete failures. Given our goal of learning about these tools and demonstrating their application, we have had to exclude cases where attempts to measure service delivery have failed.

Readers will notice that this volume focuses mostly on health and education. These areas are where these tools are most developed, but they are not the only areas where these tools may be applied. Surveys such as the Indonesia Family Life Survey (discussed in chapter 15 by Beegle), the Living Standards Measurement Study (chapter 16 by Scott), and the

Indonesia Governance and Decentralization Survey all measure different areas where the state provides services to citizens. Administrative data may also represent a powerful tool for understanding projects that do not revolve around health or education, as shown in chapter 4 by Lanjouw and Özler. Thus, as you read through chapters that focus on one sector, it is important to keep in mind that many of the tools may be fruitfully applied to other areas of service delivery.

The final section of this chapter provides a detailed road map to this book, but, now, it is worth spending a bit more time on the conceptual overview of the volume. A better understanding of service delivery will enable policy makers to increase the efficiency and effectiveness with which resources are translated into welfare outcomes. There are four main ways in which the measurement of service delivery may be used to achieve this. First, service delivery information may be used to increase accountability by helping to strengthen the ties through which information and sanctions flow between providers, clients, and the government units that fund providers. Second, service delivery data may be used to deepen our understanding of poverty and inequality and to target a policy response. This information will enable the more effective formulation of policy as the conditions the poor face become more well understood, and it will enable resources to be directed more successfully to the poor. Third, the measurement of service delivery is critical to rigorous impact evaluation. Through careful evaluation aimed at answering key questions of design and the resulting effects, existing programs may be adjusted to boost their effect. Finally, service delivery data may be used for policy-relevant research to answer a range of questions about the way providers and clients interact and about the way facilities function. Let us now examine the potential uses of service delivery in greater depth.

Making Use of Service Delivery Data

Accountability

Measures of service delivery represent a vehicle for holding service providers to account for the quality and quantity of the services they provide. This accountability is critical in any well-functioning system, but it is particularly important if the underlying system is in flux because of sectorwide policy changes or large national governance changes such as decentralization. One useful distinction in capturing and using these data is to think of the paths of accountability from the provider to the client and also from the supervising

FIGURE 1.2 Key Relationships of Power

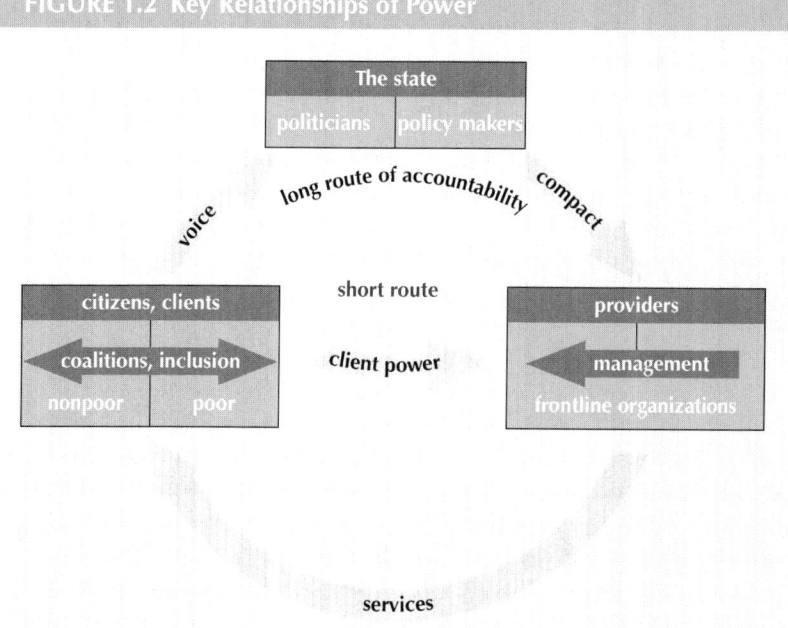

Source: World Bank 2003.

agency (the government body) to the provider. Figure 1.2, taken from *World Development Report 2004,* provides a framework for thinking about these two paths.

In terms of measurement tools for service provider accountability, we can think of the relationship between providers and citizens as being measured in terms of satisfaction (as well as the realized demand for services), while monitoring offers information for the state-provider relationship.

Satisfaction

The measurement of service delivery can represent a powerful mechanism for obtaining feedback from client to providers. Although a complaint box at a local facility is a good initial step, the tools examined in this volume represent a more organized and balanced way to obtain comprehensive feedback for providers. The satisfaction of users with the services they are relying on may be measured through tools such as citizen report cards (see chapter 3 by Amin and Chaudhury and chapter 7 by Lindelow and

Wagstaff), questions in household surveys, and exit polls (see chapter 14 by Lundberg). The satisfaction measures might include opinions on, for example, the length of the waits to see a doctor, the teacher's performance, and the politeness of nurses. This information may be presented directly to facility staff or be used by government supervisors to give voice to clients about their concerns. This type of user feedback, particularly if it is repeated and associated with appropriate incentives by government agencies responsible for oversight, may become a powerful path of accountability from providers to clients. It is important to keep in mind, however, that user satisfaction may not, in fact, be correlated with more objective measures of quality. For example, in chapter 14, Lundberg finds that measures such as whether patients were given physical examinations, whether their pulse was taken, or whether stethoscopes were used are not significantly correlated with patient satisfaction. In addition, as Amin and Chaudhury note, measures of satisfaction also show a built-in bias created by expectations, which may be based not only on the past performance of a facility, but promises made by politicians, reports in news media, and other contextual factors.

Monitoring

When the state is seeking to measure the performance of service providers, the first best option is administrative data. There are a few important attributes that these data should possess to be effective. First, they need to be collected routinely to ensure timely feedback for decision making. Second, they should be of sufficient quality to provide useful information. Third, they should be of adequate breadth to capture key activities, but also sufficiently narrow so as to avoid an unnecessary burden on frontline service providers. Finally, once these other conditions have been met, the effectiveness of the data depends on their actual use in monitoring and helping improve the performance of service providers. Chapter 5 by Galasso, chapter 6 by Behrman and King, and chapter 4 by Lanjouw and Özler in this volume show how administrative data may be used to draw inferences about program performance. Indeed, high-quality administrative data represent a key link between monitoring and impact evaluation (discussed next) because they supply information on important aspects of program implementation such as costs and service utilization rates. These data serve important monitoring functions, but they may also be used to enhance the design and results of a more thorough evaluation.

In a number of contexts, however, administrative data systems are too weak to provide effective monitoring. The primary goal should be to improve these systems, and, in the meantime, facility surveys (which are a much more expensive way of collecting data) may suffice. Indeed, using facility surveys as a replacement for administrative data in a regular program of monitoring would be akin to providing four-wheel drive vehicles for urban driving rather than fixing the roads.

It is important to bear in mind that facility surveys may be used to address other monitoring tasks and thus are a significant complement to high-quality administrative data. One use of facility surveys involves collecting data in a swath that is much broader than is feasible through regular monitoring (see the discussion in Lindelow and Wagstaff, for example) and at a level of detail that would overwhelm routine reporting. Another complementary use of facility surveys might involve verifying administrative data in cases in which service providers have a strong incentive to misreport (see the discussion of the measurement of absenteeism in Amin and Chaudhury, for instance). A final example is offered in chapter 12 by Serneels, Lindelow, and Lievens, who show how qualitative facility-level work may help us understand the incentives, motivations, and behavior that lie behind the data captured by regular monitoring systems or quantitative facility surveys.

As noted in several of the chapters in this volume, administrative data almost always only supply information on those people actually using a given service. There are a number of situations in which an analyst would also need data on those people who are not using a service (or at least not the service provided by the government). For instance, such data would be useful if the government were trying to understand why service utilization at a given clinic or school is low: is the underlying issue the awareness among potential users about the existence of a service at a given facility, or is the underlying issue the quality of the service? In those cases, administrative data, combined with a household survey, might provide information on the differences between users and nonusers. Furthermore, to compare a service at a government facility with other services, either administrative data or survey data on private facilities are needed. Ultimately, this type of analysis would lead to a thorough market analysis that may be beyond the purview of most routine monitoring systems, and we therefore discuss it in the section on research uses below.

Monitoring does not take place only at the level of facilities and of interactions with clients. A key feature of an effective monitoring system is the ability to keep track of goods and other resources as they travel through the system to the end users. This process may be achieved in part through administrative data, but periodic surveys and audits are a critical complement. One example of these types of tools is Public Expenditure Tracking Surveys, which are discussed in depth in the chapters by Filmer (9), Lindelow (7), and Wane (8). Those surveys provide in-depth information on the flows and losses of resources through a system. However, as Lindelow and Wane both point out, a serious attempt to carry out a Public Expenditure Tracking Survey inevitably raises questions about what should be classified as embezzlement or fraud and what should be classified as inefficiency and what should be classified as legitimate reallocations of resources. When conducted in an atmosphere of openness to dialogue, those surveys may help shape not only regular monitoring systems but also the thinking about allocation rules in government.

Understanding Poverty and Inequality and Targeting the Policy Response

Accurate measurements of service delivery are important tools in understanding poverty and inequality and in properly targeting the policy response to these problems. Whether we adopt a multidimensional notion of poverty and are concerned with outcomes such as health and education as ends in their own right, or rely on a narrower definition and believe that health and education are instrumental to improving income, these tools will help us fathom the processes through which health and education are or are not produced. Although the accountability mechanisms discussed above represent a critical means of ensuring that the voices of the poor are heard, they may also be put to diagnostic and analytic use in improving policy. This approach would include measuring service delivery with a particular emphasis on the levels and quality of the services available to the poor and then using this information to develop a targeted policy response.

Understanding Poverty and the Service Environment of the Poor

At a fundamental level, the Living Standards Measurement Study surveys, given their focus on the correlates and determinants of poverty, are ideally placed to help us understand poverty. However, as Scott notes in chapter 16, the surveys were not originally designed to provide information on service access or on the use and (especially) the quality of services for the poor and others. This approach has changed somewhat over time, and Scott counts 14 or so cases where a Living Standards Measurement Study survey has included a facility component. The prevailing method of the study to assess services (similar to the Indonesia Family Life Survey discussed by Beegle in chapter 15) is to sample those facilities most likely to be used by households, rather than starting from a national sample frame of, for example, all possible facilities. Given that this approach takes the household as the starting point for sampling, but also that it is explicitly designed to link household and facility data, it represents a powerful means for examining the relationship between poverty and service provision.

Unlike the Living Standards Measurement Study and the Indonesia Family Life Survey wherein facility and household data are integrated by design, the school survey in Ukraine examined by Bekh and others in chapter 11 shows us a case where this design may be achieved (with some difficulty) by adding a facility survey that, after the fact, may be linked with a living standards survey. In this case, one of the uses of the survey was to look at the effects of institutional change and the contribution of the quality of education to equality and household well-being.

Targeting the Policy Response

Linked household and facility surveys such as the Living Standards Measurement Study (LSMS) and the Indonesia Family Life Survey provide a powerful set of tools to target a policy response by providing a straightforward method to correlate poverty and service delivery. However, in the development of a policy response that focuses on service delivery, care must be taken to separate out those measures of quality that reflect the underlying poverty (and, hence, that call for a broader development strategy) and those that are due to deficiencies in service delivery. This distinction is clearly made in chapter 13 by Das and Leonard, who use the example of the measurement of service delivery quality in health through the measurement of the number of doctors who follow a given protocol. They argue that the results may be driven by the education level of the patients (for example, because the patients encourage the doctors or make their jobs easier) rather than some underlying quality of the physicians. For one to measure dimensions of quality that directly capture the quality of the underlying service providers, it is necessary to test the skills of doctors directly through a tool such as vignettes. Das and Leonard show us that, in the vignette studies they review, the poor are being served by doctors of lower quality and that an appropriate policy response would, therefore, involve finding a way to bring more competent doctors to poor districts.

Sometimes, however, the basic physical condition of a facility or the presence of a service provider may be the primary concern. One area where rapidly implemented facility surveys, combined with household data, may be of use in developing a targeted response is in the planning and execution of a reconstruction program following a natural disaster. In chapter 10 by Frankenberg and others, we can see how the surveys used in the Study of the Tsunami Aftermath and Recovery serve this purpose in the case of rebuilding after the recent tsunami in Indonesia. Clearly, the surveys (here combined with geographical information such as satellite pictures) provide evidence on facilities that have been wiped out and providers who have been killed. However, as the authors caution, a well-targeted response to the disaster does not simply consist of rebuilding and repairing previously existing facilities. Indeed, the household and facility surveys are useful in shedding light on population shifts and the resulting changes in the demand for services within the places affected by the tsunami. The surveys thus also provide insights into effects beyond the physically damaged zones. For example, some of the affected populations move to other areas, where they create additional demand for services, and this needs to be taken into account in targeting reconstruction aid.

Evaluation, Especially Impact Evaluation

Measurements of service delivery are critical in any program evaluation where the process or output of facilities is a subject of examination. However, when we are trying to establish a clear link between inputs and impacts, the best option, if feasible, is to use the tools of impact evaluation. Impact evaluation tackles one of the fundamental problems of evaluation: what would have happened to the beneficiaries of a program or a policy in the absence of the program? Because individuals either receive or do not receive a program, impact evaluation techniques seek to construct a comparison group or counterfactual that proxies for the outcome among the beneficiaries or treatment group in the absence of the intervention. This comparison group is chosen according to criteria that cause the characteristics of the group (both those characteristics that are observed by the evaluator and those that are not) to be as similar as possible to the characteristics of the group receiving the intervention. By using appropriate methods of statistical analysis to compare the two groups at a point at which the program is expected to have already had some effects, we are able to provide a rigorous link between program inputs and impacts.[1] This type of evidence provides a critical input into an informed policy debate. Indeed, returning to figure 1.2, we may think of this type of evidence as strengthening citizen–government links (by demonstrating the validity of a program) and government–provider links (by demonstrating which interventions have the greatest effect).

There are three main ways in which the measurement of service delivery may be used in impact evaluation. The first way is the most straightforward: we may use administrative data to estimate whether or not there are any program effects or any effects related to an additional time of exposure to a program. The second way looks at the effect of management on service delivery. The third way examines how the effect of interventions varies in the context of providers of different quality. If we are to make the distinction between these latter avenues of analysis clear, let us think of two types of interventions we might wish to evaluate. In the first case, the management of a facility is the subject of the intervention. For example, such an intervention might include changes in the incentives workers face, how feedback is provided, which transactions are monitored, and a host of other options. In this instance, the measurement of service delivery will provide a core set of data for the evaluation. In the second case, we may think of an intervention that provides added inputs, such as textbooks or medicines, or new inputs altogether. In this case, we may use service delivery data to understand how variations in the quality of the provider (or in the heterogeneity of treatment) affect the impacts we are examining. Let us now analyze those three ways of measurement in greater depth.

Evaluating Marginal (or Any) Program Impacts

In the simplest case of impact evaluation, we want to know whether a program has had any effect on individual welfare outcomes. To do this, we are likely to need data on individuals and household survey data or administrative data that cover both the treatment group and comparison group. Although those would be the most useful, they are not service delivery measurement tools. However, in some instances, we may use service delivery data as a proximate indicator of program impacts. For example, given a vaccine of proven effectiveness in clinic trials, the evaluation may need to rely instead on measurements of the number of children who are properly vaccinated in both the treatment and control groups. Although this examination does not reveal the welfare impact we are really concerned about (child mortality), it produces a quick assessment of whether the program is more effectively providing a treatment that we know contributes to a reduction in child mortality. For this assessment to be a viable option, however, it is essential that the service delivery data we use include information on both the treated group and the comparison group.

Chapter 5 by Galasso highlights another way we may apply service delivery data to measure program impacts. Galasso discusses the measurement of the effect of additional exposure to a program (the marginal effect of increased duration). She examines an intervention that a pilot test has shown to be effective. As the evaluation is brought to scale, her goal is to determine the effectiveness of the intervention in different socioeconomic settings. In this case, the program collected data on the phasing in of the project and implementation over time and also on recipient outcomes (such as malnutrition rates). Combining this information with data on local characteristics allows for estimates of the impact of additional exposure to the program, as well as insights into which communities would benefit most from the intervention.

Evaluating a Change in Management

If the aim is to evaluate the effect of a change in management, two levels of effect are likely to be of interest. First, the ultimate goal of a change in public service management is to improve the welfare of clients; so, the evaluation will likely include measurements of client outcomes (for example, literacy rates or the incidence of vaccine preventable disease) through household surveys or administrative data, as discussed above. However, those welfare effects may take a fair amount of time to become manifest; meanwhile, it may be useful to collect proximate indicators that measure improvements in the quality of service delivery. We are also interested in changes in service delivery outcomes in their own right, because a subsidiary goal of a change in management is, hopefully, to encourage facilities to perform more effectively. Chapter 14 by Lundberg discusses data collected as part of an evaluation of an experiment with performance-based contracts in the Ugandan health sector. In the study examined by Lundberg, private not-for-profit providers were randomly allocated to different treatments with varying amounts of financial autonomy and bonus payments. To evaluate the effects of these different contract types, the research team collected household data, conducted exit surveys, and carried out facility surveys.

Using Service Delivery Data to Capture the Effects of Variations in Treatment

The two sorts of cases outlined earlier, wherein service delivery data are used to look at the direct effects of an intervention, are common in the literature. Less common is the approach whereby data on service delivery are used to complement data on individual beneficiary outcomes to analyze the effects of heterogeneity in treatments when the intervention under evaluation is focused on providing new inputs rather than on changing the management structure among service providers. The idea is to measure individual impacts through a tool such as a household survey or, if feasible, administrative data. By itself, this approach will usually be applied to estimate an average treatment effect. However, all individuals do not face the same service environment: variations in the attributes of providers will lead to variations in program effects on individuals that will not be evident if only the average treatment effect is examined. To understand which elements of service delivery matter more or less in producing these individual-level effects, we may use measurements of the attributes of the delivery of services to determine what is most important in achieving greater program impact.

For example, take a program that seeks to promote child literacy by providing one textbook for each child instead of obliging children to share textbooks. The government is not sure about the efficacy of this program, so it randomly chooses a group of pilot schools to receive the additional textbooks. In the simplest impact evaluation, we might measure child literacy after enough time has passed and examine the treatment schools (that is, the pilot schools) with the comparison group of schools. Let's say this program increases literacy by 10 percentage points. Although we might be happy with this result, we might make more effective policy recommendations for the scaling-up of this program by complementing our analysis with service delivery data. For instance, as the program is starting, we might collect data on variables such as teacher absenteeism, the quality of roofs in the school, and teacher education levels. It could turn out that the program has a much greater effect if the school has a roof (the books will not become wet, and children will be more likely to use the books anyway if they are not exposed to the elements). Some of those effects will be obvious to anyone familiar with education program design, but some may be counterintuitive. An examination of this type will allow prioritization among scarce resources by showing which factors are more important.

Another example of the use of service delivery data to understand the heterogeneity in treatment is contained in chapter 6 by Behrman and King. The authors show the importance of being aware of differences in implementation speed. This awareness would take into account the possibility that providers are initially learning about a program (and, so, implementation is less effective) or, in contrast, that providers may be more motivated because they are pioneering a program (and therefore exert greater effort). Behrman and King apply those considerations in an evaluation of an early childhood development program in the Philippines and show that adequately measuring the duration of treatment is quite important in measuring the impact of a program.

Policy-Relevant Research

Data on service delivery permit the examination of a host of research questions. Impact evaluation is one obvious area, but chapter 2 by Lindelow and Wagstaff suggests three other broad areas for consideration. The first of those is the establishment of links between quality and client outcomes. The realm in which we define quality, be it the satisfaction of clients, the quality of facility infrastructure, the skill of the provider, or other dimensions, will guide us in the choice we make among measurement tools. The data may then be linked to client outcomes so that we may understand whether or not the different measures of quality are important and which of them are more important.

A second area of research involves understanding the demand for services. This work seeks to elucidate the factors that influence the level of utilization of services and what may be causing this level to deviate from the optimum. This analysis requires a significant amount of data on potential clients and actual clients, as well as on the service environment. This environment will likely include not only public and private providers, but also formal and informal providers. As Lindelow and Wagstaff note in the case of health, the accurate description of this environment may be tricky because many surveys only include the nearest facilities. Other surveys (for example, the Indonesia Family Life Survey discussed by Beegle in chapter 15) take a broader approach and sample all known facilities, as well as all the facilities that are used. However, as a number of chapters in this volume indicate, attempts to describe the service environment within which households make their choices require careful attention to survey design, particularly the sampling method.

A third strand of research seeks to unpack the functioning of facilities in a manner that is more in-depth than basic monitoring. This research tackles efficiency within and across facilities by looking at how inputs are used to provide different levels of service. This type of work is able to address the issue of whether human and physical capital is being used in the appropriate proportions, whether facilities are operating at the optimal size, and what inputs are being wasted. Given the focus on the production process within facilities, this type of research will require in-depth facility data supplied through a well-functioning administrative system or through facility surveys.

Many of the chapters in this volume discuss these and other research questions that service delivery measurement tools have been used to address (for example, see chapter 4 by Lanjouw and Özler on inequality and project choice). An exciting aspect of these chapters is the fact that they show

how, in many cases, the same data may be used for both routine program monitoring and in-depth research, thereby providing a range of feedback for improving the design of policies.

The Structure of This Book

This volume does not need to be read straight through; each chapter is meant to be freestanding. Nonetheless, a useful place to start might be chapters 2 and 3 (part I), which are designed to provide an overview of the different tools in health and education. In health, the focus has been more on facility surveys, and Lindelow and Wagstaff, therefore, use this as their point of departure. Amin and Chaudhury provide an introduction to methods for measuring service delivery in education.

Part II discusses administrative data and how they may be used to understand program design and program effects. In chapter 4, Lanjouw and Özler discuss administrative data and their uses in understanding the link between inequality and project choice. Galasso, in chapter 5, also uses administrative data, in this case to analyze the effects of a nutrition program in Madagascar. In chapter 6, Behrman and King discuss the ways in which the duration of exposure may affect project impacts and examine this in the case of an early childhood development program in the Philippines.

Part III presents the trials and tribulations involved in tracking public spending data. In chapter 7, Lindelow discusses general problems with defining the concept of leakage and provides an example of a survey in Mozambique. Wane, in chapter 8, offers some insight into complications in comprehending budgets and presents a case in Chad. In chapter 9, Filmer provides a transition to part IV by discussing both Public Expenditure Tracking Surveys and Quantitative Service Delivery Surveys in the context of Indonesia and Papua New Guinea.

Part IV focuses on a range of facility surveys. In chapter 10, Frankenberg and others open with a discussion of the advantages of combining facility survey data with a range of data sources to assess health and education services in Indonesia following the tsunami. In chapter 11, Bekh and others analyze a school survey in Ukraine. Chapter 12, by Serneels, Lindelow, and Lievens, offers us insights into the use of qualitative work, particularly to guide the ultimate choice among quantitative instruments, in the context of examining absenteeism in Ethiopia and Rwanda. In chapter 13, Das and Leonard review and discuss experiences with the use of vignettes to measure quality in the health sector.

Part V focuses on cases in which household and facility surveys are combined. In chapter 14, Lundberg compares client satisfaction and perceived quality among health facilities in Uganda using exit polls and household surveys. Beegle, in chapter 15, discusses the Indonesian experience with linking health facility, school, and household surveys. In chapter 16, Scott provides a broad overview of the incorporation of service provider data into Living Standards Measurement Study surveys.

Part VI concludes by pulling together some of the general lessons that may be derived from the applications of service delivery measurement that are described in the chapters.

Note

1. For more on impact evaluation methods, see Ravallion, forthcoming, and the papers and resources at http://www.worldbank.org/impactevaluation.

References

Filmer, Deon, Jeffrey S. Hammer, and Lant H. Pritchett. 2000. "Weak Links in the Chain: A Diagnosis of Health Policy in Poor Countries." *World Bank Research Observer* 15 (2): 199–224.

Grosh, Margaret E., and Paul W. Glewwe, eds. 2000. *Designing Household Survey Questionnaires for Developing Countries: Lessons from 15 Years of the Living Standards Measurement Study.* 3 vols. Washington, DC: World Bank; New York: Oxford University Press.

Lewis, Maureen A. 2006. "Governance and Corruption in Public Health Care Systems." Center for Global Development Working Paper 78, Center for Global Development, Washington, DC.

Ravallion, Martin. Forthcoming. "Evaluating Anti-Poverty Programs." In *Handbook of Development Economics,* Vol. 4, ed. T. Paul Schultz and John Strauss. Amsterdam: North-Holland.

World Bank. 2003. *World Development Report 2004: Making Services Work for Poor People.* Washington, DC: World Bank; New York: Oxford University Press.

2

Assessment of Health Facility Performance

An Introduction to Data and Measurement Issues

Magnus Lindelow and Adam Wagstaff

Over the past 20 years, household surveys have considerably improved our understanding of health outcomes and health-related behavior in developing countries. For example, data from surveys such as the Living Standards Measurement Study (LSMS) surveys and the Demographic and Health Surveys (DHS) program have shed light on the nature and determinants of health outcomes, while providing information on health-related behavior, including household expenditure on health care and the utilization of health services. Although these and other surveys have strengthened the foundations for policy design and implementation, they have also highlighted the need to understand the supply side of service delivery more thoroughly. The supply-side perspective has also gained importance because many health systems have had to grapple with real or perceived problems of inefficiency, low quality, inequality, and unsustainable financing.

In this context, health facility surveys have come to make up an important source of information about the characteristics and activities of health facilities and about the financing and institutional arrangements that support

This chapter was originally prepared as a background paper for the World Bank workshop "Health Facility Surveys," Washington, DC, December 12, 2001. We are grateful to Xiaodong Cai for assistance with revisions.

service delivery. Although those surveys all have the health facility as the focal point, they vary in at least four important dimensions. First, they have different goals. Some of the surveys aim to deepen understanding of the ways in which health facility characteristics influence health-seeking behavior and health outcomes. Others make the facility the focus of analysis and emphasize issues such as cost, efficiency, and quality. Still other surveys are designed to illuminate the broader context of service delivery, including links among providers or between providers and the government. Second, the scope and nature of the data collected by surveys differ. For example, although many surveys collect data on inputs, not all collect data on costs or on the clinical dimensions of health care quality. Third, surveys collect data in different ways and adopt different approaches to measurement. Fourth, surveys vary in the uses to which the data are put. In some cases, the attention is on research. In others, the principal application has been use as a tool in designing interventions or in monitoring and evaluating programs.

In this chapter, we provide an introduction to health facility surveys and the methodological approaches that underpin them. Although the focus is on health facility surveys, the chapter also draws attention to other sources of data for assessing and understanding the performance of health facilities. For example, household or community surveys are a major tool for shedding light on the perceptions of actual or potential clients. Moreover, in developed countries, administrative data from hospitals and other facilities play an important part in assessing costs and quality. Although administrative data can also be a key source of information in developing countries, surveys tend to play a more significant role given the incompleteness and limited reliability that plague routine data.

The chapter is organized as follows. In the next section, we discuss the motivation for various health facility surveys. The subsequent section provides details on the types of data that have been collected in the surveys and on measurement issues. The following section outlines some of the uses of facility data. In the last section, we offer conclusions, including a discussion of the lessons learned and of emerging themes. The chapter also includes an annex that summarizes key information about selected health survey programs.

The Motivation for Health Facility Surveys

Provider-Household Links

Health facility surveys have often been motivated by the desire to understand the links among the availability of health facilities, household health-

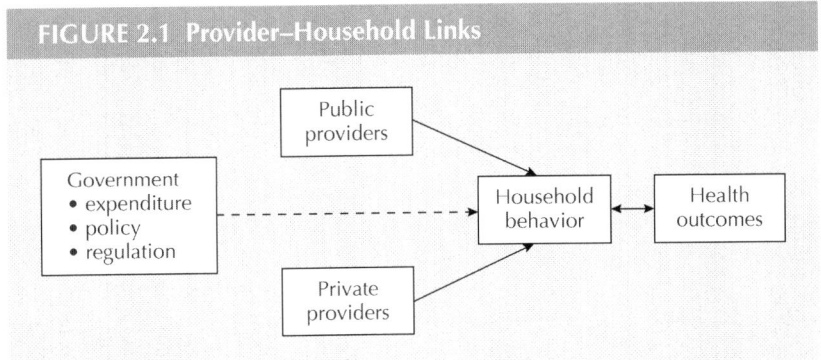

FIGURE 2.1 Provider–Household Links

Source: Compiled by the authors.

seeking behavior, and health outcomes among households (see figure 2.1). Indeed, a number of health facility surveys have been implemented with the explicit purpose of feeding into analyses of household-level data. Although household-level behavior and outcomes are shaped in large part by factors within the household (income, education, location, and so on), the characteristics of local health care providers may be an important determinant of health service utilization, the effectiveness of health care interventions, and the client perceptions.

Work on the links between households and providers dates back to the 1970s, when the World Fertility Survey started to collect data to measure the impact of health service availability on fertility and mortality (see Turner et al. 2001). Initially, data were collected at the community level through interviews with key community informants. This practice was continued in the context of the DHS program, which took over from the World Fertility Survey in 1984. Many LSMS surveys have also included community modules for the collection of information on the availability of public services, for example.

Visiting the actual providers was a natural extension of the collection of community data on service delivery. In the late 1980s, a number of LSMS surveys (such as the ones on Côte d'Ivoire and Jamaica) experimented with health facility surveys and school surveys to complement the household data. A more systematic approach, called Situation Analysis, was introduced in 1989 by the Population Council, an international nonprofit nongovernmental organization. The focus was on family planning and reproductive health services. At least in part, the approach was motivated by findings emerging from the DHS program that weaknesses on the supply side were important in explaining low contraceptive prevalence (see Miller et al. 1997, 1998). The Situation Analysis was based on a representative sample of service delivery units and included structured interviews with managers and facility staff, inventory reviews, direct observation of clinic facilities and the availability of equipment and consumables, reviews of service statistics, direct observation of client-provider interactions, and interviews with clients of family planning and maternal and child health services. More recently, facility surveys have been implemented in conjunction or in coordination with DHS household surveys. Known as Service Provision Assessments, those surveys are ambitious in scope; they seek to supply information about the characteristics of health services, including extensive information about quality, resource availability, and infrastructure.

Measuring and Understanding Provider Performance

In some surveys, the facility rather than the household has been the main object of interest. Facility data may serve in program monitoring or evaluation, but they may also form the basis of empirical work on the determinants of facility performance. For example, how may we account for differences across providers in key dimensions of performance such as quality, costs, and efficiency? The facility surveys designed to explore provider-household links have generally offered little insight into these issues. Figure 2.2 illustrates the

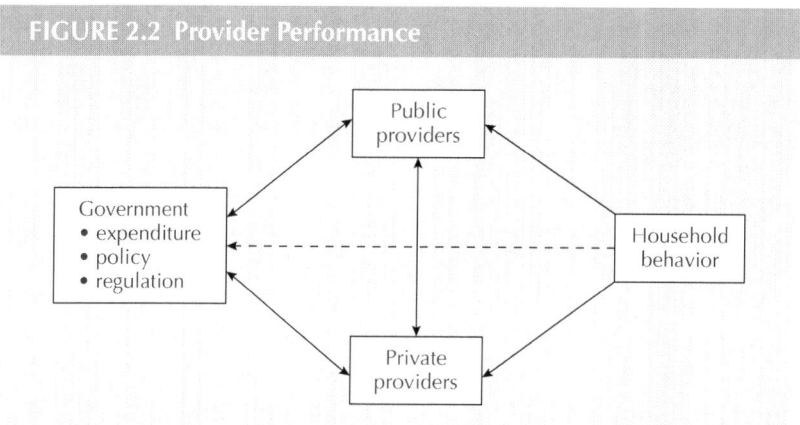

FIGURE 2.2 Provider Performance

Source: Compiled by the authors.

complex institutional and organizational environment that influences the performance of health care providers. This environment operates through the financing, support, regulation, and oversight provided by the administrative levels upstream from the facilities; the competitive environment in which the facilities are operating; and the oversight, accountability, and influence exercised by households and communities.

Quality, Costs, and Efficiency

In principle, data on inputs, costs, and outputs should be provided by a well-functioning management information system. However, where such systems are weak or otherwise deficient, a survey approach may be valuable. On this basis, some surveys have focused explicitly on the analysis of costs and efficiency, often with the aim of eliciting insights into the differences between government and private providers (for example, see Bitran Dicowsky 1995; Wouters 1993).

Facility surveys have also been used to examine the ways other purchasing reforms have affected provider performance. This examination has included efforts relating to the design and impact of provider payment reforms. For instance, detailed cost data are needed for fee-setting, and facility surveys may play a role in estimating costs (see Waters, Abdallah, and Santillán 2001; Waters and Hussey 2004). Moreover, although evaluations of the impact of provider payment reforms tend to rely on administrative data, facility surveys may also play an important role, particularly in contexts where the administrative data are weak. For example, a study of the impact of capitation payment methods in Thailand has drawn on interviews with managers and staff in health facilities (see Mills et al. 2000).

Facility surveys have also been used to study purchasing reforms, such as changes in contracting procedures. Baseline and follow-up facility survey data, in combination with household data, have been used to study the effect of new contracting arrangements in primary care in Cambodia (Bhushan, Keller, and Schwartz 2002; Loevinsohn 2000), and semistructured interviews with service purchasers and service providers have been used to understand various dimensions of the contracting experience with private general practitioners in South Africa (Palmer and Mills 2003). Health facility surveys have also been undertaken to examine the interface between government and providers and to clarify the link between public spending and health outcomes (Filmer, Hammer, and Pritchett 2000). Public Expenditure Tracking Surveys (PETSs), for example, have been motivated by a desire to determine whether the money spent on health actually reaches front-line health care facilities. These tracking surveys seek to answer this question by following the flow of public resources through various layers of the administrative hierarchy to individual service providers and by developing quantitative estimates of fiscal leakage according to data collected through structured questionnaires. Tracking surveys have shown that, as a consequence of leakage and delays in the transfer of financial and in-kind resources to health facilities, as well as low efficiency in the use of resources, more spending does not necessarily imply more or better public services (see Gauthier 2006; Lindelow, Kushnarova, and Kaiser 2006; Reinikka 2001; Reinikka and Svensson 2006). The need for this type of tool has increased in the wake of debt-reduction initiatives and a move toward sectoral and budgetary support under a country-owned policy framework.

Health Workers

The behavior and performance of health workers are receiving growing attention (see Hongoro and Normand 2006; JLI 2004; WHO 2006). Health workers may be viewed as agents for multiple principals, including patients, communities, and government agencies with responsibilities for the delivery of health services. In general, the challenge is to induce health workers to exert effort in a range of areas: clinical tasks, psychosocial interaction with patients, administration, the maintenance of hygienic standards, and so on. In addition, there is a need to restrain opportunistic behavior by health workers (such as overcharging or pilfering inputs). Agency problems in the health sector are the subject of a considerable theoretical and empirical literature.[1] This literature has highlighted the way multiple tasks and principals, and vague and poorly observed objectives impose limits on contractibility. As a result of this feature of the health sector, intrinsic motivation in the form of professional ethics or norms may be important by, in effect, creating a self-enforcing contract (see Deci 1975; Dixit 1997, 2002; Franco, Bennett, and Kanfer 2002; and Wilson 1989).

The agency issues in the health sector give rise to a number of important conceptual, empirical, and methodological questions. For example, what are the key performance issues in various countries? How do different incentive regimes influence performance? What is the role of professional norms, commitment, and trust in the motivation and behavior of health workers? Is intrinsic motivation stronger or more important in certain types of organizations? How should we approach the measurement of the performance, incentives, and motivation of health professionals? Although facility surveys have tried to address some of those questions, the supporting evidence is sparse, particularly in developing countries.

Links among Providers

Another potential motivation for health facility surveys is the examination of the interactions among providers. In the countries of the Organisation for Economic Co-operation and Development, the effect of competition on provider behavior has received attention in recent years (see Dranove and Satterthwaite 2000; Glied 2000; Miller and Luft 1997, 2002; Propper, Burgess, and Green 2004; Propper and Söderlund 1998; Propper, Wilson, and Söderlund 1998; for a review, see Cookson and Dawson 2006). There is also some evidence on the link among providers in developing countries. For example, Gertler and Molyneaux (1997) report an increase in fees among private sector providers in response to an increase in user fees in public facilities. However, although similar research might clearly benefit from health facility surveys, such surveys are typically not designed to address these issues.

Which Data to Collect and How to Collect Them

Health facility surveys have served widely differing purposes. The choice of approach, as well as the scope and precise content of the survey instruments, reflects those differences. Depending on the survey, data have been collected on inputs, costs, outputs, quality, staff behavior and perceptions, and the institutional and organizational environment. Different approaches have been used to collect data, including facility questionnaires; health worker questionnaires, sometimes involving tests of clinical skills; observations of facility characteristics; and direct observation of patient-client interactions. This section reviews the types of data that have been collected in facility surveys and the different approaches that have been used.

Inputs

The collection of facility input data is a standard feature of most facility surveys. There are three primary reasons for collecting the data. First, information about the availability and quantity of inputs may be used to assess the adequacy of resources at the facility level. Second, related to resource adequacy, the availability and characteristics of inputs at the facility level affect the range, quality, and effectiveness of the services provided. Finally, in combination with price information, data on inputs are required for the analysis of costs. Data on some facility inputs are often available in administrative records at the national or subnational level. A survey approach is typically motivated by a lack of confidence or a lack of detail in such records.

Inputs may be divided into capital and recurrent inputs. (Capital inputs are often defined as inputs that last for more than one year, such as vehicles, equipment, buildings, and other infrastructure.) Many surveys collect some data on the characteristics of basic facility infrastructure, such as types of buildings, sources of water and electricity, and the availability of toilets or latrines. Information on the availability and state of repair of means of transportation (vans, automobiles, motorcycles, bicycles, and so on) is often collected because those assets may be significant contributors to facility costs and because the availability of transportation reduces delays in responding to emergency situations, permits outreach services, and may help reduce interruptions in the delivery of supplies. Similarly, on the premise that the absence of certain well-functioning equipment has an adverse effect on the ability of a facility to provide effective health services, some surveys collect data on the quantity or availability of equipment involved in the delivery of medical or related services.

Recurrent inputs primarily consist of personnel, supplies (drugs, vaccines, other medical supplies, nonmedical supplies), and operation and maintenance services (primarily for vehicles and buildings). The number and mix of staff are important characteristics of the health facility; they have an effect on the range of services that may be provided and the technical competence with which the services are delivered, as well as overall cost. Most surveys, therefore, collect data on the number of various categories of staff and, sometimes, additional information on qualifications, education and training, and terms of employment. For the purposes of costing, data on salaries and other benefits are also often collected.

Many surveys collect information on the availability of essential drugs and vaccines. Sometimes, other medical and nonmedical consumables have also been included as items in questionnaires. Information about the current availability or the frequency and duration of stock-outs may compose an important quality indicator. Additional quality information may be gleaned from data on drug prescription practices and drug charging. However, for the purposes of costing, data collection must probe beyond questions about stocks, prescriptions, and charges and consider the flow of drugs and other inputs to facilities.

Given the physical nature of inputs, the approaches to data collection are not particularly controversial. Basic input data—for example, on infrastructure characteristics, the availability of certain types of equipment, or the frequency and duration of drug stock-outs—may be gathered through interviews with facility directors. If there are reasons to believe that the information reported by the facility staff may be inaccurate, direct observation of inputs by enumerators may be advisable. (This observation permits the verification of the drugs actually in stock at the time of the interviews, as well as an assessment of the state of repair and level of functioning of essential inputs such as refrigerators to maintain the cold chain.) A record review is required if data on the *flow* of resources to the facility (for instance, the number of drug kits received in a six-month period) or historical data are needed. However, this approach relies on the availability and reliability of facility records (such as stock cards), and these conditions are often not met. Because of the paucity of records, some input data are best collected at administrative levels above the facilities. Those data may include payroll data, as well as information on the supply of medical and nonmedical supplies to the sampled facilities.

The collection of comparable data at different levels (such as facility and district administration data) also provides a basis for verification. Although those types of cross-checks may be useful, data from different levels are often difficult to reconcile. This difficulty may be caused by irregularities or poor recordkeeping. If these issues are not anticipated, they may lead to serious problems in interpretation ex post. (For a detailed discussion of those challenges, see chapter 7, on public expenditure tracking in Mozambique, in this volume.)

Costs

Costs arise from the use of various scarce resources such as staff time, drugs, facilities, and so on in the production of health services. (For some purposes, it may be desirable also to capture costs on the patient side, such as waiting times.) Information on costs is an important management tool and is also a necessary input in the analysis of cost-effectiveness and efficiency.

Many cost studies rely on administrative data (for example, see Dor 1994; Bitran Dicowsky and Dunlop 1993; Anderson 1980). We may refer to this as a top-down approach. Although it may be a convenient and relatively cheap way of gathering data, the scope for analysis may be limited by poor quality and insufficient disaggregation. These problems are likely to be particularly severe in developing countries and among primary health care providers. Also, records of this nature on nongovernmental organizations and for-profit providers may not exist or be available.

In contrast to the top-down approach, bottom-up costing proceeds by quantifying the use of resources by facilities.[2] In bottom-up costing, a trade-off must be made between the amount of detail and the sample size. At one end of the spectrum, a survey might collect data on key inputs in the production of services from a large number of facilities. At the other end, a full resource costing may consider a more comprehensive range of inputs and might include the allocation of costs to specific service categories. This resource may take the form of a time-and-motion study and a recording of all goods and services (direct and indirect) associated with different categories of services. Detailed studies of this kind tend to rely on samples that are considerably smaller.[3]

In any costing exercise, joint inputs—that is, inputs that are used in the production of more than one type of service—make up a considerable challenge. For example, most facility staff are involved not only in the provision of outpatient services, but also in immunizations, deliveries, and inpatient care. Similarly, certain pieces of equipment may be shared across many categories of services. How should shared costs be attributed among the different activities? The task may be accomplished either on the basis of ad hoc assumptions or by using survey information, for example, on the proportion of staff time spent on various types of activities.[4] There are, however, some fundamental methodological concerns associated with the analysis of these types of data. In particular, the exercise is typically time intensive, and attention is usually restricted to one or a few health care providers. Moreover, in a multi-input, multi-output context in which facilities may substitute between inputs depending on the scale and scope of activities, it is far from clear how accounting-based unit cost estimates should be interpreted.

Outputs, Activities, and Throughputs

It is possible to conceptualize service delivery as a production process wherein the technology of production refers to the relationship between inputs on the one hand and outputs and costs on the other. How should the output of a health care provider be appropriately measured? A first issue concerns the distinction between "readiness-to-serve" capacity and rendered services. At one level, we may think that the appropriate facility output is the capacity to provide services—for example, outpatient care, immunizations, antenatal care, deliveries—rather than the actual number of cases seen. This is because households, as users of health services, play a part in influencing the level of utilization. As a result, the volume of services actually delivered is not entirely under the control of providers. For example, low levels of utilization may be due to low population density or good overall health status in the catchment area. Insofar as variation in output across facilities is driven by these types of factors, service capacity appears as a conceptually appealing measure of output, at least for the purpose of efficiency analysis. However, in many cases, the divergence between service capacity and rendered services is at least partly caused by factors that are within the discretion of the facility.

A second issue to consider in the measurement of outputs is the heterogeneity of service outputs. There are different sources of this heterogeneity. Thus, quality may differ considerably over time, across health care facilities, and even between individual clients at a given facility. For example, a thorough outpatient consultation with a doctor and a rushed consultation with a poorly trained nursing aide are different services. This issue may create serious problems of comparability across time and space. Moreover, within a particular service category, there may be notable variation in case mix and case complexity.[5] For instance, a given number of inpatient episodes may be made up of different cases or conditions across hospitals or clinics (cardiology, orthopedics, intensive care, and so on). Similarly, within each case category, inpatient episodes may range from cases requiring simple interventions and limited monitoring to highly complex cases in which a spectrum of material and human resources is required. Differences in case mix may arise from differences in the socioeconomic characteristics of the population in provider catchment areas or because more complex cases may seek out providers with particular characteristics. This approach leads to problems in comparability. (The problems may be partly overcome; for a detailed discussion, see Tatchell 1983.)

Finally, in addition to problems in the comparability of output measures in specific categories of interventions and services, most health care providers offer a wide range of services (the service mix). Even with a small number of aggregated categories such as inpatient days and outpatient visits, the question arises: how is one to compare the quantity of outputs across facilities with different service mixes? A standard technique for dealing with multi-output production is the construction of an output index using market prices as weights. This approach is not appropriate in the health sector, however, because output prices often do not reflect economic costs (or may not exist).[6] For certain types of analysis, the issue may be avoided. For example, if we are concerned with the estimation of costs, multiple outputs may be included as independent variables.[7]

In practice, most facility surveys have opted to measure output according to the units of the services actually rendered, that is, outpatient visits, immunizations, and so on. Although this option may be unsatisfactory in some respects, it is often the only practical option. Moreover, many of the problems in the measurement and conceptualization of health facility outputs may be overcome if the service data are sufficiently disaggregated.

Quality

The concept of health care quality is difficult to define. In general, the need for the concept of quality stems from the considerable heterogeneity of health services, which is only partly observable and not fully reflected in prices. It is commonly held that, however defined, the quality of health services may have a large impact on health outcomes, health-related behavior, and patient satisfaction. It is, therefore, not surprising that many facility surveys have tried to capture some dimensions of quality.

According to a commonly used definition, health care quality pertains to the management of a personal health problem by a health care practitioner (Donabedian 1980). Donabedian suggests that the most direct approach to the assessment of health care quality is to focus on the process of care—that is, the activities of the health care provider—and to evaluate this process against established technical, professional, and ethical norms. An alternative is to assess quality indirectly through an analysis of structure and outcome. Structural dimensions of health care include the tools and resources that health care providers have at their disposal and the physical and organizational setting in which care is delivered. These dimensions are relevant through their impact on the probability of a good process and outcome. In contrast, outcome refers to the change in a patient's current or future health status that may be attributed to health care, as well as changes in patient attitudes (including satisfaction), health knowledge, and health-related behavior.

Each approach to measurement has given rise to a multitude of indicators and other measurement approaches.[8] In developed countries, recent efforts to measure the quality of care have tended to rely primarily on administrative data and have focused on process and outcome measures because structure measures are not considered adequate in assessing safety and effectiveness. For example, indicators such as cancer survival rate, stroke fatality rate, immunization rates, and waiting time for surgery were included as key indicators in a recent Organisation for Economic Co-operation and Development (OECD) project to strengthen the measurement of health care quality (see Kelley and Hurst 2006). All countries included in the project were able to report reliably on most of the indicators on the basis of routine data. Because of weaknesses in management information systems and incomplete population coverage of the health care system, these types of indicators do not tend to be practical in developing countries. Instead, health facility surveys play a more important role, with a focus on a combination of inputs, the consultation process, and beneficiary or client perceptions.

Measuring Quality through Inputs

The most common approach to the measurement of the structural dimension of quality is the collection of data on the availability and quantity of inputs considered important for the delivery of services. Quality may then be proxied by focusing on particular inputs, such as drugs. Alternatively, composite quality indexes may be constructed (for example, see Garner, Thomason, and Donaldson 1990). This type of data may be used to analyze the relationship between quality, health outcomes, and behavior. However, although structural indicators of quality have the benefit of being easy to measure, they are likely to be inadequate or incomplete as measures of quality.

Measuring Quality Through Clinical Vignettes, Consultation Observation, and Simulated Patients

In response to the inadequacies of structural measures of quality, some studies have tried to collect data on the clinical competence of health professionals or the process of care. The general principle is that level of knowledge or actual case management may be assessed against established norms of diagnosis and treatment. The most common method for assessing such process quality involves clinical vignettes and consultation observation. In addition, some surveys have asked questions about general facility procedures, for example, sterilization, the disposal of needles, and so on.

Clinical vignettes assess clinical skills by presenting health workers with hypothetical cases and seeking to elicit information about the way in which the workers would handle such cases. This approach has the advantage of permitting a considerable degree of structure in the survey instruments, thus limiting—although not eliminating—the need for technical skills among the enumerators (for example, see Peabody et al. 1994; Thaver et al. 1998; Leonard and Masatu 2005; Das and Hammer 2005). In contrast, consultation observation entails using medically qualified enumerators who observe the case management of health workers in the respective facilities.[9] While the skill requirements for this type of survey may be prohibitive in many contexts, the approach has the advantage of permitting a more comprehensive assessment of the process of care.

Both clinical vignettes and consultation observation have advantages. Assuming that the provider effectively applies clinical knowledge in case management and that observation bias is not significant, we would expect a close correspondence in quality measures between vignettes and clinical observation. There is some evidence in the United States that this is the case (Peabody et al. 2000), but it is not clear that these findings may be generalized.[10] Indeed, recent studies (Das and Hammer 2004; Leonard, Masatu, and Vialou 2005) suggest that, at least in developing countries, there is often a considerable gap between knowledge and practice and that this gap varies with incentives and practitioner characteristics. Moreover, because of observation bias whereby the presence of data collectors who are observing close at hand temporarily improves clinical practice, the gap may be even wider than these studies indicate (Leonard and Masatu 2006).

One way to overcome the problem of observation bias is to use simulated or fake patients who visit doctors unannounced and relate to the doctors standard, fictitious case scenarios (describing, for example, a case of diarrhea or sexually transmitted disease). Although controversial, this approach has been used to study patient–provider interactions in a wide variety of contexts, including hospitals and physician offices (high-income countries) and drug retail outlets and family planning providers (low-income countries) (see Madden et al. 1997). Data have typically been collected not only on the technical quality of care (appropriateness of treatment, prescriptions, and information), but also on costs and psychosocial interactions.

Measuring Quality Through Beneficiary Perceptions

The assessment of quality through structure and process characteristics is premised on a set of established norms for clinical effectiveness. An alternative approach to assessing the quality of care is to ask beneficiaries about their perceptions. Patient satisfaction is important in its own right as an objective of health care, but it is also important as an indicator of the structure, process, and outcome of health care, and it is important because of its effect on client behavior. Patient satisfaction is typically assessed through interviews with actual or potential patients. Data on actual patients may be collected through exit polls. Exit polls are easy and inexpensive to administer in conjunction with facility surveys. Their main limitation is that they fail to capture the perceptions of nonusers and may result in biased assessments of the status of service delivery. If one is to obtain a more representative picture of the perceptions of users (actual and potential), it is necessary to sample all households or individuals in the community. This sampling tends to be more expensive. However, broad, multitopic household surveys, such as the LSMS, have included questions on client perceptions of services, and these types of surveys may be a valuable source in assessing the performance of service delivery.

Whatever the source, there are, nonetheless, considerable problems in interpreting subjective perceptions of health care quality. In part, this is due to courtesy bias, whereby individuals may provide responses they deem socially acceptable.[11] But it is also the case that subjective perceptions of quality are based on client beliefs and views about health care norms and standards. Evidence from the United States suggests that respectfulness and attentiveness bear little relation to technical health care quality and that individuals are only able to assess the former effectively (see Cleary and Edgman-Levitan 1997; Edgman-Levitan and Cleary 1996). This relationship may not always be the case. For example, one study of quality in family planning has found a high degree of consistency between objective and subjective measures of quality (Bessinger and Bertrand 2001). However, even where this consistency may be the situation on average, systematic differences in the way quality is assessed and rated across demographic and socioeconomic groups may render client perceptions poor proxies for objective assessments of the dimensions of quality.

There is also a host of approaches that seek to gather community-based evidence on service delivery. This includes service delivery surveys, report cards on public services, and other related approaches. For example, the Ministry of Health in Uganda has implemented the Yellow Star Program, which evaluates health care facilities on a quarterly basis using 35 indicators and disseminates findings to the community (McNamara 2006). Likewise, citizen report cards on public services have been developed and supported by civil society in a number of countries over the past decade. The first scorecard survey was implemented in Bangalore, India, in 1993; it focused on issues such as the behavior of staff, the quality of services, and the information provided (see Paul 2002). Similar approaches have since been implemented in other cities in India and in other countries, for example, Ghana, the Philippines, and Ukraine (see McNamara 2006). These approaches should not generally be described as facility surveys, nor are they always limited to the health sector. Rather, the purpose is to use a range of tools—for instance, household interviews, focus groups, institutional reviews of service providers, and interviews with service providers—to elicit information about the general awareness and experience of services and about opinions on prices, quality, waiting times, courtesy, and so on. Despite their simplicity, the approaches may be useful in the formulation of hypotheses about service delivery, as well as in the design of quantitative surveys. Moreover, they can be an effective monitoring and advocacy tool (see Ravindra 2004).

Health Worker Motivation and Performance

Notwithstanding the obvious importance of health worker behavior and motivation to quality and efficiency, there are few examples of surveys that focus on these issues. McPake et al. (1999) focus on the informal economic activities of health workers in Uganda. The survey team collected data through a complex set of instruments for a full month in a small sample of facilities. Those data were then triangulated to construct estimates of overcharging and the divergence between the amounts of drugs supplied to facilities and the amounts actually prescribed. Other studies and surveys, sometimes with a significant qualitative component, have similarly tried to shed light on issues such as absenteeism, informal charging, pilfering, and dual job-holding and have centered their attention on the role of low pay, poor working conditions, low levels of motivation, weak accountability mechanisms, and private sector opportunities (see Belli, Gotsadze, and Shahriari 2004; Di Tella and Savedoff 2001; Ferrinho et al. 2004; Ferrinho, van Lerberghe, and Cruz Gomes 1999; Killingsworth et al. 1999; Lewis 2000, 2007; and Lindelow and Serneels 2006). Absenteeism has also been the focus of large-scale facility surveys that have relied on unannounced facility visits to identify absent health workers (see Chaudhury et al. 2006; Chaudhury and Hammer 2004; and Banerjee, Deaton, and Duflo 2004).

From a different perspective, Franco, Bennett, and Kanfer (2002) and Kanfer (1999) propose a framework for analyzing health worker motivation that emphasizes determinants at the individual, organizational, and sociocultural levels. Using this framework, Franco et al. (2004) have collected data on health worker motivation and performance in hospitals in Georgia and Jordan, relying on both contextual analysis and structured interviews to assess the determinants and outcomes of motivational processes. These studies have not explicitly sought to link health worker performance and measures of motivation.

The Institutional and Organizational Environment

Because health care providers do not generally operate in a competitive market and because of the prominence of distributive concerns in health sector policy, the performance of health care providers is typically assessed with reference to multiple criteria, including allocative and technical efficiency, quality of care, and equity. Many facility surveys have found considerable variation in the dimensions of facility performance. Yet, there are few examples of surveys that have set out to explain this variation. In large part, this reflects the difficulty in measuring performance and its determinants.

Performance along different dimensions is likely to be a function of several features of the operational environment, including financing and support systems, provider autonomy, market context, and oversight and accountability (see Preker and Harding 2003). Provider incentives are shaped in important ways by how the providers are paid and by the rules that govern the retention and use of operational surpluses. Governmental facilities and, in some cases, nongovernmental facilities often depend, at least partially, on government budgetary financing, as well as on other government support systems (for example, for the supply of drugs and vaccines), and the effectiveness of these systems may therefore influence performance.

Currently, the empirical evidence on the impact that different features of the operational environment have on facility performance in developing countries is limited. A number of studies examine the impact of new provider methods, but these studies are based mainly on administrative data.[12] Cross-sectional facility survey data have been used to study the effect of various features of the institutional and financing environment on performance (for example, see Somanathan et al. 2000). However, the measurement and estimation challenges make persuasive identification difficult.[13] There have also been a number of recent efforts to collect data on resource flows from the central level to service delivery units with a view to assessing whether actual spending is consistent with intended allocations. The surveys have typically also used instruments at the provincial or district level to identify capacity and system weaknesses, management practices, and information asymmetries (for a review, see Lindelow, Kushnarova, and Kaiser 2006).

How Facility Data Have Been Used

Monitoring, Evaluation, and Accountability

Household surveys have long served as the basis for regular assessments of health status and living standards more generally. Current well-known household surveys include the DHS program, the LSMS surveys, and the Multiple Indicator Cluster Surveys. Similarly, semistandardized surveys of health care providers—for example, Service Provision Assessments or Situation Analysis Studies—have provided valuable assessments of health care quality, infrastructure, utilization, and availability. Thus, a recent survey in Kenya has found that, although contraceptive services, drugs, and materials are widely available, compliance with infection control procedures, including the sterilization of equipment and the sterilization of needles, is poor (see Macro International 2000). Moreover, consultation observation has revealed that the diagnostic process is frequently unsatisfactory and that clients are provided with incomplete or insufficient information to weigh their treatment options or to comply with treatment regimes properly. Aside from its uses in research on the determinants of health outcomes and health-related behavior, this type of information is valuable in the design of health sector strategies and interventions. Repeat surveys permit the monitoring of changes in quality over time.

Household and facility surveys are also being carried out as components in the monitoring and evaluation of specific projects or programs. As noted by Mills (1997) and Mills, Rasheed, and Tollman (2006), a broad array of health sector reforms has been proposed in recent years notwithstanding the fact that there is currently little empirical evidence to vouch for the effectiveness of such reforms. In this context, efforts aimed at regular assessments and ex post evaluations are of particular importance.

The ongoing Multi-Country Evaluation of IMCI Effectiveness, Cost, and Impact represents an example of the role that facility surveys may play in the monitoring and evaluation of health sector interventions. Worldwide, there are 30 countries at different stages of implementation of the integrated management of childhood illness (IMCI) strategy; among these, Bangladesh, Peru, Tanzania, and Uganda are participating in the evaluations. The purpose of the evaluations is to document the effects of IMCI interventions on health worker performance, health systems, and family behavior; determine the extent of measurable impact on health outcomes; and describe the costs of implementation (see WHO 2001). The evaluations have involved the design of dedicated facility survey instruments, and the results of the facility surveys have been important in assessing the impact of the IMCI on quality and costs.[14]

Health facility surveys also formed part of the evaluation strategy for the Bolivian Social Investment Fund, which was established in 1991 to direct public service investments to poor communities. Surveys were collected in 1993 and 1997 and included households, communities, and service delivery units. The surveys demonstrated clear improvements in infrastructure and equipment, as well as increased utilization rates and reduced mortality rates (Newman et al. 2002).

Evaluations relying on health facility surveys have also been undertaken under the umbrella of Measure Evaluation (see http://www.cpc.unc.edu/measure/). For example, a health facility survey was carried out in Paraguay in 1998 to identify and quantify the effects of a decentralization reform. Management authority over the provision of basic health services was being transferred from the central government to municipal governments. The authority involved control over issues of cost, efficiency, basic health service quality, patterns of health service use, and equity. The design of the study included pre- and postdecentralization elements, and there was a control group. The focus was on family planning, maternal health, and infant and child health (Angeles et al. 1999).[15]

Three rounds of household and facility surveys were carried out in Uganda, in 1995, 1997, and 1999, as components of the ongoing Delivery of Improved Services for Health Project in reproductive health. The purpose of the surveys was to measure changes in the knowledge and behavior involved in a project on reproductive, maternal, and child health (Katende et al. 1999; Katende, Gupta, and Bessinger 2003).[16]

Measure Evaluation has used health facility surveys to evaluate programs such as the Vision and Compass projects in Nigeria (Agha et al. 2003; Keating 2006), the Rural Service Delivery Partnership in Bangladesh (Angeles and Hutchinson 2003), and family planning programs in Uganda (Okullo et al. 2003).

Facility surveys may be used in budget monitoring and the examination of accountability issues in contexts in which routine budget reporting systems are weak. For example, the aim of the first Public Expenditure Tracking Survey carried out in Uganda was to identify the reason primary school enrollment rates remained stubbornly low despite a substantial increase in public spending in the early 1990s (see Ablo and Reinikka 1998; Reinikka 1999). The survey sought to clarify whether funds being allocated by the central treasury to primary schools actually reached the schools. This involved collecting data from a sample of schools and from administrative units upstream from the schools. The study provided powerful evidence of the ways weak governance and lack of accountability may hamper the process of budget implementation. It found that, on average, only 13 percent of the total yearly capitation grant from the central government had reached the sample schools in 1991–95; 87 percent had been used for purposes unrelated to education or had otherwise disappeared. Interestingly, the access to funds varied in systematic ways according to school size, school income, and the share of qualified teachers.

A number of tracking surveys have been implemented in the health sector (Gauthier 2006; Lindelow, Kushnarova, and Kaiser 2006). In many cases, poor recordkeeping and unclear allocation rules have hindered the measurement of fiscal leakage. Notwithstanding these limitations, tracking surveys have often proved useful. Beyond identifying leakage, they may help diagnose delays and other budget execution problems that may seriously undermine service delivery. They also contribute to understanding the way resources are allocated and used at lower levels of government. For example, a recent tracking study has focused on resource allocation and management, planning and budgeting, and human resource management in Brazil's Unified Health System and has shown how weaknesses in the system have undermined incentives and performance accountability (World Bank 2007). In other surveys, the focus has been on the service delivery unit, including consideration of the relationship between the facility and the administrative system upstream. This approach may involve facility surveys, but also citizen surveys and scorecard schemes. For example, the original Bangalore Scorecard, designed and implemented by the Public Affairs Center, a local nongovernmental organization in Bangalore, India, questioned a sample of both rich and poor users about their perceptions of the city's public services. The aim of the survey was to rate public agencies in terms of staff behavior, the quality of service, and the information provided. The survey generated significant feedback on public services, helped identify weaknesses in service delivery, and became a powerful advocacy tool for change (see Paul 2002).

Research

Health Care Quality and Health Outcomes

Data on health care quality are becoming widely available, and the body of empirical research on the link between health care quality and health outcomes has grown. There is now evidence that certain characteristics of health care providers and their relationships with clients are important determinants of health outcomes. For example, a number of studies have found a positive correlation between health service infrastructure and characteristics, such as the number of clinics or doctors per capita, and health indicators, including child mortality rates, fertility rates, indicators of nutritional status, and anthropometric indicators (see Benefo and Schultz 1994; Frankenberg and Thomas 2001; Hossain 1989; Lavy et al. 1996; Rosenzweig and Schultz 1982; Rosenzweig and Wolpin 1982; Thomas, Lavy, and Strauss 1996; for a review of the evidence, see Wouters 1991; Frankenberg 1995; Alderman and Lavy 1996). There is also a literature based on DHS data focusing specifically on family planning and contraceptive use (see Beegle 1995; Feyisetan and Ainsworth 1996; Mroz et al. 1999; Steele, Curtis, and Choe 1999). Finally, Peabody, Gertler, and Leibowitz (1998) provide evidence of the ways in which low quality in the care process—relating to clinical knowledge, adherence to diagnostic and treatment protocols, and so on—affects health outcomes and behavior. They find that, while none of the structural measures of quality have statistically significant effects, women who have access to complete examinations (the care process) had infants who weighed, on average, 128 grams (about 0.28 pounds) more at birth than other infants.

Health Care Quality and Health-Seeking Behavior

One of the conduits through which health care quality affects health outcomes is client behavior, including both care-seeking behavior (the utilization of health services) and adherence behavior (compliance with treatment regimes, follow-up visits, and referrals). However, concern with quality was limited in early studies of health care demand. To the extent that it was considered at all, quality was treated as an unobserved variable pertaining to the type of provider rather than the individual provider (see Gertler, Locay, and Sanderson 1987; Gertler and van der Gaag 1990).

More recent studies have used cross-sectional data to examine the effect of a series of structural quality variables on health-seeking behavior (see Akin, Guilkey, and Denton 1995; Lavy and Germain 1994; Litvack and Bodart 1993; Mwabu 1986). Generally, the studies demonstrate a significant and sometimes large statistical correlation between quality and utilization.[17] A challenge in analyzing the link between quality and utilization is the empirical characterization of the quality environment of households.[18] In some surveys, data on quality are collected only from the closest facility. In this case, the linking of households and facility data is easy, but the risk of omitted variable bias is considerable, particularly among households in urban areas. In other cases, the sample of facilities is more extensive, but linking remains a challenge. Hong, Montana, and Mishra (2006) use data from a geographic information system to link households to the closest provider and find that the quality of family planning services is an important determinant of the use of intrauterine devices. Other studies (for example, Jensen and Stewart 2003) have sought to characterize the quality environment by using summary measures for facilities within geographical units (such as the municipality).

A few studies have used data on quality from multiple facilities to examine facility choice. This literature provides a powerful illustration of the problem of using data on quality from the closest facility to study the relationship between quality and behavior or outcomes. It has been shown that many households bypass the closest facility in favor of a more distant facility and that quality is an important factor in this choice (Akin and Hutchinson 1999; Leonard, Mliga, and Mariam 2003).

Efficiency Analysis and the Econometric Estimation of Cost Functions

Information on cost functions may be useful in examining a number of questions. Are health facilities undercapitalized or overcapitalized? Are they technically inefficient in that they fail to produce the maximum output from the inputs they use? Do they use inputs in the wrong proportions? Do facilities vary in the degree of inefficiency? Are facilities in the public sector less efficient than private ones? Should facilities specialize or provide a broad range of services? There is a large literature on these topics in the industrialized world. A much smaller literature exists on the developing world. Wagstaff and Barnum (1992) review the four principal studies up to 1992 (Ethiopia, Kenya, Nigeria, and Peru).

Few of the studies to date clarify the issue of whether health facilities have too little or too much capital. Anderson's (1980) study of Kenyan hospitals is inconclusive on the overcapitalization issue. The published results of the studies in Ethiopia (Bitran Dicowsky and Dunlop 1993) and Nigeria (Wouters 1993) are consistent with overcapitalization, but Wagstaff and Barnum (1992) warn against taking the results too literally.

Data from health facility surveys have been used to assess the efficiency of health care providers. Because of the difficulty of applying the concept of allocative efficiency in the public sector, many studies of efficiency restrict their attention to technical efficiency.[19] Barnum and Kutzin (1993) use a frontier model to test for inefficiency in their sample of Chinese hospitals, but find none.[20] Dor (1987), in his study of Peruvian hospitals, does not use a frontier model, but includes a dummy variable in his cost function to indicate whether the hospital is operated by the Ministry of Health or the Social Security Institute. His findings suggest that Ministry of Health hospitals are more efficient. Wouters (1993), in her study of Nigerian facilities, explores the issue of input mix inefficiency. In her sample, she finds evidence of underemployment among health workers relative to other workers, and she finds evidence of greater relative inefficiencies in the private sector.

Another important issue confronting policy makers is whether hospitals should be encouraged to specialize or to provide a broad range of services. Should hospitals, for example, provide both inpatient and outpatient care? Should hospitals providing inpatient services aim to treat most types of cases or should they specialize? In many studies of health facilities, the functional form used in the regression analysis is too restrictive to explore economies of scope. Of the four studies surveyed by Wagstaff and Barnum (1992), only the Bitran Dicowsky and Dunlop (1993) study of Ethiopian hospitals employs a specification that is sufficiently general to avoid prejudgments on the issue of economies of scope. The results imply mild economies of scope, which is similar to the results reported by Barnum and Kutzin (1993) in their analysis of Chinese hospitals.

The research has addressed questions about scale economies in the provision of health care. In the multiproduct situation (for instance, where hospitals are treating inpatient and outpatient cases), one needs to rely on the concept of *ray* economies of scale; this concept shows how costs change when all outputs are increased in the same proportion. Some studies have prejudged this issue because of the choice of specification. For example, Dor (1987) implicitly assumes that the product-specific index of economies of scale is equal to 1 for all outputs. Bitran Dicowsky and Dunlop (1993) find slight product-specific diseconomies of scale, but also find ray economies of scale. Wouters (1993) finds ray economies of scale, but, in contrast to Bitran Dicowsky and Dunlop, also finds product-specific economies.

One recent study looked at both economies of scale and economies of scope among public hospitals in Vietnam (Weaver and Deolalikar 2004). It found that costs were significantly higher in central hospitals and lower in district hospitals relative to provincial hospitals. The analysis also indicated roughly constant returns to scale at central hospitals, but large diseconomies of scale at provincial hospitals. Modest economies and diseconomies of scale were found in district hospitals. There were large economies of scope among central and provincial general hospitals.

Conclusions

What are the lessons that emerge from past experiences with health facility surveys, and what should be on the empirical agenda now for the future? Because many of the issues of interest concern the interactions among various units in the system, it is necessary to look beyond a single part of the system. Indeed, this is precisely the rationale behind the first community and facility surveys implemented in conjunction with the DHS program and the LSMS surveys. However, while these surveys have taught us a great deal about how health behaviors and outcomes relate to service availability and provider characteristics, many questions remain. This is true not only of the relationships among households, the community, and the provider, but also in respect of the strategic interactions among the various providers and between the administrative and logistical system and downstream facilities.

Another point is that there are difficult methodological issues to resolve concerning the measurement of quality, costs, outputs, and performance. For example, the chapter notes the disparate approaches to measuring health care quality. Is there an emerging best practice? Will it be possible to design simple ways of collecting meaningful and consistent data on quality? Is it reasonable to view health care quality as a facility characteristic? Actual client experience may be endogenous to client characteristics and previous client behavior. For example, both the structural and the process characteristics of care may depend on how much is paid and on client characteristics such as income, social standing, education, and assertiveness of the client. This process would mean that individuals perceive their visits to health care providers differently and also receive different treatments. Progress in the measurement of quality is important in monitoring and in adding value to research on health outcomes and health-related behavior. The disparate approaches to measuring health care quality and the sometimes inconsistent findings largely reflect the quality of the available data. Similar methodological issues exist in the measurement of costs and outputs.

Surveys have been more effective at documenting variations in the quality and efficiency of facility performance than at explaining variations across facilities and countries. We do not know enough about the possible merits of private and nongovernmental providers or about whether general prescriptions may be undertaken in the institutional context in which public providers operate. There are a number of instructive examples of surveys that have focused on detailed performance measurements, including staff perceptions and behavior. Some of those surveys have also achieved progress in the systematic capture of features of the institutional and organizational environment that may be important determinants of performance. However, this is an open research agenda; there is no consensus on which features of the facility and its environment matter for performance or on how we should go about measuring these features. Notwithstanding the inherent difficulties involved in this research, the widespread and well-documented problems of quality and efficiency in health care provision suggest that the potential payoffs from advances in the research are considerable.

What has been the impact of health facility surveys? This question is difficult to answer not least because of the considerable differences in the focus and motivation of the surveys. The impact has probably not been as great as it might have been. In many cases, data have been underutilized and survey findings have not been integrated in the policy process. Although this shortcoming is not universal, it raises important challenges. Ultimately, achieving impact requires a degree of involvement by policy makers in the design and implementation of surveys, as well as in the dissemination and use of survey findings. In part, this depends on attuning the survey approach to the needs and requirements of a particular context. However, survey findings generally gain force if they may be generalized and compared across the findings of other surveys. An important challenge is, therefore, to improve consistency across surveys over time and across countries. This challenge would require agreement about core methodological issues, possibly in the form of core facility modules that will permit international analyses of health system performance.

<u>ANNEX 2.1</u>

A REVIEW OF HEALTH
FACILITY SURVEYS

This annex provides an overview of selected health facility surveys. It offers a brief description of each survey. This review should not be considered comprehensive; the aim has been to cover important and accessible facility survey initiatives in the health sector. The focus is on survey *programs* and not individual survey efforts. Where appropriate, selected references and background readings are suggested.

Demographic and Health Surveys (DHS)

The DHS program has been an important source of individual and household health data since 1984. The design of the DHS draws on the experiences of the World Fertility Survey and the Contraceptive Prevalence Surveys, but includes an expanded set of indicators on population, health, and nutrition.[21]

Like some of the World Fertility Surveys, many of the DHS program surveys have included tools to collect community data. These service availability modules are not true facility surveys, but they collect relevant information from community informants. They have been aimed at gathering objective information on the facilities and services available especially to women in communities, focusing particularly on family planning services.

Research and Publications

Beegle, Kathleen. 1995. "The Quality and Availability of Family Planning Services and Contraceptive Use in Tanzania." Living Standards Measurement Study Working Paper 114, World Bank, Washington, DC.

Feyisetan, Bamikale James, and Martha Ainsworth. 1996. "Contraceptive Use and the Quality, Price, and Availability of Family Planning in Nigeria." *World Bank Economic Review* 10 (1): 159–87.

Mroz, Thomas A., Kenneth A. Bollen, Ilene S. Speizer, and Dominic J. Mancini. 1999. "Quality, Accessibility, and Contraceptive Use in Rural Tanzania." *Demography* 36 (1): 23–40.

Steele, Fiona, Sian L. Curtis, and Minja Choe. 1999. "The Impact of Family Planning Service Provision on Contraceptive-Use Dynamics in Morocco." *Studies in Family Planning* 30 (1): 28–42.

The Living Standards Measurement Study

The LSMS was established by the World Bank in 1980 to explore ways to improve the nature and quality of the household data being collected by governmental statistical offices in developing countries. LSMS surveys are multitopic; they are designed to produce data permitting four types of analysis: (1) simple descriptive statistics on living standards, (2) monitoring data on poverty and living standards over time, (3) descriptions of the incidence and coverage of government programs, and (4) measurements of the impact of policies and programs on household behavior and welfare (Grosh and Glewwe 2000). The first surveys were implemented in Côte d'Ivoire and Peru. Other early surveys followed a similar format, although considerable variation has been introduced since then.

The household questionnaire forms the heart of an LSMS survey. It typically includes a health module that provides information on (a) health-related behavior, (b) the use of health services, (c) health expenditures, (d) insurance status, and (e) access to health services. The level of detail of the health section has varied across surveys. Complementary data are typically collected through community and price questionnaires. In fact, over half the LSMS surveys conducted before 1997 included community and price questionnaires. Community questionnaires are administered to community informants separately; they seek information on infrastructure, employment opportunities, availability of credit, and public services, including schools and health facilities.[22]

In some LSMS surveys, detailed data have been collected on service providers (health facilities or schools). In the health sector, facility surveys have been implemented in Côte d'Ivoire (1987), Jamaica (1989), and Vietnam (1998). The facility surveys have been included to provide complementary data primarily on the prices for health care and medicines and on health care quality. Health facilities have rarely been the object of analysis in research based on LSMS surveys. Data on quality may cover dimensions of structure (staffing, equipment, drugs, and so on) and process (diagnosis, treatment, attentiveness, and staff attitude). The facility surveys have sometimes also covered private health care providers (Jamaica).

Experiences with LSMS Health Facility Surveys

Jamaica. A survey of health care facilities was carried out in September 1990. The data were meant to complement the expanded health module of the 1989 LSMS survey. All public health facilities and a sample of private providers were surveyed. Data collection was based on four distinct health service questionnaires: public primary, private primary, public secondary or tertiary, and private secondary or tertiary. At the primary level, the questions related to catchment areas, facility characteristics, patient services, immunizations, personnel, beds, transportation, drug supplies and equipment, family planning services, and maternal health services.[23] There were slight differences in the questionnaires administered to public and private facilities. The survey instruments for the secondary and tertiary levels included more detailed questions on facility characteristics, personnel, and equipment. In the household surveys, detailed data were collected on episodes of illness and patterns in care seeking, including the names of the facilities visited (World Bank 2001).

Côte d'Ivoire. The survey instruments for Côte d'Ivoire preceded the Jamaica survey, and they are much more limited. The facility questionnaire includes many of the same sections found in the Jamaica survey, but the sections in the latter are more comprehensive. No specific data on family planning and maternity care services were collected in Côte d'Ivoire, and no attempt was made to capture the process dimensions of health care quality.

Vietnam. The 1998 Vietnam LSMS survey included school and health facility surveys. The health facility survey was limited in scope and detail relative to the Jamaica and Côte d'Ivoire surveys. It collected information on distance to different enumeration areas, staffing, areas of operation, number of beds, service range, equipment and drug availability, and cost of services and drugs.

Research and Publications

Lavy, Victor Chaim, John Strauss, Duncan Thomas, and Philippe de Vreyer. 1996. "Quality of Health Care, Survival, and Health Outcomes in Ghana." *Journal of Health Economics* 15 (3): 333–57.

Peabody, John W., Paul J. Gertler, and Arleen A. Leibowitz. 1998. "The Policy Implications of Better Structure and Process on Birth Outcomes in Jamaica." *Health Policy* 43 (1): 1–13.

Thomas, Duncan, Victor Chaim Lavy, and John Strauss. 1996. "Public Policy and Anthropometric Outcomes in Côte d'Ivoire." *Journal of Public Economics* 61 (2): 155–92.

Gertler, Paul J., and Jennie I. Litvack. 1998. "Access to Health Care during Transition: The Role of the Private Sector in Vietnam." In *Household Welfare and Vietnam's Transition*, ed. David Dollar, Paul W. Glewwe, and Jennie I. Litvack, 235–56. World Bank Regional and Sectoral Studies. Washington, DC: World Bank.

Situation Analysis Studies

Situation analyses were introduced as a tool for program evaluation by the Population Council in 1989. In general, situation analyses may be described as a comprehensive approach to the systematic assessment of the readiness of family planning and reproductive health programs to deliver services (see Miller et al. 1998). The development of the tool was stimulated by indications from DHS program surveys that weaknesses in service delivery were important in explaining low contraceptive prevalence rates in many countries.

The first situation analysis was carried out in Kenya. Subsequently, situation analyses have been conducted extensively, including in 11 African countries. The situation analysis approach is based on a representative sample of service delivery units within a geographical area of interest. It includes structured interviews with managers and facility staff, inventory reviews, direct observation of clinic facilities and the availability of equipment and consumables, reviews of service statistics for 12 months, nonparticipant direct observation of client-provider interactions in family planning services, and interviews with clients of family planning and maternal and child health services. The general approach has been modified in some cases to address broader sets of concerns.

Situation analysis studies have provided clear evidence of the poor state of service delivery in many countries. Documented problems include inadequate stocks of contraceptives, lack of basic infrastructure and equipment, and insufficient adherence to diagnostic and treatment protocols. Through the implementation of follow-up studies, it has been possible to measure changes over time and to assess the impact of policies aimed at improving service delivery. Data have been used in areas such as the design of family planning programs, training initiatives, and the formulation of sectoral strategies.

Research and Publications

Miller, Kate, Robert Miller, Ian Askew, Marjorie C. Horn, and Lewis Ndhlovu. 1998. *Clinic-Based Family Planning and Reproductive Health Services in Africa: Findings from Situation Analysis Studies.* New York: Population Council.

Miller, Robert, Andrew Fisher, Kate Miller, Lewis Ndhlovu, Baker Ndugga Maggwa, Ian Askew, Diouratie Sanogo, and Placide Tapsoba. 1997. *The Situation Analysis Approach to Assessing Family Planning and Reproductive Health Services: A Handbook.* New York: Population Council.

RAND Surveys

The RAND Corporation has supported the design and implementation of Family Life Surveys (FLS) in developing countries since the 1970s (see http://www.rand.org/labor/FLS/). Currently available country surveys include Bangladesh (1996), Guatemala (1995), Indonesia (1993, 1997, 1998, and 2000), and Malaysia (1976–77 and 1988–89). The surveys in Bangladesh and Indonesia are now discussed in detail.

The Indonesia Family Life Survey

The Indonesia Family Life Survey is an ongoing, multitopic longitudinal survey. It has aimed to provide data for the measurement and analysis of a range of individual- and household-level behaviors and outcomes. The survey has collected data at the individual and household levels, including indicators of economic well-being, education, migration, labor market outcomes, fertility and contraceptive use, health status, use of health care and health insurance, intrahousehold relationships, and participation in community activities. In addition, community-level data are collected. The data collection includes detailed surveys of service providers (including schools and health care providers) in the selected communities. The first wave of the survey was conducted in 1993/94 and covered approximately 7,000 households. The second wave and a survey on a subsample (25 percent) of households designed to assess the effects of Indonesia's economic crisis were conducted in 1997 and 1998, respectively, and a third wave was implemented in 2000. Reinterview rates of over 90 percent were achieved beginning with the second wave.

For the health facility survey, visits to local health care providers were carried out, and staff representatives were interviewed about the staffing, operations, and uses of the facilities. The surveys covered (a) public health centers and branch centers; (b) private clinics and doctors, midwives, nurses, and paramedics; and, (c) community health posts. For each community, up to three governmental health centers, six private clinics, doctors, and so on, and two community health posts were surveyed. Health care providers were selected on the basis of information supplied by household respondents about the locations where they normally seek care.

Distinct questionnaires were used for each sort of provider to reflect differences in the organization and scope of the services. In general, the questionnaires collected data on the availability and price of services, laboratory tests, and drugs; the availability of equipment and supplies; and direct observation of cleanliness and other features that might influence patients to choose a service. In addition, five hypothetical patient scenarios or vignettes were presented to the relevant health workers to assess the familiarity of the workers with the patient care process. The vignettes covered the provision of intrauterine devices, the provision of oral contraceptives, prenatal care, treatments for children exhibiting vomiting and diarrhea, and treatments for adults with respiratory ailments.

The Matlab Health and Socio-Economic Survey

The Matlab Health and Socio-Economic Survey was implemented in Matlab, a rural region in Bangladesh, in 1996. The general focus of the survey was on issues relating to health and well-being among rural adults and the elderly, including the effects on health status and health care utilization of socioeconomic characteristics, health status, the characteristics of social and kin networks and the related resource flows, community services, and infrastructure. The study included a survey of individuals and households, a specialized outmigrant survey (a subsample of individuals who had left the households in the primary sample since 1982), and a community provider survey. The provider survey covered several types of health care providers, including governmental health complexes, family welfare centers, traditional practitioners, and community health workers. Separate instruments were used for each type of provider, although there were similarities in content. Clinical vignettes were administered to all providers.

Research and Publications

Frankenberg, Elizabeth. 1995. "The Effects of Access to Health Care on Infant Mortality in Indonesia." *Health Transition Review* 5 (2): 143–63.

Frankenberg, Elizabeth, Bondan Sikoki, and Wayan Suriastini. 2003. "Contraceptive Use in a Changing Service Environment: Evidence from Indonesia during the Economic Crisis." *Studies in Family Planning* 34 (2): 103–16.

Frankenberg, Elizabeth, and Duncan Thomas. 2001. "Women's Health and Pregnancy Outcomes: Do Services Make a Difference?" *Demography* 38 (2): 253–65.

Gertler, Paul J., and John W. Molyneaux. 1994. "How Economic Development and Family Planning Programs Combined to Reduce Indonesian Fertility." *Demography* 31 (1): 33–63.

Molyneaux, John W., and Paul J. Gertler. 2000. "The Impact of Targeted Family Planning Programs in Indonesia." *Population and Development Review* 26 (supplement): 61–85.

Measure Evaluation

Measure Evaluation is a collaborative project among several academic and research institutions and donor organizations (see http://www.cpc.unc.edu/measure/). The main purpose of the project is to develop and apply effective monitoring and evaluation methods to delivery systems in family planning; maternal health; infectious diseases; sexually transmitted diseases, especially HIV/AIDS; and nutrition. Measure Evaluation operates in collaboration with programs in developing countries, the U.S. Agency for International Development, and other international donor agencies to (a) improve performance monitoring systems for tracking outcomes; (b) identify appropriate indicators, test relevant indicator measurement procedures and tools, and establish appropriate data collection and storage systems; and (c) evaluate interventions, including cost-effectiveness. As a component of a general work program, the Measure Evaluation project has provided technical support in the design, implementation, and analysis of a range of health facility surveys. Examples include Paraguay (decentralization) and Uganda (the Delivery of Improved Services for Health project).

Research and Publications

Angeles, Gustavo, Rubén Gaete, and John F. Stewart. 2002. "Cost and Efficiency of Reproductive Health Service Provision at the Facility Level in Paraguay." Working Paper WP-02-45, Carolina Population Center, University of North Carolina at Chapel Hill, Chapel Hill, NC.

Angeles, Gustavo, John F. Stewart, Rubén Gaete, Dominic Mancini, Antonio Trujillo, and Christina I. Fowler. 1999. "Health Care Decentralization in Paraguay:

Evaluation of Impact on Cost, Efficiency, Basic Quality, and Equity, Baseline Report." Measure Evaluation Technical Report 4, Carolina Population Center, University of North Carolina at Chapel Hill, Chapel Hill, NC.

Katende, Charles, Ruth E. Bessinger, Neeru Gupta, Rodney Knight, and Cheryl Lettenmaier. 1999. "Uganda Delivery of Improved Services for Health (DISH) Evaluation Surveys." Measure Evaluation Technical Report 6, Carolina Population Center, University of North Carolina at Chapel Hill, Chapel Hill, NC.

Katende, Charles, Neeru Gupta, and Ruth E. Bessinger. 2003. "Facility-Level Reproductive Health Interventions and Contraceptive Use in Uganda." *International Family Planning Perspectives* 29 (3): 130–37.

Multicountry Evaluation of the Integrated Management of Childhood Illness

There is a considerable history of facility surveys by the World Health Organization. Originally, health facility instruments focused on issues relating to child mortality and morbidity, and survey instruments were often disease specific (that is, they were designed to evaluate specific programs or projects), for example, acute respiratory infections and diarrhea. The principal interest lay in assessing the quality of care and the effect of the quality of treatment on household behavior and health outcomes. Hence, facility surveys were typically accompanied by exit polls or household surveys (coverage surveys).

Recently, integrated surveys have become an important element in ongoing multicountry evaluations of the IMCI. The IMCI Strategy was developed by the United Nations Children's Fund and the World Health Organization to address five leading causes of childhood mortality, namely: malaria, pneumonia, diarrhea, measles, and malnutrition. The three main components addressed by the strategy are improved case management, improved health systems, and improved family and community practices. Worldwide, 30 countries are at various stages in the implementation of the IMCI. Integrated instruments for cost and quality evaluations have been developed and implemented (or are being implemented) for Bangladesh, Tanzania, and Uganda. The purpose of the evaluations is to (a) document the effects of IMCI interventions on health worker performance, health systems, and family behavior; (b) determine the measurable impact of the IMCI Strategy on health outcomes (particularly, in reducing under-five morbidity and mortality); (c) describe the cost of IMCI implementation at the national, district, and health facility levels; (d) enhance the sustainability of the IMCI and other child health strategies by providing a foundation for improvements in implementation; and (e) support planning and advocacy for childhood interventions by ministries of health in developing countries and national and international partners in development.

Research and Publications

Amaral João, Eleanor Gouws, Jennifer Bryce, Álvaro Jorge Madeiro Leite, Antonio Ledo Alves da Cunha, and Cesar G. Victora. 2004. "Effect of Integrated Management of Childhood Illness (IMCI) on Health Worker Performance in Northeast-Brazil." *Cadernos de Saúde Pública, Rio de Janeiro* 20 (Sup 2): S209–S219.
Arifeen, S. E., J. Bryce, E. Gouws, A. H. Baqui, R. E. Black, D. M. Hoque, E. K. Chowdhury, M. Yunus, N. Begum, T. Akter, and A. Siddique. 2005. "Quality of Care for Under-Fives in First-Level Health Facilities in One District of Bangladesh." *Bulletin of the World Health Organization* 83 (4): 260–67.
Armstrong Schellenberg, J., T. Adam, H. Mshinda, H. Masanja, G. Kabadi, O. Mukasa, T. John, S. Charles, R. Nathan, K. Wilczynska, L. Mgalula, C. Mbuya, R. Mswia, F. Manzi, D. de Savigny, D. Schellenberg, and C. Victora. 2004. "Effectiveness and Cost of Facility-Based Integrated Management of Childhood Illness (IMCI) in Tanzania." *Lancet* 364 (9445): 1583–94.
Armstrong Schellenberg, J., J. Bryce, D. de Savigny, T. Lambrechts, C. Mbuya, L. Mgalula, K. Wilczynska, and the Tanzania IMCI Multi-Country Evaluation Health Facility Survey Study Group. 2004. "The Effect of Integrated Management of Childhood Illness on Observed Quality of Care of Under-Fives in Rural Tanzania." *Health Policy and Planning* 19 (1): 1–10.
WHO (World Health Organization). 2001. "The Multi-Country Evaluation of IMCI Effectiveness, Cost, and Impact (MCE): Progress Report May 2000-April 2001." Report WHO/FCH/CAH/01.15, Department of Child and Adolescent Health and Development, World Health Organization, Geneva.

Notes

1. A sizable literature deals with the incentive issues that arise because of the asymmetry of information between patients and providers. See Arrow (1963) for an early contribution; see also McGuire (2000); Frank (2004); and Goddard, Mannion, and Smith (2000).
2. In general, it is possible to observe five categories of resources among facilities: (a) staff time; (b) supplies, medicines, and other consumables; (c) facility administration and overhead (for example, utilities); (d) equipment; and (e) buildings and other physical infrastructure. Some costs are incurred at higher levels and are therefore not observed at the facilities. These costs include, for example, training, supervision, and central and subnational administration. Costing is primarily based on input and price data. However, for some inputs, market prices may not be available, and some values must be imputed to derive total cost estimates.

3. For example, Lewis, La Forgia, and Sulvetta (1996) study only a single hospital, although in considerable detail. The study estimates service-specific costs for outpatient, inpatient, and emergency care, taking into account the case mix, clinical norms, and indirect and imputed costs, as well as the depreciation of physical infrastructure and equipment.

4. Step-down analysis is a standard methodology for distributing aggregate costs across departments (cost centers), and, ultimately, to final service categories (with measurable outputs). A variant of step-down allocation is activity-based costing, which seeks to supersede generic assumptions by allocating overhead costs to specific services (for example, by allocating such costs pro rata on the basis of the direct costs). This methodology is meant to overcome the problems of attribution that arise because of scale and scope economies (Chan 1993). For a review of issues in the allocation of overhead costs, see, for instance, Drummond et al. (1997).

5. This observation was pointed out by Feldstein (1967), who found that differences in case mix represented an important explanation for variation in ward costs per case among hospitals.

6. Composite output indexes may be constructed on the basis of ad hoc weights. If the limitations of the resulting output measures are squarely recognized, such measures may provide a useful means of summarizing information.

7. Similarly, for the estimation of a production function, Wouters (1993) suggests, as an estimation strategy, that outputs be included as dependent variables. Although convenient, the approach imposes strong assumptions about the production technology.

8. For example, the quality assurance methodology includes among the dimensions of quality diverse issues such as technical competence, access to services, effectiveness, interpersonal relations, efficiency, continuity, safety, and amenities (DiPrete Brown et al. 1993). This may make sense in an operational context, where the objective is to design practical interventions aimed at improving outcomes and to promote comprehensive monitoring. However, this all-encompassing notion of quality is less helpful from an analytical perspective, where the emphasis is on the coherent modeling of empirical phenomena and on valid and reliable measurement. Narrowing down the definition of health care quality is, however, far from easy. For example, Bessinger and Bertrand (2001) describe the difficult process of reducing the number of indicators of quality in family planning services from 200 to 25. Even after this considerable simplification, the recommended approach requires data collection through consultation observation, a facility audit, and interviews with clients.

9. Examples include Leonard, Mliga, and Mariam (2003) and Das and Hammer (2004). Consultation observation, sometimes accompanied by gold standard reexamination and patient interviews, has been a feature of some of the IMCI evaluation efforts. Recent examples include Naimoli et al. (2006), Arifeen et al. (2005), and Osterholt et al. (2006). It is also possible to carry out reviews of patient records or chart abstractions. However, this approach relies on records that are often unavailable or inadequate in developing countries (see Peabody et al. 2000).

10. As noted by Peabody et al. (2000), the costs in time and effort of complying with diagnostic and treatment procedures in a clinical vignette are negligible. This is

not the case in a clinical setting. As a result, we would expect vignettes to be biased in favor of high quality in a context where external and internal incentives for compliance are low. Reflecting this concern, Leonard, Mliga, and Mariam (2000) report evidence from Tanzania that, while most clinicians know how to deal with certain tracer conditions in theory (on the basis of written examinations), observations reveal that many do not apply the proper procedures in a clinical setting.

11. For example, Bitran Dicowsky (1995) finds that, regardless of facility scores on the quality of diagnostic and treatment norms and the availability of drugs and supplies, patients generally report being satisfied with the treatments they receive and indicate that they would return for future treatment. Atkinson (1993) has suggested that positive and negative comments about health care are typically not reducible to satisfaction and dissatisfaction and that a more careful methodology is required to collect meaningful qualitative data on patient perceptions.

12. New methods of paying health care providers have been introduced throughout the world in recent decades. For a detailed discussion, see, for instance, OECD (2004); Langenbrunner et al. (2005); Bitran Dicowsky and Yip (1998).

13. Panel data are more likely to generate convincing estimates, but there are few examples of the use of repeated facility surveys to study the impact of institutional or organizational reform. Angeles et al. (1999) set out to compare facility performance (costs) before and after decentralization, but the second round of the survey has not yet been completed.

14. The facility survey instruments are described at http://www.who.int/imci-mce/Methods/HF_survey.htm. On the impact of the IMCI on quality and costs, see Amaral et al. 2004; Arifeen et al. 2005; Armstrong Schellenberg et al. 2004; and Gouws et al. 2004.

15. A second round of data collection is planned, but it has been delayed because the implementation of decentralization has been occurring more slowly than anticipated.

16. A separate facility survey was also conducted in 2002 to monitor and evaluate follow-up activities in the Delivery of Improved Services for Health Project II (DISH and Measure Evaluation 2003).

17. However, in many studies, as Gertler and Hammer (1997) note, this may reflect the effect of utilization on pricing policy and quality rather than the other way around.

18. The linking of household and facility data raises important sampling issues. These issues are discussed in considerable detail in Turner et al. (2001).

19. Efficiency concepts were originally developed in analyses of the performance of firms. It is customary to distinguish between technical and allocative efficiency (Farrell 1957). Technical efficiency refers to the maximization of output with a given set of inputs. Allocative efficiency refers to the substitution among inputs at different prices to achieve minimum cost. For a detailed discussion, see Fried, Lovell, and Schmidt (1993).

20. The recent literature on efficiency among health care providers in the industrialized world has primarily used a statistical frontier model (see Dor 1994; Førsund, Lovell, and Schmidt 1980; Li and Rosenman 2001; López Casanovas and Wagstaff 1996; Rosko 1999, 2001; Vitaliano and Toren 1994; Wagstaff 1989; and Zuckerman, Hadley, and Iezzoni 1994). Approaches in developing countries have been more eclectic.

21. The World Fertility Survey was a collection of internationally comparable surveys of human fertility carried out in 41 developing countries in the late 1970s and early 1980s. The project was conducted by the International Statistical Institute, with financial support from the U.S. Agency for International Development and the United Nations Population Fund. For additional information on the DHS program, see http://www.measuredhs.com/aboutdhs/history.cfm. For further reading on the history and implications of the World Fertility Survey and the Contraceptive Prevalence Surveys, see Cornelius (1985). For details on the Contraceptive Prevalence Surveys, see Lewis (1983).

22. In health, surveys have included questions on the type of health care providers available in the community, the cost of treatments and medicines, travel times to respective providers, the available means and cost of transportation, and public health services and programs, including immunization programs and information campaigns. In some countries, community-level data have been sufficiently detailed to permit analysis of the relationship between health care infrastructure and health-seeking behavior and outcomes (for example, LSMS surveys in Ghana in 1987/88, 1991/92, and 1998/99; Guyana in 1992/93; Pakistan in 1991; and Tanzania in 1991 and 1993).

23. On maternity care, the questionnaires sought to assess the process of care. This approach was undertaken by reviewing a range of services and activities with the appropriate staff members and asking the staff members whether the respective services were included in a standard prenatal visit. Information was also sought on the nature of the groups of women thus served.

References

Ablo, Emmanuel Y., and Ritva Reinikka. 1998. "Do Budgets Really Matter?: Evidence from Public Spending on Education and Health in Uganda." Policy Research Working Paper 1926, World Bank, Washington, DC.

Agha, Sohail, Gabriela Escudero, Joseph Keating, and Dominique Meekers. 2003. "Nigeria (Bauchi, Enugu, Oyo) Family Planning and Reproductive Health Survey 2002: Health Facility Survey Results." Measure Evaluation Technical Report 16B, Department of International Health and Development, Tulane University, New Orleans.

Akin, John S., David K. Guilkey, and E. Hazel Denton. 1995. "Quality of Services and Demand for Health Care in Nigeria: A Multinomial Probit Estimation." *Social Science and Medicine* 40 (11): 1527–37.

Akin, John S., and Paul L. Hutchinson. 1999. "Health-Care Facility Choice and the Phenomenon of Bypassing." *Health Policy and Planning* 14 (2): 135–51.

Alderman, Harold, and Victor Chaim Lavy. 1996. "Household Responses to Public Health Services: Cost and Quality Tradeoffs." *World Bank Research Observer* 11 (1): 3–22.

Amaral João, Eleanor Gouws, Jennifer Bryce, Álvaro Jorge Madeiro Leite, Antonio Ledo Alves da Cunha, and Cesar G. Victora. 2004. "Effect of Integrated Management of Childhood Illness (IMCI) on Health Worker Performance in Northeast-Brazil." *Cadernos de Saúde Pública, Rio de Janeiro* 20 (Sup 2): S209–S219.

Anderson, D. L. 1980. "A Statistical Cost Function Study of Public General Hospitals in Kenya." *Journal of Developing Areas* 14 (2): 223–35.

Angeles, Gustavo, and Paul Hutchinson. 2003. "Evaluation of the Rural Service Delivery Partnership (RSDP), Bangladesh." Measure Evaluation Bulletin 6: 35–41, Carolina Population Center, University of North Carolina at Chapel Hill, Chapel Hill, NC.

Angeles, Gustavo, John F. Stewart, Rubén Gaete, Dominic Mancini, Antonio Trujillo, and Christina I. Fowler. 1999. "Health Care Decentralization in Paraguay: Evaluation of Impact on Cost, Efficiency, Basic Quality, and Equity, Baseline Report." Measure Evaluation Technical Report 4, Carolina Population Center, University of North Carolina at Chapel Hill, Chapel Hill, NC.

Arifeen, S. E., J. Bryce, E. Gouws, A. H. Baqui, R. E. Black, D. M. Hoque, E. K. Chowdhury, M. Yunus, N. Begum, T. Akter, and A. Siddique. 2005. "Quality of Care for Under-Fives in First-Level Health Facilities in One District of Bangladesh." *Bulletin of the World Health Organization* 83 (4): 260–67.

Armstrong Schellenberg, J., T. Adam, H. Mshinda, H. Masanja, G. Kabadi, O. Mukasa, T. John, S. Charles, R. Nathan, K. Wilczynska, L. Mgalula, C. Mbuya, R. Mswia, F. Manzi, D. de Savigny, D. Schellenberg, and C. Victora. 2004. "Effectiveness and Cost of Facility-Based Integrated Management of Childhood Illness (IMCI) in Tanzania." *Lancet* 364 (9445): 1583–94.

Arrow, Kenneth J. 1963. "Uncertainty and the Welfare Economics of Medical Care." *American Economic Review* 54 (5): 941–73.

Atkinson, Sarah J. 1993. "Anthropology in Research on the Quality of Health Services." *Cadernos de Saúde Pública, Rio de Janeiro* 9 (3): 283–99.

Banerjee, Abhijit V., Angus S. Deaton, and Esther Duflo. 2004. "Wealth, Health, and Health Services in Rural Rajasthan." *American Economic Review* 94 (2): 326–30.

Barnum, Howard N., and Joseph Kutzin. 1993. *Public Hospitals in Developing Countries.* Baltimore: Johns Hopkins University Press.

Beegle, Kathleen. 1995. "The Quality and Availability of Family Planning Services and Contraceptive Use in Tanzania." Living Standards Measurement Study Working Paper 114, World Bank, Washington, DC.

Belli, Paolo, George Gotsadze, and Helen Shahriari. 2004. "Out-of-Pocket and Informal Payments in Health Sector: Evidence from Georgia." *Health Policy* 70 (1): 109–23.

Benefo, Kofi Darkwa, and T. Paul Schultz. 1994. "Determinants of Fertility and Child Mortality in Côte d'Ivoire and Ghana." Living Standards Measurement Study Working Paper 103, World Bank, Washington, DC.

Bessinger, Ruth E., and Jane T. Bertrand. 2001. "Monitoring Quality of Care in Family Planning Programs: A Comparison of Observations and Client Exit Interviews." *International Family Planning Perspectives* 27 (2): 63–70.

Bhushan, Indu, Sheryl Keller, and J. Brad Schwartz. 2002. "Achieving the Twin Objectives of Efficiency and Equity: Contracting Health Services in Cambodia." ERD Policy Brief 6, Economics and Research Department, Asian Development Bank, Manila.

Bitran Dicowsky, Ricardo. 1995. "Efficiency and Quality in the Public and Private Sectors in Senegal." *Health Policy and Planning* 10 (3): 271–83.

Bitran Dicowsky, Ricardo, and David W. Dunlop. 1993. "The Determinants of Hospital Costs: An Analysis of Ethiopia." In *Health Economics Research in Developing Countries,* ed. Anne Mills and Kenneth Lee, 250–71. Oxford: Oxford University Press.

Bitran Dicowsky, Ricardo, and Winnie C. Yip. 1998. "A Review of Health Care Provider Payment Reform in Selected Countries in Asia and Latin America." Major Applied Research 2, Working Paper 1, Partnerships for Health Reform, Abt Associates, Bethesda, MD.

Chan, Yee-Ching Lilian. 1993. "Improving Hospital Cost Accounting with Activity-Based Costing." *Health Care Management Review* 18 (1): 71–77.

Chaudhury, Nazmul, and Jeffrey S. Hammer. 2004. "Ghost Doctors: Absenteeism in Rural Bangladeshi Health Facilities." *World Bank Economic Review* 18 (3): 423–41.

Chaudhury, Nazmul, Jeffrey S. Hammer, Michael Kremer, Karthik Muralidharan, and F. Halsey Rogers. 2006. "Missing in Action: Teacher and Health Worker Absence in Developing Countries." *Journal of Economic Perspectives* 20 (1): 91–116.

Cleary, Paul D., and Susan Edgman-Levitan. 1997. "Health Care Quality: Incorporating Consumer Perspectives." *JAMA* 278 (19): 1608–12.

Cookson, Richard, and Diane Dawson. 2006. "Hospital Competition and Patient Choice in Publicly Funded Health Care." In *The Elgar Companion to Health Economics*, ed. Andrew M. Jones, 221–32. Cheltenham, U.K.: Edward Elgar.

Cornelius, Richard M. 1985. "The World Fertility Survey and Its Implications for Future Surveys." *Journal of Official Statistics* 1 (4): 427–33.

Das, Jishnu, and Jeffrey S. Hammer. 2004. "Strained Mercy: The Quality of Medical Care in Delhi." Policy Research Working Paper 3228, World Bank, Washington, DC.

———. 2005. "Which Doctor?: Combining Vignettes and Item Response to Measure Clinical Competence." *Journal of Development Economics* 78 (2): 348–83.

Deci, Edward L. 1975. *Intrinsic Motivation.* New York: Plenum Press.

DiPrete Brown, Lori, Lynne Miller Franco, Nadwa Rafeh, and Theresa Hatzell. 1993. "Quality Assurance of Health Care in Developing Countries." Quality Assurance Methodology Refinement Series. Quality Assurance Project, Bethesda, MD.

DISH (Delivery of Improved Services for Health) and Measure Evaluation. 2003. "Uganda Delivery of Improved Services for Health (DISH) Facility Survey 2002." Measure Evaluation Technical Report 14, Delivery of Improved Services for Health, Kampala, Uganda; Carolina Population Center, University of North Carolina at Chapel Hill, Chapel Hill, NC.

Di Tella, Rafael, and William D. Savedoff, eds. 2001. *Diagnosis Corruption: Fraud in Latin America's Public Hospitals.* Washington, DC: Latin American Research Network, Inter-American Development Bank.

Dixit, Avinash K. 1997. "Power of Incentives in Private Vs. Public Organizations." *American Economic Review Papers and Proceedings* 87 (2): 378–82.

———. 2002. "Incentives and Organizations in the Public Sector: An Interpretative Review." *Journal of Human Resources* 37 (4): 696–727.

Donabedian, Avedis. 1980. *The Definition of Quality and Approaches to its Assessment.* Vol. 1 of *Explorations in Quality Assessment and Monitoring.* Ann Arbor, MI: Health Administration Press.

Dor, Avi. 1987. "Estimates of Cost Functions for the Peruvian Hospital Sector: Some Policy Implications." Unpublished report, Urban Institute, Washington, DC.

———. 1994. "Non-Minimum Cost Functions and the Stochastic Frontier: On Applications to Health Care Providers." *Journal of Health Economics* 13 (3): 329–34.

Dranove, David, and Mark A. Satterthwaite. 2000. "The Industrial Organization of Health Care Markets." In *Handbook of Health Economics,* ed. Anthony J. Culyer and Joseph P. Newhouse, 1A: 1093–1139. Handbooks in Economics 17. Amsterdam: Elsevier North-Holland.

Drummond, Michael F., Bernard J. O'Brien, Greg L. Stoddart, and George W. Torrance. 1997. *Methods for the Economic Evaluation of Health Care Programs.* Oxford Medical Publications. New York: Oxford University Press.

Edgman-Levitan, Susan, and Paul D. Cleary. 1996. "What Information Do Consumers Want and Need?" *Health Affairs* 15 (4): 42–56.

Farrell, M. J. 1957. "The Measurement of Productive Efficiency." *Journal of the Royal Statistical Society* A: 120 (3): 253–90.

Feldstein, Martin S. 1967. *Economic Analysis for Health Service Efficiency: Econometric Studies of the British National Health Service.* Contributions to Economic Analysis 51. Amsterdam: North-Holland.

Ferrinho, Paulo, Maria Carolina Omar, Maria de Jesus Fernandes, Pierre Blaise, Ana Margarida Bugalho, and Wim van Lerberghe. 2004. "Pilfering for Survival: How Health Workers Use Access to Drugs as a Coping Strategy." *Human Resources for Health* 2 (1): 4. http://www.human-resources-health.com/content/2/1/4.

Ferrinho, Paulo, Wim van Lerberghe, and Aurélio da Cruz Gomes. 1999. "Public and Private Practice: A Balancing Act for Health Staff." *Bulletin of the World Health Organization* 77 (3): 209–10.

Feyisetan, Bamikale James, and Martha Ainsworth. 1996. "Contraceptive Use and the Quality, Price, and Availability of Family Planning in Nigeria." *World Bank Economic Review* 10 (1): 159–87.

Filmer, Deon, Jeffrey S. Hammer, and Lant H. Pritchett. 2000. "Weak Links in the Chain: A Diagnosis of Health Policy in Poor Countries." *World Bank Research Observer* 15 (2): 199–224.

Førsund, Finn R., C. A. Knox Lovell, and Peter Schmidt. 1980. "A Survey of Frontier Production Functions and of Their Relationship to Efficiency Measurement." *Journal of Econometrics* 13 (1): 5–25.

Franco, Lynne Miller, Sara Bennett, and Ruth Kanfer. 2002. "Health Sector Reform and Public Sector Health Worker Motivation: A Conceptual Framework." *Social Science and Medicine* 54 (8): 1255–66.

Franco, Lynne Miller, Sara Bennett, Ruth Kanfer, and Patrick Stubblebine. 2004. "Determinants and Consequences of Health Worker Motivation in Hospitals in Jordan and Georgia." *Social Science and Medicine* 58 (2): 343–55.

Frank, Richard G. 2004. "Behavioral Economics and Health Economics." NBER Working Paper 10881, National Bureau of Economic Research, Cambridge, MA.

Frankenberg, Elizabeth. 1995. "The Effects of Access to Health Care on Infant Mortality in Indonesia." *Health Transition Review* 5 (2): 143–63.

Frankenberg, Elizabeth, and Duncan Thomas. 2001. "Women's Health and Pregnancy Outcomes: Do Services Make a Difference?" *Demography* 38 (2): 253–65.

Fried, Harold O., C. A. Knox Lovell, and Shelton S. Schmidt, eds. 1993. *The Measurement of Productive Efficiency: Techniques and Applications.* New York: Oxford University Press.

Garner, Paul, Jane Thomason, and Dayl Donaldson. 1990. "Quality Assessment of Health Facilities in Rural Papua New Guinea." *Health Policy and Planning* 5 (1): 49–59.

Gauthier, Bernard P. 2006. "PETS-QSDS in Sub-Saharan Africa: A Stocktaking Study." Unpublished working paper, World Bank, Washington, DC.

Gertler, Paul J., and Jeffrey S. Hammer. 1997. "Strategies for Pricing Publicly Provided Health Services." Draft working paper, World Bank, Washington, DC.

Gertler, Paul J., Luis Locay, and Warren C. Sanderson. 1987. "Are User Fees Regressive?: The Welfare Implications of Health Care Financing Proposals in Peru." *Journal of Econometrics* 36 (1–2): 67–88.

Gertler, Paul J., and John W. Molyneaux. 1997. "Experimental Evidence on the Effect of Raising User Fees for Publicly Delivered Health Care Services: Utilization, Health Outcomes, and Private Provider Response." Unpublished working paper, RAND Corporation, Santa Monica, CA.

Gertler, Paul J., and Jacques van der Gaag. 1990. *The Willingness to Pay for Medical Care: Evidence from Two Developing Countries.* Washington, DC: World Bank; Baltimore: Johns Hopkins University Press.

Glied, Sherry. 2000. "Managed Care." In *Handbook of Health Economics,* ed. Anthony J. Culyer and Joseph P. Newhouse, 1A: 707–53. Handbooks in Economics 17. Amsterdam: Elsevier North-Holland.

Goddard, Maria, Russell Mannion, and Peter Smith. 2000. "Enhancing Performance in Health Care: Theoretical Perspectives on Agency and the Role of Information." *Health Economics* 9 (2): 95–107.

Gouws, E., J. Bryce, J. P. Habicht, J. Amaral, G. Pariyo, J. A. Schellenberg, and O. Fontaine. 2004. "Improving Antimicrobial Use among Health Workers in First-Level Facilities: Results from the Multi-Country Evaluation of the Integrated Management of Childhood Illness Strategy." *Bulletin of the World Health Organization* 82 (7): 509–15.

Grosh, Margaret E., and Paul W. Glewwe, eds. 2000. *Designing Household Survey Questionnaires for Developing Countries: Lessons from 15 Years of the Living Standards Measurement Study.* 3 vols. Washington, DC: World Bank; New York: Oxford University Press.

Hong, Rathavuth, Livia Montana, and Vinod Mishra. 2006. "Family Planning Services Quality as a Determinant of Use of IUD in Egypt." *Health Services Research* 6 (1): 79.

Hongoro, Charles, and Charles Normand. 2006. "Health Workers: Building and Motivating the Workforce." In *Disease Control Priorities in Developing Countries,* 2nd ed., ed. Dean T. Jamison, Joel G. Breman, Anthony R. Measham, George Alleyne, Mariam Claeson, David B. Evans, Prabhat Jha, Anne Mills, and Philip Musgrove, 1309–22. Washington, DC: World Bank; New York: Oxford University Press.

Hossain, Shaikh I. 1989. "Effect of Public Programs on Family Size, Child Education, and Health." *Journal of Development Economics* 30 (1): 145–58.

Jensen, Eric R., and John F. Stewart. 2003. "Health Facility Characteristics and the Decision to Seek Care." *Journal of Development Studies* 40 (1): 79–100.

JLI (Joint Learning Initiative). 2004. *Human Resources for Health: Overcoming the Crisis.* Cambridge, MA: Joint Learning Initiative, Global Equity Initiative, Harvard University.

Kanfer, Ruth. 1999. "Measuring Health Worker Motivation in Developing Countries." Major Applied Research 5, Working Paper 1, Partnerships for Health Reform, Abt Associates, Bethesda, MD.

Katende, Charles, Ruth E. Bessinger, Neeru Gupta, Rodney Knight, and Cheryl Let-
    tenmaier. 1999. "Uganda Delivery of Improved Services for Health (DISH) Evalu-
    ation Surveys." Measure Evaluation Technical Report 6, Carolina Population Center,
    University of North Carolina at Chapel Hill, Chapel Hill, NC.
Katende, Charles, Neeru Gupta, and Ruth E. Bessinger. 2003. "Facility-Level Repro-
    ductive Health Interventions and Contraceptive Use in Uganda." *International Family
    Planning Perspectives* 29 (3): 130–37.
Keating, Joseph. 2006. "Nigeria Baseline Health Facility Survey, 2005." Technical
    Report TR-06-39B, Carolina Population Center, University of North Carolina at
    Chapel Hill, Chapel Hill, NC.
Kelley, Edward, and Jeremy Hurst. 2006. "Health Care Quality Indicators Project: Ini-
    tial Indicators Report." OECD Health Working Papers 22, Organisation for Economic
    Co-operation and Development, Paris.
Killingsworth, James R., Najmul Hossain, Yuwa Hedrick-Wong, Stephen D. Thomas,
    Azizur Rahman, and Tahmina Begum. 1999. "Unofficial Fees in Bangladesh: Price,
    Equity and Institutional Issues." *Health Policy and Planning* 14 (2): 152–63.
Langenbrunner, Jack C., Eva Orosz, Joseph Kutzin, and Miriam Wiley. 2005. "Pur-
    chasing and Paying Providers." In *Purchasing to Improve Health Systems Performance*,
    ed. Josep Figueras, Ray Robinson, and Elke Jakubowski, 236–64. European Observa-
    tory on Health Systems and Policies Series. Maidenhead, Berkshire, England: Open
    University Press.
Lavy, Victor Chaim, and Jean-Marc Germain. 1994. "Quality and Cost in Health Care
    Choice in Developing Countries." Living Standards Measurement Study Working
    Paper 105, World Bank, Washington, DC.
Lavy, Victor Chaim, John Strauss, Duncan Thomas, and Philippe de Vreyer. 1996.
    "Quality of Health Care, Survival, and Health Outcomes in Ghana." *Journal of
    Health Economics* 15 (3): 333–57.
Leonard, Kenneth L., and Melkiory C. Masatu. 2005. "The Use of Direct Clinician
    Observation and Vignettes for Health Services Quality Evaluation in Developing
    Countries." *Social Science and Medicine* 61 (9): 1944–51.
———. 2006. "Outpatient Process Quality Evaluation and the Hawthorne Effect."
    Social Science and Medicine 63 (9): 2330–40.
Leonard, Kenneth L., Melkiory C. Masatu, and Alex Vialou. 2005. "Getting Doctors
    to Do Their Best: Ability, Altruism and Incentives." Unpublished working paper,
    University of Maryland, College Park, MD.
Leonard, Kenneth L., Gilbert R. Mliga, and Damen Haile Mariam. 2000. "Bypassing
    Health Centers in Tanzania: Revealed Preference for Quality." Unpublished working
    paper, University of Maryland, College Park, MD.
———. 2003. "Bypassing Health Centers in Tanzania: Revealed Preference for Observ-
    able and Unobservable Quality." *Journal of African Economies* 11 (4): 441–71.
Lewis, Gary L. 1983. "The Contraceptive Prevalence Survey Project: Content and
    Status." *Population Index* 49 (2): 189–98.
Lewis, Maureen A. 2000. *Who Is Paying for Health Care in Eastern Europe and Central
    Asia?* Washington, DC: World Bank.
———. 2007. "Informal Payments and the Financing of Health Care in Developing
    and Transition Countries." *Health Affairs* 26 (4): 984–97.

Lewis, Maureen A., Gerald M. La Forgia, and Margaret B. Sulvetta. 1996. "Measuring Public Hospital Costs: Empirical Evidence from the Dominican Republic." *Social Science and Medicine* 43 (2): 221–34.

Li, Tong, and Robert Rosenman. 2001. "Cost Inefficiency in Washington Hospitals: A Stochastic Frontier Approach Using Panel Data." *Health Care Management Science* 4 (2): 73–81.

Lindelow, Magnus, Inna Kushnarova, and Kai Kaiser. 2006. "Measuring Corruption in the Health Sector: What Can We Learn from Public Expenditure Tracking and Service Delivery Surveys." In *Global Corruption Report 2006: Corruption and Health,* Transparency International, 29–37. London: Pluto Press.

Lindelow, Magnus, and Pieter Serneels. 2006. "The Performance of Health Workers in Ethiopia: Results from Qualitative Research." *Social Science and Medicine* 62 (9): 2225–35.

Litvack, Jennie I., and Claude Bodart. 1993. "User Fees Plus Quality Equals Improved Access to Health Care: Results of a Field Experiment in Cameroon." *Social Science and Medicine* 37 (3): 369–83.

Loevinsohn, Benjamin. 2000. "Contracting for the Delivery of Primary Health Care in Cambodia: Design and Initial Experience of a Large Pilot-Test." Paper, Flagship Program on Health Sector Reform and Sustainable Financing, World Bank Institute, Washington, DC. http://info.worldbank.org/etools/docs/library/48616/oj_cambodia.pdf.

López Casanovas, Guillem, and Adam Wagstaff. 1996. "Hospital Costs in Catalonia: A Stochastic Frontier Analysis." *Applied Economics Letters* 3 (7): 471–74.

Macro International (2000). "Survey Looks at Service Delivery in Kenya's Health Facilities." *DHS+ Dimensions* 2 (2): 4–5.

Madden, Jeanne M., Jonathan D. Quick, Dennis Ross-Degnan, and Kumud K. Kafle. 1997. "Undercover Careseekers: Simulated Clients in the Study of Health Provider Behavior in Developing Countries." *Social Science and Medicine* 45 (10): 1465–82.

McGuire, Thomas G. 2000. "Physician Agency." In *Handbook of Health Economics,* ed. Anthony J. Culyer and Joseph P. Newhouse, 1A: 461–536. Handbooks in Economics 17. Amsterdam: Elsevier North-Holland.

McNamara, Peggy L. 2006. "Provider-Specific Report Cards: A Tool for Health Sector Accountability in Developing Countries." *Health Policy and Planning* 21 (2): 101–09.

McPake, Barbara, Delius Asiimwe, Francis Mwesigye, Mathias Ofumbi, Lisbeth Ortenblad, Pieter Streefland, and Asaph Turinde. 1999. "Informal Economic Activities of Public Health Workers in Uganda: Implications for Quality and Accessibility of Care." *Social Science and Medicine* 49 (7): 849–65.

Miller, Kate, Robert Miller, Ian Askew, Marjorie C. Horn, and Lewis Ndhlovu. 1998. *Clinic-Based Family Planning and Reproductive Health Services in Africa: Findings from Situation Analysis Studies.* New York: Population Council.

Miller, Robert, Andrew Fisher, Kate Miller, Lewis Ndhlovu, Baker Ndugga Maggwa, Ian Askew, Diouratie Sanogo, and Placide Tapsoba. 1997. *The Situation Analysis Approach to Assessing Family Planning and Reproductive Health Services: A Handbook.* New York: Population Council.

Miller, Robert H., and Harold S. Luft. 1997. "Does Managed Care Lead to Better or Worse Quality of Care?" *Health Affairs* 16 (5): 7–25.

————. 2002. "HMO Plan Performance Update: An Analysis of the Literature, 1997–2001." *Health Affairs* 21 (4): 63–86.

Mills, Anne. 1997. "Improving the Efficiency of Public Sector Health Services in Developing Countries: Bureaucratic Versus Market Approaches." In *Marketizing Education and Health in Developing Countries: Miracle or Mirage?*, ed. Christopher Colclough, 245–74. IDS Development Studies. New York: Oxford University Press.

Mills, Anne, Sara Bennett, Pomtep Siriwanarangsun, and Viroj Tangcharoensathien. 2000. "The Response of Providers to Capitation Payment: A Case-Study from Thailand." *Health Policy* 51 (3): 163–80.

Mills, Anne, Fawzia Rasheed, and Stephen Tollman. 2006. "Strengthening Health Systems." In *Disease Control Priorities in Developing Countries*, 2nd ed., ed. Dean T. Jamison, Joel G. Breman, Anthony R. Measham, George Alleyne, Mariam Claeson, David B. Evans, Prabhat Jha, Anne Mills, and Philip Musgrove, 87–102. Washington, DC: World Bank; New York: Oxford University Press.

Mroz, Thomas A., Kenneth A. Bollen, Ilene S. Speizer, and Dominic J. Mancini. 1999. "Quality, Accessibility, and Contraceptive Use in Rural Tanzania." *Demography* 36 (1): 23–40.

Mwabu, Germano M. 1986. "Health Care Decisions at the Household Level: Results of a Rural Health Survey in Kenya." *Social Science and Medicine* 22 (3): 313–19.

Naimoli, Joseph F., Alexander K. Rowe, Aziza Lyaghfouri, Rijimati Larbi, and Lalla Aicha Lamrani. 2006. "Effect of the Integrated Management of Childhood Illness Strategy on Health Care Quality in Morocco." *International Journal for Quality in Health Care* 18 (2): 134–44.

Newman, John, Menno Pradhan, Laura B. Rawlings, Geert Ridder, Ramiro Coa, and José Luis Evia. 2002. "An Impact Evaluation of Education, Health, and Water Supply Investments by the Bolivian Social Investment Fund." *World Bank Economic Review* 16 (2): 241–74.

OECD (Organisation for Economic Co-operation and Development). 2004. *Towards High-Performing Health Systems.* OECD Health Project Policy Studies. Paris: Organisation for Economic Co-operation and Development; Washington, DC: Brookings Institution Press.

Okullo, J., Q. Okello, H. Birungi, I. Askew, B. Janowitz, C. Cuthbertson, and F. Ebanyat. 2003. "Improving Quality of Care for Family Planning Services in Uganda." Report, Regional Center for Quality of Health Care, Institute of Public Health, Makerere University, Kampala, Uganda.

Osterholt, Dawn M., Alexander K. Rowe, Mary J. Hamel, William D. Flanders, Christopher Mkandala, Lawrence H. Marum, and Nyokase Kaimila. 2006. "Predictors of Treatment Error for Children with Uncomplicated Malaria Seen as Outpatients in Blantyre District, Malawi." *Tropical Medicine and International Health* 11 (8): 1147–56.

Palmer, Natasha, and Anne Mills. 2003. "Classical Versus Relational Approaches to Understanding Controls on a Contract with Independent GPs in South Africa." *Health Economics* 12 (12): 1005–20.

Paul, Samuel. 2002. *Holding the State to Account: Citizen Monitoring in Action.* Bangalore, India: Books for Change.

Peabody, John W., Paul J. Gertler, and Arleen A. Leibowitz. 1998. "The Policy Implications of Better Structure and Process on Birth Outcomes in Jamaica." *Health Policy* 43 (1): 1–13.

Peabody, John W., Jeff Luck, Peter Glassman, Timothy R. Dresselhaus, and Martin Lee. 2000. "Comparisons of Vignettes, Standardized Patients, and Chart Abstractions: A Prospective Validation Study of Three Methods for Measuring Quality." *JAMA* 283 (13): 1715–22.

Peabody, John W., Omar Rahman, Kristin Fox, and Paul J. Gertler. 1994. "Quality of Care in Public and Private Primary Health Care Facilities: Structural Comparisons in Jamaica." *Bulletin of the Pan American Health Organization* 28 (2): 122–41.

Preker, Alexander S., and April Harding, eds. 2003. *Innovations in Health Service Delivery: The Corporatization of Public Hospitals*. Health, Nutrition and Population Series. Washington, DC: Human Development Network, World Bank.

Propper, Carol, Simon Burgess, and Katherine Green. 2004. "Does Competition between Hospitals Improve the Quality of Care?: Hospital Death Rates and the NHS Internal Market." *Journal of Public Economics* 88 (7–8): 1247–72.

Propper, Carol, and Neil Söderlund. 1998. "Competition in the NHS Internal Market: An Overview of Its Effects on Hospital Prices and Costs." *Health Economics* 7 (3): 187–97.

Propper, Carol, Deborah Wilson, and Neil Söderlund. 1998. "The Effects of Regulation and Competition in the NHS Internal Market: The Case of General Practice Fundholder Prices." *Journal of Health Economics* 17 (6): 645–73.

Ravindra, Adikeshavalu. 2004. "An Assessment of the Impact of Bangalore Citizen Report Cards on the Performance of Public Agencies." ECD Working Paper 12, Operations Evaluation Department, World Bank, Washington, DC.

Reinikka, Ritva. 1999. "Using Surveys for Public Sector Reform." PREMnotes, 23, World Bank, Washington, DC.

———. 2001. "Recovery in Service Delivery: Evidence from Schools and Health Centers." In *Uganda's Recovery: The Role of Farms, Firms, and Government*, ed. Ritva Reinikka and Paul Collier, 343–70. Regional and Sectoral Studies. Washington, DC: World Bank.

Reinikka, Ritva, and Jakob Svensson. 2001. "Explaining Leakage of Public Funds." Policy Research Working Paper 2709, World Bank, Washington, DC.

———. 2006. "Using Micro-Surveys to Measure and Explain Corruption." *World Development* 34 (2): 359–70.

Rosenzweig, Mark R., and T. Paul Schultz. 1982. "Child Mortality and Fertility in Colombia: Individual and Community Effects." *Health Policy and Education* 2 (3–4): 305–48.

Rosenzweig, Mark R., and Kenneth I. Wolpin. 1982. "Governmental Interventions and Household Behavior in a Developing Country: Anticipating the Unanticipated Consequences of Social Programs." *Journal of Development Economics* 10 (2): 209–25.

Rosko, Michael D. 1999. "Impact of Internal and External Environmental Pressures on Hospital Inefficiency." *Health Care Management Science* 2 (2): 63–74.

———. 2001. "Cost Efficiency of US Hospitals: A Stochastic Frontier Approach." *Health Economics* 10 (6): 539–51.

Somanathan, Aparnaa, Kara Hanson, Tamara Dorabawila, and Bilesha Perera. 2000. "Operating Efficiency in Public Sector Health Facilities in Sri Lanka: Measurement and Institutional Determinants of Performance." Small Applied Research Paper 12, Partnerships for Health Reform, Abt Associates, Bethesda, MD.

Steele, Fiona, Sian L. Curtis, and Minja Choe. 1999. "The Impact of Family Planning Service Provision on Contraceptive-Use Dynamics in Morocco." *Studies in Family Planning* 30 (1): 28–42.

Tatchell, Michael. 1983. "Measuring Hospital Output: A Review of the Service Mix and Case Mix Approaches." *Social Science and Medicine* 17 (13): 871–83.

Thaver, Inayat H., Trudy Harpham, Barbara McPake, and Paul Garner. 1998. "Private Practitioners in the Slums of Karachi: What Quality of Care Do They Offer?" *Social Science and Medicine* 46 (11): 1441–49.

Thomas, Duncan, Victor Chaim Lavy, and John Strauss. 1996. "Public Policy and Anthropometric Outcomes in Côte d'Ivoire." *Journal of Public Economics* 61 (2): 155–92.

Turner, Anthony G., Gustavo Angeles, Amy O. Tsui, Marilyn Wilkinson, and Robert J. Magnani. 2001. "Sampling Manual for Facility Surveys: For Population, Maternal Health, Child Health, and STD Programs in Developing Countries." Measure Evaluation Manual 3, Carolina Population Center, University of North Carolina at Chapel Hill, Chapel Hill, NC.

Vitaliano, Donald F., and Mark Toren. 1994. "Cost and Efficiency in Nursing Homes: A Stochastic Frontier Approach." *Journal of Health Economics* 13 (3): 281–300.

Wagstaff, Adam. 1989. "Estimating Efficiency in the Hospital Sector: A Comparison of Three Statistical Cost Frontier Models." *Applied Economics* 21 (5): 659–72.

Wagstaff, Adam, and Howard N. Barnum. 1992. "Hospital Cost Functions for Developing Countries." Policy Research Working Paper 1044, World Bank, Washington, DC.

Waters, Hugh R., Hany Abdallah, and Diana Santillán. 2001. "Application of Activity-Based Costing (ABC) for a Peruvian NGO Healthcare Provider." *International Journal of Health Planning and Management* 16 (1): 3–18.

Waters, Hugh R., and Peter Hussey. 2004. "Pricing Health Services for Purchasers: A Review of Methods and Experiences." *Health Policy* 70 (2): 175–84.

Weaver, Marcia, and Anil Deolalikar. 2004. "Economies of Scale and Scope in Vietnamese Hospitals." *Social Science and Medicine* 59 (1): 199–208.

WHO (World Health Organization). 2001. "The Multi-Country Evaluation of IMCI Effectiveness, Cost, and Impact (MCE): Progress Report May 2000–April 2001." Report WHO/FCH/CAH/01.15, Department of Child and Adolescent Health and Development, World Health Organization, Geneva.

———. 2006. *The World Health Report 2006: Working Together for Health.* Geneva: World Health Organization.

Wilson, James Q. 1989. *Bureaucracy: What Government Agencies Do and Why They Do It.* New York: Basic Books.

World Bank. 2001. "Jamaica Survey of Living Conditions (JSLC), 1988–98: Basic Information." Unpublished report, Poverty and Human Resources, Development Research Group, World Bank, Washington, DC.

————. 2007. "Brazil: Governance in Brazil's Unified Health System (SUS): Raising the Quality of Public Spending and Resource Management." Report 36601-BR, Brazil Country Management Unit, Human Development Sector Management Unit, Poverty Reduction and Economic Management Unit, Latin America and the Caribbean Region, World Bank, Washington, DC.

Wouters, Annemarie. 1991. "Essential National Health Research in Developing Countries: Health-Care Financing and the Quality of Care." *International Journal of Health Planning and Management* 6: 253–71.

————. 1993. "The Cost and Efficiency of Public and Private Health Care Facilities in Ogun State, Nigeria." *Health Economics* 2 (1): 31–42.

Zuckerman, Stephen, Jack Hadley, and Lisa Iezzoni. 1994. "Measuring Hospital Efficiency with Frontier Cost Functions." *Journal of Health Economics* 13 (3): 255–80.

3

An Introduction to Methodologies for Measuring Service Delivery in Education

Samia Amin and Nazmul Chaudhury

Education has become a global priority. The Millennium Development Goals, adopted at the United Nations Millennium Summit in 2000, include universal primary education as one of eight objectives to be achieved by 2015. Enhancing the quantity and quality of education service delivery is integral to achieving this goal of Education for All. To improve the performance of the schooling sector, we need ways and means to evaluate performance. This chapter provides an overview of methods to measure the quality of education service delivery.

Widespread consensus on the importance of education stems from extensive research on the macroeconomic, social, and private returns to education. Many studies have linked education to more rapid economic growth and lower levels of poverty and inequality (see Barro and Sala-i-Martin 1995; Birdsall, Ross, and Sabot 1995; Mankiw, Romer, and Weil 1992; Lau, Jamison, and Louat 1991; Birdsall and Londoña 1997). Education also yields high private and social returns at the microeconomic level; it is correlated with higher individual earnings, as well as improved health and reproductive choices (see Psacharopoulos 1985, 1994; Schultz 1997, 2002, 2003; Strauss and Thomas 1995). These findings and a growing belief that education is an intrinsic good have convinced policy makers that universal education is a key ingredient in economic and social development.

Despite the greater emphasis on schooling, the provision of education in developing countries remains far from effective (Glewwe 1999; Hanushek 1995; Harbison and Hanushek 1992; Lockheed and Verspoor 1991). Although there has been steady progress in increasing primary school enrollments, challenges persist. Primary school net enrollment rates in low- and middle-income countries had only reached 78 percent by 2004 (World Bank 2006). Primary school completion rates are even more sobering. Only 47 of 163 countries examined have achieved universal primary completion (UNESCO 2005). According to *World Development Report 2004*, if countries do not improve on their rate of progress, "universal primary completion would come only after 2020 in the Middle East and North Africa, after 2030 in South Asia, and not in the foreseeable future in Sub-Saharan Africa" (World Bank 2003, 112).

Given that 8 in 10 of the world's children are living in low- and middle-income countries, enhancing the capacity of the education sector in these countries is crucial. Two major problems must be addressed simultaneously to respond to this need. First, the quantity of schooling must be increased. Today, 100 million school-age children are out of school (UNESCO 2005). Second, attention must be paid to the effectiveness of education service delivery. The *Global Monitoring Report 2007* indicates that rapid expansion in enrollment has not resulted in increased levels of learning and stresses that improving the quality of outcomes is as critical as increasing access (World Bank 2007a).

Extensive research has been conducted in developed countries on the quality of the delivery of education services. Research on education in developing countries has focused primarily on the quantity of education. If increased access to education is to help enhance economic and social development, then careful attention will also have to be paid to promoting good standards of education everywhere.

Improvement is predicated on the ability to diagnose the existing state of education service delivery. This chapter provides an overview of the methodologies and instruments used to assess education service delivery. The next section identifies the purposes for which data on education are used and how these purposes determine the design of instruments. The subsequent section examines the major types of instruments used to collect data on education quality. The last section concludes with an assessment of the relationships among the instruments considered in the chapter.

Using Data on Education

Data on education are crucial for diagnosing and improving the state of education. National policy makers need data to make administrative decisions (how and where resources should be allocated), to monitor progress (how the resources are being used), for process evaluation (how the resource distribution mechanisms operate), and for impact evaluation (how do additional resources affect target outcomes). Researchers use data on education to understand the determinants of quality, the interventions that improve the education sector, and the contexts in which these interventions succeed or fail. In gaining insights on the kinds of data required for these myriad purposes and the nature of the instruments needed for collecting the data, the following issues are relevant: (a) How representative must the survey be? (b) Which type of indicator should be used as a metric of quality? and (c) What is the primary source of data?

Representativeness of the Survey

Surveys may be representative along two dimensions: the proportion of schools represented and the proportion of school-going and school-age children represented. Instruments measuring education quality differ in the sample sizes they select. Some provide detailed information on a small sample, while others cover the universe of schools or school-age children. Analyses of quality may be based on data sets that fall anywhere along this spectrum, as shown in figure 3.1.

Policy makers and education officers typically need information on the universe of schools and school-age children to make administrative decisions and monitor progress in specific regions. For this purpose, they require census information. Analysts hoping to understand the determinants

FIGURE 3.1 Scope of the Instrument

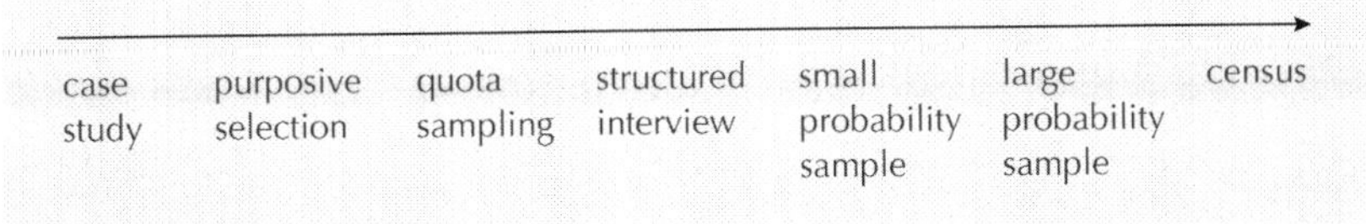

| case study | purposive selection | quota sampling | structured interview | small probability sample | large probability sample | census |

Source: Scott 2007.

and correlates of household decision making on education nationwide may wish to consider surveys with large probability samples rather than a full census given that the socioeconomic information in most census surveys is limited. Evaluators seeking to gauge the effectiveness of a policy restricted to a particular region may be able to work with an even smaller sample.

Indicators of Quality

The kind of data desired depends on the quality indicator used by the people making administrative decisions, monitoring progress, conducting evaluations, or trying to understand the correlates or determinants of quality. Studies on education vary widely in focus because there is no single, readily identifiable indicator for the measurement of the quality of service delivery in the education sector. Identifying an indicator of quality is difficult because "education is a multi-input, multi-output system with a poorly defined process of production" (Chapman and Carrier 1990, 9). Education outcomes are born of a long process involving the transformation of allocated resources into improved standards of education. Analyzing the supply of education entails looking at the inputs (planned and actual) dedicated to education, the process by which the inputs are utilized, the outputs generated by service providers, and the outcomes that result.

Decision makers and analysts choose different points along this service delivery chain to identify indicators that measure the effectiveness of an education system. Some consider *inputs* as evidence of effective service delivery. These inputs may compose material inputs, such as blackboards, utilities, and textbooks, and less tangible inputs, such as the curriculum, teacher quality, pedagogical practice, classroom organization, and the school management structure (Glewwe 2000). Although some analyses of education quality look at planned inputs, such as budget allocations or teacher hiring plans, most investigate disbursed inputs, such as education expenditure, and realized inputs, such as the number and size of schools or other school characteristics (Glewwe 2000). Other analyses gauge effectiveness based on the *process* by which officials transform allocated budgets into realized inputs; they, therefore, measure inefficiencies in management, such as the leakage of funds and teacher absenteeism. Alternatively, *outputs*, such as enrollments, student attendance, primary school completion rates, and class repetition rates, may be used as indicators of quality. Finally, some analyses use *outcomes*, such as learning achievement or private returns to education, as measures of the effectiveness of education provision. These sorts of studies are rarely simple tabulations of student performance; they usually also investigate correlates of achievement that relate to inputs, processes, or outputs. Individual studies tend to focus on a few indicators rather than a wide range (Glewwe 2002).

Depending on the data user's primary purpose and the stage of economic development of the country under study, certain types of indicators are measured more frequently than others. Users interested in developing countries, for example, tend to focus on the measurement of inputs and consider outputs to a lesser degree, whereas users interested in developed countries tend to devote more energy to the measurement of outcomes and processes.

Data Sources

Most studies may also be categorized according to whether their primary sources of information are (a) government data, (b) school data, (c) household and community data, or (d) student data. The first two encompass the supply side of education by looking at the sponsors and front-line providers of education. The latter two analyze actors on the demand side by looking at consumers, who are referred to as client-citizens in *World Development Report 2004* (World Bank 2003). Input and process indicators are more readily found in government data and school data sets, whereas output and outcome indicators are often found in household, community, and student surveys.

Education outcomes are the result of a complex interplay among governments, schools, communities, households, and students. Different types of instruments and sources of data illuminate different aspects of this puzzle. Consider a program seeking to improve educational facilities by distributing capitation grants to schools. Education officials will need government administrative data to disburse the transfer and to monitor whether it is properly administered in each village. School data may be necessary for understanding how the money is transferred from central or local governments to the facilities and how the facilities use the money. Household data may be needed to see how households modify their behavior in light of this investment in school facilities. Finally, student data may illustrate the effect of improved facilities on student performance. The same intervention may, therefore, be analyzed from several angles using widely different data sources.

Surveys often draw on more than one type of data source. A Public Expenditure Tracking Survey (PETS), for example, solicits data from government officials and front-line service providers. Similarly, household surveys with facility modules may gather information from households and from schools. Our classification is based on the nature of the primary source of data. We now portray the different instruments designed to collect data from each of the four types of sources.

Types of Surveys

This section describes the key types of studies measuring the quality of education service delivery and analyzes how they differ based on the breadth of coverage and the quality of the indicators chosen.

We start with an overview of government data, which have traditionally been used to evaluate the performance of the education sector. Two sources of government data are budget allocation records and national administrative records.

We then consider microlevel school surveys, which gather facility data. Microlevel school surveys fall into three subcategories: the PETS, the Quantitative Service Delivery Survey (QSDS), and the teacher absenteeism survey.

We also look at household and community surveys, which investigate how household and community data are used to weigh the quality of education service delivery. Those instruments include household surveys, citizen report cards, and community scorecards.

Finally, we look at surveys of student achievement. Student surveys measure educational achievement, often using it as an indicator of the quality of the education sector. There is a vast literature on student achievement in developed countries. This chapter touches on these studies briefly, while devoting itself principally to the growing body of research on educational achievement in developing countries.

Government Data

National studies seeking indicators of service delivery frequently use government administrative records to count the number of schools administered by the state, the number of teachers employed, and the number of students enrolled. Most governments collect data on educational facilities. Government-level data have been the traditional source of information for investigations of the education sector. For example, the World Education Indicators program of the UNESCO Institute for Statistics and the

Organisation for Economic Co-operation and Development gather data on 19 middle-income countries. They rely heavily on national administrative records to obtain gross and net enrollment rates. Existing national administrative data are attractive because no additional expenditure is necessary for data collection. National administrative data are also appealing to researchers because of the breadth of the coverage because many governments try to collect data on all the schools they administer or regulate. Preliminary assessments of education quality also often rely on government data relating to budgetary commitments to education and national administrative data on schooling indicators.

A few developing countries try to gather information on both public and private schools. For example, the government of Pakistan completed a national education census in 2005 that encompassed all educational institutions. However, it is important to note that national government data do not typically capture information on all the schools in a country. Schools are usually administered by the government or the private sector (in the case of for-profit and not-for-profit entities). In some countries, certain categories of private schools are subsidized by the government, for example, government-aided high schools in Bangladesh. In such cases, government-aided private schools are also included in a government's national school database. Nonetheless, in most countries, schools that do not receive government support (such as pure private schools in Bangladesh) or that operate as unregistered schools (such as unaided unregistered primary school madrassas in Bangladesh) are left out of national school databases. Thus, there is often no government data on private schools. Because the private sector is becoming a significant provider of affordable schooling for the poor, exclusive reliance on government data may therefore result in a misleading and incomplete picture of the education sector (see Andrabi, Das, and Khwaja 2005a, 2005b; Tooley and Dixon 2005).

Budget Allocations

A government's commitment to providing quality education is often assessed on the basis of its budget allocations to education. Analyses of government budgetary expenditure essentially examine planned and disbursed inputs dedicated to improving the quantity and quality of the education system. The World Bank's *World Development Indicators*, the UNESCO World Education Indicators, and the OECD Education at a Glance all gather information on annual budget allocations by governments to education. While expenditure data provide a rough guide to the relative importance of education on a government agenda, they offer little insight into how much of the allocated money ultimately reaches service providers.

Public expenditure reviews, which were developed by the World Bank, permit more thorough examinations of the size, nature, and sustainability of government education budgets. The reviews attempt to estimate the size of the education sector and examine the contexts of cost, supply, and demand in schooling. They seek to clarify whether government intervention is the best way to enhance the quantity and quality of education delivery, whether government and donor spending is being used efficiently and effectively to maximize the quality of education service delivery and the social benefits of education, and whether public expenditures on education are benefiting the intended target groups. The reviews investigate the systemic challenges to improvement in the education sector that stem from the way in which budget allocations are planned. They examine the link between macroeconomic conditions and sectoral planning to evaluate a government's ability and preparedness to maintain and improve the existing quality of education service delivery.

To some extent, the reviews examine government-household relations by analyzing the relative benefits different societal groups derive from government investments in education. The reviews include benefit incidence, which analyzes the distribution of public funding across segments of the population grouped by expenditure quintiles (or deciles). Those countries in which the poor (based on levels of consumption) receive most of the expenditure on education have progressive spending on education. Countries in which the wealthy benefit more from education expenditure have regressive spending.

A public expenditure review of education spending in Bolivia reveals, for instance, that expenditure on primary education is progressive, whereas expenditure on secondary and tertiary education is regressive. In the primary education sector, students from the poorest 40 percent of families receive almost 50 percent of total primary school expenditure, whereas students belonging to higher-income families in the top 40 percent of the income distribution receive only 30 percent of the expenditure (see table 3.1). At the secondary level, students from higher-income families receive a larger proportion of funding than do students from lower-income families. This increase is because students from poorer families show higher dropout and repetition rates in secondary school and form a smaller per-

	Quintile 1 (poorest)	Quintile 2	Quintile 3	Quintile 4	Quintile 5 (richest)	
TABLE 3.1 Public Expenditure on Education in Bolivia by Household Income Quintile, 2002 *(percent)*						
Level	Quintile 1 (poorest)	Quintile 2	Quintile 3	Quintile 4	Quintile 5 (richest)	Total
Primary	24	23	21	18	14	100
Secondary	12	20	21	22	25	100
University	2	4	14	28	52	100
Other tertiary	6	9	19	29	37	100

Source: World Bank and IDB 2004.

centage of the secondary school student population. At the university level, public expenditure is entirely regressive: public funding through universities benefits students from higher-income quintiles since they are overrepresented at the university level (see World Bank and IDB 2004).

A good public expenditure review will not rely on government data alone. Indeed, an effective review requires the use of many of the different survey tools outlined in this chapter, including household surveys, achievement tests, and facility surveys. Government capacity to conduct meaningful public expenditure reviews might be improved by gathering performance data on nongovernmental education service providers. This improvement would enable governments to make more informed comparisons of government efficiency relative to other service providers and to assess whether government interventions are the most effective way to provide education. This provision is a core objective of the review process. Studies pointing to the lower costs incurred by private schools and the consequent rise of private schooling options that are affordable for the poor in the developing world indicate that private schools may be more efficient than public schools in some instances (Jimenez, Lockheed, and Wattanawaha 1988; Tooley 2005).

National Administrative Records

Traditional assessments of education service delivery rely on administrative records on schooling collected by national governments. Government agencies collect administrative data at regular intervals, often annually, on indicators ranging from the number of public schools to enrollment rates per grade per school. Many systems also collect information on teachers and school principals. They collect these data for every public school in the country and then use them to make regional and district comparisons (Postlethwaite 2004). Many education ministries use education management information systems (EMISs) in the collection of this administrative data. The international community has dedicated much investment to helping governments adopt such systems to track schooling sector resources. The United Nations Educational, Scientific, and Cultural Organization, in collaboration with bilateral donors, has taken the lead in convincing developing countries to adopt EMIS infrastructures and in assisting them in this task.

Although EMISs vary substantially from country to country, most EMISs include data on students (enrollment, age, and repetition), data on teachers (experience and placement), and school inventory data (location, number of classrooms, and equipment). EMISs do not usually collect data on performance, school finances, cost accounting, material provisioning, or internal management programs (World Bank 2005).

An EMIS may improve efficiency by offering data on the allocation of resources, curbing the effects of bad decisions, and highlighting areas in which resources are poorly applied. An EMIS may furnish indicators of the quality of service delivery by accentuating the relationship between need and supply, thereby permitting gap analysis (Chapman and Carrier 1990). Most national and subnational governments collect data on school facilities because they are unable to make effective administrative decisions without such a full census. To allocate resources efficiently, they must understand the specific requirements and capacities of particular villages, districts, or towns. Administrative data are necessary for monitoring the progress of individual districts and villages and comparing the performance of schools from village to village. Unlike household and facility surveys, which typically do not cover multiple schools in a single village, administrative data are especially valuable in identifying intravillage disparities in school performance. Administrative data may also be useful in evaluations. They add a spatial dimension to evaluations by supplying data on neighboring schools, which survey instruments often do not cover because of their smaller sample sizes. If excellent monitoring data are collected regularly, an EMIS may likewise facilitate ex post evaluations by providing baseline data.

The utility of EMIS data is subject to three constraints. The first constraint is difficulty of access. Governments tend to be proprietary about administrative data. Government officials are reluctant to make data widely available, and they may even be reluctant to share it internally across ministries and departments. (A notable exception is the National Institute of Statistics of Cambodia, which disseminates EMIS data and information on other surveys through its Web site, at http://www.nis.gov.kh/.)

The second constraint is the lack of consistency in the indicators tracked from year to year. When data fields are changed frequently, constructing panel data sets and making comparisons across time become problematic, and this constraint reduces interest in the data.

The most serious constraint is the lack of support for strengthening EMIS data sufficiently so that they may be used for administrative decision making. This leads to a disregard for data reliability. This Achilles' heel stems from the fact that EMISs rely almost exclusively on self-reporting from schools. A standardized form is typically sent to headmasters for completion. Data fields are frequently left empty by the headmasters, and the information that is supplied is often inaccurate. The most common inaccuracies revolve around enrollments (essential for the calculation of gross enrollment rates) and the ages of students (essential for the calculation of net enrollment rates). Moreover, enrollment figures are often overstated for political reasons, and this tendency is exacerbated in public-aided schools where government financing is tied to enrollments. Age-specific data are unreliable primarily because headmasters enter the ideal age of students based on grade rather than the actual age, which generates substantial underestimates of delayed enrollments and net enrollment trends.

Few EMISs are accompanied by dependable audit systems, which adds to the concerns about credibility and consistency. Sometimes, EMIS data are inaccurate because of a shortage in data collection capacity. This typically results in incomplete coverage, missing data on many public schools, and poor information quality generally. A more systemic and enduring problem is the existence of significant incentives for misreporting. Effective information systems expose inefficiencies in the performance of the people who are responsible for providing information. Greater flows of accurate information may aid decision makers in lobbying for policy prescriptions, but they may also restrict the autonomy of decision makers by introducing unwelcome levels of accountability (Chapman 1990). Consequently, there are few incentives for accurate reporting and many incentives to doctor data.

To be effective, an EMIS must be integrated within a broader monitoring and evaluation system geared to the users of the system. Guinea offers an example. By the early 1990s, Guinea had acquired an unusually well-developed EMIS infrastructure thanks to financial and technical assistance from the U.S. Agency for International Development and the World Bank. In 1997, an interdepartmental government team initiated a dialogue with teachers, parent associations, education inspectors, and ministry officials on the need to devise a list of indicators defining the characteristics of a quality school. The EMIS was integrated within the monitoring system that was created to supply this need. EMIS data were used to determine which schools were quality schools (Crouch and Spratt 2001). EMIS data were also used extensively by local, regional, and national planners as a guide in teacher recruitment and new school construction in 1999 and 2000. Donors were intent on funding rural classroom construction, but the EMIS data helped illustrate that overcrowding in urban classrooms was a more pressing problem. EMIS statistics also showed that several hundred schools were being underutilized, primarily in rural areas. This indicated that stimulating demand rather than increasing supply was a more appropriate policy intervention in rural areas. Similarly, EMIS data on teacher deployment helped in the identification of geographical areas with shortfalls or oversupplies in teaching staff. Local and regional education officers were required to make adjustments in cases where schools were overstaffed. The EMIS in Guinea has been a success because of a fortunate confluence of capacity and demand. The surge in demand for EMIS data in the late 1990s helped create additional incentives to improve technical capacity (World Bank 2005).

More frequently, however, an EMIS tends to have a limited role in informing policy. This is partly because education ministries concentrate on improving the technical aspects of the system rather than on making the system user-friendly or on carefully analyzing the data output. If end users are uninterested in utilizing the outputs of an information system, the system administrators have fewer incentives to maintain data quality and accuracy. The unreliability of the data means that policy makers will become even less likely to use the system. The key to a good national administrative information system thus lies in creating serious demand for reliable data. Where data quality is under national scrutiny, the risks of exposure for incorrect data submissions are higher and the incentives for creating data audit systems are greater. Where statistics are regularly produced but rarely used, data quality is likely to be poor.

EMIS and similar national administrative systems may also be improved through the establishment of an effective data audit system to carry out periodic data checks on random samples of schools and impose penalties on misreporting by school and education officials. To provide a comprehensive picture of the education sector and become the definitive source of data on education service delivery, national administrative systems would have to collect information on all schools, irrespective of whether they are public, private, or nonprofit.

Microlevel School Surveys

Microlevel surveys have become important tools in measuring the quality of service delivery. They are now being used to analyze the share of allocated education budgets that reaches providers and the efficiency of schools in the utilization of resources. There are often great differences in the resources allocated to education and the funds the front-line providers—the schools—actually receive and use. Measurements of education service delivery, proxied by information on the number of schools or teachers, may therefore be greatly enhanced by data on budget allocations and school resource inputs and applications (Dehn, Reinikka, and Svensson 2003).

There are two major types of microlevel surveys: the PETS and the QSDS. A PETS assesses how much money actually reaches the front-line service providers, the schools. A QSDS is a multipurpose provider survey that analyzes how efficiently schools utilize the resources they receive. PETSs and QSDSs are often carried out in tandem (Das 2002; Sundet 2004).

Taken together, PETSs and QSDSs measure the difference between what is allocated to education and what consumers receive. They highlight the complex transformation from public budgets to services by boosting the observability of both outputs and actions (see Dehn, Reinikka, and Svensson 2003). We now discuss the key features of the PETS and QSDS methodologies. We also examine a hybrid version of these surveys that is used to investigate teacher absenteeism.

The Public Expenditure Tracking Survey

A PETS compares budget allocations to actual spending in the education sector. Data on budget allocations capture the money spent on education by the government, but not the financial resources received by schools. Discrepancies between budget allocations and budget disbursements are frequent; discrepancies between disbursed budgets and realized budgets (the money that reaches the front-line service providers) are also frequent. Unfortunately, funds are often lost during the transformation of allocated finances into actual inputs. A PETS tracks the flow of funds from the central government through different tiers of administration down to front-line service providers. These types of surveys explore the role of the relationship and interactions between governments and schools in determining the quality of education.

The first PETS study was devised and executed in Uganda in the late 1990s to investigate the reason increases in education budgets had not resulted in greater primary school enrollments. The hypothesis was that the data on budget allocations for the delivery of services were inaccurate because funds were being captured by officials and politicians at various tiers of local government. In the absence of reliable public accounts tabulating actual spending, a five-year survey was conducted that catalogued output and spending by government primary schools.

The survey results overwhelmingly favored the hypothesis that funds were being captured by local officials. Between 1991 and 1995, an average of only 13 percent of the annual per capita grant for students allocated among all schools by the central government actually reached the schools. Approximately 70 percent of the schools received none of the designated funding. Widespread dissemination of these findings by the Ugandan government shamed local and district officials into tracking expenditure flows more closely. A government information campaign was initiated that advertised monthly education disbursements to districts. This campaign was coupled with a new government regulation requiring schools to display information publicly on the funds they had received, thereby allowing the public to compare disbursements with receipts and monitor expenditure flows. The information campaign was extraordinarily effective at spurring reform. By the end of the 1990s, an estimated 90 percent of the allocated funds were reaching the designated facilities (Dehn, Reinikka, and Svensson 2003).

Since the Uganda study, PETSs have been conducted in several countries. The first step in a PETS is the identification of the structure of the education hierarchy, the structure of the resource flows from governments to schools (that is, how funds are allocated and distributed), and the institutions and actors involved. By itself, this exercise is extraordinarily instructive. One of the most valuable contributions of a PETS investigation in Peru was the information it generated on the disarray in the education hierarchy. The unit of analysis in a PETS tends to range from finance and education ministries to local government bodies and schools. A series of quantitative and qualitative assessments using survey instruments is conducted to measure budget flows in and out of the administrative layers identified during the first stage. Schools are then surveyed to determine the financial inputs they actually receive (World Bank 2001). Great care must be taken to ensure that the data collected at various levels are comparable and can be cross-checked with information from other sources.

It is recognized in microlevel surveys that agents have strong incentives to misreport expenditures. In a PETS, this tendency is countered by collecting data as close to the source as possible. For example, to verify funding, enumerators may use records kept by schools for their own use (such as check receipts) rather than official figures reported by or to education officials. Moreover, information is triangulated in a PETS by comparing data collected from other local, regional, and national providers of education in government, for-profit private entities, and the nonprofit sector (Dehn, Reinikka, and Svensson 2003). A good understanding of the data sources and of the incentives available to respondents to share or obscure data is crucial in designing microlevel surveys that capture accurate information. For example, public officials and suppliers in Uganda routinely collaborated to inflate the procurement prices of the goods supplied to schools. They were then able to siphon away some of the funds allocated to schools, while meeting accounting requirements. Accounting data on expenditures, procurement contracts, and receipts do not capture this leakage. Suppliers and public officials (including audit and accounting staff) colluding in this practice would have no incentive to respond honestly and identify the leakage. During the PETS in Uganda, the true value of realized inputs into education (and the losses caused by corruption) were measured by conducting inventories of the equipment, supplies, and other expenditure items received by schools and then setting a monetary value to these using locally prevailing prices. The PETS thus revealed that a large share of resources were being diverted.

Expenditure tracking surveys have evolved from diagnostic studies to sources of information on service provider behavior and incentives. In particular, the PETS methodology has been adapted to measure corruption. Because a PETS provides disaggregated data, it may also be used to pinpoint the administrative levels at which corruption occurs (Reinikka and Svensson 2003). By providing information on the distribution of resources among schools, a PETS permits an analysis of the equity in the distribution of government resources among schools (Sundet 2004).

A PETS not only allows estimates of average leakage rates but also shows the distribution of leakage, thus permitting an examination of the distributional effects of corruption. In Uganda, the 13 percent leakage rate masked great variation in the grants received across schools; some schools were receiving substantially less than others. Poor students were dispro-portionately affected because their schools tended to receive little, often close to nothing, whereas schools in more affluent communities managed to secure a larger share of resources. Consequently, in contrast to budget allo-cations, actual education spending in Uganda was regressive, and the socioeconomic status of recipients determined the incidence of funding (Reinikka and Svensson 2003). A PETS may, therefore, highlight the differ-ence between intended and actual effects and more accurately explore the benefit incidence of government spending on education. Conducting a PETS may be quite difficult in practice, however, because of poor record-keeping on expenditures. Discrepancies in expenditure records may sometimes stem from incorrect data entry rather than from the capture of funds by cor-rupt officials. (See chapters 7–9 for extensive discussions of the difficulties in implementing a PETS.)

The Quantitative Service Delivery Survey

Whereas a PETS dissects the flow of funds, a QSDS measures the efficiency with which allocated resources are used. The central focus of the QSDS is the front-line service provider. The QSDS is a multipurpose survey that typically collects data on (a) characteristics of the facility (size, ownership structure, type, hours of operation), (b) inputs measured in monetary terms (teacher and staff salaries, textbooks), (c) outputs (enrollments, graduation rates), (d) quality (student satisfaction, student test performance), (e) financ-ing (sources of funding, amount and type of funding, reliability of funding streams), and (f) management structures, oversight, and incentives (audits, reporting and recordkeeping policies, staff absenteeism). Incorporating information on these six core areas in each QSDS creates a certain level of standardization and allows for comparison among QSDS studies across multiple waves, sectors, and countries (World Bank 2003).

A QSDS typically involves a range of data collection techniques, including the gathering of quantitative data from facility records and inter-views with staff. As in a PETS, taking data from multiple sources permits data triangulation and cross-validation. A QSDS measures the efficiency of resource utilization in schools and provides a baseline for measuring the effect of reforms over time. Carrying out multiple QSDSs over time allows one to see whether the efficiency of educational institutions improves after interventions. A QSDS is occasionally paired with a survey of beneficiaries for a benefit incidence analysis. Such an analysis computes the distribution of public spending across demographic groups by allocating per unit subsidies (for example, expenditure per student) based on individual utilization rates among public services. QSDSs and the facility questionnaires included in household surveys are similar in content. QSDSs tend to be more intensive and lengthy.

The Teacher Absenteeism Survey

Teacher absenteeism surveys are hybrids; they combine elements of the PETS and the QSDS. They investigate a particular indicator of resource utilization and provider efficiency: whether all teachers are present. The premise of such an analysis is that, where provider absenteeism is high, a traditional PETS or QSDS may offer misleading estimates of the quality and extent of service delivery. This result is because teacher absenteeism is a form of resource capture that has not been accounted for in traditional PETS or QSDS methodologies. For example, a PETS will typically count actual expenditure on teacher salaries as a measure of schooling inputs. Similarly, a QSDS may calculate efficiency by measuring teacher-student ratios based on the number of teachers employed by schools. In practice, high rates of teacher absenteeism may mean that these measures are not good proxies for actual inputs into the education system.

Teacher absenteeism surveys combine aspects of a PETS and a QSDS to derive more accurate estimates of expenditure flows and resource utilization. Given that an average 75 percent of recurrent school expenditures are allocated for teacher salaries, teacher absenteeism surveys are similar to a PETS in that they try to measure whether expenditure on schooling translates into actual service delivery (Bruns, Mingat, and Rakotomalala 2003). Similar to a QSDS, teacher absenteeism surveys also attempt to measure the quality of schooling since teacher attendance is integral to quality and to the opportunities students are offered to receive instruction from qualified teachers.

Teacher absenteeism surveys examine the relationship between incentives for attendance and actual attendance patterns. Many developing countries have highly centralized education systems, weak local accountability, and strong teacher unions. The incentives for absenteeism are considerable (Chaudhury et al. 2006). A study of six developing countries has found that, on average, 19 percent of teachers are absent at any one time from primary schools. (The levels of absenteeism are almost twice as high in the health sector.)

Even attendance does not fully capture teacher input since, oftentimes, the presence of a teacher in school does not automatically translate into the delivery of a service. In India, three-quarters of employed teachers were in attendance at the time of the survey (that is, a 25 percent rate of teacher absenteeism), but barely half of the teachers who were present were actually engaged in teaching activities. This number held true despite the extremely broad definition of teaching activities, which might include cases in which teachers were monitoring a class rather than teaching (Chaudhury et al. 2004).

In some places, such as Peru, nonpecuniary incentives, including professional pride and concern for societal regard, motivate high teacher attendance, though penalties for absenteeism are lacking. The Peru study is based on the premise that, if social pressure and a sense of obligation to a community are deterrents to teacher absenteeism, then teachers who were born in or who now live in areas near the school should be less likely to be absent. Surveys have revealed that schools with teachers born in districts close to the school do, indeed, tend to show lower rates of absenteeism, up to 6 percentage points lower, and these effects are significant (see Alcázar et al. 2006).

Surveys aimed at measuring teacher absenteeism gather facility-level data. Enumerators make unannounced visits to primary schools to check on the attendance of teachers. To investigate correlates of teacher absenteeism, the surveys also collect data on teacher characteristics (age, gender, experience, educational background, and position), school characteristics (infrastructure, facilities, and utilities), and community characteristics (parental literacy, wealth, and location). Studies in Bangladesh, Ecuador, India, Indonesia, Peru, and Uganda have found that teacher absence is concentrated in poorer and more remote areas. Higher-ranking providers with more power, such as headmasters, tend to be absent more often. Men are absent more often than women, and local teachers tend to be absent less. Whereas pay does not appear to have a dramatic effect on teacher absence, the quality of infrastructure is correlated to absence. This concept is plausible. In countries where job security is high and the lack of penalties makes absenteeism an easy option, the quality of the working environment is likely to play a larger role in the decisions of teachers to go to work (Alcázar et al. 2006; Chaudhury et al. 2005, 2006).

The methodology for such surveys relies on direct physical observation of teacher attendance, coupled with interviews of directors and teachers. Enumerators rely on teacher rosters and schedules obtained from school principals; they list the teachers to be observed and interviewed. They do not use the rosters to determine attendance, but rather to determine sur-

vey strategy. Attendance is tabulated by direct observation during unannounced visits. Enumerators typically perform the survey in two phases:
first, to tabulate teacher attendance and, then, to interview teachers. They
usually visit the school twice to confirm patterns of attendance and, if possible, to interview teachers who were absent during the first visit. Multiple
visits allow enumerators to confirm the validity of the data, document
trends in teacher absenteeism, and assess whether absenteeism is a problem restricted to a few teachers or a more widespread phenomenon affecting a large proportion of staff. Repeated absences among the same small set
of teachers indicate an administrative problem that may be remedied
through better management. Absenteeism among a large share of teachers
indicates a more deeply rooted institutional problem that may require an
overhaul of incentive structures in the education system.

Assessing Microlevel Surveys

Microlevel surveys may provide an extraordinary richness of detail on
school quality and provider behavior. They allow thorough, in-depth examinations of the providers of education and multipronged analyses of interactions among players, processes, and procedures at different levels of an
education hierarchy. Microlevel surveys may be administered to public
(government-funded) and government-aided private schools and may
therefore facilitate a performance comparison among schools. There is great
scope for linking facility surveys with other instruments, including household surveys. More innovative PETSs such as the one conducted in Zambia have extended the scope of these studies. The Zambia PETS combined
school surveys, household surveys, and learning achievement tests among
pupils to measure the effect of inputs on results and the impact of government funding on schooling decisions taken by households.

Microlevel surveys fill a crucial gap left by administrative data systems. These systems are unable to gather detailed provider information
because this approach imposes an excessive reporting burden on school
staff. Microlevel surveys that target a sample of schools and do not require
self-reporting are thus a viable option. Microlevel surveys are also preferable
if the data being solicited may be self-incriminating (such as those relating
to absenteeism) and are unlikely to be readily disclosed by providers to
superintendents.

A well-conducted PETS, QSDS, or teacher absenteeism survey offers
invaluable insights into the efficiency and quality of schooling, but there are
constraints on implementation. First, they are time-consuming and expensive

to conduct. They consist of multiple questionnaires, each tailored to different units of analysis, and they must be carefully field-tested. Given the complexity of the questionnaires, it is usually necessary to require that enumerators be more well educated and more intensively trained than enumerators in standard household surveys. This requirement adds substantially to the costs.

Second, designing facility surveys presents challenges. Innovative ways of circumventing the incentives for providing misinformation must be devised. A well-designed PETS, for example, depends on a thorough understanding of the budget game, the formal and informal rules determining budget allocations and resource flows. If formal or strict allocation rules have not been established (often the case, particularly at the district or facility level), it will be more difficult to design effective techniques to determine the amounts of money allocated to a particular region or facility. Although it gives governments more flexibility in improving the allocation of funds and adapting policy in light of the findings from a PETS, the lack of hard rules makes a PETS diagnosis more difficult in the first place.

Third, poor data collection by education officials and poor recordkeeping by schools impede the implementation of facility surveys. Those problems may emerge at the outset of the survey design process. Many developing countries do not have a reliable census of schools. Sample frames may have to be constructed that draw on data from other sources, such as administrative records maintained by the central government or by donor organizations active in the sector.

Given the expense of microlevel surveys, sample sizes tend to be relatively small. Although the surveys collect far more data on any given school in the sample sets, EMISs capture information on far more schools. Conversely, surveys that encompass a greater number of schools tend to collect fewer details and are less rigorous about triangulating data. In effect, there appears to be a trade-off between quantity and quality in data collection. This trade-off exists not simply because of budget constraints, but also because of concerns over data quality. Selecting the optimal sample size involves a choice between minimizing sampling errors, which arise because a sample is being selected rather than the entire population, and minimizing nonsampling errors, which are caused by poor survey implementation. Sampling errors decrease with sample size, whereas nonsampling errors increase with sample size. In facility surveys such as a PETS or a QSDS, nonsampling errors are of greater concern because the data are often highly disaggregated and complicated to collect and the survey instruments are more complex and therefore more difficult to administer. Sampling issues become particularly acute when a PETS and a QSDS are combined. In a PETS, enumerators may want to survey a large number of local government administrations. This entails reducing the number of provider facilities sampled in each district. From the point of view of a QSDS, however, it is often more informative to select more providers in fewer districts to capture intradistrict variation among facilities (Reinikka and Smith 2004).

Household and Community Surveys

This section describes studies that rely on households and communities as the primary source of information on the quality of education service delivery. Unlike microlevel facility surveys that focus on the supply side, household and community surveys tend to evaluate the quality of schooling by relying on data gathered among consumers of education. Household surveys are important because they provide data on all school-age children, not merely those children enrolled in public schools. By providing data on the universe of school-age children, they allow estimations of total enrollment rates and facilitate insights into private versus public school enrollment rates. Most EMISs do not contain credible age data on students (see elsewhere above). Thus, household surveys that provide more reliable data on the ages of children are essential for robust estimates of net enrollment rates.

Household and community surveys are particularly important in the context of developing countries because of the extraordinary decision-making power households in these countries have in choices relating to investments in human capital, such as education. "In many developing economies, the household and family are key economic decision-makers and intermediaries, whereas as development progresses some of these roles are taken over either by the market or by the state" (Strauss and Thomas 1995, p. 1885). For example, basic education is now compulsory in all developed countries, and the state guarantees access to public education. However, in most developing countries, families are often free to decide whether children receive any schooling and bear much of the financial burden and the direct and indirect costs associated with this choice. Where households have such extraordinary power over education investment decisions, their perceptions of school quality become particularly important.

For policy makers and analysts conducting impact evaluations of schooling, understanding household decision making is valuable. Household surveys permit them to account for behavioral responses by households in the face of policy interventions. Consider a randomized evaluation of textbook provision that has resulted in an increase in learning. For a policy maker to select an optimal policy based on this information, it would be useful to know whether the increase in learning was generated because: (a) people were too poor to buy textbooks prior to the intervention, in which case distributing money or vouchers may be the solution; (b) the bookshop was too far away, implying that a bookshop should be established; or (c) household bargaining issues are at play, and distributing textbooks is appropriate. In each case, the policy prescription is different. Household surveys are able to supply these sorts of data that illuminate the dynamics underlying changes in outcomes.

Multitopic Household Surveys

Household surveys have long been used as a source of information on household choices on expenditures and other issues. Systematic data collection on households began over 200 years ago with the gathering of family budget data in England by Davies (1795) and Eden (1797). By the mid-1800s, this sort of data was being used to make generalizations about household decisions. By the end of World War II, large-scale nationwide surveys were being conducted in many countries. These surveys included developing countries such as India, where the annual National Sample Survey was initiated in 1950 (Grosh and Glewwe 1995).

In addition to national surveys financed by governments, international organizations such as the United Nations and the World Bank, as well as bilateral organizations, have supported the collection of household survey data in developing countries since the 1970s. These programs include the World Bank's Living Standards Measurement Study (LSMS), the U.S. Agency for International Development's Demographic and Health Surveys (DHS) Program (initially known as the World Fertility Survey), and the Multiple Indicator Cluster Survey (MICS) conducted by the United Nations Children's Fund. Organizations such as the RAND Corporation and the International Food Policy Research Institute have also conducted household surveys in developing countries. Regional surveys include the Social Dimensions of Adjustment Program in Sub-Saharan Africa and the Improving Surveys of Living Conditions Program in Latin America and the Caribbean.

We now briefly delineate the key characteristics of the three most widely used types of household surveys: the LSMS surveys, the DHS Program surveys, and the MICS. We also describe key features of RAND Corporation's Family Life Surveys because of their pioneering role in the development of innovative surveys in the 1960s and their influence on the design of the LSMS, DHS, and MICS instruments.

LSMS surveys (http://www.worldbank.org/LSMS). The LSMS surveys are multitopic surveys that investigate multiple aspects of household welfare and behavior (see Grosh and Glewwe 1995). They are meant to provide a comprehensive picture of living standards (Deaton 1997). The primary objectives of these detailed household surveys are to (a) establish a consumption-based measure of household welfare and (b) document other nonincome dimensions of poverty, particularly in relation to household investments in human capital. In studies of the determinants of educational outcomes using microlevel data, it is essential to control for household incomes. Unfortunately, most developing countries do not have systematic data on household incomes. Furthermore, in many settings, consumption is a better proxy for permanent income given the variable nature of income streams (and other factors).

Because they supply detailed data on living standards, including education (for example, current enrollment and grade completion in schools), LSMS surveys have become an important source of data for describing household decision making on investments in education. By looking at the choice of goods reflected in household production functions, household survey data allow us to estimate the value households place on schooling. This value is partly influenced by the quality of the education services available. Information on household decisions on enrollment and educational attainment (that is, number of years of schooling) are indirect measures of the quality of education service delivery (Strauss and Thomas 1995). Nonetheless, one must be aware that larger economic forces may also be at work. Thus, though the quality of schools in a particular region may be high, households might still choose to maintain or lower their investments in the education of their children if they perceive, for instance, that the demand for educated labor is weak in local markets.

Government policies that affect school quality may alter household decisions on enrollment and educational attainment. For example, a study of the effects of school characteristics on learning in Ghana has found that repairing leaking roofs and providing blackboards in classrooms significantly raise the number of years students remain in school (Glewwe 1999). Household surveys allow us to capture the impact of such policy changes on education outputs and outcomes (see Glewwe 2005; for detailed treatment of how household survey data may be used to estimate such impacts, including the impact on household behavior, see Deaton 1997).

An LSMS survey typically consists of three kinds of questionnaires: a household questionnaire, a community questionnaire, and a price questionnaire. The household questionnaire and the community questionnaire usually contain modules on education. Special facility questionnaires are included when more detailed information is needed on education and health facilities. The facility modules examine provider-household relationships. They elaborate on the relationships between school access, school quality, and key household welfare indicators.

Household questionnaires, community questionnaires, and facility modules in surveys collect different sorts of data on education. Household questionnaires provide information on the children in a household who are attending school, the frequency of school attendance, the cost of schooling to the household, and the activities of the children after they leave school. However, they provide limited information on school characteristics (Glewwe 2000). Judgments on school quality are gleaned indirectly through the analysis of household choices in the consumption of education. Household questionnaires also sometimes seek information on other measures of school quality such as educational attainment, school repetition, and wage returns to education (Schultz 2003).

Community questionnaires collect basic information on the location and quality of nearby educational facilities. They seek to supplement household questionnaires or reduce the length and scope of household questionnaires by gathering information on conditions common to a local community. They are, however, usually used only in rural areas where the boundaries of local communities are more readily identifiable. Community questionnaires, therefore, tend to rely on information provided by relatively few individuals. For this reason, they are often heavily subjective and typically supply statistics on the availability of educational facilities, but little information on school characteristics (Grosh and Glewwe 1995).

School questionnaires are more detailed. They collect information on teacher presence, student attendance, and the availability of supplies (World Bank 2003). Specialized education modules have been included in a few LSMS surveys, most notably those in Ghana, Jamaica, and Vietnam. These modules differ from household and community questionnaires because they collect information from schools. They are quite similar to facility-level surveys such as the QSDSs in this regard, but they are more easily linked to the relevant households than are the QSDSs because the household and facility modules are part of the same survey exercise, which is carried out in tandem using harmonized identifiers.

DHS program surveys (http://www.measuredhs.com; http://www.eddata global.org). The DHS program is funded by the U.S. Agency for International Development and administered by Macro International to supply data and analysis on population, health, and nutrition, especially among women and children, in developing countries. DHS program surveys were first undertaken in 1984 by the Institute for Resource Development, which was acquired by Macro International in 1989. The DHS program was folded into the U.S. Agency for International Development's multiproject Measure as Measure DHS+ between 1997 and 2003. In 2003, additional collaborating organizations joined in the new Measure DHS project. The DHS program has helped 75 countries conduct over 200 surveys. DHS program surveys are nationally representative household surveys with large sample sizes, ranging from 5,000 to 30,000 households. They are typically conducted every five years. The core questionnaires gather data primarily on health-related issues through questions on marriage, fertility, family planning, reproductive health, child health, and HIV/AIDS.

The core questionnaires consist of a household questionnaire and a women's questionnaire. The household questionnaire collects information on members of a household, including age, sex, relationship to the head of household, education, parental survivorship, and residence. The questions relating to education in the household questionnaire investigate whether each household member who is 5 years or older has ever attended school, the highest level of school attended, and the highest grade completed. For household members who are between the ages of 5 and 24, information is collected on school attendance, including level and grade, at any time during the current or the most recent school year. The responses to the questions are used to calculate gross and net attendance rates and repetition and dropout rates. In the women's questionnaires, additional questions on education are asked of women who are between the reproductive ages of 15 and 49. Women with less than secondary schooling are asked to read a simple sentence to assess their reading ability for the calculation of literacy rates in the country. They are asked about their participation in literacy promoting programs to gauge adult participation in literacy programs.

The U.S. Agency for International Development has also created a specialized education survey called DHS EdData that may be linked with a DHS Program survey or carried out separately. DHS EdData surveys have been conducted in Egypt, Ghana, Guinea, Malawi, Nicaragua, Uganda, and

Zambia. In the case of DHS EdData surveys that are linked to regular DHS program surveys, a subsample of surveyed DHS households is revisited, and data are collected from parents and guardians of school-age children. In stand-alone DHS EdData surveys, a nationally representative sample is independently chosen and surveyed. DHS EdData household surveys examine household demand for education. They provide information on the reasons for attendance or nonattendance among school-age children, expenditures on schooling, parental perceptions of school quality and the benefits of schooling, distances and travel times to schools, and the frequency of and reasons for pupil absenteeism. In 1999, DHS program surveys and DHS EdData surveys began to include questions on primary school repetition and dropout rates.

DHS EdData surveys collect little information on school facility characteristics directly from providers. They focus instead on school usage by households and parental perceptions of school quality. Unlike the education modules in the LSMS, little or no information is collected from schools or teachers. So far, the Measure DHS project has not developed provider surveys similar to the Service Provision Assessment surveys that it has adopted in the health sector. These assessment surveys collect extensive data on the quality of health facilities directly from health providers and communities. They examine costs, the availability of services, infrastructure, quality of care, and the components of care. The information from suppliers gathered through these assessments may be coupled with consumer information collected in DHS program surveys to provide a fairly comprehensive picture of health service delivery. DHS program surveys and DHS EdData surveys, in contrast, allow only evaluations of education service delivery based on information provided by consumers.

DHS program surveys are popular because the sample sizes are large and the samples are nationally representative. The use of nationally representative samples allows researchers to attach population weights to the samples and extrapolate findings to particular areas of interest. Because DHS program surveys are often carried out periodically, at five-year intervals, trends in education quality may be highlighted. A wealth index has been created based on asset data from DHS program surveys. The index may be used as a substitute for consumption-based permanent income measures in estimates of education attainment functions (Filmer and Pritchett 1998).

DHS program surveys have drawbacks. They gather information solely from education consumers, not providers. Unlike LSMS data, the DHS data do not include information on household income, consumption, or expenditure. Therefore, it is not possible to use them to construct household production functions that capture educational decisions in economic terms (Grosse, Klasen, and Spatz 2005; Wagstaff 2000).

MICS (http://www.childinfo.org/MICS2/Gj99306k.htm). The MICS methodology was developed by the United Nations Children's Fund in the mid-1990s to track global progress on goals relating to the welfare of children and women by providing internationally comparable and statistically rigorous data. The first round of the MICS program was conducted in 1995 and encompassed 60 countries. A second round carried out in 2000 expanded the number of indicators included in the survey. A third round was conducted in 2006 to measure progress toward the Millennium Development Goals. Each MICS has at least three modules: a household questionnaire, a questionnaire on children, and a questionnaire on women. Optional modules are also available.

The household questionnaire has an education module. The module asks if household members aged 5 or above have ever attended school or preschool, the highest level of schooling attended, and the highest grade completed. For household members aged 5–24, the questionnaire collects data on schools attended during the current school year, the number of days attended, the level and grade attended, whether the individual attended school or preschool in the preceding year, and the grade attended during that year. The MICS women's questionnaire, administered to women aged 15–49, collects data on school attendance, the highest level of school attended, and the grade completed. Respondents who have only had primary or nonstandard education are asked to read a simple sentence to test their literacy. The MICS child questionnaire collects data on children under 5 from mothers or caretakers. It includes a question on attendance at any organized learning or early childhood program. A MICS is typically carried out by government organizations with the assistance of the United Nations Children's Fund and other partners. The usefulness of MICS data is limited by the fact that the MICS samples are not usually nationally representative. Like a DHS program survey, a MICS does not capture the income and expenditure decisions of households and is therefore used less frequently by economists.

Family Life Surveys (http://www.rand.org/labor/FLS/). The RAND Corporation, in collaboration with national research institutions, conducts detailed household and community surveys in developing countries. These surveys, particularly the Malaysian Family Life Surveys in 1976–77, pioneered the adoption of experimental surveys in the 1960s and 1970s. Their innovative methodology has been emulated in the LSMS and DHS (Glewwe 2000). Family Life Surveys have been conducted in Bangladesh, Guatemala, Indonesia, and Malaysia. They gather current and retrospective data on households and communities. With the exception of the Guatemala survey, which deals primarily with family health, the surveys all collect data on the educational histories of adults and children, as well as detailed data on schools. The Family Life Survey carried out in Bangladesh included cognitive tests on language skills and mathematics.

Family Life Surveys have a far smaller geographical focus relative to the LSMS, DHS, or MICS. The variations in design and focus in the four country surveys limit the potential for cross-national comparisons. Repeat surveys have allowed the construction of longitudinal data sets that capture trends in education service delivery in Bangladesh, Indonesia, and Malaysia.

The LSMS, DHS, MICS, and the Family Life Surveys all evaluate school quality mostly by considering household decisions relating to education. Some LSMS surveys may include facility questionnaires to gather data on school characteristics, but most multitopic household surveys do not do so.

Citizen Report Cards

We now look at surveys that directly measure citizen and community perceptions regarding the quality of education service delivery.

Citizen report cards are surveys that capture consumer perceptions of the quality of public services and gauge client satisfaction. Data on education quality are usually collected as part of surveys that ask respondents to rate a wide range of providers. Citizen report cards have been used to aggregate feedback from the public on school provision.

This methodology was first popularized in Bangalore, India, by a group of civil society institutions seeking to address poor standards of service delivery. The survey consisted of a combination of ratings and detailed questions on specific aspects of service provision such as staff behavior, service quality, and responsiveness.

Citizen report cards collect data at the household and individual levels. The data may then be aggregated to provide more macrolevel data. Information is gathered through questionnaires that typically take three to six months to administer. Feedback and findings are disseminated later through media reports.

Citizen report cards typically capture demand-side perceptions, but they offer little systematic information on school characteristics. They investigate what respondents think of service delivery, but not why they hold these opinions; they do not identify causal relationships. Citizen report cards are not meant to function as accurate gauges of the quality of schools, but rather as catalysts to galvanize public debate and civic engagement. User ratings are inherently subjective because they vary relative to consumer expectations regarding government performance. These report cards may not serve as benchmarks because there are no common baselines or standards that are shared by reviewers. Expectations (and therefore scoring standards) tend to vary not only between countries, but between different regions in the same country. A comparison of the results of citizen report card surveys conducted in the Indian states of Bihar and Kerala offers a vivid illustration. The two states lie on opposite ends of the spectrum in the effectiveness of education service delivery. Although standards of education are undeniably higher in Kerala, the school ratings expressed by residents of Kerala are lower than those expressed by inhabitants of Bihar. This is because the expectation concerning quality standards in state services is entirely different in the two states. Kerala residents, used to a more efficient state, simply expect more (see Public Affairs Center, http://www.pacindia.org/rcrc).

Report cards function primarily as a means of generating public awareness, stimulating debate, voicing public discontent, and pressuring governments into improving service delivery and adopting more citizen-friendly services. In Bangalore, for example, the report cards have been instrumental in creating public pressure for reform and have led to improvements in governance. However, the effect of report cards often hinges on wide distribution and, more important, on their effectiveness in convincing policy makers (Ravindra 2004).

Community Scorecards

Community scorecards are qualitative monitoring tools used to monitor and evaluate service delivery performance by communities. They combine elements of social audits, community monitoring, and citizen report cards. They are similar to citizen report cards in that they capture collective community perceptions and opinions on the quality of service delivery and educational facilities in the local area.

The scorecards are being used with increasing frequency. Part of their appeal lies in the relatively short time frame required for implementation, ranging from three to six weeks. Information from community scorecards is location specific and, unlike the information from citizen report cards, may not be aggregated to provide information at various levels (municipality, city, state). This finding is because information is collected through focus group discussions rather than the randomized survey questionnaires used in citizen report cards. Ensuring that consensus is reached among the focus group participants in scoring services in a community is heavily dependent on the skill of the moderators. Community scorecards are highly subjective measures of quality; although they reveal community perceptions of quality, they do not systematically examine school characteristics that might determine these opinions (Sundet 2004).

Citizen report cards tend to be an urban phenomenon, while community scorecards are more common in rural areas where community boundaries are more easily identifiable. Citizen report cards allow demographic information to be gathered on respondents such as age, gender, and marital status. This collection is more difficult in the case of the focus groups involved in generating the community scorecards.

Furthermore, the use of focus groups in community scorecards to create aggregate assessments of service quality means there is the possibility the views of some individuals or groups may be dominating those of other individuals. Meanwhile, though respondents are assured their views are heard in citizen report cards, the polling methodology may result in bias. For example, some citizen report card surveys are conducted by randomly selecting names from a phone directory; this may have the unintended effect of restricting the sample to those who are sufficiently affluent to possess telephones.

The primary function of citizen report cards and community scorecards is not to provide comparable indicators of quality, but to serve as a means of strengthening relationships of accountability among consumers, governments, and service providers. The framework of accountability described in *World Development Report 2004* (World Bank 2003) indicates that there is no direct accountability of the provider to the consumer in situations in which the government takes responsibility for services in sectors such as education, health, water, electricity, and sanitation. Instead, accountability travels by a long route: citizens influence policy makers who then exert pressure on providers (see figure 3.2).

If the relationships along this route of accountability collapse, the quality of service delivery begins to deteriorate to the detriment of human development outcomes. This deterioration may occur when citizens do not have sufficient influence over policy makers or when policy makers have limited ability to monitor, reward, or penalize service providers. Improving the performance of the education sector hinges in

FIGURE 3.2 Framework of Accountability Relationships

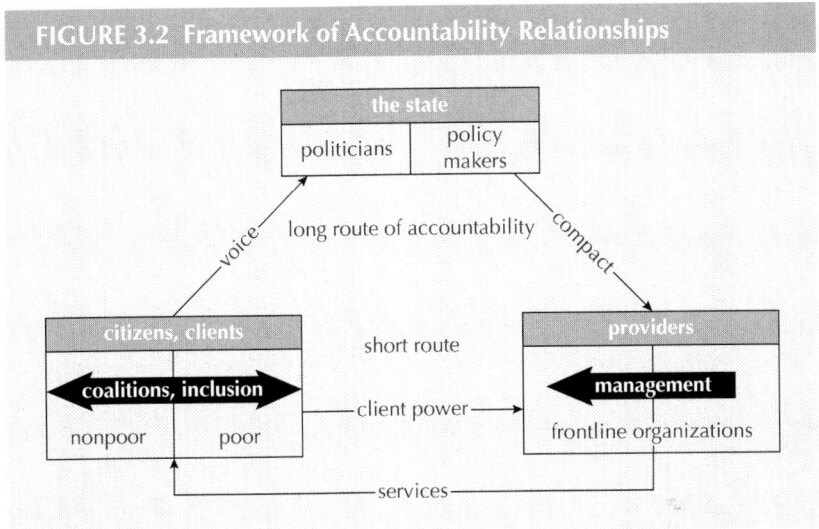

Source: World Bank 2003.

part on the ability to strengthen ties of accountability. The quality of service delivery is augmented by government measures that convert long routes of accountability into direct answerability between providers and consumers, mirroring traditional market relationships. These measures include school voucher schemes or scholarships that allow consumers to influence providers by exercising choice. Citizen report cards and community scorecards do not provide direct choice, but they do offer an avenue for pressuring policy makers, who may then exert their influence over providers to improve the delivery of services in education and other sectors.

Surveys of Student Achievement and Educational Attainment

Surveys of educational attainment measure the quality of the schooling system on the basis of education outcomes, that is, changes in student achievement. Studies of achievement were initially used simply to provide indicators of schooling performance, particularly in studies in which they served to highlight cross-country differences in achievement. They quickly evolved into instruments for diagnosing factors that affect student achievement.

There is a caveat to the use of education outcomes as indicators of service delivery: they are often deeply influenced by factors exogenous to school quality, such as student, household, and community characteristics. For example, many studies have found positive correlations among household income, wealth, and student achievement (see Dahl and Lochner 2005; Shonkoff and Phillips 2000; Levy and Duncan 1999; Blau 1999; Conley 1999). Achievement outcomes should, therefore, be used only as indicators of schooling quality once the influence of student backgrounds has been carefully taken into account.

A significant amount of research has been conducted in developed countries on the degree to which schools may affect student achievement apart from the influence of family and community characteristics. Student achievement is measured in a variety of ways. Most studies of student achievement consist of tests measuring cognitive performance in mathematics, reading comprehension, and science. More expansive tests (limited mostly to developed countries) include subjects such as geography, nonverbal reasoning, computers in education, and second-language acquisition (Porter and Gamoran 2002).

Typically, studies of educational achievement consist of tests and background surveys administered to students and, less frequently, to teachers and principals. Some surveys, such as the Trends in International Mathematics and Science Study and the Civic Education Study conducted by the International Association for the Evaluation of Educational Achievement (IEA), have included case study components. The Trends in International Mathematics and Science Study also includes a large-scale classroom video component in which mathematics and science instruction is examined by videotaping and analyzing teaching practices in over 1,000 classrooms globally.

Research on educational achievement has followed different trajectories in developing and developed countries. Research into education in the United States began toward the end of the 19th century, and tests on educational achievement were designed primarily in the United States by agencies such as the Educational Testing Service. By 1969, national sample testing surveys were being undertaken on a regular basis in the United States (Postlethwaite 2004). Concern about student performance on these tests, which became particularly acute in the United States in the early 1980s following the publication of the report *A Nation at Risk: The Imperative for Educational Reform* (National Commission on Excellence in Education 1983), spurred further study of the effect of a wide array of factors on learning (Gordon 2003). These factors include teacher performance, classroom and school management structures, curriculum content, and school culture. Surveys of educational achievement in industrialized countries are extensive and span a wide variety of topics and methodologies.

In developing countries, the focus used to be primarily on access to schooling. Studies of achievement were undertaken much later. Although a spurt of new research in recent years has augmented our knowledge, the depth and breadth of inquiry into the impact of school characteristics remain limited, especially relative to developed countries (Fuller 1990). However, since the 1990s, there has been a large number of studies on the impact of school characteristics on learning. The nascent, but rapidly growing literature on educational achievement in developing countries falls into two types. The first type includes national surveys and country-level research conducted by national governments, development agencies, and academics. The second type comprises international studies seeking to gather comparable cross-national data on educational performance in multiple countries.

Country-Level Research

Governments in developing countries conduct national studies of educational achievement primarily to gauge the performance of the education sector at a particular point in time and to track changes over time (Postlethwaite 2004). Governments taking stock of the education system at a given moment are often interested in making comparisons among regions within a country. Governments tracking changes over time are more interested in trends in student achievement and changes in the disparities in educational performance among pupils and schools.

Studies investigating the influence of school characteristics on student achievement usually examine the impact of one or more of the following four categories of school characteristics: (a) school expenditures and material inputs, (b) teacher quality, (c) teacher practice, and (d) school management structure and school policies.

Few studies attempt to examine the entire range of school characteristics that might influence student performance. Individual studies usually analyze the impact of a few factors. Studies of correlations of material inputs and student achievement often begin by exploring the relationship between school expenditure per pupil and student achievement. Investigations of the influence of discrete material inputs investigate a range of school characteristics, including class size, textbook availability and use, and the availability of desks, laboratories, and school feeding programs (Fuller 1990).

The studies tend to focus on the impact of discrete material inputs rather than the way these inputs are mobilized (Fuller 1990). Fewer studies examine the role and influence of teachers in schools. There are two categories in the analyses of the influence of teachers. The first looks at teacher quality based on professional background. Teaching background is usually measured through indicators such as length of schooling, postsecondary teacher training, and length of experience. Some surveys probe teacher quality by administering tests to teachers.

The second category of teacher impact studies examines the effects of teacher practices on student achievement. The studies focus on indicators such as the length of the school day, the number of hours of instruction on specific subjects, and the assignment of homework. Other indicators, including length of time spent explaining classroom instructional materials or the number and variety of instructional activities, have received less coverage in the literature on educational achievement in developing countries.

Investigations into school management and structure analyze the qualifications and role of headmasters, including the length of postsecondary schooling, length of teaching experience, salary levels, and share of ownership in the school (Fuller 1990). Some surveys also analyze decision-making processes and the division of responsibilities between the teaching staff and headmasters. For example, the Learning and Educational Achievement in Punjab Schools surveys in Pakistan include questions on who is responsible for the design of lesson plans and the choice of textbooks (see Andrabi, Das, and Khwaja 2006; World Bank 2007b). School advancement policies relating to the repetition of grade levels by low-achieving students are another factor examined in research.

International Studies

International studies were initiated in developing countries in 1958 by the IEA, an international conglomerate of research institutes and ministries of education (Lockheed and Verspoor 1991). Cross-national studies quickly became popular because they highlighted disparities in achievement, and this proved effective in mobilizing support for education reform.

The largest and most comprehensive international studies are being conducted by the IEA, the Southern and Eastern Africa Consortium for Monitoring Educational Quality, and the Program for International Student Assessment. All three international studies focus on assessing student performance in reading and mathematics. The Program for International Student Assessment and the IEA also concentrate heavily on science, and, from early on, the IEA has diversified into testing in other subject areas, including literature, foreign languages, and civic education.

The IEA undertook its first study in 1958 with a seminal 12-country testing project among 13-year-olds in Belgium, England, Finland, France, the Federal Republic of Germany, Israel, Poland, Scotland, Sweden, Switzerland, the United States, and the former Yugoslavia (see http://www.iea.nl). By the late 1970s, the IEA had begun conducting periodic surveys of key subject areas on a regular basis. These surveys gathered longitudinal data on performance indicators and other factors that influence education outcomes (IEA 2005). The IEA subsequently initiated several series of studies, including the Trends in International Mathematics and Science Study, the Pre-Primary Project, the Written Composition Study, and the Reading Literacy Study. The earlier studies focused primarily on developed and upper-middle-income countries, but, by the 1970s, the IEA studies had come to include India, Islamic Republic of Iran, and Thailand. In subsequent years, the studies encompassed low- and lower-middle-income countries such as Armenia, Bulgaria, Colombia, Arab Republic of Egypt, Ghana, Indonesia, the former Yugoslavia, Moldova, Morocco, Nigeria, Papua New Guinea, the Philippines, Serbia, Swaziland, the Syrian Arab Republic, Tunisia, Republic of Yemen, and Zimbabwe.

The *Southern and Eastern Africa Consortium for Monitoring Educational Quality* is a network of education ministries in the southern Africa subregion that aims to build the capacity of ministry planners to undertake large-scale educational policy research (see http://www.sacmeq.org). The consortium conducts cross-national education research projects on reading literacy and mathematics achievement. The aim is to identify weaknesses in educational systems. The consortium has conducted two major cross-national studies. The first was carried out between 1995 and 1999 in Kenya, Malawi, Mauritius, Namibia, Tanzania, Zambia, and Zimbabwe. The second study was conducted between 2000 and 2003 by ministries of education in Botswana, Kenya, Lesotho, Malawi, Mauritius, Mozambique, Namibia, the Seychelles, South Africa, Swaziland, Tanzania (mainland), Tanzania (Zanzibar), Uganda, and Zambia.

The *Program for International Student Assessment,* administered by the Organisation for Economic Co-operation and Development, was initiated in 2000 (see http://www.pisa.oecd.org/). The program pools expertise from participating countries, of which the governments jointly define the agenda. It targets 15-year-olds in these participating countries to assess the extent to which students completing compulsory education have acquired skills in reading, mathematical, and scientific literacy. Testing occurs in rounds

(2000, 2003, and 2006; the next round is set for 2009). The program was initially designed primarily for countries in the Organisation for Economic Co-operation and Development, but 27 of the 56 countries included in the latest round of the assessment (2006) are not members of this organization. These include Azerbaijan, Brazil, Bulgaria, Colombia, Indonesia, Jordan, the Kyrgyz Republic, Montenegro, the former Yugoslavia, Thailand, and Tunisia.

Other international studies include the Monitoring Learning Achievement Project of the United Nations Children's Fund and the United Nations Educational, Scientific, and Cultural Organization; the Programme d'analyse des systèmes éducatifs des pays de la Conférence des Ministres de l'Education des pays ayant le français en partage (Program of Analysis of the Education Systems of Countries Participating in the Conference of Ministers of Education of French-Speaking Countries), which covers many French-speaking African countries; and the study of South American school systems coordinated by the United Nations Educational, Scientific, and Cultural Organization's Regional Bureau for Education in Latin America and the Caribbean and conducted by the Latin American Laboratory for the Assessment of the Quality of Education.

Conclusion

This chapter has focused on the supply of data and the methodologies available to measure service delivery in education. The key to the impact of better measurements of performance in the delivery of services is the demand for pertinent information by policy makers. If there is more emphasis on the production of data and less on analysis and dissemination, data systems will remain ineffective. The political economy of the use of data merits further study.

The chapter describes the instruments used to illuminate various features of the education sector, and it draws attention to the limits and possibilities of each methodology. Which is the ideal instrument for measuring the quality of education? The answer depends on the aim of each study, the way the study wishes to define quality, and the resources available for the research. No single methodological instrument provides a comprehensive assessment of the delivery of education.

We have highlighted the wide variety of metrics that may be used to evaluate the efficiency and quality of education service delivery. Sometimes, the variations in the choices of the sources of data are purely a function of the indicators selected as metrics of quality. For example, studies on enrollment decisions by parents necessarily rely on household surveys because household members are likely to be the only people to have this information. At other times, different studies look to disparate sources for information on the same indicators. For instance, depending on the interest of the study, data on student enrollments might be sought through government administrative records, facility surveys, or household surveys.

The nature of the data will depend on the source. It is important to be cognizant of this and of the distinct advantages and disadvantages peculiar to the data supplied by specific sources. Administrative data may be used to measure enrollment because they encompass a larger number of schools. Because the data are self-reported, however, they may contain inflated or deflated enrollment numbers if school staff have incentives to exaggerate or underreport the size of student populations. Household surveys will capture information about children in or out of school in any sampled household, but may not capture accurate enrollment numbers for individual schools. Facility survey data allow for direct observation and the verification of student enrollments at the sampled schools, but may not capture information on all schools in a locality.

The choice of the instrument may also be constrained by cost and by the size requirements of the study sample. Instruments differ greatly in the breadth of the samples, the depth of the analysis, and costs. There are trade-offs between data coverage and data quality and reliability. A facility survey such as a PETS or a QSDS may yield the most intensive type of information, but, if resources are limited and a greater sample size is necessary, this sort of survey may not be feasible. An EMIS may provide superior coverage among schools, but the quality of the data may be suspect given that the data are often insufficiently audited.

Rather than attempting to construct instruments that cover all aspects of education service delivery, one may prefer to seek ways to link data sets that have been created using different instruments. Administrative data with clear geographical coding (such as postal codes) may be used so as to allow for at least some data aggregation across various sources. Pooling data becomes more feasible if each type of study includes a geographic information system technology component. A geographic information system is essentially a computer-based tool for tabulating, storing, editing, manipulating, analyzing, and plotting spatially referenced data (Korte

2001). By providing unique identifiers for each source of information (such as schools and households) and sharing those identifiers across data sets, the system eases links among different types of data. If geographically referenced data are available, a QSDS may be linked to a household survey to yield a more complete picture of how schools, households, and communities interact to determine education outcomes. The usefulness of a geographic information system depends on the quality and accuracy of the data supplied by the system and the degree to which studies rely on comparable identifiers and mapping tools. The value of data linked using comparable identifiers and coordinates likewise depends on comparability across the periods covered by the various surveys and resources.

Over the longer term, however, pooling ad hoc surveys and data sources may not be sufficient for providing the information needed to improve quality. Government officials must begin thinking in terms of developing a carefully planned system of surveys that is tailored to their data needs (Scott 2007). Optimally, such a system would include a mix of administrative, household, facility, and student achievement surveys, as well as information on the variations in the timing of these surveys. For example, it is often not feasible for governments to conduct a full school census every year. Between the census rounds, it might be necessary to undertake a sample survey on the basis of a panel design or a random-rotating panel design. Furthermore, to improve transparency, governments should delegate a PETS, QSDS, or teacher absenteeism survey to an independent survey firm or research organization. Although these surveys may be administered on a sample basis as well, it is important to update them every few years to gauge any impact of policy changes on improvements in the quality and governance of the education system. Table 3.2 shows a possible framework for evaluating data needs. More often than not, governments will be obliged to choose among competing data requirements. For example, the data demands of domestic administrative entities are likely to clash with donor demands for annual data on the progress toward the achievement of the Millennium Development Goals. Ultimately, governments must assess the competing demands for data and the resources available so as to pick the combination of instruments and timelines most suited to the particular situation. This selection is often a difficult exercise in practice.

In planning such systems, governments must be clear about the types of data they expect each component to provide and the timeline for each sort of survey. Ideally, to ensure coordination among these various surveys, governments should develop a regular program of periodical surveys sup-

TABLE 3.2 Evaluating Data Needs

Type of indicator	Data requirement	Type of instrument	Frequency
Input	Financial and physical indicators	Administrative data collection	Monthly
Process	Resource distribution and utilization process indicators	PETS, QSDS, teacher absenteeism surveys	Every 3 years
Output	Usage indicators	Administrative data collection, school census	Annually
		Household surveys	Every 3 years
Outcome	Achievement indicators	Student achievement tests	Every 3 years
Impact	Indicators on improvements in living standards	Household surveys	Every 3–5 years

Source: Compiled by the authors.

ported by adequate resource allocations rather than planning and undertaking ad hoc surveys one at a time (Scott 2007). This development will allow national statistics offices to accumulate capacity, avoid losses in institutional memory, exploit economies of scale, and become more flexible and responsive to government data needs. By ensuring that policy makers and the public are able to rely on data becoming available on a predictable basis from specified data producers, such a program may encourage greater use of the data in decision making and generate additional demand for reliable data. Building capacity in the use of data in decision making would certainly be instrumental in improving the quality of education for all.

References

Alcázar, Lorena, F. Halsey Rogers, Nazmul Chaudhury, Jeffrey S. Hammer, Michael Kremer, and Karthik Muralidharan. 2006. "Why Are Teachers Absent?: Probing Service Delivery in Peruvian Primary Schools." *International Journal of Educational Research* 45: 117–36.

Andrabi, Tahir, Jishnu Das, and Asim Ijaz Khwaja. 2005a. "Private Schooling: Limits and Possibilities." Unpublished working paper, Department of Economics, Pomona College, Claremont, CA.

———. 2005b. "Students Today, Teachers Tomorrow?: The Rise of Affordable Private Schools." Unpublished working paper, Department of Economics, Pomona College, Claremont, CA.

———. 2006. "A Dime a Day: The Possibilities and Limits of Private Schooling in Pakistan." Policy Research Working Paper 4066, World Bank, Washington, DC.

Barro, Robert J., and Xavier Sala-i-Martin. 1995. *Economic Growth.* McGraw-Hill Advanced Series in Economics, New York: McGraw Hill.

Birdsall, Nancy, and Juan Luis Londoña. 1997. "Asset Inequality Does Matter: Lessons from Latin America." OCE Working Paper 344, Office of the Chief Economist, Research Department, Inter-American Development Bank, Washington, DC.

Birdsall, Nancy, David Ross, and Richard H. Sabot. 1995. "Inequality and Growth Reconsidered: Lessons from East Asia." *World Bank Economic Review* 9 (3): 477–508.

Blau, David M. 1999. "The Effect of Income on Child Development." *Review of Economics and* Statistics 81 (2): 261–76.

Bruns, Barbara, Alain Mingat, and Ramahatra Rakotomalala. 2003. *Achieving Universal Primary Education by 2015: A Chance for Every Child.* Washington, DC: World Bank.

Chapman, David W. 1990. "The Role of Education Management Information Systems in Improving Education Quality." In *Improving Educational Quality: A Global Perspective,* ed. David W. Chapman and Carol A. Carrier, 217–42. New York: Greenwood Press.

Chapman, David W., and Carol A. Carrier, eds. 1990. *Improving Educational Quality: A Global Perspective.* New York: Greenwood Press.

Chaudhury, Nazmul, Jeffrey S. Hammer, Michael Kremer, Karthik Muralidharan, and F. Halsey Rogers. 2005. "Teacher Absence in India: A Snapshot." *Journal of the European Economic Association* 3 (2–3): 658–67.

———. 2006. "Missing in Action: Teacher and Health Worker Absence in Developing Countries." *Journal of Economic Perspectives* 20 (1): 91–116.

Chaudhury, Nazmul, José R. López-Cálix, Nancy Córdoba, Jeffrey S. Hammer, Michael Kremer, Karthik Muralidharan, and F. Halsey Rogers. 2004. "Teacher Absence and Incentives in Primary Education: Results from a National Teacher Tracking Survey in Ecuador." In *Background Papers,* Vol. 2 of *Ecuador, Creating Fiscal Space for Poverty Reduction: A Fiscal Management and Public Expenditure Review.* World Bank Report No. 28911-EC, 2: 139–67. Washington, DC: World Bank and Inter-American Development Bank.

Conley, Dalton. 1999. *Being Black, Living in the Red: Race, Wealth, and Social Policy in America.* Berkeley, CA: University of California Press.

Crouch, Luis, and Jennie Spratt. 2001. "EMIS Success in South Africa and Guinea: Insights from Practitioners." *TechnKnowLogia* 3 (1): 36–38.

Dahl, Gordon B., and Lance Lochner. 2005. "The Impact of Family Income on Child Achievement." NBER Working Paper 11279, National Bureau of Economic Research, Cambridge, MA.

Das, Jishnu. 2002. "Delivering Education in Zambia: A Guide to Expenditure and Service Delivery Surveys." Public Services Research, August, Development Research Group, World Bank, Washington, DC.

Davies, David. 1795. *The Case of Labourers in Husbandry Stated and Considered.* Bath, United Kingdom: printed by R. Cruttwell.

Deaton, Angus S. 1997. *The Analysis of Household Surveys: A Microeconometric Approach to Development Policy.* Washington, DC: World Bank; Baltimore: Johns Hopkins University Press.

Dehn, Jan, Ritva Reinikka, and Jakob Svensson. 2003. "Survey Tools for Assessing Performance in Service Delivery." In *The Impact of Economic Policies on Poverty and Income Distribution: Evaluation Techniques and Tools,* ed. François Bourguignon and Luiz A. Pereira da Silva, 191–212. Washington, DC: World Bank; New York: Oxford University Press.

Eden, Frederick Morton. 1797. *The State of the Poor: A History of the Laboring Classes in England, with Parochial Reports.* 3 vols. London: printed by J. Davis.

Filmer, Deon, and Lant H. Pritchett. 1998. "The Effect of Household Wealth on Educational Attainment: Demographic and Health Survey Evidence." Policy Research Working Paper 1980, World Bank, Washington, DC.

Fuller, Bruce. 1990. "What Investments Raise Achievement in the Third World?" In *Improving Educational Quality: A Global Perspective,* ed. David W. Chapman and Carol A. Carrier, 17–44. New York: Greenwood Press.

Glewwe, Paul W. 1999. *The Economics of School Quality Investments in Developing Countries: An Empirical Study of Ghana.* New York: St. Martin's Press.

———. 2000. "Education." In *Designing Household Survey Questionnaires for Developing Countries: Lessons from 15 Years of the Living Standards Measurement Study,* ed. Margaret E. Grosh and Paul W. Glewwe, 1: 143–75. Washington, DC: World Bank; New York: Oxford University Press.

———. 2002. "Schools and Skills in Developing Countries: Education Policies and Socioeconomic Outcomes." *Journal of Economic Literature* 40 (2): 436–82.

———. 2005. "Using Multi-Topic Household Surveys to Improve Poverty Reduction Policies in Developing Countries." In *Household Sample Surveys in Developing and Transition Countries,* ed. United Nations, 355–66. Studies in Methods ST/ESA/STAT/SER.F/96. New York: Statistics Division, Department of Economic and Social Affairs, United Nations.

Gordon, David T., ed. 2003. *A Nation Reformed: American Education 20 Years after a Nation at Risk.* Cambridge, MA: Harvard Education Press.

Grosh, Margaret E., and Paul W. Glewwe. 1995. *A Guide to Living Standards Measurement Study Surveys and Their Data Sets.* Washington, DC: World Bank.

Grosse, Melanie, Stephan Klasen, and Julius Spatz. 2005. "Creating National Poverty Profiles and Growth Incidence Curves with Incomplete Income or Consumption Expenditure Data: An Application to Bolivia." Discussion Paper 129, Ibero-America Institute for Economic Research, Georg-August-Universität Göttingen, Göttingen, Germany.

Hanushek, Eric A. 1995. "Interpreting Recent Research on Schooling in Developing Countries." *World Bank Research Observer* (10) (2): 227–46.

Harbison, Ralph W., and Eric A. Hanushek. 1992. *Educational Performance of the Poor: Lessons from Rural Northeast Brazil*. Washington, DC: World Bank; New York: Oxford University Press.

IEA (International Association for the Evaluation of Educational Achievement). 2005. "Brief History of IEA." International Association for the Evaluation of Educational Achievement. http://www.iea.nl/brief_history_of_iea.html.

Jimenez, Emmanuel, Marlaine E. Lockheed, and Nongnuch Wattanawaha. 1988. "The Relative Efficiency of Public and Private Schools: The Case of Thailand." *World Bank Economic Review* 2 (2): 139–64.

Korte, George B. 2001. *The GIS Book: How to Implement, Manage, and Assess the Value of Geographic Information Systems*. 5th ed. Clifton Park, NY: OnWord Press.

Lau, Lawrence J., Dean T. Jamison, and Frederic F. Louat. 1991. "Education and Productivity in Developing Countries: An Aggregate Production Function Approach." Policy Research Working Paper 612, World Bank, Washington, DC.

Levy, Dan Maurice, and Greg J. Duncan. 1999. "Using Sibling Samples to Assess the Effect of Childhood Family Income on Completed Schooling." JCPR Working Paper 168, Northwestern University and University of Chicago Joint Center for Poverty Research, Chicago and Evanston, IL.

Lockheed, Marlaine E., and Adriaan M. Verspoor. 1991. *Improving Primary Education in Developing Countries*. New York: Oxford University Press.

Mankiw, N. Gregory, David Romer, and David N. Weil. 1992. "A Contribution to the Empirics of Economic Growth." *Quarterly Journal of Economics* 107 (2): 407–37.

National Commission on Excellence in Education. 1983. *A Nation at Risk: The Imperative for Educational Reform*. Commission report, U.S. Department of Education, Washington, DC.

Porter, Andrew C., and Adam Gamoran. 2002. "Progress and Challenges for Large-Scale Studies." In *Methodological Advances in Cross-National Surveys of Educational Achievement*, ed. Andrew C. Porter and Adam Gamoran, 1–24. Washington, DC: National Academies Press.

Postlethwaite, T. Neville. 2004. *Monitoring Educational Achievement*. Fundamentals of Educational Planning 81. Paris: International Institute for Educational Planning, United Nations Educational, Scientific, and Cultural Organization.

Psacharopoulos, George. 1985. "Returns to Education: A Further International Update and Implications," *Journal of Human Resources* 20 (4): 583–604.

———. 1994. "Returns to Investment in Education: A Global Update." *World Development* 22 (9): 1325–43.

Ravindra, Adikeshavalu. 2004. "An Assessment of the Impact of Bangalore Citizen Report Cards on the Performance of Public Agencies." ECD Working Paper 12, Operations Evaluation Department, World Bank, Washington, DC.

Reinikka, Ritva, and Nathanael Smith. 2004. *Public Expenditure Tracking Surveys in Education*. Paris: International Institute for Educational Planning, United Nations Educational, Scientific, and Cultural Organization.

Reinikka, Ritva, and Jakob Svensson. 2003. "Survey Techniques to Measure and Explain Corruption." Policy Research Working Paper 3071, World Bank, Washington, DC.

———. 2004. "Local Capture: Evidence from a Central Government Transfer Program in Uganda." *Quarterly Journal of Economics* 119 (2): 678–704.

Schultz, T. Paul. 1997. "Demand for Children in Low Income Countries." In *Handbook of Population and Family Economics,* ed. Mark R. Rosenzweig and Oded Stark, 1A: 349–430. Handbooks in Economics 14. Amsterdam: Elsevier North-Holland.

———. 2002. "Why Governments Should Invest More to Educate Girls." *World Development* 30 (2): 207–25.

———. 2003. "Evidence of Returns to Schooling in Africa from Household Surveys: Monitoring and Restructuring the Market for Education." Center Discussion Paper 875, Economic Growth Center, Yale University, New Haven, CT.

Scott, Kinnon. 2007. "Assessing Information Needs, Survey Alternatives, and Alternative Surveys." PowerPoint presentation at the course "Poverty and Inequality Analysis," module 1, "Multitopic Household Surveys," Development Economics Vice Presidency, World Bank, Washington, DC, January 23.

Shonkoff, Jack P., and Deborah A. Phillips, eds. 2000. *From Neurons to Neighborhoods: The Science of Early Childhood Development.* Washington, DC: National Academies Press.

Strauss, John, and Duncan Thomas. 1995. "Human Resources: Empirical Modeling of Household and Family Decisions." In *Handbook of Development Economics,* ed. Jere R. Behrman and T. N. Srinivasan, 3A: 1883–2023. Handbooks in Economics 9. Amsterdam: Elsevier North-Holland.

Sundet, Geir. 2004. "Public Expenditure and Service Delivery Monitoring in Tanzania: Some International Best Practices and a Discussion of Present and Planned Tanzanian Initiatives." HakiElimu Working Paper 04.7, HakiElimu, Dar es Salaam, Tanzania.

Tooley, James. 2005. "Private Schools for the Poor." *Education Next* (2005) 4: 22–32.

Tooley, James, and Pauline Dixon. 2005. *Private Education Is Good for the Poor: A Study of Private Schools Serving the Poor in Low-Income Countries.* Washington, DC: Cato Institute.

UNESCO (United Nations Educational, Scientific, and Cultural Organization). 2005. *EFA Global Monitoring Report 2006: Education for All, Literacy for Life.* Paris: UNESCO Publishing.

Wagstaff, Adam. 2000. "Socioeconomic Inequalities in Child Mortality: Comparisons across Nine Developing Countries." *Bulletin of the World Health Organization* 78 (1): 19–29.

World Bank. 2001. "Expenditure Tracking and Service Delivery in the Education Sector in PNG." Concept Note, October 16, World Bank, Washington, DC.

———. 2003. *World Development Report 2004: Making Services Work for Poor People.* Washington, DC: World Bank; New York: Oxford University Press.

———. 2005. "Education Management Information Systems: Guidelines and References for Putting Information Systems to Work in Education." Advisory report, Education Advisory Service, World Bank, Washington, DC.

———. 2006. *World Development Indicators 2006.* Washington, DC: World Bank.

———. 2007a. *Global Monitoring Report 2007: Millennium Development Goals, Confronting the Challenges of Gender Equality and Fragile States.* Washington, DC: World Bank.

————. 2007b. "Pakistan, Learning and Educational Achievements in Punjab Schools (LEAPS): Insights to Inform the Education Policy Debate." Draft report, Human Development Sector Unit, South Asia Region, World Bank, Washington, DC.

World Bank and IDB (Inter-American Development Bank). 2004. "Bolivia: Public Expenditure Management for Fiscal Sustainability and Equitable and Efficient Public Services." Economic Report 28519-BO, World Bank, Washington, DC.

4

Administrative Data in a Study of Local Inequality and Project Choice

Issues of Interpretation and Relevance

Peter Lanjouw and Berk Özler

In a recent paper (Araujo et al. 2006), we investigate whether income distribution at the local level affects project choice in the Fondo Inversión Social de Emergencia (Social Investment Fund, FISE) in Ecuador. We focus on the community choice among projects on a social fund menu. Our main interest is in understanding the role played by elites in community decision making.[1] Specifically, we examine whether a community's decision to apply for a latrine project (a private good that mostly benefits the poor) is negatively influenced by the level of inequality in the community. We find that communities with higher levels of estimated (consumption) inequality are less likely to implement such projects. Once inequality is controlled for, however, we find that the larger the share of the poor in a community, the greater the likelihood that the community will receive pro-poor projects.[2]

Although local inequality may result in projects that are less pro-poor than they might have been otherwise, it might still be possible that, without some inequality, the village may not have gotten access to any social fund project at all. It has been argued, for example, that local elites "can act benevolently and play a positive leadership role" (World Bank 2005, 162). Given that most FISE projects provide at least some benefits to the poor, the effect of local inequality on project choice might be counteracted by its effect on the likelihood of receiving funds for any type of project. We, therefore, also

111

ask whether local inequality enhances the probability that a community will be selected for *any* FISE project. The results suggest that, conditional on village characteristics, such as demographics, community needs, political affiliation, and poverty, inequality is actually negatively correlated with the likelihood of obtaining a FISE project. Hence, in our study, greater influence by local elites (proxied by consumption inequality) does not seem to increase the chances that the community will receive project funds, and it may actually decrease the chances of receiving projects that provide (excludable) benefits to the poor.

This chapter provides a brief description of the principle data sources on which the analysis described above has been based. We raise a number of issues with respect to our use of administrative data. We do this seeking to highlight weaknesses and concerns that (a) may have been encountered (and possibly resolved) in other settings, and (b) affect the robustness of the conclusions that we are able to draw in our analysis.

The Data and Empirical Setting

The empirical analysis undertaken in the Araujo et al. (2006) study brought together data from a variety of sources to allow for a statistical investigation of the impact of local inequality on choice in the FISE program, while controlling for a wide range of community characteristics and circumstances.

The Ecuador Social Fund

The FISE program was established in March 1993. It was a new type of instrument in the social policy toolbox, and the Ecuadoran government presented it as a program that would be targeted so as to compensate the poor for some of the costs of the macrostabilization program that had been implemented to cut inflation. FISE was created with resources from international organizations (the U.S. Agency for International Development, the Inter-American Development Bank, the Andean Finance Corporation, and the World Bank), matched by local funds. It was administered by an agency under the direct supervision of the president of Ecuador and had a board of managers composed of representatives of various ministries (social welfare, education, health, labor, finance, agriculture, and information).

FISE financed small projects that had been identified, chosen, managed, and implemented by local governments and local organizations. The resources might be used on five types of projects: social infrastructure, socioeconomic infrastructure, social services, institutional development, and productive community investments.[3] However, FISE would not cover the operational budgets of an organization. Over its first year, the fund executed 608 projects nationally for a total of US$9.3 million. Indirectly, when the projects involved construction, the fund created employment for local contractors, as well as for local unskilled labor.

Before approaching communities, FISE would establish central targets concerning the share of the budget that might be spent on the different types of projects. In addition, it incorporated geographical targeting criteria by allocating proportionally more resources to communities with higher poverty rankings.

FISE used a participatory approach. Regional offices brought together community organizations and local governments to promote the program and to issue guidelines for project preparation. In these sessions, FISE indicated its priorities in terms of the types of projects for which resources were available. In addition, attendees were provided with reference costs for different sorts of projects; they might use this information in preparing their applications.

Once FISE approved a project, an implementing agency or contractor was chosen, and a representative of the community was appointed to ensure that the contract was honored during project execution. Although there are no records describing community processes of project selection, community representatives were granted power of attorney by the communities for which they were acting as agents. In addition to these monitoring efforts, technical supervision was provided by FISE.

Project-Level Administrative Data

The FISE program was accompanied by the introduction of a computer-based management information system (MIS) that was intended to assist with monitoring the project cycle and the overall performance of the project. The MIS database provides information on the choice, number, and location of projects, key dates (of application, approval, and completion), the size of the FISE transfer, the amount of community counterpart funding, and the name of the implementing agency (a contractor, a nongovernmental organization, the community itself, and so on). Our data source on projects is the MIS. There have been two criteria in our selection of data on projects: there had to have been an application for the project between May 1993 and January 1996, and the application had to have been granted. Information is available on a total of 2,876 projects. The MIS data reveal that many parroquias applied for and were granted more than one FISE project.

For the purposes of the Araujo et al. (2006) study, the key variables of interest were the type of project and the name and location of the community (parroquia) that had requested the project. Table 4.1 breaks down the projects that were analyzed in the study. The table shows the percentage of the projects across types. Slightly more than one-third of the projects (34 percent) involve the acquisition of school equipment and supplies. FISE program documents indicate that equipment included items such as blackboards and desks, but there was an explicit prohibition against the acquisition of schoolbooks.

Another 32 percent of the projects entailed the construction of new school rooms or school buildings. Although projects supplying school equipment included the delivery of goods in kind, the construction projects involved transfers of funds that were used to pay contractors for the construction work. Another difference between equipment-acquisition projects and construction projects is that the latter generally involved significant counterpart funding by the community requesting the project. Equipment projects did not require communities to provide counterpart funding.

A third sizable category of projects focused on the construction of latrines (13 percent of all projects). These projects were central to the analysis in Araujo et al. (2006) for two main reasons. First, latrines are used largely by the poor in rural Ecuador (see table 4.2). Evidence from household surveys indicates that nonpoor households are far more likely to use

TABLE 4.1 Distribution of FISE Projects by Type, 1993–96

Project type	Number of projects	Share of total projects (percent)
School (infrastructure)	920	32
School (equipment and supplies)	977	34
Latrines	377	13
Sewerage	132	5
Water supply	129	5
Health care	115	4
Other	226	7
Total	2,876	100

Source: Araujo et al. 2006.
Note: "Other" includes roadwork, agroindustries, irrigation, erosion control, crafts, adult training centers, statues, murals, and public laundries.

TABLE 4.2 Access to Toilets and Latrines by Quintile of Per Capita Household Consumption percent			
Quintile	Toilet	Latrine	None
Poorest quintile	44.5	12.0	43.4
2nd	45.8	15.4	38.7
3rd	51.1	18.4	30.5
4th	56.7	17.4	25.9
Richest quintile	73.9	9.7	16.4
Richest 1 percent	98.1	1.9	0.0

Source: Araujo et al. 2006.

other forms of sanitation infrastructure, such as toilets with connections to a networked water supply or septic tanks. Second, the latrines constructed through the FISE program are best seen as private goods that accrued to households that had not previously had access to sanitation infrastructure. Project documents indicate that beneficiary households obtaining such latrines had to provide the land on which the latrine was to be constructed. Each beneficiary household received a latrine, and the latrine was intended for the household's exclusive use.[4] The donation of land constituted the main form of counterpart provisioning by the beneficiaries for these projects. (Counterpart funding in financial terms, while not zero, was generally a small percentage of the overall project value.)

The empirical analysis in Araujo et al. (2006) takes as the unit of observation all parroquias in rural Ecuador. For each parroquia, an indicator was created to show whether or not it had received a FISE project. A separate indicator was produced showing whether a parroquia received *at least* one latrine project.[5] These parroquia-level project variables served as the principal variables of interest. The study sought to assess the extent to which the values taken by these indicators were affected by the characteristics of the parroquias, such as poverty or inequality.

Poverty and Inequality Estimates for the Parroquias

The next key set of indicators in the Araujo et al. (2006) study consists of information on inequality and poverty among parroquias. Such information is generally unavailable from conventional data sources. Distributional outcome indicators are typically calculated from household surveys, such as the World Bank's Living Standards Measurement Study surveys, and are often based on relatively small samples. While such surveys are usually designed to be representative at the national level and sometimes also allow for reliable estimates of inequality and poverty on a broad stratum (coastal, highland, or forest regions, for example), the sample size is typically far too small to yield reliable estimates of distributional outcome measures among small communities such as parroquias. Moreover, the sampling design of household sample surveys such as the Living Standards Measurement Study surveys are often complex and involve both stratification and clustering. As a consequence, only a relatively small subset of communities would be included in the sample. A typical Living Standards Measurement Study–style household survey might comprise an overall sample of 5,000 households built up from a set of, say, 500 communities (selected out of a universe of, perhaps, 10,000 communities), from within which 10 households have been randomly selected.

Household sample surveys may be useful sources of information on a wide variety of important indicators, and they may permit broad inferences at the national or, possibly, regional level. It is less clear how such a data set might yield estimates of distributional outcomes at the community level. First, as noted above, only a subset of communities would likely be represented in the data. Second, even in the subset of communities that is represented in the survey sample, the sample of households per community would typically be far too small to allow for a reliable estimate of economic welfare. The problem would likely be most acute with measures of community-level inequality.

If one is to obtain a reliable estimate of inequality for a small community, the sample of households drawn from that community generally has to be much larger than the 10–20 households per cluster that is commonly found in Living Standards Measurement Study–style household surveys. This point may be illustrated through data from a study on Palanpur, a small village in northern India analyzed by Lanjouw and Stern (1998). Palanpur is located on the Gangetic Plain of western Uttar Pradesh, India. The village has been the subject of intense study by economists starting in the late 1950s. A unique feature of this effort is that detailed income data were collected on *all* households in the village in four waves (1957–58, 1962–63, 1974–75, and 1983–84). It is thus possible to calculate the true level of income inequality in Palanpur, that is, calculated over all households in the village over time.

To assess the reliability of inequality estimates that are based on a sample of village households, we draw repeated samples of a given size from the Palanpur data set and calculate a set of inequality measures. The variation across these sample estimates provides an indication of the degree of error that is associated with the attempt to describe village inequality based on a single sample of households rather than on the whole population. Table 4.3 reports on this exercise with the Palanpur data from the 1983–84 survey year. True income inequality in Palanpur, as measured by the Gini coefficient, is 0.307. If a sample of seven households were drawn randomly from the population of 143 households, inequality measured across the seven households would provide an unreliable estimate of the truth. Drawing such a sample 100 times and calculating inequality for each repetition yields such widely varying estimates of village inequality that one would be able to declare with only 95 percent confidence that true inequality lay somewhere between 0.105 and 0.415. For the Gini coefficient, this figure is a wide range in measured inequality. If, instead of seven households, the sample had comprised 14 households, the precision of the sample-based inequality estimates would be only slightly better. The 95 percent confidence interval for the Gini coefficient would now span the range between 0.162 and 0.405. Only when the sample consists of at least 40 households (from a total village population of 143 households) would the sample-based inequality estimates start to look reasonable (the coefficient of variation is 10 percent; see table 4.3). With measures of inequality other than the Gini, the precision of sample-based estimates, even for samples of 40, remains unreliable.

The implication of the exercise described earlier is a caution against undertaking an analysis such as that presented in Araujo et al. (2006) in which community-level inequality estimates, based on small samples, are included as regressors in econometric models. At a minimum, the coefficients on such inequality estimates will be biased downward (because the massive sampling error leads to attenuation bias). More likely, because the measurement error also presents among other regressors, even determining the direction of the bias will be difficult.

To circumvent these difficulties, the Araujo et al. (2006) study analyzes the relationship between project choice and inequality at the community level based on small area estimates of inequality for each community. The small area estimation methodology was developed by Elbers, Lanjouw, and Lanjouw (2002, 2003), who combined household survey data with population census data. Essentially, they used the household survey data to impute into the population census an estimated consumption level for every

TABLE 4.3 Standard Errors Based on 100 Simulated Samples of the Palanpur 1983–84 Population

Sample size[a]	Gini coefficient		General entropy, c = 0.5		General entropy, c = 2	
	Standard error[b]	95% confidence interval	Standard error[b]	95% confidence interval	Standard error[b]	95% confidence interval
7 (5)	30	0.105–0.417	90	−0.096–0.334	59	−0.023–0.287
14 (10)	21	0.162–0.405	55	−0.013–0.267	48	0.001–0.256
28 (20)	12	0.223–0.370	30	0.056–0.218	26	0.070–0.218
42 (30)	10	0.245–0.359	26	0.067–0.210	20	0.088–0.204
Truth	0	0.307	0	0.140	0	0.149

Source: Lanjouw and Stern 1998.

a. The sample size is the number of households; this is followed, in parentheses, by the percentage of all households in the village. The total number of households in the village is 143. The sampling is without replacement.

b. The standard error is shown as a percentage of the point estimate.

household in the country and then calculated community-level inequality (and poverty) measures from these imputed consumption estimates.

More specifically, the Elbers, Lanjouw, and Lanjouw (2002, 2003) methodology involved estimating a model of per capita consumption, y_h, using 1994 household survey data (the *Encuesta de condiciones de vida* of the National Institute of Statistics) and limiting explanatory variables to those that were also found in and were strictly comparable to the population census of 1990. The model regressed (log) per capita consumption on a set of household-level demographic, occupational, and educational variables, as well as census variables calculated at the level of the census tract and other levels of aggregation above the household level:

$$\ln y_h = x_h \beta + u_h, \qquad (4.1)$$

where $x_h\beta$ is a vector of k parameters, and u_h is a disturbance term satisfying $E[u_h | x_h] = 0$.

The model in the equation (4.1) was estimated using the survey data; it allowed for an intracluster correlation in the disturbances (for more details, see Elbers, Lanjouw, and Lanjouw 2002, 2003). Failing to take account of spatial correlation in the disturbances would have resulted in underestimated standard errors. Different models were estimated for each region, while census mean variables and other aggregate-level variables were included in each model to capture latent cluster-level effects. All regressions were estimated with household weights. Heteroskedasticity in the household-specific part of the residual was also modeled, limiting the number of explanatory variables so as to be cautious about overfitting. Before the simulation, the estimated variance-covariance matrix was used to obtain generalized least square estimates of the first-stage parameters and their variance.

Because the disturbances for households in the census are always unknown, Elbers, Lanjouw, and Lanjouw (2002, 2003) estimated the expected value of a given welfare indicator based on the observable characteristics of the census households and the model of expenditure in the equation (4.1). This expectation may be denoted as:

$$\mu_v = E[W | X_v, \xi], \qquad (4.2)$$

where X_v is a matrix of observable characteristics, and ξ is the vector of model parameters, including those that describe the distribution of the disturbances.

In constructing an estimator of μ_v, the unknown vector ξ was replaced by consistent estimators, $\hat{\xi}$, from the survey-based consumption regression, yielding $\hat{\mu}_v$. Because such an expectation is generally analytically intractable, simulation was applied to obtain the estimator, $\tilde{\mu}_v$.

The estimates of poverty and inequality produced for Ecuador on the basis of the earlier methodology are described in greater detail in Demombynes et al. (2004) and Elbers et al. (2004). These studies document the considerable heterogeneity across parroquias in Ecuador in relation to poverty and inequality. At the aggregate level, rural poverty rates are generally highest in the Amazon rain forest in the Oriente Region in the eastern part of the country. However, at the local level, pockets of significant poverty are also discernable in the mountainous Sierra Region in the central part of the country and along the coast in the Costa Region. Elbers et al. (2004) note that the level of inequality varies markedly across parroquias; they emphasize that there should be no presumption that inequality is somehow lower in poorer communities.

Additional Control Variables

In addition to the poverty and inequality estimates that are of primary interest in an investigation of the determinants of project choice, Araujo et al. (2006) also include control variables intended to capture the influence of other factors.

From the 1990 census data, they have calculated population figures for the provinces and the parroquias. This data source has also permitted calculation of the percentage of the population of indigenous ethnic origin in each parroquia. These demographic characteristics might be thought to influence project choice in a variety of ways and, in the case of population, have also been important in the assessment of the targeting of the FISE program on poor communities. Project documents are explicit in noting that the targeting of FISE funding was to be based on a combination of measured poverty and the population in the provinces (although the targeting was based on an ad hoc map entirely unrelated to the poverty map derived from the small area estimation procedure described above). A simple correlation study finds no significant association between the presence of a FISE project and the incidence of poverty in a parroquia. At first glance, this study suggests that targeting has been poor. However, when there is a control for the parroquia population, the association becomes positive and strongly significant (Araujo et al. 2006). Similar to the situation described by Paxson and Schady (2002) in the case of a social fund in Peru, the geographical targeting in Ecuador's FISE program appears to have been rather good in the sense that the program reached those regions with large populations of poor people.

Census data have also been exploited to construct proxies for various sorts of infrastructure needs among individual parroquias. From the census, the percentage of households in each parroquia that are connected to a piped sewerage network has been calculated, as have the percentage of households that use modern toilet facilities (flush toilets or toilets connected to septic tanks), the percentage of households with access to a piped water supply, and the percentage of children (ages 5 to 12) enrolled at school.

Other control variables included in the Araujo et al. (2006) analysis have captured geographical differences. One is the distance of each parroquia from Quito, the capital of Ecuador and the seat of the central government. This variable is computed as a linear distance based on the geographical coordinates of the parroquias. The method yields an imperfect estimate of proximity, as it does not measure actual travel times between the pairs of locations. For ease of interpretation, distance has been expressed in kilometers. Data on geographical coordinates have been obtained through the Sistema Integrado de Indicadores Sociales del Ecuador (Integrated System of Social Indicators of Ecuador); they do not cover all parroquias in the country. For locations for which no geographical coordinates are available, the coordinates of the closest parroquia have been imputed. These imputations have been carried out based on visual inspection of a map.

A second geographical variable takes the value of 1 if the parroquia is the administrative capital of the canton in which it is located. Such parroquias are plausibly more closely connected to the government than others.

Following Schady (2000), the Araujo et al. (2006) study also recognizes the possible role of political influences on the distribution of FISE expenditures. As with the social funds in many other countries, the FISE program provided for the creation of an independent agency set up in parallel to established ministries of the government. In Ecuador, this agency was essentially run by the Office of the President. It is certainly conceivable that a project such as FISE might be used by the Presidency for purposes other than the official objectives of the project. Araujo et al. (2006) have examined provincial results from the second round of the 1992 presidential elections, as published by the Tribunal Supremo Electoral Ecuatoriano, the agency overseeing the electoral process in the country. This election was the last national election prior to the creation of FISE, and, in fact, FISE was established during the administration of the Partido Unidad Republicana, the winning party in the election. In the study, the share of votes obtained by this party in the total number of votes in a province was calculated. The higher this percentage, the more inclined the central government might be, according to the interpretation, to reward a particular province with FISE funding.

A second indicator aimed at capturing the nonmarginality of a particular province from a political point of view. This measure was based on the absolute deviation from 50 percent in the presidential vote in a particular province. As has been argued in Schady (2000), building on points in Dixit and Londregan (1996), the central government might wish to influence voting behavior in swing provinces, that is, provinces in which either the government's majority is precarious, or the government is close to gaining a majority. Thus, on the basis of this argument, the more nonmarginal a province, the less likely the province would be to receive a FISE allocation.

The Limitations of the Administrative Data

In working with the MIS data from Ecuador's FISE program, we have encountered six main areas or dimensions within which the limitations of those data have become apparent to us and which have had the effect of curtailing the strength of the inferences that we have been able to draw from the analysis in Araujo et al. (2006). Overcoming the weaknesses might dramatically enhance our ability to refer to such data in the kind of studies with which we have been concerned. Our intention in this chapter is to highlight these limitations with a view toward stimulating reflection on ways in which such data might be made more useful.

A Selected Sample of Communities

The MIS database on the FISE projects that are analyzed in Araujo et al. (2006) provides details on a large set of variables associated with all projects carried out in each of Ecuador's parroquias during the first phase of this social fund in the early 1990s. Information is supplied on the name and location of each parroquia. Projects are classified according to the nature of the intervention that has been undertaken (networked water provision, latrine construction, school or health post construction, road upgrading and maintenance, and so on). Key project dates are entered (dates of application, approval, and completion). The value of the FISE investment and the value of counterpart funding provided by each parroquia are listed. Finally, the name of the soliciting agency or institution is supplied. More than 2,800 projects are described.

About 65 percent of Ecuador's 915 parroquias in rural areas had at least one FISE project. Yet, our data are not able to tell us anything about the 35 percent of parroquias that did not receive a project. Crucially, we are not able to ascertain through the MIS data whether these parroquias did not receive a project because their application for a project was denied or whether these parroquias simply did not request a project.

A simple addition to the MIS database—whereby all parroquias are taken as the domain of analysis and a basic indicator is calculated showing whether a community's application had been received and rejected, received and accepted, or simply not received—would have permitted more detailed analysis of how local inequality affects local decision making.

The Parroquia as the Unit of Analysis

In rural Ecuador, parroquias average around 1,000 households. This unit of aggregation clearly conforms to the traditional administrative divisions of the country. However, questions remain. Is a parroquia also a community? Are local community decisions taken in the parroquias or in smaller units such as villages? Little is known about the number of parroquias that encompass several villages or about the mechanisms for and the extent of cooperation and coordination across villages within parroquias. Although the MIS database on the FISE program contains a wealth of information on individual projects in parroquias, it is not clear whether the communities that are making the choices and undertaking the activities recorded in the database are acting on behalf of entire parroquias or perhaps only some communities within the parroquias. The failure of the MIS database to reflect these possible complexities raises some doubts as to the suitability of the data for the purposes to which they have been put in Araujo et al. (2006).

The Designation of Public versus Private Goods

The Araujo et al. (2006) paper places a good deal of weight on the ability to designate certain FISE projects as private goods rather than public goods. Specifically, the analysis is predicated on the idea that latrine construction involves the construction of latrines for the private use of beneficiary households. In addition, it is argued that these latrines are private goods that are primarily of interest to the poor. This latter argument is justified by appealing to an analysis of household survey data indicating that only poor households make use of latrines; richer households either have access to septic tanks or are connected to sewerage systems. Without clear confirmation of these conjectures, it appears that some of the key elements of the arguments made in Araujo et al. (2006) must still be considered somewhat speculative.

The Classification of Projects by Type

The MIS database drawn on in the Araujo et al. (2006) paper classifies projects according to the nature of the intervention that has been undertaken in each parroquia. Such a classification already offers a considerable amount of detail. Yet, inevitably, it is not as much detail as one might have liked for an analysis of local project choice. In particular, as described above, the Araujo et al. (2006) paper sorts among the FISE projects according to whether they relate to public goods or private goods. Distinguishing between education and health projects or between latrine and rural road projects, however, does not provide sufficient detail to allow one to, for example, determine whether a project involves the construction of school buildings or the provision of desks and blackboards. It may be plausibly argued that, although the former might be (at least partially) public goods, the latter are much more likely to be excludable. If, as a general principle, a database supplies data at the greatest possible level of detail, then analysts might aggregate *up* for their specific purposes, thereby telling a more credible and nuanced story.

How FISE Projects Were Selected

A clear feature of Ecuador's FISE program and of social funds in other countries is that projects are identified, planned, implemented, and (at least partially) financed by communities themselves. In Ecuador, participatory mechanisms are supposed to be followed to ensure that projects represent the choice of a community as a whole rather than the choice of one or several individuals in the community. Yet, there is precious little detail in either the MIS data or in documents accompanying the project files on precisely the way community views are mobilized and the way these views influence decision making. The Araujo et al. (2006) analysis is predicated on the assumption that some kind of democratic decision making was achieved, although, it must be supposed, individuals are not all equal in terms of voting power. Whether this analysis is a reasonable way in which to set up the analysis is difficult to establish unambiguously. An MIS database that provides more detail on such factors would be of great value in permitting a thorough inquiry into the way participation affects the supply of publicly provided goods and services.

Multiple Projects per Parroquia

In the first phase of Ecuador's social fund program, some 2,876 projects were implemented in slightly fewer than 600 parroquias. On average, nearly five projects were implemented per parroquia. The projects varied. They involved different types of interventions that were requested by different agencies, approved and implemented at different times, and supported by different levels of financing and counterpart funding. Yet, the MIS data are not satisfactory in terms of providing information project by project. In particular, the data are sometimes simply aggregated across projects in a particular parroquia to determine the total amount of counterpart funding supplied by the parroquia, and then this information is entered among the MIS data for that parroquia. Thus, although the database provides sufficient detail to suggest that an analysis may be undertaken at the project level, close scrutiny reveals that the data are not complete in all relevant dimensions. The Araujo et al. (2006) study thus had to be undertaken at the parroquia level; in particular, it became necessary to select as the central unit of observation a parroquia in which *at least one latrine project* had been implemented rather than a more nuanced criterion that would have permitted analysis, for example, of the amount of funding received for latrine projects per parroquia.

Conclusions and Recommendations

Empirical investigations of the relationship between particular characteristics of the public provisioning of goods and services at the local level and the characteristics of the localities receiving these goods and services may help us understand the impact of policy and learn to design more effective public interventions. Such investigations have been rare, or they have been limited in scope because of the substantial informational requirements.

Recent years have seen a number of developments that promise to resolve or at least relax these data constraints. Rapid advances in geographic information systems analysis and techniques have brought a wealth of detailed, spatially referenced information into the ambit of such investigations. Growing experience with the small area estimation methodology and the increased availability of unit-record census data are offering analysts unprecedented opportunities to construct detailed, wide-ranging profiles of the socioeconomic characteristics of the communities within a country. Perhaps most significantly, more widely available and comprehensive MIS databases are providing more detail on the processes governing the selection, design, financing, and implementation of interventions at the local level. The study by Araujo et al. (2006) represents an example of how these disparate data sources may be brought together to analyze the relationship between the way interventions at the local level operate and the characteristics of the localities in which they are being carried out.

To realize the potential of such research applications, however, one must allow the different data sources to speak to each other. In particular, the types of data assembled in MIS databases and the way in which they are structured might bear reexamination. An appealing feature of data based on a geographic information system or a census (such as the small area poverty and inequality estimates) is that these essentially modular data may be neatly aggregated and disaggregated between the very detailed microlevel and the national level. Census data, for example, may be tabulated to provide information on population characteristics at the national, provincial, community, household, and even individual levels. Ideally, MIS data would also allow a similar decomposition from the aggregate to the individual.

In the Araujo et al. (2006) study, a number of limitations in the MIS database were encountered that constrained the nature of the conclusions that might be reached. Several of those limitations may be linked to the unwieldy architecture of the database. First, although the FISE program had a nationwide ambit, information was entered only for those parroquias in which a project was implemented. A minor adjustment to the data-entry procedures would have allowed researchers also to distinguish between parroquias that failed to receive a project because of a failure to apply for a project and parroquias that failed to receive a project because of the rejection of a project application. Second, the MIS database was built up with the parroquia as the lowest unit of analysis. Information on projects was entered at the parroquia level even when it was not clear that projects always applied at that level (as opposed to some subparroquia level such as the village).

Because of the decision to enter data at this somewhat aggregated level, the researchers were frustrated in their ability to link projects to subparroquia-level characteristics. Third, consistent with the decision to enter project information at the parroquia level, the MIS database does not consistently provide details on individual projects within a given parroquia. Rather, information about all projects undertaken within a parroquia is sometimes aggregated across projects to yield a single line entry for the parroquia. Fourth, the MIS data analyzed in Araujo et al. (2006) rely on a classification of projects according to the kind of intervention undertaken. However, for the purposes of the study, the classification turned out to be coarse. Key details about specific interventions were not retained, and this hampered the reclassification of projects into interventions relating to public versus private goods.

A common theme in this description of the limitations of the MIS data analyzed by Araujo et al. (2006) is the entry of the data into the MIS at a level of aggregation that was higher than the level strictly possible. The factors that led to the decision to do this are not clear. In part, cost considerations may have played a role. Possibly, computational constraints may also have influenced thinking. It is likely that, over time, computational constraints have become less binding. Without additional information, it is difficult to assess how much more costly it would have been to produce the MIS data in a more detailed format. Yet, it is also conceivable that, to some extent, decisions were taken without a good idea of the potential benefits of a more detailed MIS database. The purpose of this chapter has been to stress that the availability of detailed and comprehensive MIS data may yield benefits beyond the original purpose of the databases by supporting broader analysis and research. Important questions that are relevant to policy may be addressed. Such benefits should be evaluated against the additional costs of ensuring that the MIS data are made available at the greatest level of detail possible.

Notes

1. Bardhan and Mookherjee (2000) argue that the net effect of various local factors on outcomes in a decentralized setting, such as superior local information and greater capture by local elites, is theoretically ambiguous. They call for more empirical assessments of projects. Dasgupta and Kanbur (2001, 2003) analyze the relationship between within-community inequality and local public goods provisioning.
2. Another paper that examines the issue of democracy and local choice in infrastructure projects is Rosenzweig and Foster (2003). The paper shows that increases in the population weight of the poor result in increases in the likelihood that villages

with elected panchayats in India will receive pro-poor projects (such as roads), though this is not the case for villages with more traditional leadership structures.
3. The term community is used here as a synonym of *parroquia* (parish), the smallest administrative unit in Ecuador.
4. A separate category of FISE projects that are designated "public toilets" are more readily seen as public goods and are kept separate from the latrine category in table 4.1. These represented around 4 percent of all FISE projects.
5. There is also information available on the number of projects of each type received by communities and on the amount of funding (both FISE and local counterpart) provided for each project. However, these data seemed unreliable for use in the empirical analysis. For example, for projects involving in-kind transfers, such as equipment and supplies, the funding was usually entered as zero in the MIS database. Furthermore, the total amount of funding the community or the applicant received sometimes seems to have been entered under one project line, while the rest of the projects are recorded as zero. For this reason, Araujo et al. (2006) were unable to use these data to check the robustness of the results with respect to the manner in which the dependent variable was defined.

References

Araujo, María Caridad, Francisco H. G. Ferreira, Peter F. Lanjouw, and Berk Özler. 2006. "Local Inequality and Project Choice: Theory and Evidence from Ecuador." Policy Research Working Paper 3997, World Bank, Washington, DC.

Bardhan, Pranab, and Dilip Mookherjee. 2000. "Capture and Governance at Local and National Levels." *AEA Papers and Proceedings* 90 (2): 135–39.

———. 2005. "Decentralizing Antipoverty Program Delivery in Developing Countries." *Journal of Public Economics* 89, 675–704.

Dasgupta, Indraneel, and Ravi Kanbur. 2001. "Class, Community, Inequality." Working Paper WP 2001–24, Department of Applied Economics and Management, Cornell University, Ithaca, NY.

———. 2003. "Community and Anti-Poverty Targeting." Working Paper WP 2003–37, Department of Applied Economics and Management, Cornell University, Ithaca, NY.

Demombynes, Gabriel M., Chris Elbers, Jean O. Lanjouw, Peter F. Lanjouw, and Berk Özler. 2004. "Producing an Improved Geographic Profile of Poverty: Methodology and Evidence from Three Developing Countries." In *Growth, Inequality, and Poverty: Prospects for Pro-Poor Economic Development,* ed. Rolph van der Hoeven and Anthony Shorrocks, 154–75. United Nations University–World Institute for Development Economics Research Studies in Development Economics. New York: Oxford University Press.

Dixit, Avinash K., and John Londregan. 1996. "The Determinants of Success of Special Interests in Redistributive Politics." *Journal of Politics* 58 (4): 1132–55.

Elbers, Chris, Jean O. Lanjouw, and Peter F. Lanjouw. 2002. "Micro-Level Estimation of Welfare." Policy Research Working Paper 2911, World Bank, Washington, DC.

———. 2003. "Micro-Level Estimation of Poverty and Inequality." *Econometrica* 71 (1): 355–64.

Elbers, Chris, Peter F. Lanjouw, Johan A. Mistiaen, Berk Özler, and Ken Simler. 2004. "On the Unequal Inequality of Poor Communities." *World Bank Economic Review* 18 (3): 401–21.

Lanjouw, Peter F., and Nicholas Stern, ed. 1998. *Economic Development in Palanpur over Five Decades.* Oxford: Clarendon Press.

Paxson, Christina, and Norbert R. Schady. 2002. "The Allocation and Impact of Social Funds: Spending on School Infrastructure in Peru." *World Bank Economic Review* 16 (2): 297–319.

Rosenzweig, Mark R., and Andrew D. Foster. 2003. "Democratization, Decentralization, and the Distribution of Local Public Goods in a Poor Rural Economy." BREAD Working Paper 010, Bureau for Research and Economic Analysis of Development, Center for International Development at Harvard University, Cambridge, MA.

Schady, Norbert R. 2000. "The Political Economy of Expenditures by the Peruvian Social Fund." *American Political Science Review* 94 (2): 289–304.

World Bank. 2005. *The Effectiveness of World Bank Support for Community-Based and -Driven Development: An OED Evaluation.* Washington, DC: Operations Evaluation Department, World Bank.

5

What May Be Learned from Project Monitoring Data?

Lessons from a Nutrition Program in Madagascar

Emanuela Galasso

The main rationale for collecting monitoring data is to facilitate the monitoring of program or project performance over time. Such data have been mainly viewed as a management tool for observing program evolution over time, providing timely information on the extent to which a project is implemented according to a design or a plan, and, in the case of any shortcoming, in creating the information base to redress the problem. Monitoring data represent a particular subcategory of administrative data. They have a specific feature: by construction, the monitoring database contains only information relevant to monitoring the implementation of participating units. The monitored activities are explicitly set up as a result of the program and are, therefore, not yet captured in any nationwide administrative data source.

The objective of this chapter is to reflect on the potential use of such data as a tool for analytical work and in making inferences about the impact of programs.

In general, the use of administrative data for analytical or evaluation purposes has been mainly limited to the United States in the context of large-scale evaluations of labor market programs and social assistance programs. (See Heckman, Lalonde, and Smith 1999 for a comprehensive synthesis of such evaluations of active labor market programs in Europe and the United States.)

There are few examples of analogous work in developing countries, where such work falls into two main categories. The first group uses administrative data, combined with complementary census-based data, to gauge the effectiveness of targeting. Ravallion (2000) uses monitoring data, matched with poverty maps, to estimate targeting performance and variations in performance over time in a workfare program in Argentina.[1] This analytical work is an example of how to use such data to provide rapid evaluative feedback to policy makers on one key dimension of program performance, namely, targeting.

A second group in the analytical work based on administrative data focuses specifically on inferences about program impacts. Large, low-cost samples of administrative data are used to study the impact of an intervention (generally schooling) on various outcomes (test scores, school enrollments, and progress in school).[2] Administrative data are available on both participants and nonparticipants in programs, and the causal impacts of programs are usually identified through a clean evaluation design whereby the exogenous variation arises from a natural experiment (such as a lottery) or clear eligibility rules (such as eligibility thresholds in program assignments).

But what about using monitoring data to make inferences about impacts? This chapter illustrates the potential and challenges of such an application and isolates the set of questions that may or may not be posed with such a source of data in this context. Because the information is limited to areas of intervention only (or treated individuals, facilities, or communities), these data have generally been used only to describe trends in participating communities: comparisons between, before, or, better, at the beginning of an intervention and during or after the intervention (reflexive comparisons). However, one may not credibly assume that these trends measure the impact of a program: it is difficult to believe that all the changes shown by outcome indicators may be attributed to the effects of a program and that the selection bias averages out to zero.[3]

This extreme data selection process characterized by the collection of data only after the onset of a program and only on program participants implies that one is not able to estimate a credible counterfactual (that is, what would have happened in the absence of the program) and, therefore, the common parameters that are of interest in the evaluation literature relying on this counterfactual (such as average treatment effects and average treatment effects on the treated). We argue here that these same data would allow us to estimate a different counterfactual and, therefore, a different parameter of interest, namely, the *marginal* effects of the increased duration of a program or, put differently, the differences in the cumulative effects of the program over different lengths of time.

The case study examined here involves the Seecaline program, a large-scale community-based nutrition program in Madagascar. The example draws heavily on Galasso and Yau (2006), where we use monitoring data on the program to estimate the *marginal* or *differential* effects of increased program duration on nutritional outcomes. The objective is to compare, at any given point in time, the nutritional outcomes among communities that have experienced differential lengths of program exposure.

Why is this parameter useful? Information on average treatment effects is generally used to perform cost-benefit analyses to determine whether activities are worth pursuing. Suppose instead that—as in the case of Seecaline—the effectiveness of the intervention has already been established through a small-scale pilot exercise, the decision to adopt the intervention has already been taken, and the program needs to be expanded to a large scale. In a context of limited resources, the program would have to be phased in gradually across different geographical areas. Understanding the socioeconomic characteristics of the areas in which the marginal impact of the intervention is greatest may provide guidance in establishing a sequence in the geographical expansion of the program across many administrative units or other sorts of units.

Community nutrition programs typically target children in the critical age of 0 to 3 months and promote behavioral change in the context of existing resources through improved knowledge on child feeding practices and childcare. Monthly growth monitoring through weight measurements at any given age represents the focal point around which communities are mobilized to raise awareness on the problem of malnutrition and to become engaged in improving hygiene, childcare, and nutrition practices. As a by-product, in our case, monthly information on the regular activities of participating communities is generated by local community nutrition workers who are in charge of coordinating community program sites.[4]

For our study, we have relied on data on 3,000 project sites followed over four years. The program was phased in gradually through an entry process at the end of each year staggered over several years so as to cover about one-third of the target population of children aged 0–3 months nationally. So the study could maximize the geographical coverage, the implementation of the program was contracted out to local nongovernmental organizations (NGOs) that had been put in charge of supporting and supervising the program sites. The average length of exposure of a community to the program was about two years (see figure 5.1). The attractiveness of this case study

FIGURE 5.1 Proportion of Sites That Joined the Seecaline Program over Time, 1999–2003

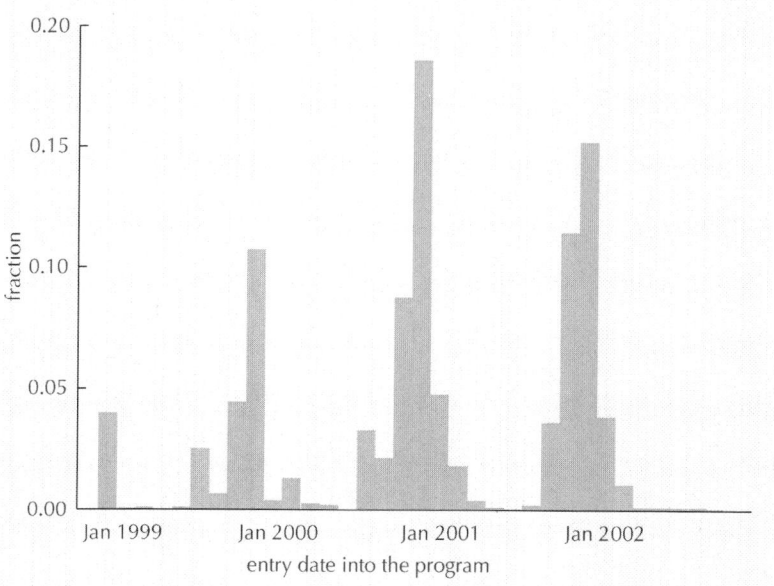

Source: Galasso and Yau 2006.
Note: The joining date is defined by the date of the first growth monitoring measurement. Each vertical bar represents the fraction of program sites that opened in each quarter. The joining date of a site is defined as the date of the first growth monitoring measurement.

arises from the fact that, as an integral part of the performance indicators monitored over time, the monitoring database includes information not only on input and output indicators, but also on final outcome indicators of particular relevance (malnutrition rates and take-up rates). In what follows, we first review the advantages and limitations of monitoring data as illustrated in practice by the case study at hand (the next section) and then describe the issues and the methodological challenges (the subsequent section).

Advantages and Challenges of Using Administrative (and Monitoring) Data

The use of monitoring data that, by definition, become available as a by-product of the program may be attractive for several reasons:

- *Cost factor:* Data that become available as part of day-to-day monitoring of program performance may represent a low-cost source of information for analytical work. In the Seecaline program, the information is a subset of a large record of observations maintained by community nutrition workers in each site registry. NGO supervisors regularly aggregate summary results derived from the registries up to the provincial and the central levels as part of the monitoring process.

- *Scale and sample size:* By construction, the monitoring data represent the entire treated population. This aspect of the data is attractive if one wishes to disaggregate the results through subgroup analysis. Decomposing the analysis by specific groups is particularly important for programs that use communities or facilities as the unit of analysis. In such settings, outcomes are correlated across individuals within the communities or facilities (the clustering effect). Household surveys generally rely on inadequate sample sizes to allow this sort of analysis to be performed within reasonable budget limits. In our example of a community-based intervention, we wanted to test whether the differential effects varied systematically with some key environmental factors that affect the child health production function (such as incidence relative to weather shocks, geographical remoteness, poverty rates, and access to safe water) and are spatially heterogeneous.

- *Time dimension:* This element of the data has been collected since the launch of the program to facilitate the monitoring of performance over time. Long-time horizons and high data frequency in the observations are not usual features of survey data. The focus of the analysis of Seecaline has been the first four years of operation; monthly records on program activities were maintained at all program sites. The time dimension has generally been exploited for descriptive purposes, such as analyses of program participation or trends. In the Seecaline program, trends in preharvest and post-harvest malnutrition rates and average program take-up rates were considered key performance indicators. Nonetheless, the descriptive analysis does not help us understand the reasons for the trends. Note that participating communities are observed only after they have joined the program; the nature of the panel data is, therefore, unbalanced.

- *Intermediate outcomes, outputs:* The database usually provides detailed information on program outcomes and process indicators that are revealing about the channels through which the program is having an effect. In the Seecaline program, for instance, records on the activities of the nutrition workers (such as number of home visits, which is a proxy for the outreach of the workers), community participation at nutrition sessions and cooking demonstrations, the free distribution of micronutrients (including vitamin A supplements and deworming tablets), and emergency food supplementation are also maintained in the registries and appear among the monitoring data. One key, attractive feature of community nutrition programs is that, by design, they also monitor a welfare outcome, namely, malnutrition rates.

Against these advantages are many limitations and practical issues if the objective is to use these data to infer something about a program's impact:

● *Missing data question:* The first and most challenging feature of this type of data is that, by construction, monitoring data are collected only in participating villages or at program sites. In the absence of strong identification assumptions, the purposive placement of the program renders the extrapolation of the results to nonparticipating areas difficult.

Might it be possible to circumvent this limitation by tackling the underlying constraint and extending the data collection effort to villages, other communities, and facilities that have not received the program? The answer depends on the nature of the key variable of interest.

In the first scenario, the outcome variable (incidence of underweight children in our example) would otherwise be available only through household surveys. In our case study, this type of data are collected by service delivery agents (community workers and NGO supervisors) who are put in place directly as a result of the program. Under these circumstances, it is difficult to envision that the data collection effort might be extended to all villages that are not receiving the program. Even restricting the effort to the villages scheduled to participate in the program at some point in the near future might be challenging with respect to the costs, logistics, and planning. In many instances, eligible districts are identified first, and the choice of program sites within these districts is made only at a later stage. An updated list of current and potential program sites might not be available sufficiently in advance to collect baseline data before the launch of the program at a site. However, there might still be scope for triangulating the monitoring data with survey data to gain insights into underlying trends without the effects of the program. For instance, a survey might be appropriately planned and undertaken in nonintervention areas at a smaller scale, at a higher level of geographical aggregation (regions, provinces), and at regular intervals over time.

In the alternative scenario where data on the outcome variable of interest are also regularly collected for other administrative purposes (for example, tests scores in the case of an education intervention), the lack of linkability is a major constraint (see later). The objective would be to use these additional sources of data to form a nonprogram group that may be followed over time and compared with the program group.

* *Level of disaggregation of the monitoring data:* It is common in most monitoring data systems that only a subset of the extensive information recorded at the unit level of intervention is transmitted upward to higher administrative entities. As a consequence, much of the richness of the information on the unit level is lost to the system. Important information on variations in outcome and process indicators is overlooked in the process of aggregation. From a management perspective, it would be useful to learn more, for instance, about the characteristics of those sites that have experienced worsening trends in take-up.

In the Seecaline program, monthly information on several basic outcome indicators (take-up rates and malnutrition rates) was entered digitally only at the level of aggregation produced by the NGOs, not at individual sites or communities. This information was subsequently reduced into summaries by provincial and national administrators for performance monitoring during the program.

For our analysis, the technical counterparts at the central and provincial offices and the NGO supervisors at all the program sites cooperated in providing and entering data on a more extensive set of indicators once a month. The data were reported on the basis of each site registry from the onset of the program until the end of 2002. The ex post data entry was time-consuming given that the paper registries had to be collected at all sites by the NGO supervisors and the data had to be entered retrospectively. The commitment and cooperation of the technical counterparts were crucial in the process. However, we argue that, at only a little extra expenditure, the unit-level information might be regularly entered and stored at a central data-sharing site. These data might then be viewed at any time for descriptive and analytical work. The case study formed the starting point for a discussion with the technical counterparts about restructuring the monitoring data system during the next phase of the program.

* *Limited information on socioeconomic characteristics:* Most administrative databases maintain little or no information on covariate socioeconomic

characteristics of individuals or communities.[5] This limitation may be partially overcome if one is able to merge geographical identifiers of the location of the communities of the program participants with census-based information on the socioeconomic characteristics of the intervention areas. This use of different data sources at low levels of geographical disaggregation may become more common in developing countries, many of which rely regularly on standardized geographical codes or geo-references in data collection.

In our example, the monitoring data have been merged with and complemented by three additional sources of information to form a rich set of conditioning variables. First, we have used a commune census that contains detailed information on the demographic and socioeconomic characteristics of all communes in the country (including remoteness, principal economic activities, and access to infrastructure).[6] Second, we have used commune-level estimates of poverty from the poverty map developed by Mistiaen et al. (2002), who combined the 1993 household survey with the population census collected in the same year. The technique permits the estimation of consumption-based measures of poverty and inequality at low levels of geographical disaggregation. Third, in the program, additional administrative information was collected on the location of each site (distance between the site and the center of the commune). Basic information was also collected on each partner NGO that was in charge of a site (such as size, number of personnel, whether the NGO is a local or national organization, and the experience and sector of activity of the NGO before joining Seecaline).

Keeping track of such complementary data exercises (involving census or administrative data) is instrumental to creating an integrated monitoring and evaluation system. Having all these data sources readily available at a central point where they may be shared across different programs would facilitate the use of these data in analytical work enormously.

Linkability: Standardized identification codes are crucial to the ability to link unit records across different regions and over time. Likewise, those who might wish to realize the potential of using various data sources in a complementary or supportive fashion must address the practical reality that the geographical identifiers (or program codes) should be uniform across administrative, survey, and census data. Many programs lack a system of numerical identifiers and rely on names of localities in their data collections. Many of the resulting databases are characterized by misspelled or shortened names and by different local and official language versions of locational names, all of which may vary from the codes found in other databases. The use of the information consistently is thus a challenge. This major practical issue should be dealt with as a priority in the strengthening of monitoring and evaluation systems in developing countries.

In the process of putting together the data, we worked closely with our technical counterparts to construct a set of codes for each intervention site based on geographical identifiers drawn from the population census. The codes were subsequently adopted for systematic application during the program monitoring process. Relying on the census as the standard for geographical codes (and the use of geo-references wherever possible) seems to be the most natural approach; it is less prone to errors of duplication and lends itself easily to the goal of sharing data across programs and sectors.

Data quality: There is an important caveat against using monitoring data or administrative data in general: how is one to assess the quality of the information contained in the database? As Heckman, Lalonde, and Smith (1999, p. 1867) put it: "Too much emphasis has been placed on formulating alternative econometric methods for correcting for selection bias and too little given to the quality of the underlying data. Although it is expensive, obtaining better data is the only way to solve the evaluation problem in a convincing way."

In the case of monitoring (and administrative) data, data quality will depend on various factors. Proper training and periodic supervision will ensure that the data are recorded and entered properly. Built-in quality checks at data entry will help iron out possible inconsistencies in the data (incorrect dates, codes, fields, values, and so on). Reliability issues are more difficult to tackle. It may be argued that local agents might have an incentive to overstate or understate the results if they are held accountable based on performance or if they are trying to attract more resources, for example. In practice, it is more difficult to manipulate data in a systematic way if the level of detail is substantial in the data that must be provided upward in a national system. Nonetheless, ultimately, the only way to ensure reliability is to verify and triangulate the data with other data sources whenever possible.

Ultimately, the quality of the data will depend on whether the data are used actively as a management tool by program administrators. One advantage of the data in the Seecaline program, or any community-based nutrition program, is that monitoring is an integral part of the program goal: monthly child-growth monitoring is the focal point around which community mobilization, counseling, and food supplementation activities to improve child nutritional status are organized. The collected data are used locally to trigger monthly community meetings where community nutrition workers discuss the nutritional situation with the community. Great attention is attached to training the community nutrition workers to keep track of outcomes within the sites. The NGO supervisors are responsible for supporting the community nutrition workers in properly collecting data on all program activities. The unit-level report drawn from the registries at each site and submitted each month is detailed. Systematic over- or underreporting in the results would require a high level of sophistication.

Questions to Address through the Data to Make Inferences about Program Impact

What may we infer about program effectiveness with a large longitudinal database on outcomes in the communities of program participants? A time trend on these communities does not provide any information on a counterfactual time trend in the absence of the program. Given the available data, we are able to isolate only the differential impact of the duration of the program in intervention areas.

Obviously, a simple comparison among communities with different lengths of program exposure is likely to produce biased estimates because the timing of program entry is not likely to be random. For this reason, we exploit our knowledge about the program phase-in process to model the selection among a large set of data according to different program durations.[7] From a methodological point of view, we adapt an empirical methodology first developed by Behrman, Cheng, and Todd (2004), who propose a matching estimator for this marginal effect for cases in which no comparison group data are available. Behrman, Cheng, and Todd use data on participants only to measure the marginal impact of the program at *one* point in time as the length of exposure to the program increases. In this chapter, we calculate the average differential returns to exposure and exploit the panel dimension of our monitoring data to compute the differential effect of the program *at different points in time* as the length of exposure increases at one-year intervals (one extra year and two extra years).

The data limitations imply that these exposure effects may be estimated only by making some assumptions in the analysis. Because only postprogram data are available, one should separate out time effects and duration effects. We do so by comparing two sets of communities at the same point in time; we implicitly assume that any time effect would be the same among communities independently of the length of exposure.

A summary of the key results is presented in table 5.1. We show that the differential effects are positive: communities exposed for one additional year or two additional years to the program exhibit, on average, malnutrition rates that are 7 to 8 percentage points lower among all age groups together. The effect is statistically significant only among the younger age group (0–6 months) with one extra year of exposure (see figure 5.2). With two years of additional exposure, the gains materialize among older children (7–12 months and 13–36 months). The results on the age-ranking suggest that the program's impact materializes over time and that the younger children stand to gain more because a larger fraction of their lives has been affected by the program. We used the panel dimension of the monitoring data to show that these differential effects are decreasing over time. Over time, the duration of exposure increases among both sets of communities, and shorter exposure communities begin catching up. However, these differential returns do not converge to zero, suggesting that there may be learning effects involved in the program.

We also performed the same analysis by restricting the population to subgroups according to key socioeconomic characteristics of the area of intervention, such as poverty levels, incidence of cyclones, length of the lean season, and access to drinkable water. Poverty levels are a proxy for the average level of economic conditions and resource and nutrient availability. Cyclones, the greater length of the lean season, and the lack of access to safe water are all factors that enhance the likelihood of morbidity and, hence, the likelihood of growth faltering. The subgroup analysis showed that the differential effects of exposure are higher in areas with scarcer resources (higher poverty rates), as well as areas that are more vulnerable to disease. The results suggest that, in a context in which a program is phased in gradually, it pays to target communities that are poorer and more disease-prone first.

The analysis has formed the starting point of an effort to rethink the structure of the monitoring data system before the next phase of the program.

Conclusions

Monitoring data are an integral part of the process of learning about the performance of any social program. Yet, the data still represent an underused source of data for analysis, especially in developing countries. In this chapter, we argue that certain features of this data source (low cost, large scale, and

TABLE 5.1 Differential Program Treatment Effects, by Age Group

Quarter	Exposure for one extra year			Exposure for two extra years		
	0–6 months	7–12 months	13–36 months	0–6 months	7–12 months	13–36 months
2001 Q4	−0.10[a]	−0.06[a]	−0.03[a]	−0.09[a]	−0.10[a]	−0.09[a]
	[−0.13,−0.07]	[−0.08,−0.04]	[−0.05,−0.01]	[−0.12,−0.06]	[−0.12,−0.08]	[−0.12,−0.06]
2002 Q1	−0.09[a]	−0.03[a]	−0.01	−0.11[a]	−0.10[a]	−0.09[a]
	[−0.12,−0.06]	[−0.05,−0.01]	[0.03,0.01]	[−0.14,−0.01]	[−0.12,−0.07]	[−0.11,−0.06]
2002 Q2	−0.09[a]	−0.05[a]	0.00	−0.10[a]	−0.11[a]	−0.10[a]
	[−0.12,−0.06]	[−0.05,−0.02]	[−0.02,0.03]	[−0.13,−0.08]	[−0.13,−0.09]	[−0.12,−0.05]
2002 Q3	−0.08[a]	−0.04[a]	0.00	−0.08[a]	−0.07[a]	−0.08[a]
	[−0.11,−0.06]	[−0.05,−0.02]	[−0.01,0.02]	[−0.10,−0.07]	[−0.09,−0.05]	[−0.10,−0.05]
2002 Q4	−0.05[a]	−0.03[a]	0.01	−0.06[a]	−0.04[a]	−0.04[a]
	[−0.087,−0.05]	[−0.05,−0.01]	[−0.008,0.039]	[−0.08,−0.04]	[−0.07,−0.02]	[−0.05,−0.02]
2002, average	−0.08	−0.04	0	−0.09	−0.08	−0.08

Source: Galasso and Yau 2006.

Note: The range of numbers in the square brackets indicates the bootstrapped confidence interval. The set of conditioning variables used to model the selection according to different program exposures includes province dummies, remoteness indicators (distance between communities and the nearest urban centers, the proximity of a national road), socioeconomic indicators on the communes (daily, weekly, and seasonal markets, access to water and electricity), yearly indicators of weather shocks (cyclones, flooding, droughts), and NGO characteristics (local or national NGO, years of experience in the district, number of personnel), as well as interactions between NGO characteristics and remoteness, poverty rates at the commune level (from the poverty map), and the malnutrition rate at the site at first measurement (detrended).

a. Statistically significant at the 5 percent level.

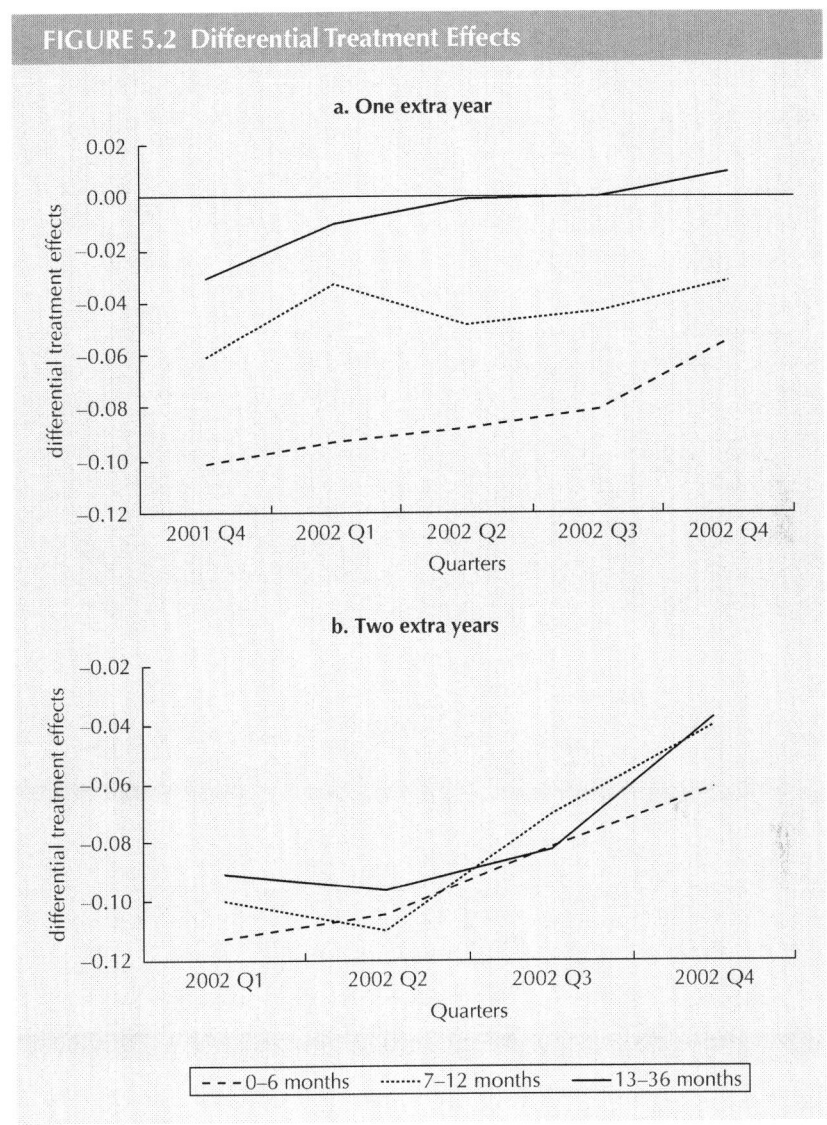

FIGURE 5.2 Differential Treatment Effects

Source: Galasso and Yau 2006.

time dimension) make it an attractive complement to survey data in analytical work. Because monitoring data are collected only on participating units, however, their use in attempting to gauge the impact of a program (relative to the counterfactual of nonparticipation) is problematic. Nonetheless, various policy issues may be of interest as regards the program impact. One such issue might be the returns to longer program exposure. This might be relevant from a policy perspective where program gains are cumulative over time and where (as in most large-scale programs) the impact is expected to be heterogeneous across socioeconomic groups or areas of a country.

This application has highlighted many practical issues that deserve attention during the design of the monitoring system that accompanies any social program. There is enormous potential for designing the system to allow these data to be merged with other administrative data and census-based data. There is scope for investing more in training and supervision in data collection, supervision, and data management so as to ensure comprehensiveness and quality. These investments would help make monitoring data an important source of information in analysis, for work on descriptive trends, and in addressing specific questions about program impact.

Notes

1. The idea is to track spending across local government areas within each province. By combining the spending data with poverty incidence data across local areas within each province, Ravallion (2000) estimates the targeting performance of the program (defined as the difference in spending on the poor and the nonpoor) and provides a methodology that helps determine the share of the targeting performance that might be attributed to various subnational levels in a decentralized setting. Van de Walle (2004) applies the same methodology on the targeting performance of public expenditure and poverty programs in Morocco.

2. For example, Angrist, Bettinger, and Kremer (2006) exploit the random feature of the assignment of school vouchers by lottery in Colombia. They use administrative records on registration and test scores for a centralized college entrance examination to study the effect on school outcomes among lottery winners; winners were more likely to take the university entrance examination as well as exhibit higher language test scores. Analogously, Chay, McEwan, and Urquiola (2005) use school-level administrative data on test scores to study the effects on beneficiaries of a school program that allocates resources based on a cutoff in scores.

3. An interesting variation on reflexive comparisons is proposed by Piehl et al. (2003), who show that sufficiently longtime series data on participants may be used to test for structural breaks and to identify impacts. On the structure of the monitoring and evaluation system for India's District Primary Education program, see the fundamental critique in Case (2006). The nonrandom selection of initial sites for intervention, coupled with

the fact that no data were collected from nonintervention areas, makes it impossible to draw any conclusions about the impact of the program.

4. In the case of the community nutrition program, the nutritional status of children is monitored by measuring the children's weight for age and height for age each month and plotting this indicator on a growth chart that displays the internationally recognized parameters for identifying children as moderately or severely malnourished. The approach is preventive in that mothers are advised if the growth of their children has faltered at levels below which it will be difficult for the children to recuperate. Without such advice, malnutrition is often not recognized by parents until it has become severe.

5. For instance, the labor literature on the impact of training programs in developed countries highlights the importance of the availability of information on labor force histories, educational attainment, family status, and geographical location as key conditioning variables in such an analysis (see Heckman, Lalonde, Smith 1999). A lack of this information would limit the possibilities for the use of empirical methods that require high-quality data (such as matching), and it would also limit the extent to which one may perform subgroup analysis.

6. The census was conducted under an International Labour Organization program in 2001 by Cornell University, in collaboration with the National Statistical Institute and the National Center for Applied Research on Rural Development (the agricultural research institute within the Ministry of Scientific Research). The census covered 1,385 (out of a total of 1,394) communes in the country. The questionnaire was administered to individual focus groups composed of residents of each commune.

7. More specifically, we used predetermined characteristics obtained in the merged data sources to model the selection of sites according to different lengths of program exposure. One key set of variables refers to remoteness and accessibility, which represents a major constraint for service delivery in Madagascar. The program was initiated mostly among the most accessible communities and was then gradually expanded to the least accessible sites. The sequential selection among sites across intervention districts was carried out through partnerships between the NGOs and the communes. In the database, we included key socioeconomic characteristics of the communes, NGO characteristics, and an interaction between remoteness and NGO characteristics. Finally, we controlled for sequential selection based on needs by including the poverty rates in the communes and the malnutrition rates at first measurement. See Galasso and Yau (2006) for more details on the phase-in process.

Bibliography

Angrist, Joshua, Eric Bettinger, and Michael Kremer. 2006. "Long-Term Educational Consequences of Secondary School Vouchers: Evidence from Administrative Records in Colombia." *American Economic Review* 96 (3): 847–62.

Behrman, Jere R., Yingmei Cheng, and Petra E. Todd. 2004. "Evaluating Preschool Programs When Length of Exposure to the Program Varies: A Nonparametric Approach." *Review of Economics and Statistics* 86 (1): 108–32.

Case, Anne. 2006. "The Primacy of Education." In *Understanding Poverty*, ed. Abhijit V. Banerjee, Roland Bénabou, and Dilip Mookherjee, 269–85. New York: Oxford University Press.

Chay, Kenneth, Patrick McEwan, and Miguel Urquiola. 2005. "The Central Role of Noise in Evaluating Interventions That Use Test Scores to Rank Schools." *American Economic Review* 95 (4): 1237–58.

Galasso, Emanuela, and Jeffrey Yau. 2006. "Learning through Monitoring: Lessons from a Large-Scale Nutrition Program in Madagascar." Policy Research Working Paper 4058, Development Research Group, World Bank, Washington, DC.

Heckman, James J., Robert J. Lalonde, and Jeffrey A. Smith. 1999. "The Economics and Econometrics of Active Labor Market Programs." In *Handbook of Labor Economics,* ed. Orley Ashenfelter and David E. Card, 3: 1865–2097. Amsterdam: Elsevier Science.

Hotz, V. Joseph, Robert Goerge, Julie D. Balzekas, and Frances Margolin, eds. 1999. "Administrative Data for Policy Relevant Research: Assessment of Current Utility and Recommendations for Development." Report, Advisory Panel on Research Uses of Administrative Data, Joint Center for Poverty Research at Northwestern University and the University of Chicago, Chicago.

Karim, Rezaul, Jennifer Coates, Gwenola Desplats, Iqbal Kabir, Yeakub Patwari, Stephanie Ortolano, Thomas Schaetzel, Lisa Troy, Beatrice L. Rogers, Robert F. Houser, and F. James Levinson. 2002. "Challenges to the Monitoring and Evaluation of Large Nutrition Programs in Developing Countries: Examples from Bangladesh." Tufts Nutrition Discussion Paper 1, Food Policy and Applied Nutrition Program, Friedman School of Nutrition Science and Policy, Tufts University, Boston.

Levinson, F. James, and Isabel Madzorera. 2005. "Recent Experience in the Monitoring and Evaluation of Nutrition-Related Projects in Developing Countries: Nine Lessons Learned." Tufts Nutrition Discussion Paper 28, Food Policy and Applied Nutrition Program, Friedman School of Nutrition Science and Policy, Tufts University, Boston.

Mistiaen, Johan A., Berk Özler, Tiaray Razafimanantena, and Jean Razafindravonoma. 2002. "Putting Welfare on the Map in Madagascar." Africa Region Working Paper 34, World Bank, Washington, DC.

Piehl, Ann Morrison, Suzanne J. Cooper, Anthony A. Braga, and David M. Kennedy. 2003. "Testing for Structural Breaks in the Evaluation of Programs." *Review of Economics and Statistics* 85 (3): 550–58.

Ratomaharo, Malalanirina. 2003. "Use of Monitoring Data for Evaluation: Case Example from Madagascar." Background note presented at the World Bank meeting "Strengthening Monitoring and Evaluation in the World Bank's Nutrition Portfolio," Health, Nutrition, and Population, World Bank, Washington, DC, May 21–22.

Ravallion, Martin. 2000. "Monitoring Targeting Performance When Decentralized Allocations to the Poor are Unobserved." *World Bank Economic Review* 14 (2): 331–45.

van de Walle, Dominique. 2004. "Do Basic Services and Poverty Programs Reach Morocco's Poor?: Evidence from Poverty and Spending Maps." Middle East and North Africa Working Paper 41, World Bank, Washington, DC.

6

Program Impact and Variation in the Duration of Exposure

Jere Behrman and Elizabeth King

Impact evaluations of social programs and policies aim to measure the key outcomes that may be attributed to an intervention. Many evaluations treat the intervention as if it were an instantaneous change in conditions that is equal across treatment groups. Many evaluations also implicitly assume that the impact on individuals is dichotomous, that individuals are either exposed or not, as might be the case in a one-shot vaccination program that provides permanent immunization; there is no consideration of the possibility that the effects are different depending on variations in program exposure. Whether the treatment involves immunization or school decentralization, the unstated assumptions are that the treatment occurs during a specified inception date, that it is implemented completely and in precisely the same way across treatment groups, and that the only important issue is simply whether one is exposed to the program or not. Indeed, if a program were fully implemented as planned, if it had a randomized design, and if the project had a dichotomous impact, then the differences in outcome measures between treatment and control groups would be sufficient to estimate impact: either the average treatment-of-the-treated (TOT) effect or the intent-to-treat (ITT) effect (see Manski 1996). However, there are several reasons why implementation is not perfect; why the duration of exposure to a treatment differs not only across treatment areas, but also across ultimate beneficiaries; and why varying lengths of program exposure might lead to different estimates of program impact.

One question that project managers and evaluators commonly raise is: how long should one wait before evaluating a program? This concern about timing is motivated partly by the belief that programs may be associated with a technical maturation period and that this determines when impact may be revealed. If one evaluates too early, one risks finding no impact. However, the solution does not lie only in waiting.

This chapter discusses various sources of differences in the duration of program exposure and the implications for impact estimates. It reviews the evidence presented by careful evaluations on the ways the duration affects impacts and discusses the types of data used by these studies to capture the duration of exposure. It presents a specific case study to illustrate some dimensions of the methodological importance of this issue and the power of combining administrative data and household survey data to measure variations in the duration of exposure across treatment areas.

Sources of Variation in the Duration of Effective Program Exposure

Effective exposure to most development programs is likely to vary considerably across treatment or beneficiary groups, and this variation may, in turn, affect estimated program impact, though many program evaluations do not control for this possibility. This variation exists for a number of reasons, including (a) implementation delays; (b) postimplementation delays in attaining full program effectiveness on the supply side, such as in the case of service providers who become proficient only after learning-by-doing; (c) reliance on program uptake by beneficiaries on the demand side; (d) age dependence of program effects; and (e) interactions between the length of exposure and program effects on individual beneficiaries. None of these situations is uncommon. We discuss them next and summarize the empirical evidence found through selected studies.

Implementation Lags

One assumption of many impact evaluations is that program implementation or the delivery of specific interventions occurs at a specific, knowable time, which is usually determined at a central program office. Yet, a program start date that is presumed to be well defined often turns out to depend on supply- and demand-related realities in the field. For example, a program requiring material inputs relies on punctuality in the arrival of these inputs, such that the timing of the procurement of the inputs by a central program office is not necessarily an accurate indicator of the moment when these inputs arrive at their intended destinations.[1] This timing problem is magnified because of the number of inputs needed to start a program and the number of suppliers involved, and this problem has consequences for impact estimates, particularly estimates of ITT effects. If there is an average gap of one year between program launch and actual implementation, then an allowance of one year after program launch would be more accurate than the date of program launch in estimating the start of program exposure. However, assuming such a constant allowance for delays may not yield an adequate approximation of exposure because of the possibility of significant variations in timing across and within treatment areas. Timing may differ across treatment areas especially in large programs that cover several states or provinces and, within each such administrative or geographical division, a large number of localities spread out over vast distances. Region or state fixed effects might control for these differences if the differences are homogeneous within a region or state and if the delays are independent of unobservable characteristics in the program areas that may also influence program impact.

Program documents typically contain official project launch dates, as well as other administrative dates, but it is much more difficult, though not impossible, to ascertain the timing of actual implementation in each treatment area. In some evaluations, this problem is partly addressed through interviews among public officials in each area; yet, when programs have many components, the variation in the duration of exposure becomes more complicated to measure. For example, in a school improvement program that involves additional weeks of teacher training and the delivery of instructional materials, the materials might arrive in schools in a treatment area at about the same time, but the additional teacher training might be achieved only over a period of several months because of differences in teacher availability. The effective program start might be pegged at the date when all teachers have completed their training, but this definition underestimates program duration in those schools where teachers have finished their training earlier. Indeed, precise and timely implementation is the exception rather than the rule in the case of programs that require concerted actions by groups of providers rather than by a centralized program management unit.

Implementation delays that are not incorporated into the estimation of impact almost surely bias the ITT estimates of program impact downward, especially if such an impact increases with the exposure of the beneficiaries who are actually treated. However, the extent of this underestimation for a given average lag across communities depends on the nature of the lags. If the program implementation delays were not random, it would matter if they are inversely or directly correlated with unobserved attributes of the treated groups that may positively affect program success. If the implementation lags are *directly* correlated with unobserved local attributes (for example, central administrators may put more effort into getting the programs started in areas that have worse unobserved determinants of the outcomes of interest), then the true ITT effects would be underestimated to a greater extent. If the implementation delays were *inversely* associated with the unobserved local attributes (for example, the management capability of local officials in program implementation may be greater in areas that are more well off in terms of the unobserved determinants of desired outcomes), then they are likely to be underestimated to a lesser extent. If the program delays were random, the extent of the underestimation would depend on the variance in the implementation lags (given the same mean lag). Greater random variance in the lags, all else being equal, would result in a greater underestimation of the ITT effects because of a larger classical random measurement error in a right-hand-side variable that biases the estimated coefficient more toward zero.

Implementation delays per se do not necessarily affect TOT estimates if the start of the treatment has been identified correctly. In some cases, the identification of the start of treatment might be relatively easy, for instance, when the dates on which beneficiaries enroll in a program may be ascertained through a household or facility survey or administrative records. In other cases, however, the identification may be more difficult, such as when beneficiaries are unable to distinguish among programs or recall their enrollment dates or when the facility or central program office does not monitor beneficiary program enrollments.[2] Nonetheless, even if the variation in treatment dates within program areas is handled adequately and enrollment dates are identified fairly accurately at the beneficiary level, nonrandom implementation delays will bias TOT estimates. Even a well-specified facility or household survey will still generate a concern that unobservables may be related to the direction and size of the program impact.

Post-Start-Up Patterns in Effectiveness: Program Vintage Effects

Given any implementation date, most programs do not immediately attain full steady-state effectiveness even if the date is conditional on actual use by beneficiaries (which may also change with program duration; see next). Consider decentralization reforms and their impact on the delivery of public services such as health care or schooling. Even the simplest form of this type of change in governance (say, the transfer of the supervision and funding of public hospitals from the national government to a subnational government) entails a shift in the accountability relationships between levels of government and between governments and providers. For example, an evaluation of the impact of Nicaragua's autonomous schools program in the 1990s used the date a school signed the contract with the government as the indicator of the date the school became autonomous. In fact, the signature of the contract was merely the first step the school would take toward school autonomy. Thus, a qualitative analysis conducted in a dozen randomly selected schools indicates that school personnel were generally not in agreement on whether their schools had become autonomous or the extent to which this might have occurred (King and Özler 1998; Rivarola and Fuller 1999). Even after the various planned and observable aspects of this reform had been implemented, the full impact of the reform (if any) on outcomes would have been felt only after a period of time, and the size of this impact might perhaps increase gradually, probably with diminishing marginal effects. This change is because the transformation of accountability relationships is not immediate and because the behavioral responses of providers and citizens may also be slow in becoming apparent. In addition, there is likely to be a learning process internal to the program. Typically, among new organizations, innovation implies initial learning such as that reflected in the well-known ogive or s-shaped learning patterns shown in figure 6.1.

If learning leads to full program effectiveness, then impact evaluations that use information from the initial period of a project, before the s-shaped learning curve has approached the asymptote for all types of relevant learning, result in downward-biased ITT and TOT impact estimates relative to the estimates that would have been obtained through evaluations relying on information only from the period after the learning asymptotes have been attained. There may be heterogeneity in this learning process so that there is a family of learning curves reflecting, for example, those programs that have better unobserved management capabilities and that, therefore, involve more rapid learning (for instance, the dashed line in figure 6.1). This learning would influence the extent to which the ITT and TOT

FIGURE 6.1 Learning Patterns

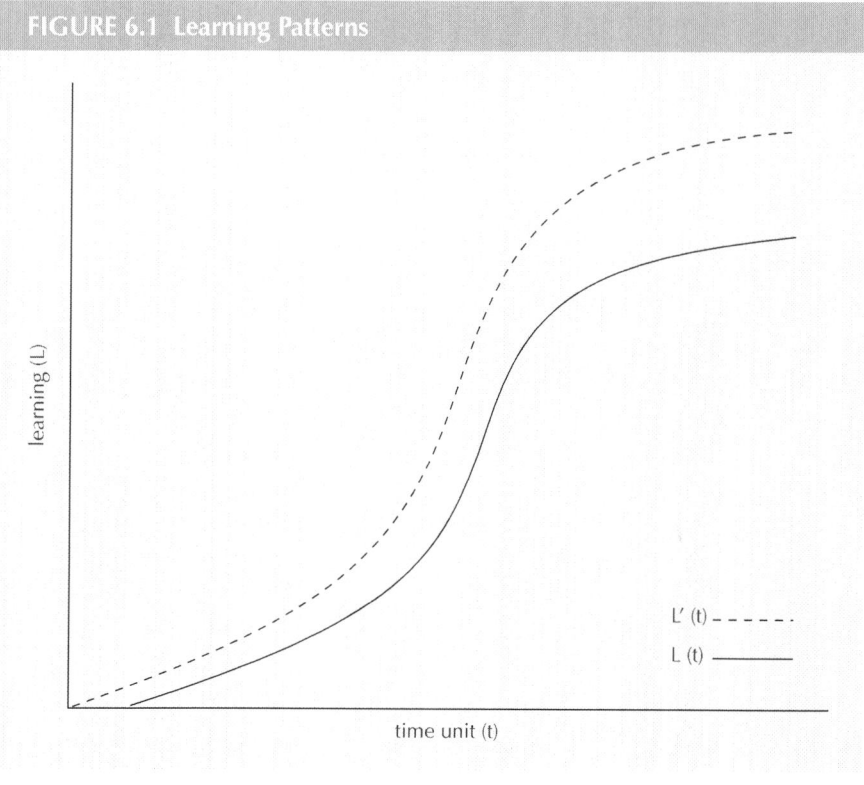

L' (t) - - - - - .

L (t) ———————

time unit (t)

learning (L)

Source: Constructed by the authors.

impacts that have been estimated before all the programs have approached sufficiently close to long-run effectiveness are downward biased. In such a case, the estimates would be underestimates of long-run effectiveness, but less so than if the heterogeneity in learning were random.

Although there is considerable emphasis in the literature on learning in new programs, another effect might be active in the opposite direction. This is the pioneering effect, whereby initial implementers exhibit extra dedication, enthusiasm, and effort during the first stages because the program represents an innovative endeavor to attain an especially important goal. If such a phenomenon exists, it would exert an opposite pull on the estimated impacts and, if sufficiently strong, might offset the learning effect, at least in the early phases of a new program. It might even result in the approach to the long-run asymptote of program effectiveness occurring from above rather than from below. Over time, however, this extra dedication, enthusiasm, and effort are likely to wane.[3] If there are heterogeneities in this pioneering effect across programs, their influence on the estimates of program effectiveness would depend on whether they are correlated with other important unobserved characteristics such as program management capabilities.

Program Subscription: Use by Beneficiaries

Another source of variation in the duration of exposure is the length of time that passes after a program is launched but before the intended beneficiaries use it. For example, the implementation of a new or expanded child immunization or nutrition program may not involve a long process once the program has been launched and inputs have been procured and delivered, but the program will be fully effective only if parents bring their children to the relevant providers. In Mexico, for example, the Progresa program (Programa de Educación, Salud y Alimentación) was carried out in seven states, where it was randomly assigned to localities that were to receive benefits starting in mid-1998 (treatment localities) or that were to receive identical benefits two years later (control localities). However, while treatment was randomly assigned at the community level, this was not so at the household level (see Behrman and Hoddinott 2005). Only 61–64 percent of the eligible children aged 4 to 24 months and only half of those aged 2 to 4 years actually received the nutritional supplements. Given the initial randomization of assignment among localities, a simple comparison between eligible children in the control and treatment localities would have been sufficient to estimate the program ITT effect had program uptake been perfect. Behrman and Hoddinott (2005) actually found no significant ITT effects, but they did find that the TOT effects were significant even after individual and household controls.

Was the undersubscription of the nutrition component in Progresa a matter of informing and convincing more parents about the benefits of the program? Again, there may be a learning process whereby potential program beneficiaries find out enough about a new program such that they actually attempt to use it. Studies of the diffusion of the Green Revolution in the mid-1960s have demonstrated the role of social learning, the process by which an individual learns about a new technology from the experiences of his neighbors (their previous decisions and outcomes) and which accounts for some of the observed lags in the adoption of high-yielding seed varieties in India at the time (see Foster and Rosenzweig 1995; Munshi 2004). For example, in rice villages, the proportion of farmers who adopted the new seed varieties rose from 26 percent in the first year following the introduction of the technology to 31 percent in the third year; in wheat villages, the proportion of adopters increased from 29 percent to 49 percent. Farmers who did not have neighbors with comparable attributes (such as farm size or unobservables) may have had to carry out more of their own experimentation, which was probably a more costly form of learning because the farmers bore all the risk of the choices they made (Munshi 2004).

School voucher programs that require interested students to apply for the voucher award also rely on the participation decisions of individuals and thus on the saturation of information about the program. In cases in which these programs are targeted to a single segment of a population, the information requirements are even greater. For instance, in Paces (Programa de Ampliación de Cobertura de la Educación Secundaria), a school voucher program in Colombia, information about the program was needed to induce both municipal government participation and student participation (Angrist et al. 2002). The program targeted low-income families by giving vouchers only to students living in neighborhoods classified among the two lowest socioeconomic strata in the country, and applicants had to present a utility bill as proof of their residency in poor neighborhoods.

The speed of the learning process may depend on many factors, including information campaigns to persuade potential beneficiaries to use the program and the extent to which the program requires active decisions by beneficiaries before there may be any impact. Indeed, if program information is randomly disseminated (perhaps as part of an evaluation), it may provide an exogenous instrument for the treatment itself. However, information campaigns for programs that attempt to improve primary school quality or to enhance child nutrition through primary school feeding programs in a context in which virtually all primary-school-age children are already enrolled would seem less relevant than such campaigns as part of a new program to improve preschool child development where there had previously been no preschool programs.

One might interpret figure 6.1 as representing the process of expanding effective demand for a program over time, whereby the asymptote is reinterpreted as referring to steady-state effective demand among potential beneficiaries (effective in the sense that the beneficiaries actually act to enroll in or use program services). This process might bias ITT estimates of program impact downward if the estimates are based on data obtained before the attainment of this steady-state effective demand. Parallel to the earlier discussion, the extent of this bias depends on whether the expansion of effective demand across program sites is correlated with unobserved program attributes so that there is less downward bias if there is a positive correlation. However, this phenomenon would not appear to affect TOT impact estimates directly, except perhaps through an indirect feedback effect of expanded demand on the learning process because the learning itself may depend directly on the volume of services that a program provides and not merely on the passage of time.

Age-Targeted Interventions

The age of beneficiaries may be one more factor in determining that the duration of exposure to a program is an important consideration in estimating impact. Early childhood development (ECD) programs such as infant feeding and preschool education offer a good example because they target children who are only eligible at a young age. Moreover, because a significant portion of a child's physical and cognitive development occurs at this young age, the returns to improvements in the living or learning conditions of the child may be particularly high, and such programs, therefore, have the potential for a noticeable impact when the child is young. Studies in the epidemiological and nutrition literatures emphasize that children age 1 to 3 years are especially vulnerable to malnutrition (Glewwe and King 2001; Engle et al. 2007). In interpreting the finding that a nutritional supplementation program in Jamaica did not produce long-term benefits for children, Walker et al. (2005) suggest that supplementation of longer duration or supplementation at an earlier age might have benefited later cognition; the prevention of undernutrition through supplementation during pregnancy and soon after birth might have been more effective than the attempt to reverse the effects of undernutrition through supplementation at an older age.

Similarly, Hoddinott and Kinsey (2001) conclude that, in rural Zimbabwe, the physical development of children ages 12–24 months is the most affected during drought shocks; those children lose 1.5 to 2.0 centimeters of growth, while older children age 2–5 do not seem to experience a slowdown in growth. Information on drought was obtained from rainfall data by area for four agricultural seasons in 1992/1993 and 1995/1996 and normalized against mean levels observed during earlier years. In addition, the authors estimate the impact of atypically low rainfall levels by including a year's delay because the food shortages would be apparent only one year after the drought, but before the next harvest was ready. In another study of rural Zimbabwe, Alderman, Hoddinott, and Kinsey

(2006) conclude that the longer the exposure of young children to civil war and drought, the larger the negative effect of these shocks on child height, but that older children suffer less than younger children in terms of growth. To estimate these longer-run impacts, the authors combine data on children's ages with information on the duration of the civil war and the episodes of drought used in their analysis, and they undertake a new household survey to trace children measured in earlier surveys in 1983–1984 and in 1987.

While the window of opportunity for early childhood nutrition is a particularly striking example of program impact that depends extensively on successful targeting by age, it is far from the only example. The conditional cash transfers for school attendance in Mexico's Progresa program, for instance, start at the third grade. However, preprogram enrollment rates were almost universal through primary school; so, the program impact on enrollments through the primary grades was very small (Behrman, Sengupta, and Todd 2005; Schultz 2004). Therefore, if the program is viewed purely as a program to increase schooling attainment, then it may be rendered much more effective with the same budget constraint if the transfers for the primary grades were eliminated to increase the transfers for the postprimary grades (see Todd and Wolpin 2006). For such reasons, the program authorities are currently considering assessing the impact of reducing or eliminating subsidies for the primary grades so as to increase them for the postprimary grades.

Estimates of ITT and TOT impacts clearly may be affected substantially by whether the timing with regard to the ages of the beneficiaries is well targeted toward such critical age ranges. We will return to these age-related issues in our case study elsewhere below that involves an ECD program.

The Duration Dependence of the Effects on Beneficiaries

A World Bank (2005) study has concluded that it took over three decades of continued support before the health sector in Bangladesh obtained clear, positive improvements in the country's maternal and child health outcomes, while such results were not clearly discernible after the first decade of assistance. However, even within the life of a single program, the duration dependence of effects is an obvious issue. The achievements of a single program during its entire existence, much less only the first few years after program launch, are likely to be modest. One reason is that programs aiming to increase learning or nutritional status inherently require the passage of time.

The accumulation of knowledge and physiological growth are cumulative processes so that there are likely to be greater gains, probably with diminishing marginal returns, from longer program exposure. The importance of the duration of exposure for beneficiaries undoubtedly varies substantially according to the program and the technology that is being provided.

Indonesia's Midwife in the Village program illustrates how the age effects and the duration of program exposure together may vary the estimates of impact. Frankenberg, Suriastini, and Thomas (2005) have evaluated this program, which was supposed to expand the availability of health services to mothers and thus improve children's health outcomes. By exploiting the timing of the (nonrandom) introduction of a midwife to a community, they are able to distinguish between children who were exposed to a midwife during the vulnerable early years of their lives and older children who were living in the same community, but who had not been exposed to a midwife when they were young. As with the studies on Zimbabwe, the authors group the sample of children by birth cohort: an older cohort born between the beginning of 1984 and the end of 1987, a middle cohort born between 1988 and the end of 1991, and a younger cohort born between 1992 and the end of 1995. For each group, the extent of exposure to a village midwife during the vulnerable period of early childhood varied as a function of whether the village had a midwife and, if so, when she had arrived. Hence, in communities that had a midwife from 1993 onward, children in the younger cohort had been fully exposed to the program in 1997, whereas children in the middle cohort had been only partially exposed. The authors conclude that partial exposure to the village midwife program conferred no benefits in improved child nutrition, while full exposure from birth yielded an increase in the height-for-age Z-score of 0.35 to 0.44 standard deviations among children age 1–4.

Behrman, Cheng, and Todd (2004) have evaluated the impact of a preschool program in Bolivia, the Proyecto Integral de Desarrollo Infantil. Their analysis explicitly takes into account the dates of program enrollment of individual children. In their comparison of treated and untreated children, they find evidence of positive program effects on motor skills, psychosocial skills, and language acquisition that are concentrated among children age 37 months and older. When they disaggregated their results by the duration of program exposure, the effects were most clearly observed among children who had been involved in the program for more than a year.

In evaluating the impact of Mexico's Progresa program, Gertler (2004) estimates two program impact models: one model assumes program impact has been independent of the duration of program exposure, and one model allows impact to vary according to the length of exposure. Treatment families were to receive a cash transfer conditional on the use of health and nutritional services. Children under age 2 years were to be immunized, visit nutrition monitoring clinics, and obtain nutritional supplements, and their parents were to receive training on nutrition, health, and hygiene; children between age 2 and 5 years were expected to have been immunized already, but were to obtain the other services. The key outcome variable was the probability of illness. Gertler finds no program impact after a mere six months of program exposure for children under age 3 years, but with 24 months of program exposure, the illness rate among the treatment group was 39.5 percent lower than the rate among the control group, a difference that is significant at the 1 percent level.

Programs that aim at skill development offer an obvious example of the importance of the duration of program exposure. Beneficiaries who attend only part of a training course are probably less likely to benefit from the course and attain the program goals than those who complete the course and course requirements fully. For example, in measuring the number of days of the training course attended by students, Rouse and Krueger (2004) distinguish between students who have completed the computer instruction offered through the Fast ForWord program and those who have not. They define completion as a function of the amount of training time completed and the actual progress of students toward the next stage of the program as reflected in the percentage of exercises at the current level mastered at a prespecified level of proficiency. Because they define the treatment group more stringently, however, the counterfactual treatment received by the control students becomes more mixed, and a share of these students are contaminated by partial participation in the program. The authors find that, among students who have received more comprehensive treatment as reflected in the total number of completed days of training and the level of achievement of the completion criteria, performance improved more quickly on one of the reading tests (but not all) that the authors use.

The duration of exposure to education programs has also been examined by Chin (2005) in India and Duflo (2001) in Indonesia. Because they are retrospective evaluations, these studies have had to depend on the availability of reliable administrative data. Both studies consider program duration as a measure of the intensity of program exposure; they use information on the region and year of birth, combined with administrative data on the year and placement of programs. In Indonesia from 1973 to 1978, more than 61,000 primary schools were built throughout the country, and the enrollment rate among children age 7–12 rose from 69 percent to 83 percent (Duflo 2001). The objective of Duflo's study was to examine the impact on the subsequent educational attainment and on the wages of the birth cohorts affected by this massive school construction program. To achieve this goal, Duflo links district-level data on the number of new schools by year and matches these data with intercensal survey data on men born between 1950 and 1972. Matching information on each individual's region and year of birth and the number of schools by region and year yields estimates of the exposure of an individual to the program. The estimates indicate that each new school per 1,000 children increased the years of education by 0.12–0.19 percent and earnings by 1.5 to 2.7 percent among the first cohort *fully* exposed to the program.

Chin (2005) uses a similar approach in estimating the impact of India's Operation Blackboard, which began in 1987. Taking grades 1–5 as the primary school grades, age 6–10 as the corresponding primary school ages, and 1988 as the first year that schools would have received program resources, Chin supposes that only students born in 1978 or later would have been of primary school age for at least one year in the program regime and, therefore, potentially exposed to the program for most of their schooling. She thus assumes away other factors such as delayed entry into school, grade repetition, and temporary school leaving that would have reduced exposure. Although the central government allocated and disbursed funds for the program for the first time in fiscal year 1987, schools probably did not receive program resources until the following school year. (Chin also supposes a one-year implementation lag.) The author considers two cohort categories: a younger cohort that was born between 1978 and 1983 and was, therefore, potentially exposed to the program and an older cohort. Several years of the All-India Educational Survey, a census of schools, provided state-level data on the number of one-teacher schools, the total number of schools, the number of teachers, and the availability of specific school inputs such as libraries and classrooms. Chin uses these data to define the duration of program exposure and concludes that accounting for duration somewhat lowers the impact as measured, but it remains statistically significant, though only for girls.

If there are duration-of-beneficiary-exposure effects, then it seems that estimates of both ITT and TOT program impacts are generally likely to be biased downward if the evaluation coverage is too short. Moreover, estimates based on short periods of exposure are not likely to be informative about issues such as the extent of diminishing marginal returns to exposure that would seem to be important as part of the information basis of policies.

A Case Study: An ECD Program in the Philippines

In this section, we present the example of a specific ECD program in the Philippines that we have been evaluating with a group of other researchers (see Armecin et al. 2006; Ghuman et al. 2005). Because program implementation was neither instantaneous nor perfect, we have explicitly examined the effect of the length of program exposure on impact. The program was initiated in the late 1990s to enable local government units in three regions to deliver a broad set of ECD-related services to pregnant women and to children under age 7.[4] To assess whether the program has improved cognitive, social, motor, and language development and health and nutrition, we collected survey data on 6,693 children in randomly selected households in three rounds over three years. The surveys covered two treatment regions, as well as one control or comparison region that had not received the program. Program assignment was nonexperimental, and so we have used difference-in-difference propensity score-matching estimators to control for a variety of observed characteristics measured at the level of the child, municipality, or *barangay* (the smallest administrative unit in the Philippines; akin to a village or district).

The ECD program assignment to municipalities or other local government units took several steps, a signal that implementation lags would be likely. First, municipalities deemed to be high risk or needy were identified on the basis of indicators such as infant mortality rate, maternal mortality rate, low birthweight, child malnutrition, and education attainment among children and women. Second, an information campaign was conducted to enlist the participation and cooperation of mayors and local health officials as program partners. Within the decentralized system in the Philippines, local government units are responsible for providing basic ECD services, supporting the organization of parent cooperatives to initiate programs, financing the salaries of service providers, and supplying counterpart funds for local ECD councils. (National agencies are expected to provide counterpart funding for the establishment and expansion of ECD programs in poor and disadvantaged communities.) Local officials thus essentially decide the menu of ECD services to be implemented in each government unit. Accordingly, we incorporate the baseline characteristics of barangay and other unit leaders in the propensity score-matching estimates.

Discussions with program managers and the analysis of field administrative data indicate that the timing of the implementation differed substantially across program areas, especially in procurement, the receipt of material inputs, and provider training. This variance implies that there have been differences in the duration of program exposure across treatment areas and, therefore, differences in the amount of time during which the interventions would have an impact.

Although the type of ECD-related services has not changed significantly because of the program, the program has substantially increased the extent of several primary health care and other services designed to promote ECD, though not evenly across services or areas. Table 6.1 shows the percentage of municipalities that had *functioning* elements of various ECD-related services during our first survey round and during our third survey round depending on whether they are in program or nonprogram regions (but see the note to the table). The data were collected through systematic interviews with local officials; they are likely based on local administrative data. Specifically, between the baseline and last round, there was a positive trend in the adoption of feeding programs, parent education programs, and home-based day care in program areas, and this positive trend was either not observed or not as strong in nonprogram areas.

We discuss elsewhere above the possible delays to program effectiveness that may result from learning. In the ECD program in the Philippines, attendance at a training course was an important learning activity for service providers. Table 6.2 shows that, by the third survey round, midwives and day-care providers in program areas were substantially more likely than

TABLE 6.1 Municipalities with ECD-Related Programs, by Region and Survey Round

Type of program	Program areas		Nonprogram areas	
	Round 1	Round 3	Round 1	Round 3
Feeding programs (%)	32.3	69.4	28.1	38.6
Parent education, effectiveness seminars (%)	77.4	100.0	68.4	63.2
Home-based day care (%)	16.1	44.4	8.8	0.0
Number of municipalities	31	36	57	57

Source: Armecin et al. 2006.
Note: Services that were being provided in all municipalities during both the first and the third rounds are omitted.

TABLE 6.2 Service Providers Who Have Received Program Training, by Type of Training

Type of training	Rural health midwife		Barangay health worker		Day-care worker		Child development worker
	Program area	Nonprogram area	Program area	Nonprogram area	Program area	Nonprogram area	Program area[a]
Parent education (%)	36.3	1.0	4.9	0	83.7	0	61.5
Management of childhood illness (%)	52.5	4.2	4.9	1.7	n.a.	n.a.	1.8
Growth monitoring (%)	45.3	10.4	16.7	0	3.4	0.0	0.9
Health care service delivery (%)	13.4	3.1	6.5	1.7	1.0	1.1	1.8
Number of providers	179	96	306	174	208	92	109

Source: Armecin et al. 2006.
Note: All data pertain to the third survey round. n.a. = not applicable.
a. Child development workers are found in program areas only.

providers in nonprogram regions to have received training in topics such as parent education, the management of childhood illness, and growth monitoring. Two-thirds of the child development workers received training in educating parents about child health, but, in fact, not all providers in the program areas had received training three years after project launch. In general, barangay health workers were less likely than other types of providers to receive training, although they were still more likely to receive training if they worked in a program barangay.

Tables 6.1 and 6.2 suggest that it would be inaccurate to assume that the eligible children in all treatment areas were exposed to the program at the same time. According to the central program office, however, the implementation delays were caused by administrative lags in the central procurement rules and centralized actions rather than by preferences or management capacity in program areas. Because of lags in disbursements, the program was not initiated in 70 percent of the program barangays until after the first round of data had been collected and, in 29 percent of the program barangays, until after the second round. During the second round, a lack of funds or delays in releasing funds was reported by 28 of the 33 municipality project teams that shared data and was the most common implementation problem named by these teams (OPS 2005).[5] All barangays had experienced the program by round 3, with one exception (accounting for 32 children), which we excluded from the analysis.

To estimate the potential program exposure of individual children, we used the administrative data on implementation from the central project management office and household survey data on each child's birth month and year and place of residence. Figure 6.2 shows that the mean length of exposure of eligible children was 14 months, with a substantial standard deviation of six months. Table 6.3 indicates the distribution of children by age in years across four exposure categories at the third survey round.[6] In estimating program impact, we have restricted our sample to children who lived in barangays that had at least four months of exposure at round 3 because children with less than four months of exposure were unlikely to have had enough contact with the program to have benefited, particularly given the start-up problems. As a result, we dropped 252 children from the analysis.

In the absence of a randomized allocation of children to the program, we established a counterfactual group using a difference-in-difference propensity score-matching method and controls for fixed unobserved characteristics (see Armecin et al. 2006). We have conditioned our estimates on

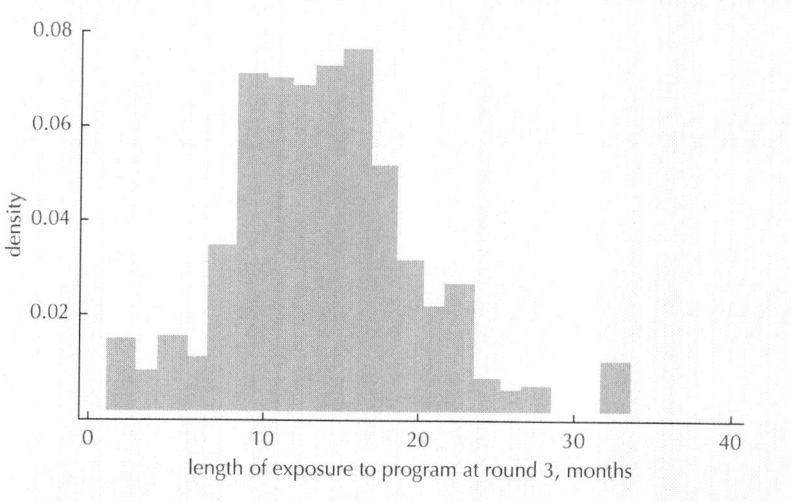

FIGURE 6.2 Distribution of the Length of Program Exposure

length of exposure to program at round 3, months

Source: Armecin et al. 2006.

the joint distribution of children's ages (at round 3) and a discrete measure of the duration of the program exposure of children. We have distinguished among duration categories of under 4 months, 4–12 months, 13–16 months, and 17 months or longer, and we have specified robust standard errors. (Since the age at round 3 is given, the exposure reported represents the

TABLE 6.3 Distribution of Children across Program Exposure Categories, by Age

Age in years	<4 months	4–12 months	13–16 months	17+ months	Total
2	4.42 (24)	33.2 (180)	32.6 (177)	29.8 (162)	100 (543)
3	6.13 (53)	33.7 (291)	28.4 (245)	31.8 (275)	100 (864)
4	6.51 (50)	34.4 (264)	28.4 (218)	30.7 (236)	100 (768)
5	5.67 (49)	39.2 (339)	24.1 (209)	31.1 (269)	100 (866)
6+	6.92 (76)	36.7 (404)	28.0 (308)	28.3 (311)	100 (1,099)
Total number	252	1,478	1,157	1,253	4,140

Source: Armecin et al. 2006.
Note: Numbers of children are in parentheses. Ages refer to children in round 3.

indicated number of months of exposure before the age at round 3.) We have chosen this strategy so as to uncover potentially valuable information about how children of different ages respond to variations in program exposure. We have estimated the impact of the program on a number of outcomes: (a) cognitive, social, motor, and language development, which has been measured using an instrument developed for the evaluation and covering gross motor skills, fine motor skills, receptive language, expressive language, cognitive development, socioemotional development, and self-help or the ability to perform routine daily activities;[7] (b) anthropometric indicators of nutrition and health status, such as height-for-age and weight-for-height (that is, the number of standard deviations below or above the widely used U.S. National Center for Health Statistics standard); (c) helminth infections six months before the survey; (d) the incidence of diarrhea; and (e) the hemoglobin levels in blood samples of children at least 6 months of age.

Our estimates are ITT effects, that is, the impact of the program, on average, for all children in a given age range within a barangay whether or not all the children in the barangay have actually received treatment. Estimating the TOT impact of the program has been conceptually complex and difficult to implement because of the following: (a) The program had several components, some new (such as child-minding and the child development workers) and some representing improvements on existing services such as growth monitoring and micronutrient supplementation. (b) The delivery of many of the program components was not centralized; thus, the actual treatment supplied through various components was difficult to ascertain and model. (c) Information campaigns about ECD in the community, as well as home visits, were an important aspect of program mechanisms. Overall, the impact of the program was not likely to depend on service utilization in ways that may be true of programs that offer a single, centralized service.[8]

The difference-in-difference method controls for all unobserved fixed variables related to the child (such as innate health), family (such as the relevant aspects of the home environment that affect ECD), and community (such as the relevant aspects of the community that may directly affect ECD and the placement of ECD-related programs) and all community variables that exhibit secular changes common across program and nonprogram areas. The propensity score-matching method utilizes information on the observed baseline characteristics of children, their families, and their communities to identify and match children in the treatment and control samples on the elements of these characteristics. For each outcome indicator, we have estimated the impact for each of 15 age-duration groups (that is, five ages at round 3 and three durations). Briefly, our ITT estimates fall into three groups: predominately positive program impacts (nine indicators), mixed or virtually no program impacts (four indicators), and predominately negative program impacts (two indicators). Armecin et al. (2006) provide the detailed estimates; below, we summarize our results with respect to the duration of program exposure.

Among children below age 4 in program areas at round 3, there was a substantial improvement in cognitive, social, motor, and language development in all seven domains relative to children in nonprogram areas. Among 2-year-olds in program areas, gross motor skills were 1.1 to 1.5 standard deviations better relative to children in nonprogram areas. Among 2- and 3-year-olds exposed to the program for at least 17 months, expressive and receptive language skills were 0.92 to 1.8 standard deviations better. Cognitive skills were 0.92 to 1.2 standard deviations better among 2-year-olds and 0.28 to 0.43 standard deviations better among 3-year-olds. The weight-for-height Z-score among older children (age 4 and above) was also significantly higher among program children relative to nonprogram children (by 0.16 to 0.27 standard deviations), though similar, positive impacts were not evident among children who had been exposed to the program for 17 months or longer.

Table 6.4 summarizes the positive and significant (at the .05 level) impact estimates for 15 age-duration categories. It gives the number of significant and positive estimates for each of the 15 age-duration groups, as well as the mean estimated impacts for each duration category and each age bracket. Though the table indicates significant positive responses primarily after fairly long durations of program exposure (for example, after 17 months for gross motor skills and after 13 months for socioemotional skills), the last two rows suggest only slight evidence for greater impact with greater duration. In particular, there is a 10 percent increase in the prevalence of positive coefficients between the shortest duration category and the other duration categories and an increase from 0.60 to 0.72 standard deviations in mean outcomes with increases in exposure. However, the last column indicates a substantial concentration of significant positive program impacts among younger children of age 2–3 in round 3. The average magnitude of the impacts is 0.90 standard deviations among 2-year-olds and 0.49 standard deviations among 3-year-olds, but only in the 0.24–0.29 range for children older than 3.

In sum, the incorporation of information about the variation in program exposure and child age is valuable because, with this information, we have

**TABLE 6.4 Distribution of Significant Positive Effects,
by Age and Months of Exposure**

| Indicator | Exposure (months) | | | | Mean impact (sample standard deviation) |
	4–12	13–16	17+	Total	
Age in years (round 3)					
2	9	7	7	23	0.90
3	4	7	7	18	0.49
4	2	3	3	8	0.26
5	4	2	3	9	0.24
6+	1	3	2	6	0.29
Total number by duration	20	22	22	64	n.a.
Mean impact by duration	0.60	0.70	0.72	n.a.	n.a.

Source: Armecin et al. 2006.
Note: Only estimates for which the results were predominately positive are included (nine of 15 indicators). n.a. = not applicable.

been able to test the extent to which program impacts have been sensitive to the duration of program exposure and the ages of the children involved in the program. We have found that the program impacts seem to vary according to the duration of exposure, although this variation is not as dramatic as the variation associated with children's ages. In particular, cognitive, social, motor, and language development among children below age 4 in program areas at the time of the final survey round improved significantly and substantially relative to the development among similar children in nonprogram areas. Younger children exhibited more rapid rates of change in psychosocial development than did older children and may thus be more receptive to interventions that aim to improve developmental outcomes. These impacts are not trivial: among 2- and 3-year-olds exposed to the program, Z-scores were 0.5 to 1.8 standard deviations higher for motor and language development. The prevalence and magnitudes of the estimated positive program impacts are much lower among older children.

Conclusions

Many impact evaluations of social programs assume that the interventions occur at specified launch dates and produce equal and constant changes in conditions among eligible beneficiary groups. This assumption is perhaps reasonable when the intervention is almost completely under the direction and control of the evaluator. In the examples we have cited (India's Green Revolution, Mexico's Progresa program, and an ECD program in the Philippines), this assumption is far from true. Indeed, there are several reasons why initial start-up costs will typically delay program effectiveness in treatment areas and thus influence the estimates of impact. This chapter discusses sources of the variation in the length of program exposure across treatment areas and beneficiaries, including (a) lags in implementation that arise from administrative or bureaucratic delays; (b) learning processes that providers and beneficiaries may have to undertake; and (c) thus, delay full program effectiveness; and (c) dependence of an effect on the ages of beneficiaries and the duration of the program.

Capturing this variation in program exposure typically requires administrative data on the design and implementation details of a program, combined with survey data on beneficiaries. Program data on the timing of implementation are likely to be available from program management units, but these data may not be available at the desired level of disaggregation, which might be the district, community, or individual depending on where the variation in timing is thought to be the greatest. The primary concern of the high-level program manager may be the disbursement of project funds and the procurement of major expenditure items, whereas the evaluator's main concern should be the moment when the funds and inputs reach treatment areas or beneficiaries. There may be too much detailed data on timing such as the procurement dates for numerous material inputs or staffing hires, and the evaluator is faced with a critical choice among these data, a choice that may be extremely difficult without in-depth institutional knowledge of the program. The administrative program data may be collected and held in local program offices that may have different (computer-based or paper-based) systems for monitoring and storage. Compiling such data on large programs that decentralize to numerous local offices would be costly.

Despite these various time and cost issues, however, establishing the duration of program exposure across treatment areas or beneficiaries is a worthwhile undertaking. The appropriate moment to implement a program evaluation may depend on the speed of diffusion of a new technology or of a social reform, but it also depends on practical considerations related to the way national and local bureaucracies operate. In the cases we have reviewed, evaluation results show that accounting for variations in length of program exposure alters impact estimates significantly; therefore, ignoring these variations may generate misleading conclusions about an intervention. For example, in our Philippine case study, the evaluation results indicate that the program has had positive impacts on several dimensions of children's physical, mental, and social development and that longer duration of program exposure increases impact somewhat, particularly among children below age 4 at the time of the evaluation. Qualitatively similar results that reveal important age-duration interactions have been obtained on ECD programs in Bolivia, Indonesia, and Mexico.

The way impact estimates are affected by variations in the length of program exposure depends on whether the source of the variations is common within a treatment area or differs within a treatment area and whether the source of the variations is random or not. If the implementation lags are homogeneous across treatment areas, a simple comparison between the beneficiaries in the treatment and control areas would be sufficient to estimate the average treatment or the ITT effects. If the delays vary across treatment areas, but not within those areas and if the variation is random or independent of unobservable characteristics in the program areas that may also affect program effectiveness, then it is possible to estimate the ITT effects, the appropriate controls for area or facility data, or the fixed effects for different exposure categories. When the source of variations in exposure across treatment areas is not random (for example, it is correlated with the management capabilities of local officials), then the ITT effects are likely to be influenced, and this calls for appropriate instruments. Implementation delays per se do not necessarily affect TOT estimates if the onset of the treatment is identified correctly. When the variations in duration of exposure occur at the level of the ultimate beneficiaries perhaps because program participation is voluntary and nonrandom, a lack of accounting for the variations will bias the TOT estimates. We have reviewed the empirical evidence in various studies on methods to address these issues.

Notes

1. In their assessment of the returns to World Bank investment projects, Pohl and Mihaljek (1992) cite construction delays among the risks that account for a wedge between ex ante (appraisal) estimates and ex post estimates of rates of returns. They estimate that, on average, projects take considerably more time to implement than expected at appraisal: six years rather than four years.

2. In two programs that we know, administrative records at the individual level were maintained at local program offices, not at a central program office, and local record-keeping varied in quality and form (for example, some records were computerized and some were not), so that a major effort was required to collect and check records during the evaluations.

3. This may be related to the so-called experimental or Hawthorne effects in experimental evaluations and possibly to scaling-up issues. Banerjee et al. (2007) present an

example of short-run effects that are significantly larger than longer-run effects. They evaluate two randomly assigned programs in urban India: a computer-assisted learning program and a remedial training program that hired young women to teach children with low literacy and numeracy skills. The remedial program raised average test scores by 0.14 standard deviations in the first year and 0.28 standard deviations in the second year of the program, while computer-assisted learning increased mathematics scores by 0.35 standard deviations in the first year and 0.47 standard deviations in the second year. One year after the programs had ended, however, the gains had fallen. For the remedial program, the gain fell to 0.1 standard deviations and was no longer statistically significant; for the computer learning program, the gain had dropped to 0.09 standard deviations, but was still significant.

4. In general, the project did not introduce new health and ECD-related services, but upgraded or improved the facilities available through existing service providers. Its innovation was to adopt an integrated, multisectoral approach to deliver a combination of services, including center-based interventions (such as day-care centers, preschools, and village or district health stations) and home-based interventions (such as household child day-care programs and home visits by health workers). To link the center-based and home-based services, new service providers, known as child development workers, were placed in all program areas. These providers were to complement the roles of midwives and health workers in providing food and nutritional supplements and monitoring children's health status and were responsible for community-based parental education on ECD.

5. Two barangays received the program inputs about a year and a half before round 1 as part of a pilot phase; so, we excluded these two barangays (which accounted for 33 eligible children). In these cases, the matching variables, measured at the baseline, were not likely to be exogenous relative to the program launch (see Armecin et al. 2006).

6. Of the original cohort of 7,922 children age 0–4, 86 percent (or 6,774 children) were successfully resurveyed in the same barangay during the first follow-up survey in 2002 (round 2) and the second follow-up survey in 2003 (round 3) (see Armecin et al. 2006).

7. The scaled scores in each of the seven domains relative to a sample of healthy children are expressed as Z-values that are measured as the number of standard deviations below the reference subsample mean. The reference group is children who reside in households where the father and mother have 12 years of schooling or more, the households are in the upper quartile of the income distribution, and the houses have cement walls and tin roofs.

8. The treatment variable is defined with respect to the timing of implementation relative to the survey rounds. For example, if the program began after round 1, we use the round 2 value for a child's visit to a health center. Because the treatment indicator refers to the year before the survey, the value attached to it may conceivably refer to a period prior to the start of the program. Because we do not know the precise timing of children's visits to health centers, we have been unable to elucidate this issue. The results indicate that, among the unmatched and matched samples of children, there is no evidence linked to any indicator that program impact is statistically significant. The sign and magnitude of the estimates tend to vary erratically across the age and duration cells. However, for the reasons given in the description of the nature of the ECD program, we think these attempts to estimate the TOT effect are not particularly informative.

References

Alderman, Harold, John Hoddinott, and William Kinsey. 2006. "Long Term Consequences of Early Childhood Malnutrition." *Oxford Economic Papers* 58 (3): 450–74.

Angrist, Joshua D., Eric Bettinger, Erik Bloom, Elizabeth M. King, and Michael Kremer. 2002. "Vouchers for Private Schooling in Colombia: Evidence from a Randomized Natural Experiment." *American Economic Review* 92 (5): 1535–58.

Armecin, Graeme, Jere R. Behrman, Paulita Duazo, Sharon Ghuman, Socorro Gultiano, Elizabeth M. King, and Nannette Lee. 2006. "Early Childhood Development through an Integrated Program: Evidence from the Philippines." Policy Research Working Paper 3922, World Bank, Washington, DC.

Banerjee, Abhijit V., Shawn Alen Cole, Esther Duflo, and Leigh Linden. 2007. "Remedying Education: Evidence from Two Randomized Experiments in India." *Quarterly Journal of Economics* 122 (3): 1235–64.

Behrman, Jere R., Yingmei Cheng, and Petra E. Todd. 2004. "Evaluating Preschool Programs When Length of Exposure to the Program Varies: A Nonparametric Approach." *Review of Economics and Statistics* 86 (1): 108–32.

Behrman, Jere R., and John Hoddinott. 2005. "Programme Evaluation with Unobserved Heterogeneity and Selective Implementation: The Mexican 'Progresa' Impact on Child Nutrition." *Oxford Bulletin of Economics and Statistics* 67 (4): 547–69.

Behrman, Jere R., Piyali Sengupta, and Petra E. Todd. 2005. "Progressing through Progresa: An Impact Assessment of Mexico's School Subsidy Experiment." *Economic Development and Cultural Change* 54 (1): 237–75.

Chin, Aimee. 2005. "Can Redistributing Teachers across Schools Raise Educational Attainment?: Evidence from Operation Blackboard in India." *Journal of Development Economics* 78 (2): 384–405.

Duflo, Esther. 2001. "Schooling and Labor Market Consequences of School Construction in Indonesia: Evidence from an Unusual Policy Experiment." *American Economic Review* 91 (4): 795–813.

Engle, Patrice L., Maureen M. Black, Jere R. Behrman, Meena Cabral de Mello, Paul J. Gertler, Lydia Kapiriri, Reynaldo Martorell, Mary Eming Young, and the International Child Development Steering Group. 2007. "Strategies to Avoid the Loss of Developmental Potential in More Than 200 Million Children in the Developing World." *Lancet* 369 (9557): 229–42.

Foster, Andrew D., and Mark R. Rosenzweig. 1995. "Learning by Doing and Learning from Others: Human Capital and Technical Change in Agriculture." *Journal of Political Economy* 103 (6): 1176–1209.

Frankenberg, Elizabeth, Wayan Suriastini, and Duncan Thomas. 2005. "Can Expanding Access to Basic Health Care Improve Children's Health Status?: Lessons from Indonesia's 'Midwife in the Village' Programme." *Population Studies* 59 (1): 5–19.

Gertler, Paul J. 2004. "Do Conditional Cash Transfers Improve Child Health?: Evidence from Progresa's Control Randomized Experiment." *American Economic Review* 94 (2): 336–41.

Ghuman, Sharon, Jere R. Behrman, Judith B. Borja, Socorro Gultiano, and Elizabeth M. King. 2005. "Family Background, Service Providers, and Early Childhood Development in the Philippines: Proxies and Interactions." *Economic Development and Cultural Change* 54 (1): 129–64.

Glewwe, Paul W., and Elizabeth M. King. 2001. "The Impact of Early Childhood Nutrition Status on Cognitive Achievement: Does the Timing of Malnutrition Matter?" *World Bank Economic Review* 15 (1): 81–113.

Hoddinott, John, and William Kinsey. 2001. "Child Growth in the Time of Drought." *Oxford Bulletin of Economics and Statistics* 63 (4): 409–36.

King, Elizabeth M., and Berk Özler. 1998. "What's Decentralization Got to Do with Learning?: The Case of Nicaragua's School Autonomy Reform." Working Paper on Impact Evaluation of Education Reforms 9 (June), Development Research Group, World Bank, Washington, DC.

Manski, Charles F. 1996. "Learning about Treatment Effects from Experiments with Random Assignment of Treatments." *Journal of Human Resources* 31 (4): 709–33.

Munshi, Kaivan. 2004. "Social Learning in a Heterogeneous Population: Technology Diffusion in the Indian Green Revolution." *Journal of Development Economics* 73 (1): 185–213.

OPS (Office of Population Studies). 2005. *A Study of the Effects of Early Childhood Interventions on Children's Physiological, Cognitive and Social Development: Results of the Longitudinal Evaluation Study.* Cebu City, Philippines: Office of Population Studies, University of San Carlos.

Pohl, Gerhard, and Dubravko Mihaljek. 1992. "Project Evaluation and Uncertainty in Practice: A Statistical Analysis of Rate-of-Return Divergences of 1,015 World Bank Projects." *World Bank Economic Review* 6 (2): 255–77.

Rivarola, Magdalena, and Bruce Fuller. 1999. "Nicaragua's Experiment to Decentralize Schools: Contrasting Views of Parents, Teachers, and Directors." *Comparative Education Review* 43 (4): 489–521.

Rouse, Cecilia Elena, and Alan B. Krueger. 2004. "Putting Computerized Instruction to the Test: A Randomized Evaluation of a 'Scientifically Based' Reading Program." *Economics of Education Review* 23 (4): 323–38.

Schultz, T. Paul. 2004. "School Subsidies for the Poor: Evaluating the Mexican Progresa Poverty Program." *Journal of Development Economics* 74 (1): 199–250.

Todd, Petra E., and Kenneth I. Wolpin. 2006. "Assessing the Impact of a School Subsidy Program in Mexico: Using a Social Experiment to Validate a Dynamic Behavioral Model of Child Schooling and Fertility." *American Economic Review* 96 (5): 1384–1417.

Walker, Susan P., Susan M. Chang, Christine A. Powell, and Sally M. Grantham-McGregor. 2005. "Effects of Early Childhood Psychosocial Stimulation and Nutritional Supplementation on Cognition and Education in Growth-Stunted Jamaican Children: Prospective Cohort Study." *Lancet* 366 (9499): 1804–07.

World Bank. 2005. "Improving the World Bank's Development Effectiveness: What Does Evaluation Show?" Evaluation report, Operations Evaluation Department, World Bank, Washington, DC.

7

Tracking Public Money in the Health Sector in Mozambique
Conceptual and Practical Challenges

Magnus Lindelow

In most health facility surveys, the facility is an object of interest in its own right. Data are collected on costs, quality, or some other facility characteristic with the objective of studying facility performance or outcomes or using facility characteristics to gain a better understanding of household behavior. However, in health systems in which providers are financed and operated by the government, health facilities are merely the final link in a broader system of public service financing and delivery. A number of recent health facility surveys have made this broader system the focus of analysis. These surveys, often referred to as Public Expenditure Tracking Surveys (PETSs) or Quantitative Service Delivery Surveys, collect data from health facilities, but also from the administrative units at local and central government levels that are charged with the financing and administration of the facilities. A central aim of these surveys has often been to determine whether funds allocated by governments to health service delivery reach the facilities that are supposed to deliver the services.

The first PETS focused on the education sector and was carried out in Uganda in 1995 (Ablo and Reinikka 1998). It was motivated by the failure of educational outcomes to respond to increases in public spending on primary education in the early 1990s. The survey, which covered 250 primary schools around the country, found that, over the five years preceding the

173

survey, schools had, in fact, received only 13 percent of the capitation grants to which they were entitled. This striking finding and the vigorous policy response by the Ugandan government that ensued led to widespread interest in the PETS approach. Tracking surveys have now been undertaken in a large number of countries and have become a standard tool for public expenditure analysis and fiduciary accountability.

Yet, many of the tracking surveys that have followed in the wake of the Uganda survey have not generated such striking findings and have not had the same impressive policy impact. Why is this so? The survey in Uganda addressed a seemingly straightforward question: do schools actually obtain the funds to which they are entitled? It turns out that this question is often difficult to answer. This chapter provides a brief overview of the conceptual and practical challenges that arise in designing and implementing tracking surveys and draws on a 2002 tracking survey in Mozambique to provide concrete examples of how these challenges appear in practice.[1]

The Challenge in Tracking Public Money

One reason for the success of the education PETS in Uganda was the fact that the design and implementation of the capitation grant made it amenable to tracking. Reliable data were available through primary schools; it was easy to establish that the funds had been released by the central level; and there were simple, explicit rules about the amounts the schools were supposed to receive.

However, tracking public money is not always so easy. Indeed, because of poor recordkeeping and other problems, the first health PETS, undertaken in Uganda in 1995 at the same time as the education PETS, did not generate clear findings. Similar problems have plagued tracking surveys in other countries. Why was the outcome of the PETS in health so different from the outcome of the PETS in education? Why have many other tracking surveys faced difficulties in measuring leakage? There are three key parts to the answer.

Dealing with Complex Resource Flows

In most developing countries, public health facilities do not each obtain one monthly budget allocation that they spend and must account for. Typically, they receive financial and in-kind resources through multiple channels that are governed by distinct, separate administrative and recording procedures.[2] At every step, there is a risk of leakage.

Salary payments—sometimes distributed to staff in cash and sometimes disbursed directly into bank accounts—are typically subject to the specific institutional arrangements regulating the overall government payroll. Salary budgets may nonetheless leak at different levels of government because administrators may simply create fictitious health workers—ghosts—and collect the salary payments on their behalf. Likewise, staff who are being paid may not show up for work or may work only irregularly.

Medical supplies, including drugs, vaccines, and other material goods, are often procured at the central or regional level and distributed to facilities in kind.[3] Facilities sustain other, minor recurrent expenditures by paying for food for patients, stationery, cleaning materials, and utilities. Budgets may be allocated for these purposes, or, if the facilities are small and isolated, the expenditure may be incurred by the local government, and the goods distributed in kind to the facilities. Expenditures on drugs and other supplies may leak during the procurement process. They may also leak during the distribution process through theft, loss, or routine disposal (for example, drugs or vaccines that have not been used before the expiration date). Similar issues arise for other nonsalary expenditures.

External financing provided by development agencies or nongovernmental organizations (NGOs) plays an important role in supporting health services in many countries. Although there are exceptions, external financing and the government budget are often managed separately, creating separate resource flows and, consequently, separate opportunities for leakage.

Because of the complex institutional arrangements involved in financing health facilities, it is usually difficult to collect data on *total* resource flows to facilities and to assess the overall leakage in facility financing. It is clear that the risk of leakage arises at facilities, local governments, and the central government and that the relative risks at the various levels are likely to vary across resource flows and contexts. A first step to successful tracking, therefore, involves mapping the respective flows, determining the scope for leakage, and establishing how the various public expenditure flows are being recorded.

The Concept of Leakage

Most tracking surveys have the explicit objective of measuring and, at least to some extent, explaining leakages in the flow of resources from the central government to individual service providers. According to the typical working hypothesis, as in Uganda, schools and health care facilities fail to receive a sizable share of the funds allocated for them.

However, though the question that tracking surveys seek to address is undoubtedly an important one, the concept of leakage has been difficult to define in practice.

Leakage is generally thought of as the difference between a resource allocation or entitlement for a particular facility for a given period and the amount of resources actually received by the facility during the relevant period. In the Uganda education PETS, the focus was on the capitation grant to schools. The grant regulations established an amount that was based on the size of the student population and that district offices were to pay to individual schools. Once it had been established that the central government had disbursed the allocation to the district offices, the allocation rule and the data collected from the schools on the funds they had received were sufficient to construct a meaningful estimate of leakage.[4]

In many places and contexts, however, there are no hard allocation rules or formal and binding budget allocations for individual service providers (see table 7.1). Instead, there may be line-item allocations to administrative units, such as districts, that exercise considerable or complete discretion over the allocation of resources among facilities. Alternatively, the allocation of resources may be guided by criteria or norms established at the central level, but allowing for discretion among local managers who may adjust outlays on the basis of need or other considerations. The absence of hard allocation rules complicates the conceptualization and measurement of leakage. Although it may still be possible to collect data on funds or other resources received by service providers, these data may not be compared with a defined entitlement or allocation to determine leakage. Of course, it is possible to compare the funds and other resources received with actual disbursements made by administrative units at higher levels of government, but this comparison represents a considerably narrower view of leakage than the view gained in a context in which the allocation rules are hard. Analysis of the data may, nonetheless, generate other insights on, for example, the delays in resource transfers or the degree of compliance with the allocation criteria governing the amount and direction of resource transfers.

Making Sense of Records

Regardless of the expenditures being tracked, data collection is typically based on structured questionnaires. Some information is gathered through interviews with the health facility staff, district administrators, and other relevant personnel. However, in contrast to qualitative, perception-based surveys,

TABLE 7.1 Examples of Allocation Rules

Type of allocation rule	Example	Implications for the assessment of leakage
Hard allocation rules	Binding prospective funding formulas (such as capitation payments) Formal budget allocations to facilities (global or line items) and strict procedures for budget changes during the implementation period	Differences between the allocations and the funds received may be established, provided reliable data are collected. Differences may be considered leakage if they are verifiably the result of administrative bottlenecks (for example, in the budget execution process). Leakage may reflect embezzlement or fraud, but may also reflect legitimate reallocations of resources.
Soft or no allocation rules	Normative allocation criteria (for example, in the allocation of drugs and staff to facilities) Informal budget allocations (global or line items) and significant local discretion in the initial allocation and in altering budget allocations Multiple facilities are part of higher-level budget entities (such as districts) with full local discretion over the allocation of resources	Differences between the allocations and the funds received may be established, provided reliable data are collected. Differences may not be considered leakage because departure from the norms or allocation criteria is permissible. Narrow leakage may be assessed by comparing the funds disbursed or the resources distributed at higher levels and the funds received. Other issues may be addressed, including consistency with allocation criteria, equity, and delays and bottlenecks in resource transfers.

Source: Compiled by the author.

tracking surveys seek to capture the quantitative information in administrative records, including budgets, expenditure accounts, receipts, drug records, and payrolls. These records may be difficult to understand. Moreover, they are often poorly maintained, reflecting a lack of capacity, weak procedures, and possibly efforts by the staff to manipulate and take advantage of the system. Data collection is demanding, and highly qualified professionals such as accountants or auditors may be best placed to undertake the work. However, unlike an audit, a PETS seeks to collect data from a large and representative sample of facilities. This feature may be the one that adds the most power to the findings of a PETS.

Organizers of a PETS thus face a trade-off: they may obtain greater scale, but at a cost in data quality. As in the first health PETS in Uganda, many surveys have struggled with records that are incomplete and riddled with errors. As a result, the accurate interpretation of discrepancies in recorded resource flows between various levels of government or between government administrative units and providers is often not evident. Do they reflect leakage or, perhaps, errors in bookkeeping?

This question points to the importance of understanding the limitations of administrative records, developing questionnaires that reflect the institutional context, training enumerators, and balancing the scope of the study in terms of content and geographical coverage and with respect to depth and quality. It also points to some important tensions in the design and implementation of tracking surveys. For example, to collect good data from administrative records, enumerators need to spend considerable time in local government offices and facilities and must rely on the support and assistance of facility staff. In some areas, the need to ensure such cooperation may conflict with other survey goals. For example, to determine the share of ghost workers or the rate of absenteeism at a facility, the visit of the enumerator at the facility needs to be unannounced.[5] In contrast, if the aim of a survey is to determine more than the presence or absence of health workers in a facility, then relying on unannounced visits may be unnecessarily costly and time-consuming and may risk undermining cooperation of the facility staff.

The Challenges in Practice: The Mozambique Tracking Survey

Mozambique is one of the poorest countries in the world.[6] Since independence in 1975, the country has made considerable progress in establishing a health system based on public financing and provision (Noormahomed and Segall 1994). Recent decades have seen rapid expansion in health facility infrastructure and health sector staff. This expansion has permitted considerable growth in aggregate service output. However, there is also evidence of notable problems in service delivery, including low technical quality, lack of drugs and equipment, low staff morale, and informal charging. In addition, little is known about the process by which resources are allocated among districts or among facilities within districts. So one could explore these issues, an Expenditure Tracking and Service Delivery Survey was implemented in 2002 with the aim of providing quantitative and representative evidence on the operation of the financing and logistical arrangements for supporting health centers and health posts and the impact of these arrangements on the capacity of facilities to deliver services.[7]

Similar to other tracking surveys, the starting point of the Mozambique survey was a concern that the resources being allocated to district health services were not reaching the facilities actually delivering the services. During the preparations for the survey, the complexities of the financing and logistical arrangements in the health sector in Mozambique became apparent (see figure 7.1). Aside from salaries, there were no financial transfers to individual facilities. Instead, facilities received in-kind resource transfers, and procurement occurred at the central, provincial, or district level depending on the specific input. The survey team thus faced a difficult choice. One option was to focus on a specific resource flow and collect detailed data that would permit a reliable assessment of leakage. There might be a risk that the impact would be limited because of the narrow focus. The alternative— the option actually chosen—was to adopt a broader focus; the risk was that the data would not permit firm conclusions on leakage.

The questionnaires and data forms included sections on three key inputs in the delivery of health services: district recurrent budgets, human resources, and drugs and other supplies (for details, see http://www.worldbank. org/research/projects/publicspending/tools/newtools.htm). In addition, data were collected on service outputs, infrastructure, and revenues from user fees. The data collection in provinces, districts, and facilities was complemented by interviews with health workers and patients.

Measuring Leakage

An immediate challenge during the Mozambique survey was the need to clarify the concept of leakage. With the exception of salary payments, the amounts of which were determined by the number and salary grade of the

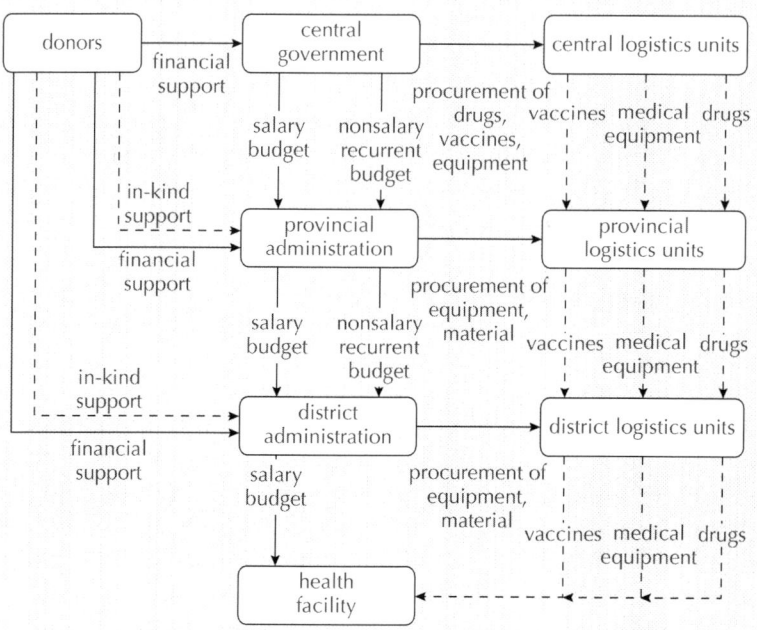

FIGURE 7.1   Financial and Resource Flows to Primary Facilities

Source: Compiled by the author.
Note: ----- In-kind support; ——— financial support.

staff at a facility, resource flows to facilities were not governed by hard allocation rules. Consider, for example, the nonsalary component of the annual
government budget. Although the budget established an explicit allocation for nonwage recurrent expenditures for the health sector in each
province, the allocation to districts within a province was merely indicative
and might easily be changed in the course of a year. In this case, should
leakage be defined relative to the initial or final allocation? The answer to
this question presumably depends on whether or not a change in an allocation may be considered part of legitimate adjustments to reflect evolving
circumstances or needs, but this difference is difficult to assess in practice.

Similar issues arise in relation to drugs and other medical supplies. Drugs
are distributed to health centers and health posts through two separate channels: prepackaged drug kits and individual drugs. The allocation of kits is
loosely based on historical patient volume, while individual drugs are distributed on the basis of requisitions by facilities. In both situations, adminis-

trators at the provincial and district levels may exercise considerable discretion over the distribution of drugs. During the survey, there was no hard allocation rule against which the actual distribution of drugs could be compared. The focus of the survey had to be limited to a narrower concept of leakage, that is, a comparison of records showing the amounts of resources distributed by higher levels in the public budget administration and records showing the amounts of resources received at lower levels of distribution and at facilities.

Even salary leakage through absenteeism or ghost workers was difficult to assess. To ensure cooperation by the facility staff, surveyors usually announced visits to facilities. The survey, nonetheless, identified a high rate of absenteeism (19 percent), although data on the reasons for the absences were not collected. The survey also sought to measure the prevalence of ghost workers in the health system by comparing staff lists at the facilities and payroll lists at higher-level administrative units. That effort became complicated because of poor data quality (see below). Moreover, more serious problems emerged with this approach, which relied on official records and facility observation. Insofar as salaries may be siphoned off by way of fictitious names on payroll lists, the leakage is unlikely to be the uncoordinated initiative of staff in primary health care facilities. Administrative staff at the local and the central levels are in a better position not only to learn of opportunities, but also to manipulate records, thereby minimizing the risk of discovery. A careful assessment of leakage through ghost workers would, therefore, have to depend on an in-depth review of records at all levels of the system. A facility-based survey alone would not suffice.

Interpreting Questionable Data

Data quality was a serious concern in most areas covered in the questionnaires. Consider, for example, the records on nonwage recurrent budget expenditures. Given that the district health offices render accounts to the provincial health offices on a regular basis, it should have been possible, in principle, to collect complete financial data at the provincial level. However, in the event, the enumerators found that financial records in almost all provinces suffered from large gaps. As a result, complete budget data were available on less than 40 percent of the districts. Moreover, the enumerators often found that the information in district records bore little relation to the information previously collected from the district health offices; there were discrepancies with provincial records in the records of approximately 75 percent of the districts (see table 7.2). These inconsistencies may have many

TABLE 7.2 Summary of the Findings of the Mozambique Tracking Survey

Finding	Nonwage recurrent budget	Drugs, vaccines, and medical supplies	Personnel and salaries
Allocation rules	Legally binding allocations are made to provinces, are explicit but changeable allocations to districts, and have no financial flows to facilities.	Nominally are allocated on the basis of facility activity, but there is considerable local discretion.	Provincial allocations are determined centrally; there is considerable discretion over staff allocations within provinces.
Source of data	Financial statements are at the provincial and district levels.	Distribution and stock records are at various levels.	Personnel records are in the provinces, districts, and facilities.
Leakage	Discrepancies exist between province and district data on 75% of the districts, but the differences do not seem systematic.	Some drugs distributed were not received, but there is much noise.	Inconsistencies in data are across the levels, but the differences do not seem systematic; 19% of facility staff were absent.

Source: Compiled by the author.

explanations, including poor recordkeeping and a failure to close annual accounts, errors in data entry, and uncoordinated updating of records to reflect budget changes during the course of a year. Yet, it is also possible that they may reflect, in some instances, willful manipulation to hide financial irregularities.

There were similar challenges in the case of drugs and in the case of human resources. The gaps in the human resource data frequently involved nonsalaried staff. For example, most provincial directorates were unable to provide information on the number of community health workers or the number of staff paid through user fees in the districts and facilities. However, even for salaried staff, it was often difficult to reconcile provincial and district data.

These data problems raise an important issue. If there are discrepancies in the information on financial resource transfers, does this mean money was somehow lost along the way? In the case of human resources, this hypothesis may be rejected because the provincial records often indicate there were *fewer* staff in districts and facilities than were actually present. If the opposite had been true, one might have supposed there were ghost workers. In the case of drugs, the survey found that, in 25–30 percent of the districts, the number of drug kits received according to district records did not correspond to the number of kits distributed according to provincial records. Similarly, the total value of the individual drugs distributed to districts according to provincial records was more than the corresponding value of the drugs received according to district records in 60 percent of the districts; the difference ranged from 10 to 90 percent. Although these findings represent strong evidence of leakage, the data also suggest that a few districts received *more* drugs than the provinces claim to have distributed. It is, therefore, possible that the observed discrepancies are driven by poor recordkeeping rather than irregularities.

Beyond Leakage

The estimation of leakage was a difficult undertaking in the Mozambican health sector. Nonetheless, the documented discrepancies in information were a clear sign of weaknesses in management and control systems. These weaknesses were undoubtedly hampering efficiency and equity in the allocation of resources and the deployment of staff. Moreover, although there is little firm evidence on leakage, the lack of control provided insufficient incentives against fraud or malfeasance.

The study also generated a number of useful findings in related areas, including bottlenecks and delays in budget execution and in the distribution of drugs and materials, human resource challenges, and inconsistencies in the implementation of user-fee policies (see table 7.3). Taken together, these findings provided the basis for three regional workshops that brought together central and local staff of the Ministry of Health and the Ministry of Planning and Finance. These workshops served to disseminate the results of the study, discuss the causes of the problems revealed through the survey, and identify possible steps in addressing the problems.

Lessons from the Mozambique Experience

The tracking survey in Mozambique was a resource-intensive, time-consuming exercise. It generated a wealth of new information and helped stimulate a productive debate about the financing and organization of primary health care services. Yet, it is pertinent to ask, with the benefit of hindsight, if the survey should have been conducted differently.

One key issue that arises is the balance between the scope and the depth of the survey. Arguably, the ambitious scope of the questionnaire came at the price of detail and data quality in particular areas. A more narrow, focused survey might have avoided some of the data collection challenges and generated more reliable leakage estimates. Yet, the areas that should have been the focus of a more narrow survey were not so apparent at the time. Meanwhile, the wide scope of the questionnaire reflected the need to satisfy a broad range of stakeholders and render the survey less threatening than a survey exercise focused exclusively on leakage might have been.

Another key issue concerns the sample design and the appropriateness of a nationally representative sample. The decision was made to reduce the risk that the results might be dismissed because they appeared specific to particular regions or areas. This specificity issue had been raised about surveys in other countries. However, the nationally representative sample increased the cost of the survey and also meant that the survey would not be able to shed much light on intradistrict allocations.

On both these issues, it may be argued that more effort should have been invested in the preparatory stages of the survey. For example, a small-scale pilot exercise in two or three districts, accompanied by detailed qualitative work and institutional reviews, would have been useful in enhancing the scope for diagnosing and understanding problems in the health care

TABLE 7.3 Key Survey Findings beyond Leakage	
Nonwage recurrent budget	There are delays in execution: in many districts, the initial budget transfer, due in January, occurred only in March or April, and monthly replenishments were frequently delayed by several months. Delays and other problems resulted in low budget execution among districts; the average execution rate was 80%, and some districts executed only 35% of the original allocation. There are dramatic disparities in district health spending per capita; these disparities may not be adequately accounted for by differences in population or differences in infrastructure.
Drugs	There are delays in drug distribution, and there is evidence of stock-outs. Individual drugs compose a large share of the drugs used in health centers and health posts, even though drug kits are supposed to be adequate. Despite the explicit aim of a needs-based distribution of drugs to facilities, there were considerable discrepancies in the number of tablets distributed per patient for six tracer drugs (for example, between 1.1 and 16 aspirins were distributed per patient episode).
Human resources	Delays in salary payments (60% of staff reported that they had received their salaries late "often" or "almost always"). Absenteeism (19% of staff were not present at the time of the visits). Low levels of health worker satisfaction existed, particularly in rural areas (75% of staff in rural facilities wanted to transfer).
User fees	Despite the existence of a national policy, the fees for consultations and medicines vary considerably across provinces, districts, and facilities; similarly, the rules on exemptions in payments for consultations and medicine vary greatly across districts and facilities. A sizable share of the revenues from user fees are not recorded by facilities (68% of the total consultation fees and 80% of the payments for medicines, based on a comparison of expected total facility receipts, given patient volume, payments reported by patients, and revenue reported by facilities).

Source: Compiled by the author.

system through a tracking survey. This pilot would have provided a foundation for a more informed decision about the merits of a survey implemented on a national scale.

Another lesson that emerges from the Mozambique survey and from surveys in other countries is the need to plan follow-up activities more carefully. Such activities might include detailed case studies and qualitative work to test the results of analyses of the study data. They might also include the design of and support for measures to address problems identified through the surveys. In the case of the Mozambique PETS, the survey team organized central and regional dissemination workshops that provided opportunities for stakeholders to discuss the study and the implications of the findings. The survey might, however, have become the starting point for a structured and sustained engagement with the Ministry of Health and the Ministry of Planning and Finance in confronting the key financial issues revealed during the study (Lindelow, Ward, and Zorzi 2004).

Conclusions

This chapter has outlined conceptual and practical challenges that arise in designing and implementing public expenditure tracking surveys. It has provided concrete examples of these challenges based on a recent tracking survey in Mozambique. Similar problems have been encountered in many other surveys. (For a discussion, see Lindelow, Kushnarova, and Kaiser 2006.) These challenges suggest that analysts and policy makers should avoid equating leakage with corruption: leakage may often be explained by administrative bottlenecks, legitimate reallocations, and other legitimate procedures.

Although the conceptual and practical challenges have prevented many surveys from generating reliable estimates of leakage, some of these surveys have produced highly policy-relevant findings. Nonetheless, policy-relevant findings—whether on leakage or other issues—may not be sufficient to justify the considerable resources required to design and implement such surveys. So, what have we learned about when and how to design and implement tracking surveys? A few lessons have emerged.

First, tracking surveys may be useful tools for diagnosing public expenditure management issues in sectors with service delivery functions. These issues include corruption, allocation decisions, compliance with administrative procedures, and accountability arrangements. However, tracking surveys are not the only tool, and, in many cases, they may not be the best tool.

For example, audits, institutional reviews, assessments of financial management procedures, and other approaches all have important advantages. The strength of the PETS approach is the attempt to collect representative quantitative data and the focus on the ways weaknesses in public expenditure management affect service delivery. This strength has not always been exploited, and many surveys have not effectively linked with other tools and approaches.

Second, if the survey is to ask the right questions and shed light on complex institutional and financing arrangements, the service financing and delivery system must be properly analyzed and understood before the survey work is initiated. Some tracking surveys have been driven by a broadly defined question and tight deadlines. Too often, expensive, large-scale surveys are launched in a rush. The results are inevitably disappointing. The design, implementation, and analysis involved in tracking surveys are time-consuming. It is often advisable to start small, for example, by performing a limited-scale pilot survey, combined with in-depth qualitative work.

Third, despite the aim of many tracking surveys to clarify leakage and other service delivery issues, the surveys tend to be more effective in diagnosis than in making inferences about the determinants of the outcomes of interest. This finding is largely because the key determinants are complex institutional factors that are difficult to measure. The scope for using *cross-sectional* data from tracking surveys in inferential quantitative analysis is therefore limited.[8] A focus on diagnosis may be useful and appropriate in many contexts, but diagnosing leakage or other problems in the absence of a process for addressing the problems may be destructive. Yet, this process is the component that is often lacking, in part because budget reform or broader public sector reforms call for expertise beyond the capabilities of the typical survey team.

Hence, tracking surveys may be useful and worthwhile exercises, but only under certain conditions. The survey must be designed to answer a clear and explicit question. If the problems in the budget and the service delivery system are already well understood, a tracking survey is likely to add little of value. Conversely, if there is no consensus on where the problems lie, more diagnostic work is required to identify the appropriate scope and focus of the survey. The problem the survey is meant to examine must be amenable to tracking. The extent to which tracking surveys may identify leakage and other problems depends on the context, including the budget system and the quality of the records, and it is therefore important to ensure that a tracking survey is the proper tool for the problem at hand.

Finally, survey findings are unlikely to have an effect if there is not an interest among key stakeholders to engage with problems and if there is not a clear process through which to build consensus on problems and develop follow-up actions. These have been the key ingredients in survey successes such as in the case of Uganda.

Notes

1. This chapter does not seek to provide a comprehensive review of expenditure tracking and service delivery surveys. For a recent review of tracking surveys in the health sector, see Lindelow, Kushnarova, and Kaiser (2006); for a discussion of education sector PETSs, see Reinikka and Smith (2004).
2. For example, in Ghana, Mozambique, and Rwanda, facilities receive practically no cash aside from user fee revenues generated at the facilities. Salaries are paid to staff directly by higher levels of government; other resources are also procured in this way and are distributed in kind to the facilities.
3. There is a rationale behind central procurement. The procurement of medical supplies requires technical skills that may be more readily available at the central level, and centralized, high-volume procurement may reduce costs. Some medical supplies are also perishable or require a cold chain; in principle, central procurement and distribution may facilitate and guarantee proper control over storage and delivery in such cases.
4. Incidents of leakage in this context do not necessarily reflect corruption and may even enhance welfare. For example, local governments may decide to reallocate resources to meet needs that are higher priorities in local communities. However, the Uganda education PETS provided anecdotal evidence that this was not the most likely explanation.
5. This approach has been the one in a number of recent studies that have found rates of absenteeism of 23 percent to 40 percent in the health sector across a range of countries (Chaudhury et al. 2006; Chaudhury and Hammer 2004). Although unannounced visits may be an effective way of determining absenteeism, these studies do not shed much light on the reasons staff are absent.
6. Gross national product per capita (Atlas method) was US$210 in 2003 (World Bank 2006). In 1997, the poverty headcount was 69 percent (MPF, UEM, and IFPRI 1998). The latest national health account data suggest that total annual health sector expenditures from all sources were only US$8.8 per capita (Yates and Zorzi 1999). Over half of spending is financed by donor agencies or nongovernmental organizations; approximately a quarter derives from government tax revenues; and slightly less than a quarter originates among households through out-of-pocket payments.
7. The survey collected data from 90 facilities, 35 district health offices, and 11 provincial health offices. The sample of health facilities was selected in two stages: a random selection of districts, followed by a random selection of facilities within each selected district. Facility users and staff members were also sampled randomly. Sampling weights were used to provide nationally representative estimates.

8. The success of repeated surveys offers scope for using a series of tracking surveys to evaluate the impact of institutional reforms. Apart from an evaluation of an information campaign in Uganda, there are few notable examples of tracking surveys used for this purpose (see Reinikka and Svensson 2004).

References

Ablo, Emmanuel Y., and Ritva Reinikka. 1998. "Do Budgets Really Matter?: Evidence from Public Spending on Education and Health in Uganda." Policy Research Working Paper 1926, World Bank, Washington, DC.

Chaudhury, Nazmul, and Jeffrey S. Hammer. 2004. "Ghost Doctors: Absenteeism in Rural Bangladeshi Health Facilities." *World Bank Economic Review* 18 (3): 423–41.

Chaudhury, Nazmul, Jeffrey S. Hammer, Michael Kremer, Karthik Muralidharan, and F. Halsey Rogers. 2006. "Missing in Action: Teacher and Health Worker Absence in Developing Countries." *Journal of Economic Perspectives* 20 (1): 91–116.

Lindelow, Magnus, Inna Kushnarova, and Kai Kaiser. 2006. "Measuring Corruption in the Health Sector: What Can We Learn from Public Expenditure Tracking and Service Delivery Surveys." In *Global Corruption Report 2006: Corruption and Health*, Transparency International, 29–37. London: Pluto Press.

Lindelow, Magnus, Patrick Ward, and Nathalie Zorzi. 2004. "Primary Health Care in Mozambique: Service Delivery in a Complex Hierarchy." Africa Region Human Development Working Paper 69, Human Development Sector, Africa Region, World Bank, Washington, DC.

MPF (Ministry of Planning and Finance), UEM (Universidade Eduardo Mondlane), and IFPRI (International Food Policy Research Institute). 1998. *Understanding Poverty and Well-Being in Mozambique: The First National Assessment (1996–97).* IFPRI monograph, International Food Policy Research Institute, Washington, DC.

Noormahomed, Abdul Razak, and Malcolm Segall. 1994. *The Public Health Sector in Mozambique: A Post-War Strategy for Rehabilitation and Sustained Development.* Macroeconomics, Health, and Development Series 14. Geneva: World Health Organization.

Reinikka, Ritva, and Nathanael Smith. 2004. *Public Expenditure Tracking Surveys in Education.* Paris: International Institute for Educational Planning, United Nations Educational, Scientific, and Cultural Organization.

Reinikka, Ritva, and Jakob Svensson. 2004. "The Power of Information: Evidence from a Newspaper Campaign to Reduce Capture." Policy Research Working Paper 3239, World Bank, Washington, DC.

World Bank. 2006. *World Development Indicators 2006.* Washington, DC: World Bank.

Yates, Robert, and Nathalie Zorzi. 1999. "Health Expenditure Review: Mozambique." Report, Management Sciences for Health, Cambridge, MA.

8

Public Expenditure Tracking Survey in a Difficult Environment
The Case of Chad

Waly Wane

M any recent studies have shown a weak relationship between outcomes and the public spending recorded in government budgets.
This result is especially clear for developing countries, human development
outcomes, and spending in social sectors, such as education and health.
Filmer and Pritchett (1999) find that, in a cross-section of countries, spending
does not seem to affect infant and child mortality rates, whereas Ablo and
Reinikka (1998) present evidence that budget allocations for primary education and health in Uganda have no bearing on the main indicators in these
sectors. The innovation introduced by Ablo and Reinikka (1998) is the
reliance on facility data. They show large discrepancies between government
data and data collected from frontline providers.

Since these findings, surveys of providers have mushroomed. New tools
known as the Public Expenditure Tracking Survey (PETS) or the Quantitative
Service Delivery Survey (QSDS) have been developed to help restore the link
between public spending and outcomes. To achieve this grand goal, these
surveys collect data from all entities involved in the service delivery process,
from the ministry of finance to the primary school or the health center.

Two main reasons are invoked for the absence of a relationship between
budget allocations and outcomes. The first is the existence of leakage in the
system, whereby providers do not obtain what they are entitled to. Second, even

191

if funds reach providers in their entirety, the latter may simply inefficiently use their resources, thus preventing these funds from fully contributing to the production of improved outcomes. The main focus of these surveys has been to assess whether publics funds allocated to frontline providers do, in fact, reach them. Along the way, these surveys try to estimate how much of the entitlements providers actually receive and to understand the determinants of leakage, if any, in the system.

Because increased budgetary resources do not guarantee improved outcomes, it is important to identify and fix bottlenecks before pouring more money into the system. It is imperative to make sure that budget increases lead to enhanced outcomes, such as the Multilateral Debt Relief Initiative or the Enhanced Heavily Indebted Poor Countries Initiative, and of incentives for developing countries to increase budget allocation to the social sectors. A PETS or QSDS may prove a powerful instrument for this purpose. However, these surveys have not always been successful. The exercise often proves less straightforward than appears at first sight (see Lindelow in chapter 7). The objective of this chapter is to share the experience of carrying out a PETS in a difficult environment. It is based on the 2004 PETS in Chad.

How to Carry Out a PETS

A PETS relies on the availability of information at all levels. Before starting the implementation of a PETS, one needs to make sure that facilities (schools or health centers) keep records on the resources they receive from the public administration. In many instances, the survey's only finding is that facilities have no records whatsoever on such resources. Although this is valuable information by itself, the finding often represents a waste of time and expenditure when it is the result of a full-blown survey. A rapid data assessment, which is a simple questionnaire administered to a few facilities, usually suffices to arrive at the same conclusion. The rapid data assessment typically aims at assessing the existence of the records (on the receipt of resources sent by the government) that form the basis for a PETS among facilities. It is, therefore, highly recommended that a rapid data assessment be carried out before launching a PETS.

Once the assessment has established that information on resource transfers is available among providers, the next task is to identify public resources that are trackable and devise a tracking strategy. The tracking strategy hinges on the allocation rules that prevail in the country. Borrowing the jargon of Lindelow in chapter 7, there are broadly two kinds of allocations rules. First, there are hard rules, which take the form of explicit formulas for allocating resources, such as capitation grants, specified budget lines for individual providers, or fixed and recorded amounts of materials assigned to individual facilities. Second, there are soft rules, whereby resources are assigned to a bigger entity, such as a region or district, that has full discretion in the allocation of the resources among facilities.

Resources that are governed by hard allocation rules are easy to track, and establishing a leakage rate is straightforward. For instance, in the case of Mali (surveyed in 2006), where each school was assigned a specific number of books by the Ministry of Education, one merely needs to contrast the book allocation as recorded in the government's documents to the number of books received by the school as assessed by the survey on the basis of school records. For capitation grants in Uganda (1996) or school grants in the case of Zambia (2002), one needs to compute how much the school is entitled to, using the government's formula, and contrast this with the amount received by the provider. The leakage rate is then defined as the ratio between how much the provider *actually* received and how much the provider *should have* received.[1]

Unfortunately, many developing countries, especially in Sub-Saharan Africa, seldom use hard allocation rules. It is highly likely that regional and district administrations enjoy a great deal of discretion in allocating resources to providers. The central government exercises much discretion itself in the allocation of resources to regions and districts.

The chapter will, therefore, focus on the implementation of a PETS in a soft allocation rules environment. The lack of allocation rules affects not only the design of a PETS, but also the definition of leakage. Indeed, leakage is traditionally computed at the provider level. Though it is possible to collect data on resources sent by the central, regional, or district administration and received by the provider, leakage according to the traditional definition does not make sense because the denominator of the ratio is no longer identified. It is still possible, though, to compute a leakage rate at the lowest administrative level that has an allocation from the national budget, be it a region or a district. Carrying out a PETS in such an environment implies at least: (a) a thorough review of the budget, (b) broadening the concept of leakage, and (c) exerting a serious effort to collect the administrative data that are crucial to any meaningful estimate of the leakage rate or other relevant indicators on the availability of public resources among frontline providers.

Understanding the Budget Game

A PETS is based on an essential understanding of the budgetary system that governs public spending. Under heavy outside pressure, most Sub-Saharan African countries have recently started to decentralize the execution of their budgets and have given more responsibility to lower levels of administration. This translates into increased budget allocations to regions and districts.

In Chad, the Ministry of Health (MoH) earmarked the lion's share of its recurrent budget in 2003 to the regions. However, this decentralization is only apparent. The MoH invokes economies of scale or lack of capacity in the regions to rationalize its subsequent decisions to execute the bulk of the regional budgets on behalf of the regions. The MoH buys drugs and materials, decides on the regional allocation, and procures the materials for the regions. Each of the regions then decides on the allocations it will make to districts and health facilities.

For the sake of example, table 8.1 shows the structure of the MoH budget for 2003. In that year, the MoH put 59.9 percent of its recurrent budget under the umbrella of the regions. However, the regions directly executed only 14.3 percent of their budgets, or 8.6 percent of the MoH recurrent budget. The share of the goods and services that were decentralized, however, reached 20.9 percent. The central government executed the remaining 79.1 percent by buying drugs and medical supplies for the regions and districts and putting in place a procurement system to deliver the goods and services.

TABLE 8.1   Ministry of Health Budget, 2003

Item	MoH budget CFAF (billions)	Regions CFAF (billions)	Regions Share (%)	Decentralized CFAF (billions)	Decentralized Share (%)
Total	33.408	n.a.	n.a.	n.a.	n.a.
Recurrent budget	13.407	8.030	59.9	1.145	14.3
Personnel	5.295	2.560	48.4	0	0
Goods and services	8.112	5.470	67.4	1.145	20.9

Source: Revised Finance Laws, Chad 2003, Ministère des Finances.
Note: n.a. = not applicable, MoH = Ministry of Health, CFAF = francs.

Regions, districts, and health facilities, therefore, obtain public resources essentially from two channels: decentralized credits and centralized purchases.

- *Decentralized credits:* Credits in the amount of CFAF 1.15 billion are executed directly by the regions and districts. The local administrative officers in charge are responsible for managing these financial resources and for redistributing purchased materials and drugs to health providers under their jurisdiction.
- *Centralized purchases:* Using the remaining CFAF 4.3 billion, the government purchases materials and medical consumables through public tendering procedures and sends the supplies to the regional and district administrations and health centers. The MoH uses no explicit allocation rule for redistributing the materials. Allocations may reflect the preferences of the MoH or demands by lower administrative levels.

Ad hoc requests constitute a third, informal channel through which lower-level entities may receive materials. Administrative officers sometimes submit specific requests for (a list of) materials directly to the MoH. Once (part of) a request has been granted and authorized, an administrative officer may go to the central warehouse with the authorization letter and carry the material, at personal expense, to the home region or district.

All the materials acquired through centralized purchases that are to be sent to the regions originate from the central MoH warehouse in N'djamena. The destination points are the MoH warehouses in the regions and districts. Resources are sent to the regions by an official MoH agent. All material exits are registered on exit slips by the central warehouse manager. When the material reaches the regional warehouse, the regional delegate verifies the list of material and certifies that the material has been received. He notes any missing material or quality problems with the material. The slips are standard administrative forms that must be collected. They constitute the backbone of the tracking exercise: the administrative data.[2]

If one wishes to compute the total regional leakage rate, the denominator would be CFAF 8.0 billion. This is well defined, but one needs to be able to track all the purchases made and sent to the regions before one may identify leakage. This is a daunting task. Fortunately, most of the time, the budget has a lower level of disaggregation, whereby each region's allocation is known. One may then sample some of the regions in which a PETS will be conducted and estimate a leakage rate for these regions. This is the typical strategy. It is still necessary, though, to track all the materials that are sent in those regions using the administrative forms. A regional leakage rate is the ratio between what the region should get and what it has been allocated.[3]

Collecting Administrative Data

Clearly, without the slips for the materials the government sent to the regions, districts, and health facilities, one would be working in a vacuum. A PETS then necessarily requires the collection, one way or the other, of the relevant administrative data. A triangulation of the data must be performed using structured questionnaires in the regions, districts, and facilities.

The collection of administrative data is often difficult in weak institutional environments. The most serious problem one faces is simply the lack of records even with the central government. Recordkeeping practices are often extremely poor. The most common form of storage for administrative data is paper. On rare occasions, one finds data on magnetic or electronic support. Even then, the data are at risk. In Chad, for instance, MoH personnel records were being managed by one person, who, through his own initiative, put all the records on computer without performing a backup. The computer had a virus. In Sub-Saharan Africa, Chad is no exception in this regard. Anecdotes abound about lost records. The collection of administrative data for the 2002 PETS in Senegal was almost impossible at the regional level. With few exceptions, newly elected officials at the local level in Senegal acknowledged that they had no records on previous fiscal years. The main reason they gave was that their predecessors had taken the books or shredded them after losing the elections in 2000. Administrative records are often the first victims of reorganizations or major housecleaning in administration buildings; they are simply thrown away to make room or reduce clutter. It is not uncommon for informal sector workers to use administrative records to make packages for their belongings.

Given all these risks facing administrative data, PETS planners must resist the temptation to design their PETS studies to span several years so as to construct a trend in leakage rates. This concept is often unrealistic. Unless there is a clear indication that the data exist, one should envision tracking the resources for only one year. The timing of the tracking exercise is essential. Planning the survey so that it may be launched two months after the end of the fiscal year is the best practice. First, this timing allows for the completion of the recordkeeping on all transactions from the previous fiscal year, which is the focus of the tracking. Most important, it increases the likelihood that the records are still being stored somewhere by the administration. In the case of Chad, we obtained the records from the Division of Material Resources, which is under the Direction of Administrative and Financial Affairs in the MoH.

Given the formula for the regional leakage rate, one needs to collect the amount of decentralized credits allocated to the regions and *all* materials sent to the regions during the fiscal year of interest. In 2003, the information on decentralized credits was available both in the national budget and at the Direction of Administrative and Financial Affairs. The information on the procured materials was more likely to be at risk. Fortunately enough, in Chad, the Division of Material Resources had all the records for 2003. The PETS team asked for and was granted access to absolutely all the records. All the slips were kept in a binder. One might obtain information on the date the shipment had been authorized, the recipient of the materials, the full list of materials sent, the quantities and prices, and also the signature and comments of the recipient. The team photocopied all the records for later use and returned the originals to the Division of Material Resources. The collection of information on resources sent by the central government was thus complete.[4] To construct the numerator of the leakage rate, one would now assess whether the intended beneficiaries received the materials. This is accomplished through structured questionnaires.

Primary Data Collection and Triangulation

The tracking module of the questionnaires was designed using the standard administrative forms for the procurement of materials so as to capture the relevant information on the forms and allow triangulation. The MoH sends hundreds of different kinds of materials, from motorcycles to hand soaps and window cleaner. A strategy must, therefore, be devised to capture the materials received by the recipients. One possibility is to replicate the strategy used at the central level; that is, photocopy all the forms found in the regions, districts, and health facilities. Unfortunately, this approach is not feasible because, among other reasons, there are no photocopy machines in rural areas. The information needs to be obtained through the questionnaires. In the future, the use of digital cameras might be useful for this purpose.

Clearly, given the space restriction on the questionnaires, it is not realistic or even possible to cover in the questionnaires all the materials sent by the MoH. A limited number of items must be chosen for tracking purposes.

These items fall into two broad categories: (a) resources of higher value that are supplied in limited numbers, such as ambulances or automobiles, and (b) resources of petty value that are supplied in large numbers. One faces certain hurdles in tracking high-value items in the sample of facilities or regions. The records may not be entirely helpful. For example, ambulances may be allocated on a rotation basis, and there is a good probability that sampled entities will receive their allocation sometime in the next few years. In contrast, a focus on the petty items that many facilities receive regularly is likely to lead to a useful triangulation of data. For instance, the Division of Material Resources has probably sent window cleaner to all regions, which have subsequently allocated some to most districts and facilities. The questionnaire thus includes a question to the regions about the amount of window cleaner received from the Division of Material Resources and sent on to districts and facilities in our sample. The district questionnaire has a question on the amount of window cleaner the districts have received from the region and the amount sent on to facilities in our sample. Finally, each facility is asked about the amount of window cleaner received from the region and the district. All the numbers must come from the records. (The selection of the materials included in the tracking process is described in the sampling subsection below.)

The triangulation is achieved by comparing the various answers. Because the regions send the petty items to providers in nonzero quantities, there are many responses that may be compared relative to the reports of the regions on the resources sent to the districts and the providers and the reports of the districts and the providers on the resources they have received. The region supplies data on each item and each beneficiary in the sample. Then, each district and provider supplies data on the amount of each resource requested and received from the region.

Tracking the numerous petty items helps build confidence in the records. The more the number of matching responses, the higher the level of confidence one may have in the collected data. In our case, for the decentralized credits, almost all the responses from the regions and districts coincide with the numbers in the budget. This analysis means that the decentralized credits have reached the regional and district administrations. For the items acquired through centralized purchase, selected for tracking, and included in the questionnaires, one must compare the data collected by the regions and districts and the forms collected from the Division of Material Resources. In our case, there is almost a one-to-one match in the data. The triangulation has, therefore, worked well at least at the regional and district levels.

Measuring Leakage Rates

In a soft or no allocation rules environment, accounting for leakage may be accomplished only at the lowest level that is a recognized recipient of public resources from the national budget. For lower levels such as frontline providers, no leakage rate may be estimated, and one must revert to another indicator (see elsewhere below). For either indicator, it is imperative to develop a methodology to account for *all* public resources that reach the administrative or operational level of interest. For a region or district, the issue boils down to the sorts of data that must be collected to arrive at the best estimate of the resources received. The issue is a bit more complex for frontline providers. The goal is to obtain a nonbiased estimate of the resources received by the average frontline provider in a region or district. The sampling strategy for pursuing this tracking goal should then ensure that the materials and the frontline providers are representative.

Sampling Issues

In Chad, 13 of the 14 regions were selected for the tracking exercise.[5] This selection meant it was possible to track all the resources, decentralized credits, centralized purchases and ad hoc requests sent by the MoH and received by the selected regions. Once all the resources received by the regions had been accounted for, a public resource leakage rate was computed for each region and for the health sector as a whole. Because tracking all the material resources the MoH procures for the regions and districts was not possible (see elsewhere above), the items selected for tracking had to be representative of the resources sent by the MoH.

The selection procedure was simple. From the hundreds of items that might have been tracked, all items that had been sent in units or that had not been sent at all to the regions, such as vehicles or luxury desks, were eliminated. From the list of remaining items, eight items were chosen at random for inclusion in the questionnaires. It was also decided to track important drugs. Using the information collected from the Central Pharmaceutical Procurement Agency, the drugs were ranked on the basis of the annual quantities delivered by the agency to its clients. The top 10 drugs were then selected for tracking. This process increased the probability that the drugs might also be found in the regions, districts, and facilities.

To capture the resources received by the frontline providers, one needs to design the sampling strategy carefully. In the ideal PETS, one should be able to account for all the resources received by facilities. A seemingly recurring pattern in countries with difficult environments is that few facilities receive public resources. A sampling strategy that neglects the large inequalities might result in a downwardly biased estimate of the amount of public funds received by frontline providers. One would, therefore, wish to capture facilities that are important recipients of public resources in one's sample, that are important recipients of public resources because of unobservable fixed effects, such as a proactive head of facility; and that are not captured by our instruments.[6] If only a handful of facilities are visited in a region or district during the survey, then the risks of missing such facilities may be great. Meanwhile, it is often impossible to conduct a PETS on the basis of a census because of the large number of facilities in the country and the resulting time and cost factors.

In Chad, an alternative sampling strategy was followed. First, within each region, one or two districts were randomly sampled with probability proportional to size (size being the number of facilities). The number of districts selected was a function of the number of districts in the region. (Districts are the lowest administrative level.) Second, for each of the selected districts, all the facilities identified prior to and during the survey were visited. Using this strategy, one may account for all the public resources that reach beneficiaries within each selected district. Finally, using pricing information on materials, as provided in MoH documents, one may compute the share represented among all items by the items (drugs) selected among centralized purchases (the drugs budget line) and then use this information to estimate the value of the resources received by regions, districts, and facilities.

Regional Leakage Rates

Now that all the administrative data have been collected and the regional questionnaires have been filled out, the computation of regional leakage rates should be possible. The denominator is simply the regional allocations as indicated in the budget data and confirmed by the government as executed. Once the triangulation of the regional data and the administrative data confirms that the data are correct, one may be confident the questionnaires administered to the regions have captured all the resources sent to the regions. The denominator of our leakage rate is then obtained simply by adding all numbers in our data set after estimating the value of the materials received through centralized purchases.

The regions have clearly received and executed all the financial resources deriving through the decentralized credits and received nearly every single item shipped to them from the MoH warehouse. There are rare cases in which regional administrative officers have reported they did not receive listed items. This lack may be caused by errors in typing or by delivery failures. In any event, the losses are minor and may be considered negligible. The leakage rate from shipments and centralized credits is, therefore, zero. Does this mean that there is no leakage at the regional level? The answer to this question would be yes if the value of the shipments to the regions were equal to the full amount the MoH retained under its control to cover the centralized purchases. After a quick computation, one finds out that the approximate value of the materials the regions received through ad hoc requests and shipments after centralized purchases is a little over CFAF 300 million. In total, the regions received 26.7 percent of the nonwage recurrent budget allocated to them. The average regional leakage rate is therefore 73.3 percent, although this masks substantial variation across regions.

The Provider Share of Public Resources

In a soft allocation rules environment, it may not be possible to estimate a classical leakage rate (see elsewhere earlier) because the facility has no defined allocation. Therefore, the denominator of the leakage is indeterminate. An important alternative indicator might be the share of, say, primary health care in the MoH budget. To this end, one needs to account for all the resources providers received from the central government, the region, and the district. The tracking module of the facility questionnaires should be designed precisely for this task. The administrative officer in charge of each facility is first asked to account for all financial resources the facility received from higher levels of government. Then, the officer must report a quantity and a date of reception from the MoH for each of the items and drugs selected during the sampling.

By thus corroborating the findings of the small rapid data assessment exercise, the enumerators found that the providers had good data on the materials they had received from various government agencies. Using the price information from the MoH, one may readily estimate the value of the medical and material resources providers received. It has been estimated that the primary health sector received 1.3 percent of the MoH nonwage recurrent budget. In a soft or no allocation rules environment, though it is not possible to estimate a leakage rate, the methodology permits one to assess the weight attached by the central government to the various sectors. Table 8.2 summarizes the receipt of public health resources by the administrative regions and the primary levels of operations.

	TABLE 8.2 Receipt of Resources at Regions and Health Facilities, 2003					
	Initial regional allocation		Resources received by regions		Resources received by health facilities	
Unit indicator	Excluding salaries	Total	Excluding salaries	Total	Excluding salaries	Total
CFAF millions	5,470	8,030	1,461	4,021	71.1	2,631
% of MoH nonwage recurrent budget	67.4	98.9	18.0	49.6	1.3	32.8
% of MoH recurrent budget	40.8	59.9	10.9	30.0	0.5	19.6

Source: Gauthier and Wane 2006.

Other Policy Issues Addressed through a PETS or QSDS

The first question of interest after the estimation of the leakage rate or the weight of the primary health sector in the country revolves around the counterintuitive, but strong conclusion that public resources have little effect in determining outcomes in health or education (see Filmer and Pritchett 1999, among others). Does this conclusion still hold once leakage is taken into account? Examining the relationship between government spending and the services provided, Gauthier and Wane (2006) find that public spending does, in fact, affect the production and delivery of services. They contrast the public spending represented in the budget and routinely used in most studies and the public spending that reaches final providers as estimated in a PETS. They thus subtract from the budget data all funds that do not reach frontline providers.

Figure 8.1 (from Gauthier and Wane 2006) shows two simple scatter plots of the relationship between public health expenditure per capita (in CFAF) and the total number of outpatient visits to primary health centers per 1,000 inhabitants by region. The first chart (a) plots outpatient visits against public spending as recorded in the budget, whereas the second chart (b) illustrates actual public health expenditures.

Figure 8.1 shows that only public resources that effectively reach the intended beneficiaries have an effect in the field. In a follow-up

FIGURE 8.1   Budgeted Versus Effective Regional Public Spending and Production in Health

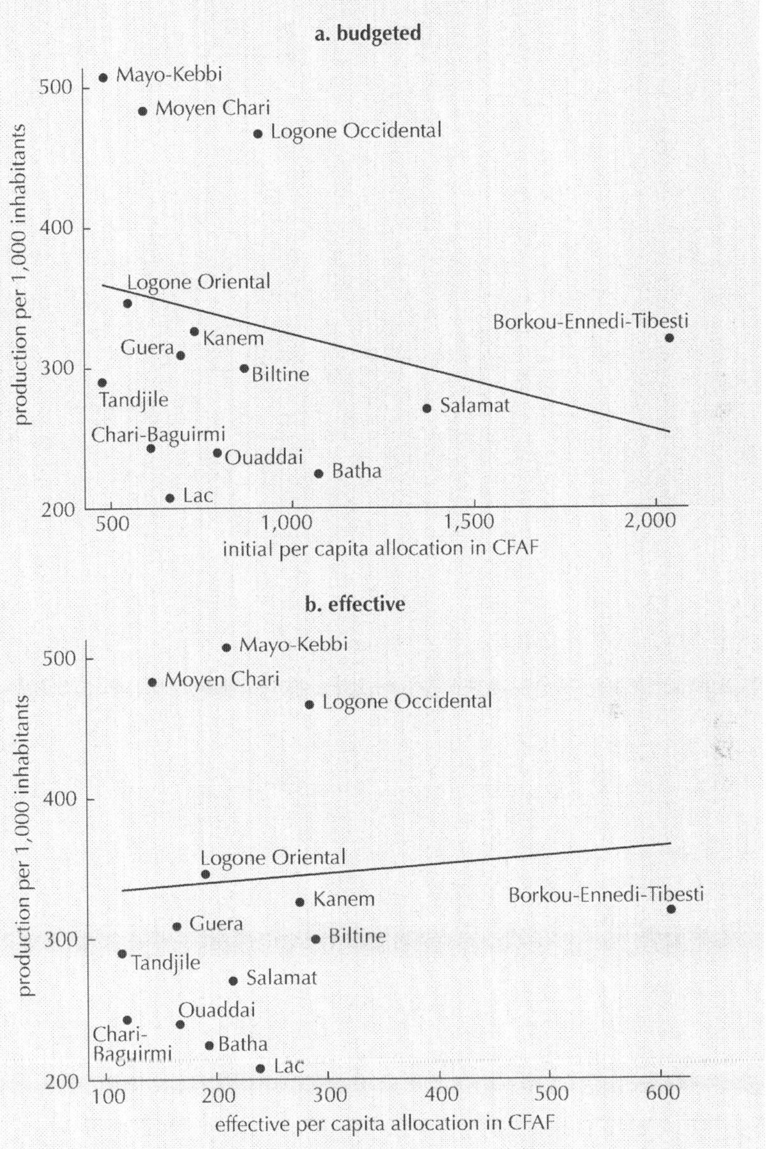

a. budgeted

Source: Gauthier and Wane 2006.
Note: Regional production is the number of outpatient visits in the health centers as shown in routine monthly reports on center activities. The data follow a bottom-up path and are consolidated by the MoH.

econometric analysis taking into account more controls, this result has been confirmed.[7] Gauthier and Wane (2006) estimate that, in Chad for 2003, if all health resources that had been planned for the regions had reached the primary health centers, the number of outpatient visits would have been more than doubled. One of the mechanisms through which this result is made possible is a decrease in the drug prices charged by facilities. Figure 8.2 shows that, in public facilities, around three-quarters of the out-of-pocket payments received from patients arise from the purchase of drugs. Gauthier and Wane (2006) also show that facilities receiving public resources set a significantly lower markup on the drugs they sell. Because the demand for health care is highly elastic to expected prices, it is likely that demand would increase because of the better financial accessibility of health care resulting from price reductions following the receipt of public resources.[8]

In addition to tracking public funds, the survey aims at clarifying the determinants of efficiency in health centers. For this purpose, the facility questionnaire also includes modules on facility characteristics, the services facilities offer, and the prices they charge, as well as modules on human resources, financing, and supervision. One of the major health issues in Chad is the maternal mortality rate, which is among the highest in the world. It has been established that, because of cultural factors, women are reluctant to visit a facility if they expect to find no women conducting antenatal visits at the facility. The share of women operating in the family planning unit of a facility should, therefore, have an impact on the number of women who seek antenatal care at the facility. This pattern clearly shows up in the data if one compares the number of women visiting not-for-profit facilities relative to other types of providers both public and private. Not-for-profit facilities tend to have more women on their staffs, in number and share, especially traditional birth attendants. There are important policy prescriptions to draw from this finding.

Staff and patient questionnaires may also be developed as companions to the facility instrument. The staff questionnaire may be used to track salaries and to assess the quality of personnel or their morale, for example. The staff questionnaire would also be valuable in determining the effect of staff structure, quality, and morale on facility output. The patient questionnaire, delivered as an exit poll, would address issues pertaining to the determinants of household demand for health care and on the perceptions of patients on the delivery of health services. The analysis of the demand for health care would be more useful if the patient data were coupled with the facility data, which might be used to control for various dimensions of quality on the supply side.

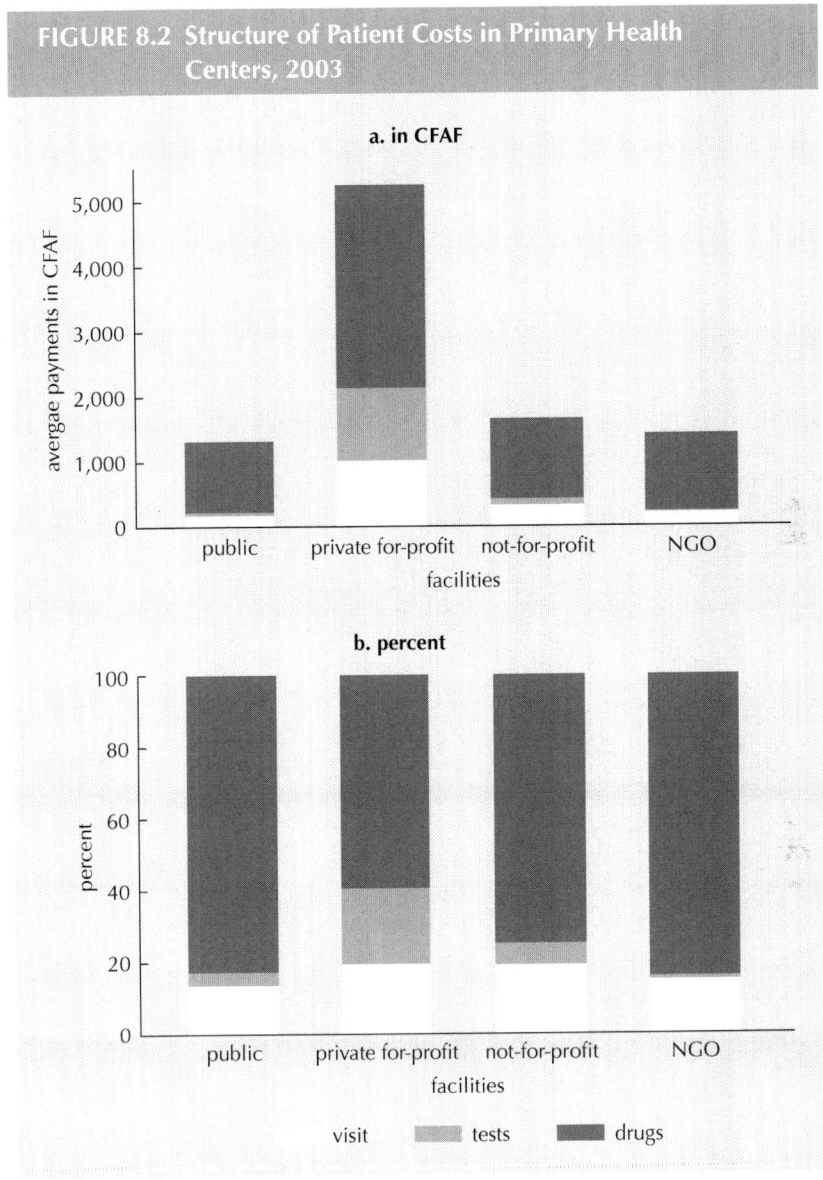

FIGURE 8.2 Structure of Patient Costs in Primary Health Centers, 2003

Source: Gauthier and Wane 2006.

Conclusions

Most PETS studies, following in the footsteps of the Uganda pioneer, have the aim of pinning down an exact estimate of the leakage rate of public resources in the sector of interest. Yet, few of these attempts meet success, and precise estimates of leakage rates largely remain an elusive objective. The two main reasons for this lack of success are the narrow classical definition of leakage and the fact that many PETS have been carried out in countries with soft or no rules for the allocation of financial and material resources.

This chapter has shown that, within such a context, sticking to the classical definition of leakage may be misleading. There is a need to broaden the definition. Indeed, in Chad, the regions received almost every single item the central level procured for them. This hints at a zero leakage rate. However, a closer look shows that the government, through the Ministry of Health, sent only about 26.7 percent of the resources they earmarked for the regions. This would lead to a 73.3 percent leakage rate at the regional level. If one is to arrive at such a number, it is necessary to collect as much administrative data as possible. Data on all the shipments of material from the central level to lower administrative levels must certainly be collected. Although administrative data are difficult to gather because they are seldom available on electronic or magnetic support in such contexts, it is imperative that the PETS planner collect all possible data with the central government.

By forsaking the goal of estimating a leakage rate at the facility level to focus on estimating a weaker indicator, such as the share of public resources received by primary health centers, the chapter has shown that, in Chad in 2003, the primary health sector received around 1.3 percent of the MoH nonwage recurrent budget. More important, the PETS study has shown that, despite many claims to the contrary, public spending does have a significant positive impact on health outcomes. However, only public resources that effectively reach the final beneficiaries contribute to the production of more positive outcomes.

ANNEXES

ADMINISTRATIVE FORMS USED
FOR TRACKING PURPOSES

ANNEX 8.1

République du Tchad
Ministère des Finances
Dépenses engagées

N'Djaména, le ___/___/___ 2003

Le Ministre des Finances du Tchad
à
Mr le Préfet du Logone Oriental à Doba

Autorisation de Dépenses N° ____
Budget de l'Etat - Exercice 2003

J'ai l'honneur de vous faire connaître que j'autorise à la date de ce jour, pour les besoins de votre préfecture, une dépense s'élevant à la somme de : quatre vingt six millions quatre cent cinquante cinq mille francs, et dont le détail se trouve ci-après :

	Imputation budgétaire		Montant des crédits délégués	Observations
	16- 99 -31- 1	Fournitures et petit matériel de bureau	2 250 000	Gestion Déleg.Sanit.
	16- 99 -31- 5	Produits d'entretien et nettoyage	2 230 000	Gestion Déleg.Sanit.
	16- 99 -32- 1	Pièces détachées moyens de transport	7 750 000	Gestion Déleg.Sanit.
	16- 99 -32- 2	Pièces détachées autres équipements	1 980 000	Gestion Déleg.Sanit.
	16- 99 -34- 2	Carburants et lubrifiants	29 000 000	Gestion Déleg.Sanit.
		Délégation sanitaire	2 500 000	Gestion Déleg.Sanit.
		District de Bebedja - Pétrole frigos	2 660 000	Gestion Dist.Bebedja
		- Autres	1 200 000	
		District de Bessao - Pétrole frigos	3 840 000	Gestion.Dist.Bessao
		- Autres	1 200 000	
		District de Doba Pétrole frigos	12 480 000	Gestion Dist.Doba
		- Autres	2 000 000	
		District de Gore Pétrole frigos	1 920 000	Gestion Dist.Doba
		Autres	1 200 000	
	16- 99 -35- 1	**Subsistances**	20 000 000	
		Hôpital de Doba	10 500 000	Gestion Hôp.Doba
		Hôpital de Goré	4 750 000	Gestion Hôp.Gorè
		Hôpital de Baibokoum	4 750 000	Gestion Hôp.Baibokoum
	16- 99 -34- 3	**Charbon, gaz et bois de chauffe**	570 000	
		Hôpital de Doba	300 000	Gestion Hôp.Doba
		Hôpital de Goré	150 000	Gestion Hôp.Goré
		Hôpital de Baibokoum	120 000	Gestion Hôp.Baibokoum
	16- 99 -35- 2	**Vaisselle et ustensiles de cuisine**	575 000	
		Hôpital de Doba	300 000	Gestion Hôp.Doba
		Hôpital de Goré	150 000	Gestion Hôp.Goré
		Hôpital de Baibokoum	125 000	Gestion Hôp.Baibokoum
	16- 99 -37- 4	Petit matériel de quincaillerie et électricité	1 000 000	Gestion Déleg.Sanit.
	16- 99 -47- 1	Entretien et réparation matériel de bureau	1 500 000	Gestion Déleg.Sanit.
	16- 99 -47- 2	Entretien et réparation matériels médico-techniqu	4 000 000	Gestion Déleg.Sanit.
	16- 99 -47- 3	Entretien et réparation autres matériels	3 600 000	Gestion Déleg.Sanit.
	16- 99 -48- 1	Entretien et réparation édifices et bâtiments	12 000 000	Gestion Déleg.Sanit.
		TOTAL	**86 455 000**	

Vous êtes en conséquence autorisés à engager des dépenses jusqu'à concurrence des crédits indiqués ci-dessus.

Enregistré
Le Chef du Service des Dépenses engagées

Pour le Ministre des Finances et par délégation
L'Ordonnateur Délégué

Vu l'AT PAAS de l'Union Européenne

Les crédits non affectés, nommément à une structure et laissés à la gestion de la DPS sont à utiliser selon les besoins, par la DPS, au profit des structures de la DPS (hôpitaux, CS, ...)

ANNEX 8.2

REPUBLIQUE DU TCHAD

Ministère de la Santé Publique

Magasin Central du MSP

N'Djaména, le 02/12/03

Bon de Sortie
N° 1026

Destinataire : Magasin préfectoral du Biltine

Origine : Magasin central

Livreur : enlevé

Date de sortie : __ / __ / __

Code Produit	Libellé Produit	Quantité	Unité	PU	Montant
000396	Ampoule 100 W	20	unité	419	8 380
000421	Boite de dérivation PM	10	unité	1 691	16 910
000399	Câble 2,5 x 2	1	rouleau 100 m	57 807	57 807
000444	Disjoncteur 10-30 A monophasé	4	unité	45 861	183 444
000427	Interrupteur simple apparent	10	unité	812	8 120

Total : 274 661

Au départ

Visa Responsable Magasin

Visa Directeur des Affaires Financières et du Matériel

Visa du Transporteur

Destinataire Date de réception : 22 12 03

Visa Responsable Magasin

Visa Responsable de la structure

Visa du Délégué Finances

Reception Conforme au tableau ci dessus

Page 1 sur 1

ANNEX 8.2 *(Continued)*

REPUPLIQUE DU TCHAD
MINISTERE DE LA SANTE
Magasin central

UNITE - TRAVAIL - PROGRES

Bordereau de Livraison N° **0 0 3**/

Destinataire: Magasin préfectoral du Logone oriental

origine:Magasin central

Code Produit	Libellé Produit	Quantité	Unité	Prix unitaire	Montant	Observations
21	Agrafeuse GM	2	unité	31 544	63 088	x
20	Agrafeuse PM	7	unité	5 564	38 948	x
494	Ajax vitre	24	flacon	2 748	65 952	x
137	Alèse	20	unité	2 500	50 000	x
128	Armoire métallique 2 portes	4	unité	226 920	907 680	x
631	Balai brosse	25	unité	2 030	50 750	x
105	Balai coco	25	unité	1 523	38 075	x
106	Balai tête de loup	20	unité	750	15 000	x
129	Banc métallique	3	unité	47 500	142 500	x
82	Bic bleu	750	unité	82	61 500	x
83	Bic rouge	750	unité	80	60 000	x
123	Bloc classeur métallique	5	unité	224 215	1 121 075	x
41	Bloc notes GF	35	unité	1 230	43 050	x
42	Bloc notes PF	35	unité	684	23 940	x
148	Blouse infirmier	25	unité	7 000	175 000	x
147	Blouse manœuvre	100	unité	4 900	490 000	x
150	Blouse sage-femme	25	unité	5 100	127 500	x
181	Boite de 10 disquettes	10	unité	12 990	129 900	x
495	Boite de punaises	9	unité	781	7 029	x
95	Boite vim	200	unité	1 425	285 000	x
113	Bombe insecticide	192	unité	906	173 952	x
96	Bouteille crèsyl	400	unité	340	136 000	x
97	Bouteille eau de javel	300	unité	328	98 400	x
143	Brancard local	6	unité	251 000	1 506 000	x
632	Brouette	6	unité	27 550	165 300	x
130	Bureau ministre importè 1 caisson	3	unité	215 000	645 000	x
131	Bureau mnistre importè 2 caissons	3	unité	343 420	1 030 260	x
10	Cachet dateur	7	unité	2 995	20 965	x
15	Cahier PF 200 pages	20	unité	697	13 940	x
651	Calculatrice 12 chiffres	3	unité	22 500	67 500	x
652	Calculatrice à bande	1	unité	80 000	80 000	x
118	Chaise dactylo	3	unité	79 000	237 000	x
120	Chaise visiteur imp	3	unité	67 200	201 600	x
580	Chambre à air 750x16	5	unité	11 492	57 460	x
31	Chemise à rabat en plastic	30	unité	1 000	30 000	x
29	Chemse à sangle	30	unité	1 100	33 000	x
32	Chemise cartonnée	300	unité	90	27 000	x
37	Chrono	20	unité	2 471	49 420	x
63	Colle liquide	15	petit tube	720	10 800	x
	Sous-total1				8 416 496	✱

Page 1

ANNEX 8.2 (Continued)

Code Produit	Libellé Produit	Quantité	Unité	Prix unitaire	Montant	Observations
153	Combinaison pulvérisateur	60	unité	12 000	720 000	ɔ
86	Coupe-papier	20	unité	2 000	40 000	x
139	Couverture 1 place	15	unité	20 172	302 580	x
81	Crayon	36	unité	31	1 116	x
98	Déodorant	96	unité	1 788	171 648	x
75	Dictionnaire français	1	unité	30 000	30 000	x
138	Drap coton 1 place	20	unité	5 636	112 720	x
151	Ensemble chirurgien	5	unité	11 000	55 000	x
68	Enveloppe GF	1000	unité	90	90 000	x
67	Enveloppe MF	1000	unité	63	63 000	x
66	Enveloppe PF	1000	unité	30	30 000	x
116	Eponge	50	unité	317	15 850	x
117	Fauteuil tournant	2	unité	144 275	288 550	x
476	Fauteuil visiteur importé	3	unité	139 000	417 000	y
17	Feutre bleu	30	unité	586	17 580	x
474	Feutre noir	30	unité	595	17 850	x
475	Feutre rouge	10	unité	874	8 740	x
610	Gants en cuir	18	paire	2 864	51 552	x
79	Gomme crayon	20	unité	323	6 460	y
653	Lampe tempête GM	15	unité	8 199	122 985	x
19	Marqueur	6	pqt de 4	2 500	15 000	x
136	Matelas local 1 place	10	unité	70 000	700 000	p
140	Moustiquaire 1 place	36	unité	8 102	291 672	y
115	paillason	8	unité	4 362	34 896	x
479	Pantalon	28	unité	7 000	196 000	x
11	Paquet de stencil	5	pqt de 50	14 173	70 865	x
478	Paquet omo de 5kg	15	unité	8 000	120 000	x
89	Parapheur	4	unité	14 000	56 000	x
100	Pelle locale	25	unité	3 359	83 975	x
57	Perforateur 2 trous	6	unité	4 561	27 366	x
58	Perforteur 4 trous	6	unité	5 500	33 000	x
93	Petit paquet omo	400	unité	356	142 400	y
92	Petite boule savon linge	1080	unité	163	176 040	x
633	Pioche	20	unité	5 075	101 500	x
621	Pneu 750x16	5	unité	175 703	878 515	y
78	Post it Gf	10	pqt de 10	1 000	10 000	y
108	Poubelle métallique	12	unité	12 358	148 296	x
634	Raclette chasse-eau avec manch	15	unité	1 885	28 275	x
2	Rame 1ère frappe	10	unité	3 722	37 220	y
3	Rame 2è frappe	10	unité	3 597	35 970	x
501	Rame duplicata	10	unité	5 372	53 720	x
1	Rame photocopie	25	unité	4 710	117 750	x
101	Rateau local	30	unité	3 239	97 170	y
527	Réchaud à pétrole GM	15	unité	15 841	237 615	y
35	Registre courrier arrivée	20	unité	2 486	49 720	x
34	Registre courrier départ	20	unité	2 483	49 660	x
36	Regitre de transmission	30	unité	2 482	74 460	x
391	Réglette néon de 0,60	20	unité	5 282	105 640	x
392	Réglette néon de 1,20	20	unité	5 912	118 240	x
99	Rouleau de papier hygiènique	720	unité	317	228 240	x
61	Rouleau de scotch transp GM	15	unité	1 894	28 410	x
601	Rouleau tuyau arrosage de 50m	3	unité	32 831	98 493	y
508	Ruban machine typex	17	unité	972	16 524	x
94	Savon toilette	1000	unité	209	209 000	x
Sous-total 2					7 234 263	

ANNEX 8.2 *(Continued)*

Code Produit	Libellé Produit	Quantité	Unité	Prix unitaire	Montant	Observations
635	Seau métallique	15	unité	6 000	90 000	X
522	seau plastic	10	unité	2 500	25 000	X
109	Serpillère	30	unité	743	22 290	X
111	Serviette FM	10	unité	5 000	50 000	X
110	Servitte PF	10	unité	3 000	30 000	X
33	Sous chemise	100	pqt de 10	300	30 000	X
73	Sous-main de bureau	9	unité	6 000	54 000	X
18	Surligneur	25	unité	660	16 500	X
142	Table de chevet métallique locale	10	unité	25 000	250 000	X
119	Table de travail importée	3	unité	127 000	381 000	X
156	Tablier manœuvre	12	unité	3 500	42 000	X
132	Tabouret en bois	4	unité	12 700	50 800	X
59	Taille crayon	8	unité	531	4 248	X
9	Tampon encreur	8	unité	1 513	12 104	X
450	Torche 2 piles	12	unité	1 233	14 796	X
114	Torchon	30	unité	487	14 610	X
26	Trombone PM	30	pqtde100	1 008	30 240	X
393	Tube néon de 0,60m	20	unité	1 113	22 260	X
394	Tube néon de 1,20	20	unité	1 285	25 700	X
644	Ventilateur plafonnier	3	unité	34 800	104 400	X
645	Ventilateur sur pied	3	unité	39 875	119 625	X
7	Vernis correcteur	7	unité	1 064	7 448	X
	Sous-total 3				1 397 021	

Total Général	17 047 780

Au départ
Visa responsable
Magasin   Visa du DAAFM /MSP

Destination   Date 14 / 03 / 2003

Visa responsable de la Structure

Visa du gestionnaire

Délégué des finances

REPUBLIQUE DU TCHAD
MINISTERE DE LA SANTE PUBLIQUE
SECRETARIAT GENERAL
DIRECTION GENERALE DES RESSOURCES
ET DE LA PLANIFICATION
DIRECTION DES AFFAIRES ADMINISTRATIVES,
FINANCIERES ET DU MATERIEL
DIVISION DES RESSOURCES MATERIELLES

N° 037/MSP/SG/DGRP/DAAFM/DRM/2003.

UNITE- TRAVAIL- PROGRES
****

Logone oriental

ORDRE DE MISSION

Il est ordonné à Monsieur **FOUDOUSSIA YOUSSOUF**, Commis de SAF du Ministère de la Santé Publique de se rendre à Doba (Logone-Oriental).

Motif : Convoyer les matériels destinés
à la **Délégation Préfectorale**
Sanitaire du Logone-Oriental.

Date de départ :   09 Septembre 2003

Durée de Mission :   Une Semaine

Moyen de transport :   Véhicule Gros porteur TLO 0643R et TLO 4909 A

Imputation budgétaire :   ETat.

N'Djaména le, **0 9 SEPT 2003**

Le Directeur Général des Ressources
et de la Planification du
Ministère de la Santé Publique

ADOUM DJIBRINE

ANNEX 8.3 *(Continued)*

Vu à l'arrivée à DOBA
le 13 Septembre 2003
Le gestionnaire DPSLOR

NISABI MASRDEAYE

Vu au départ de DOBA
le 15 Septembre 2003
Le gestionnaire DPSLOR

NISABI MASMBAYE

REPUBLIQUE DU TCHAD

Ministère de la Santé Publique

Magasin Central du MSP

N'Djaména, le 05/09/03

Bon de Sortie
N° 846

Destinataire : Magasin préfectoral du Logone Oriental

Origine : Magasin central

Livreur : enlevé

Date de sortie : ___ / ___ / _____

Code Produit	Libellé Produit	Quantité	Unité	Prix unitaire
000021	Agrafeuse GM	2	unité	31 544
000020	Agrafeuse PM	7	unité	5 564
000494	Ajax vitre	24	flacon	2 748
000137	Alèse	20	unité	2 500
000128	Armoire métallique 2 portes	4	unité	226 920
000631	Balai brosse	25	unité	2 030
000105	Balai coco	25	unité	1 523
000106	Balai tête de loup	20	unité	750
000129	Banc métallique	3	unité	47 500
000082	Bic bleu	750	unité	82
000083	Bic rouge	750	unité	80
000123	Bloc classeur métallique	5	unité	224 215
000041	Bloc note GF	35	unité	1 230
000042	Bloc note PF	35	unité	684
000148	Blouse d'infirmier	25	unité	7 000
000147	Blouse manoeuvre	100	unité	4 900
000150	Blouse sage-femme	25	unité	5 100
000181	Boite 10 disquettes	10	unité	12 990
000495	Boite de punaises	9	unité	781
000095	Boite VIM	200	unité	1 425
000113	Bombe insecticide	192	unité	906
000096	Bouteille Crésyl	400	unité	6 793
000097	Bouteille eau de Javel	300	unité	4 918
000143	Brancard local	6	unité	251 000
000632	Brouette	6	unité	27 550
000130	Bureau ministre importé 1 caisson	3	unité	215 000
000131	Bureau ministre importé 2 caissons	3	unité	343 420
000010	Cachet dateur	7	unité	2 995
000015	Cahier PF 200 pages	20	unité	697

Page 1 sur 5

REPUBLIQUE DU TCHAD

Ministère de la Santé Publique

Magasin Central du MSP

N'Djaména, le 05/09/03

Bon de Sortie
N° 846

<u>Destinataire :</u> Magasin préfectoral du Logone Oriental

Origine : Magasin central

Livreur : enlevé

Date de sortie : ___ / ___ / _____

Code Produit	Libellé Produit	Quantité	Unité	Prix unitaire
000651	Calculatrice 12 chiffres	3	unité	22 500
000652	Calculatrice à bande	1	unité	80 000
000118	Chaise dactylo	3	unité	79 000
000120	Chaise visiteur imp	3	unité	67 200
000580	Chambre à air 750 x 16	5	unité	11 492
000031	Chemise à rabats en plastique	30	unité	1 000
000029	Chemise à sangle	30	unité	1 100
000032	Chemise cartonnée	300	unité	90
000037	Chrono	20	unité	2 471
000063	Colle liquide	15	petit tube	720
000153	Combinaison pulvérisateur	60	unité	12 000
000086	Coupe-papier	20	unité	2 000
000139	Couverture 1 place	15	unité	20 172
000081	Crayon	36	unité	31
000098	Déodorant	96	unité	1 788
000075	Dictionnaire français	1	unité	30 000
000138	Drap coton 1 place	20	unité	5 636
000151	Ensemble chirurgien	5	unité	11 000
000068	Enveloppe GF	1 000	unité	90
000067	Enveloppe MF	1 000	unité	63
000066	Enveloppe PF	1 000	unité	30
000116	Eponge	50	unité	317
000117	Fauteuil tournant	2	unité	144 275
000476	Fauteuil visiteur importé	3	unité	139 000
000017	Feutre bleu	30	unité	586
000474	Feutre noir	30	unité	595
000475	Feutre rouge	10	unité	874
000610	Gants en cuir	10	paire	2 864
000079	Gomme crayon	20	unité	323

Page 2 sur 5

ANNEX 8.3 *(Continued)*

REPUBLIQUE DU TCHAD

Ministère de la Santé Publique

Magasin Central du MSP

N'Djaména, le 05/09/03

Bon de Sortie
N° 846

Destinataire : **Magasin préfectoral du Logone Oriental**

Origine : Magasin central

Livreur : enlevé

Date de sortie : ___ / ___ / _____

Code Produit	Libellé Produit	Quantité	Unité	Prix unitaire
000653	Lampe tempête GM	15	unité	8 199
000019	Marqueur	6	paquet de 4	2 500
000136	Matelas local 1 place	10	unité	70 000
000140	Moustiquaire 1 place	36	unité	8 102
000115	Paillasson	8	unité	4 362
000479	Pantalon	28	unité	7 000
000011	Paquet de stencil	5	paquet de 50	14 173
000478	Paquet OMO 5 kg	15	unité	8 000
000089	Parapheur	4	unité	14 000
000100	Pelle locale	25	unité	3 359
000057	Perforateur 2 trous	6	unité	4 561
000058	Perforateur 4 trous	6	unité	5 500
000093	Petit paquet OMO	400	unité	356
000092	Petite boule savon linge	1 080	unité	163
000633	Pioche	20	unité	5 075
000621	Pneu 750x16	5	unité	175 703
000078	Post It GF	10	paquet de 10	1 000
000108	Poubelle métallique	12	unité	12 358
000634	Raclette chasse-eau avec manche	15	unité	1 885
000002	Ramé 1ère frappe	10	unité	3 722
000003	Rame 2ème frappe	10	unité	3 597
000501	Rame duplicata	10	unité	5 372
000001	Rame photocopie	25	unité	4 710
000101	Rateau local	30	unité	3 239
000527	Réchaud à pétrole GM	15	unité	15 841
000035	Registre courrier arrivée	20	unité	2 486
000034	Registre courrier départ	20	unité	2 483
000036	Registre de transmission	30	unité	2 482
000391	Réglette néon de 0,60 m	20	unité	5 282

Page 3 sur 5

REPUBLIQUE DU TCHAD

Ministère de la Santé Publique

Magasin Central du MSP

N'Djaména, le 05/09/03

Bon de Sortie
N° 846

Destinataire : Magasin préfectoral du Logone Oriental

Origine : Magasin central

Livreur : enlevé

Date de sortie : ___ / ___ / _____

Code Produit	Libellé Produit	Quantité	Unité	Prix unitaire
000392	Réglette néon de 1,20 m	20	unité	5 912
000099	Rouleau de papier hygiénique	720	unité	317
000061	Rouleau de scotch transparent GM	15	unité	1 894
000601	Rouleau de tuyau d'arrosage - 50 m	3	unité	32 831
000508	Ruban machine Typex	17	unité	972
000094	Savon toilette	100	unité	209
000635	Seau métallique	15	unité	6 000
000522	Seau plastique	10	unité	2 500
000109	Serpillère	30	unité	743
000111	Serviette MF	10	unité	5 000
000110	Serviette PF	10	unité	3 000
000033	Sous-chemise	100	paquet de 10	300
000073	Sous-main de bureau	9	unité	6 000
000018	Surligneur	25	unité	660
000142	Table de chevet métallique locale	10	unité	25 000
000119	Table de travail importée	3	unité	127 000
000132	Tabouret en bois	4	unité	12 700
000059	Taille crayon	8	unité	531
000009	Tampon encreur	8	unité	1 513
000450	Torche 2 piles	12	unité	1 233
000114	Torchon	30	unité	487
000026	Trombone PM	30	paquet de 100	1 008
000393	Tube néon de 0,60 m	20	unité	1 113
000394	Tube néon de 1,20 m	20	unité	1 258
000644	Ventilateur plafonnier	3	unité	34 800
000645	Ventilateur sur pied	3	unité	39 875
000007	Vernis correcteur	7	unité	1 064

REPUBLIQUE DU TCHAD

Ministère de la Santé Publique

Magasin Central du MSP

N'Djaména, le 05/09/03

Bon de Sortie
N° 846

<u>Destinataire :</u> Magasin préfectoral du Logone Oriental

Origine : Magasin central

Livreur : enlevé

Date de sortie : ___ / ___ / ____

Code Produit	Libellé Produit	Quantité	Unité	Prix unitaire

Au départ

Visa Responsable Magasin

Visa Directeur Général
de la Santé Publique

Visa du Transporteur

Destinataire   Date de réception : ___

Visa Responsable Magasin

Visa Responsable
de la structure

Le Transporteur

ISSA SOULEYMANE
TRANSPORTEUR
TEL:P. 841 58 41
N'DJAMENA

Page 5 sur 5

Notes

1. The leakage rate is $LF_i = \dfrac{\text{Amount Received by Facility}}{\text{Amount Allocated to Facility (by Formula or Budget Line)}}$.

2. Some of the forms used are inserted in the annexes.

3. The leakage rate in region i is $LR_i = \dfrac{\textit{Decentralized} \text{ Credits} + \Sigma \text{ Materials Received from Centralized Purchases}}{\text{Regional } i \text{ Allocation}}$.

4. In Chad, the drugs follow a different circuit, and information on drug allocations had to be collected. We followed the same process and collected data on all drug shipments to the regions, districts, and facilities from the Central Pharmaceutical Procurement Agency, which has the monopoly on the sale and delivery of drugs to public facilities.

5. There are now 18 regions in Chad, but, in 2003, at the time of the tracking exercise, there were 14 regions. The region not covered in the exercise, Borkou-Ennedi-Tibesti, forms the north of the country. It is the largest region, spanning almost half the area of the country. It is populated mainly by nomadic peoples and is not well secured. It is home to less than 4 percent of all public health facilities.

6. The sampling is of more concern in a soft or no allocation rules environment because of the existence of strong discretionary powers in the allocation of public resources. If one follows a resource that is governed by a formula, it is necessary to know only whether the resources at the provider level obey the allocation formula, which is not affected by sampling.

7. The coefficient on budgeted spending is negative, but not significant, whereas that on effective spending is positive and strongly significant.

8. The analysis by Gauthier and Wane does not supply an explanation of the finding that providers receiving public funds charge less for drugs, all other factors being equal. It is not clear whether this is a manifestation of altruism or profit-maximizing behavior.

References

Ablo, Emmanuel Y., and Ritva Reinikka. 1998. "Do Budgets Really Matter?: Evidence from Public Spending on Education and Health in Uganda." Policy Research Working Paper 1926, World Bank, Washington, DC.

Filmer, Deon, and Lant H. Pritchett. 1999. "The Impact of Public Spending on Health: Does Money Matter?" *Social Science and Medicine* 49 (10): 1309–27.

Gauthier, Bernard P., and Waly Wane. 2006. "Leakage of Public Resources in the Health Sector: An Empirical Investigation of Chad." Unpublished working paper, World Bank, Washington, DC.

Ministère des Finances, "Loi de Finances et Loi de Finances Rectificative," (Finance Law and Revised Finance Laws), 2003, République du Tchad.

9

Lessons from School Surveys in Indonesia and Papua New Guinea

Deon Filmer

This chapter contains an informal, retrospective look at a personal experience with two sets of school-focused surveys: a survey effort in Indonesia and a survey in Papua New Guinea. The objective of this chapter is to describe the survey activities and to draw out some of the lessons about activities that worked well and activities that might be carried out differently in the future. (The full set of results derived from the surveys is not described here. It is available in Filmer et al. 1998, 2001, and World Bank 2004.)

Background on the Surveys

Indonesia

The first round of the Indonesian survey was carried out in 1998. It was motivated by the recent East Asian economic crisis, the impacts of which were beginning to be felt in the country. There was concern that the crisis would have a substantial and negative impact on the education sector through a reduction in the demand for education and a reduction in the quality of the supply of schooling.

The idea behind the second round, in 2000, was to go back to most of the same schools and look at the longer-run impact of the crisis. Ultimately,

221

the panel survey aspect of the study was never fully exploited because of school openings and closings, the political turmoil in the country, and the need to redesign the sampling frame. At the time of the second round, there were many questions looming about decentralization. In the end, Indonesia undertook a big bang decentralization in 2000 whereby the responsibility for delivering primary and lower-secondary services was devolved to the district level. (There were roughly 300 districts at the time.) The survey, therefore, tried to assess the state of the financial, management, and administrative support available at the onset of this decentralization process.

Papua New Guinea

The Papua New Guinea survey was carried out in 2002. At the time, several countries had experimented with a Public Expenditure Tracking Survey or a more comprehensive Quantitative Service Delivery Survey. World Bank staff working in Papua New Guinea determined that such a survey would be useful in the context of a poverty assessment for that country, the focus of which would be on public service delivery to the poor. The primary motivation was to obtain descriptive information about the state of schools in Papua New Guinea because such information did not exist. In addition, there was a particular interest in decentralization, which entailed provincial governments exercising control over a portion of the education budget. Finally, there was a concern about leakage and, therefore, a desire to track expenditures. In the end, the survey design attempted to reflect all those interests with a heavy public expenditure tracking component.

Conducting the Surveys

In Indonesia, both survey rounds covered around 600 schools. Viewed in retrospect, this number might seem large; at the time, it seemed quite a small number given the country's size and heterogeneity. In Papua New Guinea, the survey covered about 200 schools.

In both countries, the selection of the particular areas that were surveyed was purposeful, although the purpose was quite different in each case. In Indonesia, the World Bank had ongoing projects in five provinces, and there was a perceived need to cover those provinces. Limitations in budgets and logistical support capacity also tended to restrict the scope to those areas. In addition, the sampling frame of the second round of the Indonesian survey was altered because of political unrest affecting parts of the country. This alteration meant that, among other changes, the province of Maluku was replaced by Nusa Tenggara Timur.

In Papua New Guinea, the main driver for the use of a not purely random sample was cost containment. Because so much of the country is extremely remote, the survey was clustered in 8 (of 20) provinces that were selected to represent different types of areas in the country. The approach allowed summary statistics by type of area (for example, remote provinces, coastal areas, the islands) that had reasonable coverage.

In both countries, after the provinces had been selected, districts were randomly chosen, and then, within those districts, schools were selected randomly. The sampling frames were based on national lists of schools, supplemented, where necessary, by locally constructed lists.

The structure of the survey activities in Indonesia and Papua New Guinea differed substantially. The work in Indonesia was conceived as a stand-alone project; staff at the Ministry of Education and policy makers more generally were considered the primary audience. The project was a close collaborative effort of the World Bank and the research department of the Ministry of Education. About 10 ministry staff participated in the final stages of questionnaire development. The entire team traveled to Bengkulu and went through several rounds of pilot testing and revision with the instruments. About 8 of the 10 ministry staff served as regional survey supervisors in the fielding of the survey. The structure worked well because it gave the survey and the results a home within the ministry. In addition, the procedure lowered the financial costs. There were some problems, however, because ministry staff were not survey specialists, and the learning curve was steep. In effect, there was a trade-off, and the work served as a capacity-building exercise at a slight cost in design sophistication and survey supervision.

The concept in Papua New Guinea was different. The survey effort fed into a poverty assessment, the focus of which was service delivery to the poor. The project was overseen by a working group and a steering committee that encompassed a variety of participants. Much effort went into setting up these groups, and they gave the survey substantial legitimacy at the outset. Numerous other stakeholders took part in the groups and offered input, including people in government, nongovernmental organizations, and church organizations (which are important providers of education services in Papua New Guinea). The staff at the Department of Education provided endorsement of the project and participated in the working group and the steering committee, but did not participate much otherwise. The survey task was contracted out to the National Research Institute, an independent agency that had experience in qualitative surveys and smaller-scale quantitative surveys.

Results

What Worked Well

Indonesia: At the time of the survey rounds, the conventional wisdom in Indonesia was that students were dropping out of school in droves. By documenting trends in enrollment, the survey was able to show a more nuanced picture (see figure 9.1). In particular, to the extent that the crisis was affecting enrollments, the impact was occurring in urban areas, at the secondary level, and, especially, in private or nonsecular schools. There was an important caveat, however. In a school survey, one can estimate only the number of students enrolled; one cannot estimate the enrollment *rate.* Estimating the enrollment rate requires knowing the number of children who are available to enroll in school. Because one of the effects of the economic crisis was population movement, this issue was particularly salient. Falling enrollment at a school might signify dropouts, but it might also mean that students and their families had moved. The large-scale nature of the survey meant that this potential problem was mitigated because a migrating student who had not dropped out should appear as a new entrant in a survey school somewhere else. Nonetheless, a school survey that measures enrollment is no substitute for a household survey from which a readily interpretable enrollment *rate* may be estimated.

The survey collected a substantial amount of information from respondents on perceptions of the crisis. Because the main purpose of the survey was descriptive, perceptions were considered a useful complement to the quantitative data that were being collected. The qualitative responses covered several topics. Did the respondent think the situation at the school had worsened? If so, in what ways? The crisis effects that were most frequently perceived among respondents in both primary and secondary schools were the late payment of parent school fees and other contributions, the inability to conduct extracurricular activities, and the increase in the number of students who must work. There were also significant concerns at primary schools (about declines in student achievement and student health) and at the lower-secondary level (about declines in student enrollment, increases

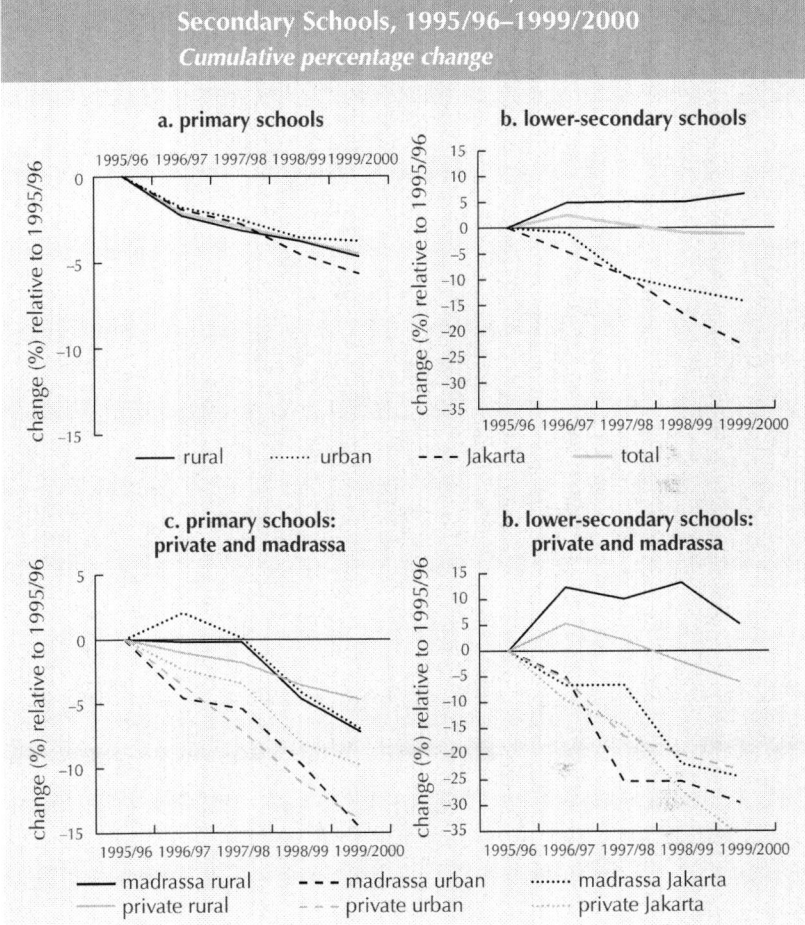

FIGURE 9.1 Student Enrollment in Primary and Lower-Secondary Schools, 1995/96–1999/2000
Cumulative percentage change

Source: Filmer et al. 2001.

in student absenteeism, and constraints on the ability of schools to hire part-time teachers). Perceptions of crisis impacts were more common in urban areas (particularly Jakarta) than in rural areas, and private schools tended to perceive more effects than did public schools.

At the time of the crisis, the government instituted a large-scale scholarship and school grants program for public and private schools. By

a. primary schools

Rupiah

8,000
7,000
6,000
5,000
4,000
3,000
2,000
1,000
0

public   public   private   private
grant   nongrant   grant   nongrant

b. lower-secondary schools

Rupiah

140,000
120,000
100,000
80,000
60,000
40,000
20,000
0

public   public   private   private
grant   nongrant   grant   nongrant

grant   local   central

Source: Filmer et al. 2001.

collecting detailed information on school incomes, the survey was able to uncover some interesting patterns. The most important finding was that local governments (the provincial and district level) were adjusting their allocations to public schools in response to the central government grants (see figure 9.2). At the primary level, the central government grant was offset almost 1 for 1 by reductions in local government spending on grant-receiving public schools; as a result, net income from government sources remained almost constant for these schools. There was no such substitution in private schools; they did not receive any of the local government funds to start with. There are similar patterns at the lower-secondary level; but, there, the magnitude of the grant was so small relative to other central sources in income that it did not make much difference in overall school income.

Another component that worked well was the documentation of changes in school fees, including the implementation of fee waivers. The proportion of schools collecting fees from parents declined at the primary level (15 percentage points) and the lower-secondary level (12 percentage points); the largest declines occurred in the first year of the crisis (1998/99). Urban schools were less likely to waive fees relative to rural schools; in Jakarta, almost no sampled lower-secondary school waived fees (compared to about 40 percent elsewhere). At the primary level, average entrance fees increased dramatically during the crisis years (mainly because of large increases in Jakarta); but, except in the case of Jakarta, the increases did not keep pace with inflation. At the secondary level, nowhere did the increases keep pace with inflation. Monthly student and examination fees also rose, on average, during the crisis years, but in no case at a greater rate than inflation.

Papua New Guinea: One of the main contributions of the survey in Papua New Guinea was the descriptive statistics on the state of schools. Such statistics had been quite limited until then. A wealth of information was generated on the average number of teachers, teacher turnover, school infrastructure, and so on, and about the variations in such indicators across the country. The survey documented the generally inferior condition of school facilities in poor or remote areas, especially classrooms and the access to other amenities. Differences between church- and government-operated schools were typically not significant. Overall, education facilities tended to be better at schools that had greater financial resources, especially higher levels of nongrant revenues per student.

One of the strongest results to emerge from the survey revolved around delays in the payment of school subsidies. These subsidies were per student grants sent to schools on a quarterly basis. Payments in quarters 1 and 3 were the responsibility of the national government; payments in quarters 2 and 4 were the responsibility of the provincial governments. The survey asked whether the subsidy for each quarter of the prior year had been received and, if so, when. As the year progressed, schools were less and less likely to receive the subsidy, especially the schools that were in remote areas (see figure 9.3). At the same time, the delays associated with each quarter increased.

The survey was also designed to measure teacher absenteeism, which ideally would have been captured through surprise visits. In the end, school visits were not a complete surprise. It was difficult to obtain consent to carry out a survey without any warning whatsoever, and it was considered somewhat dangerous to attempt a survey in this way. Schools were, therefore, given, at most, a two-week window of time during which the survey team would visit, and the enumerators would arrive without announcement

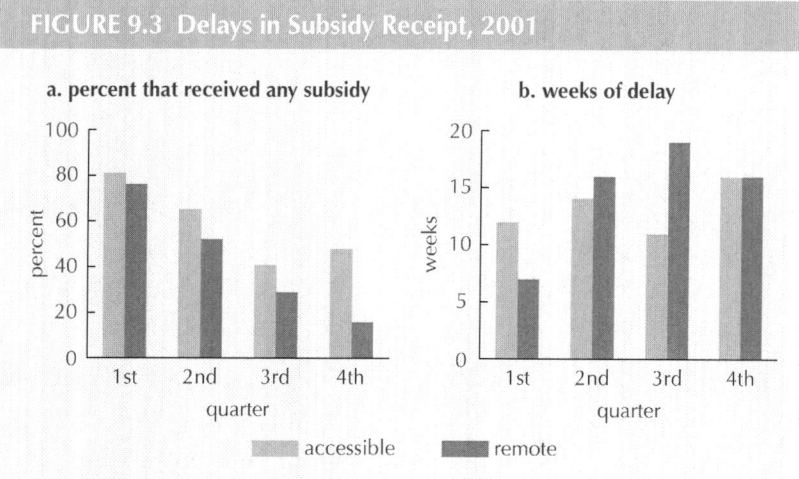

FIGURE 9.3 Delays in Subsidy Receipt, 2001

a. percent that received any subsidy

b. weeks of delay

accessible   remote

Source: World Bank 2004.
Note: 1st quarter, 3rd quarter = national government responsibility. 2nd quarter, 4th quarter = provincial government responsibility. "Accessible" and "remote" are based on an index of access to roads, towns, and various types of infrastructure and services.

within that window of time. The visit allowed a valid estimation of teacher absenteeism on the day of the visit under such conditions.

In addition to absenteeism, the study was able to compare lists of teachers who were being paid salaries according to the civil service payroll and lists of teachers who were teaching in classrooms according to records at each school. The exercise was painstaking. The lists of names were long, and the exercise had to allow for leeway; under local-level arrangements, some teachers were legitimately teaching in schools other than those to which they were officially posted. Nonetheless, the matching exercise yielded a substantial estimate for the number of ghost teachers. The estimates on ghost teachers, absenteeism, and schools that were closed because there were no teachers available allowed a credible estimate of the overall depletion in the effective supply of teachers (see figure 9.4).

What Was Hard to Do

It proved difficult to obtain reliable information on total school incomes through these surveys. High-quality data are not readily available on income from all sources, including regular government sources (such as capitation grants), irregular government sources (such as capital expenditures),

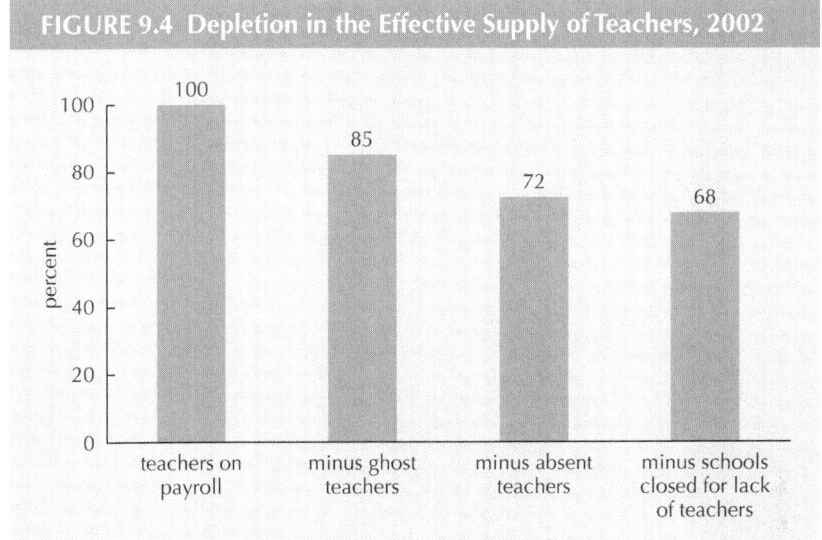

FIGURE 9.4 Depletion in the Effective Supply of Teachers, 2002

Source: World Bank 2004.

and the full panoply of school fees (registration fees, parents association fees, examination fees, and so on). In Indonesia, despite numerous prompts, it was never clear whether the survey was able to capture the full picture. Even at the pilot stage, the team of supervisors had long debates about prompting for various types of income sources, but never reached consensus. In retrospect, it probably would have been worthwhile to focus on specific components, such as those illustrated in figure 9.2.

Similarly, in Papua New Guinea, the Public Expenditure Tracking Survey component was hampered by poor recordkeeping at the school level. About half the schools had information on either revenues or expenditures, but not both; it was possible to put together a full revenue and expenditure picture for only about 30 percent of the schools. In the end, the analysis focused specifically on a school subsidy that was set at a relatively well-defined amount (it was based on specific amounts fixed by grade level), the distribution channels for this subsidy, and the intended schedule of subsidy payments. The study was able to yield revealing results on the subsidy (such as those in figure 9.3), but the overall objective of tracking total public expenditures was probably too ambitious.

One of the lessons from these surveys is that it is better, in collecting financial data, to use a survey instrument that is relatively more specific.

School principals and teachers will often only report that they have received a grant if they are prompted with the specific name of the grant. Even this reporting is not always sufficient, however. In Indonesia, for example, ministry staff would use the official name or acronym to refer to a transfer; while, at the school level, the staff would call the same transfer by a different name (often the name or acronym of older, similar school transfers that were no longer available). Enumerators need to be well trained to elicit correct financial information in such cases.

What Would be Hard to Justify Doing Again

Although enrollment trends in Indonesia proved a useful check on conventional wisdom at the time they were produced, they were of limited value as a measure of the overall *impact* on enrollments because it was difficult to establish conclusively that changes in enrollments were not being driven by changes in migration patterns. Collecting enrollment numbers, especially retrospectively, is an extremely time-consuming and tedious task. It requires careful copying of many numbers from school records to a questionnaire and is prone to transcription errors (as well as subsequent data-entry errors). Because the numbers are ultimately hard to interpret anyway, the collection of retrospective information may not be so useful. In contrast, the collection of current enrollment information is necessary for a variety of reasons, including, for example, calculating the amount expected through capitation grants.

Another lesson from these surveys revolves around the advantages inherent in the use of fewer survey instruments. In Papua New Guinea, the survey included seven instruments at the school level, one for the district office, and one for the provincial office. In the end, much of the information was extraneous. The many instruments made the school visits much longer and more complicated than they needed to be. There is a temptation to add questions to a school survey because, once the fixed cost of visiting a school is undertaken, it appears that the marginal cost is minimal. However, the marginal cost may also have to be calculated in the form of interviewer and interviewee fatigue and the resulting losses in data quality.

One instrument, the parent interview, proved particularly unhelpful in Papua New Guinea. Because of funding limitations, it was not possible to include a random sample of parents at each school. As a result, only one parent per school was interviewed. The idea was that a sample of about 200 parents would nonetheless be informative about parent perceptions.

In the end, however, this sample turned out to be potentially highly unrepresentative because it relied on parents who chanced to be available for the interviews. The instrument produced interesting quotations only by parents who happened to catch the sense of the analysis derived from the other instruments.

Warning: Bad Data-Entry Packages May Be Hazardous to Your Health

One of the hard lessons one must learn in data collection is that careful data entry is crucial. Although it may seem simple to enter data from survey instruments into Excel, SPSS, or some other software package, doing so is likely to add months to the task of data processing. Good data-entry packages that allow for real-time data checking (including ranges and skip patterns) help minimize the need for ex post data cleaning. The data cleaning is also a tedious task, made even more difficult by the growing time lag between data collection and data cleaning. Staff move to other projects as time goes on. A well-designed data-entry package (such as a suitably programmed Census and Survey Processing System, Structured Query Language package, or other such package, many of which are available free of charge) shortcuts this process and yields higher-quality data for analysis. A long delay in data cleaning potentially contributes to a reduction in the impact of the findings because it increases the risk that policy makers may consider the data to be too old to be relevant.

Conclusion

The experience of these two survey efforts has yielded lessons about what is more difficult and what is easier to do in the context of a school survey. Drawing on the author's involvement in these efforts, this chapter concludes with three main recommendations for anyone embarking on a similar exercise. First, questionnaires and interviews should be simple and straightforward. This approach lightens the load on interviewers and interviewees and helps improve data quality. Second, especially in the collection of information on financial issues, the process should be precise. This process may require a great deal of pilot testing particularly because precision may have different meanings at the school level and at the official level. Third, the data-entry process must allow for real-time data validation and verification, which will save months of data cleaning.

References

Filmer, Deon, Haneen Sayed, Boediono, Jiyono, Nanik Suwaryani, and Bambang Indriyanto. 1998. "The Impact of Indonesia's Economic Crisis on Basic Education: Findings from a Survey of Schools." Working paper, World Bank and Ministry of Education and Culture, Jakarta.

Filmer, Deon, H. Dean Nielsen, Nanik Suwaryani, and Bambang Indriyanto. 2001. "Indonesia's Primary and Junior Secondary Schools in a Post-Crisis Environment: Findings from a Follow-Up Survey of 600 Schools." Working paper, World Bank and Ministry of National Education, Jakarta.

World Bank. 2004. "Papua New Guinea: Public Expenditure and Service Delivery." Report, Washington, DC. World Bank. http://www.worldbank.org/research/projects/publicspending/tools/PNG%20QSDS%20Education/PNG.PESD.Education.Final (G).jun.2004.pdf.

10

Assessment of Health and Education Services in the Aftermath of a Disaster

Elizabeth Frankenberg, Jed Friedman, Fadia Saadah,
Bondan Sikoki, Wayan Suriastini, Cecep Sumantri,
and Duncan Thomas

On December 26, 2004, the Sumatra-Andaman earthquake shook the Indian Ocean, creating a tsunami that, around 45 minutes later, slammed into the nearby island of Sumatra, resulting in unparalleled devastation. The tsunami ultimately wreaked havoc on 10 countries and 4,500 kilometers (about 2,800 miles) of coastline throughout the region. Estimates suggest that worldwide casualties likely numbered over a quarter of a million people. The vast majority of deaths occurred in Indonesia, where some communities were almost wiped out.

Less than a year later, Hurricane Katrina swept over the Gulf Coast of the United States. Though Katrina's impact was underanticipated, her arrival had been forecast for several days, sufficient time for many to evacuate, and far fewer lives were lost.

The costs of these disasters have been huge. They underscore our limited knowledge about the way people are able to cope in the midst and in the aftermath of such catastrophes and about how the institutions that provide social services are affected by these events, respond to them, and are able to assist people in taking advantage of new opportunities that arise as rebuilding commences after the disaster. This chapter discusses a project that is designed to address such issues in the context of post-tsunami Aceh Province on the island of Sumatra.

The overall project, the Study of the Tsunami Aftermath and Recovery (STAR), seeks to provide scientific evidence on the impact of the shock associated with the 2004 tsunami on many dimensions of population health and well-being, the pace and form of the recovery process, and the roles that institutions play in helping or hindering that recovery process in the shorter and the longer term. The focus is Indonesia, the country most affected by the tsunami. Specifically, the project's goals are threefold: to document the immediate, medium-term, and longer-term consequences of the disaster on mortality, family disruption and relocation, physical and mental health, economic resources and opportunities, the housing stock, and physical infrastructure; to trace the reconstruction of lives and livelihoods in the aftermath of the disaster; and to identify the characteristics of individuals, households, and communities that may contribute to mitigating the deleterious consequences of a shock on a broad array of indicators of well-being.

To accomplish these goals, we are assembling, collecting, and analyzing uniquely rich longitudinal survey data on households, communities, and facilities in the Indonesian provinces of Aceh and North Sumatra. These data are combined with satellite-based measures of the destruction caused by the tsunami and regrowth after the tsunami. Baseline data are provided by the National Socioeconomic Survey (SUSENAS), a broad-purpose household survey conducted by Statistics Indonesia in early 2004 in tsunami-affected areas and in comparable areas that were not directly affected by the tsunami. STAR involved locating and, if possible, reinterviewing, in 2005, the same respondents first interviewed in 2004. In this chapter, we describe the project and provide a detailed discussion of the design of the community and facility components of the survey. Design features are illustrated by tables constructed from the community and facility components.

The Disaster and Its Consequences

The tsunami of December 26, 2004, was preceded by the Sumatra-Andaman earthquake, the epicenter of which was about 150 kilometers (around 95 miles) off the coast of the Indonesian province of Aceh. The quake generated a rupture some 1,900 kilometers (1,200 miles) in length, which forced the seafloor upward by about 10 meters (around 33 feet). This movement displaced a trillion tons of water and generated a tsunami surge that moved at speeds of over 800 kilometers (500 miles) an hour, slam-

ming into the nearby island of Sumatra only 45 minutes after the earthquake (see Kerr 2005; Lay et al. 2005; Marris 2005). In some instances,
the inundation reached inland 5 kilometers (over 3 miles). The tsunami was
extreme by any standards; in the previous 100 years, estimates put the
cumulative death toll associated with tsunamis at less than 10,000. Worldwide casualties from the December 26, 2004, tsunami are estimated at
around a quarter of a million people.

This disaster has had immense consequences for Indonesia. It is estimated that over 120,000 people died (see BBC 2005; Doocy et al. 2007). In
Banda Aceh, the capital of Aceh Province, about one-third of the population is thought to have died. Estimates suggest that as many as 700,000 survivors were displaced for at least a short period of time. The psychological
consequences of the tsunami among survivors are likely to be profound
and long-lasting (Frankenberg et al. 2007). In addition to whatever else
the survivors may have experienced, many witnessed the deaths of family
members and friends and were surrounded by reminders of the event,
including corpses and numerous aftershocks associated with the earthquake. Many individuals spent weeks and months looking for information
on people who were still missing.

Other costs of the disaster encompass damage to infrastructure, productive assets, and the natural environment. The World Bank estimated
the disaster's costs as of May 2005 at about US$4.5 billion, 78 percent of
which reflected damage and loss in the private sector. The costs represented 2.2 percent of the national gross domestic product and 97 percent of
the gross domestic product of Aceh Province. Full recovery was expected
to take at least five years (BBC 2005).

The disaster created new difficulties in many aspects of daily life, community relationships, and the broader economy. Vast numbers of houses,
schools, health facilities, and businesses were destroyed or damaged, along
with roads, bus and ferry terminals, fuel depots, ports, telecommunications
facilities, and water resources (Bappenas and Consultative Group on
Indonesia 2005). Teachers, health care providers, and community leaders
were among the individuals who lost their lives, and their absence has made
the reestablishment of service delivery and management more difficult.
Around 20 percent of public health facilities were destroyed, and Ministry
of Health officials estimated that rebuilding the public health infrastructure
might take up to five years (see WHO 2005; Zipperer 2005).

The consequences of the disaster were not uniformly distributed along
the west coast of the island of Sumatra. In general, the waves diminished

in force and magnitude as they traveled southeast along the coast of Aceh toward North Sumatra Province (Black 2005). The effects of the tsunami in any individual locality depended on the height of the water wave on shore, which was a complex function of the slope of the land, the wave type, the water depth, and the coastal topography (Ramakrishnan 2005). The variations in the degree of damage in such situations are extremely complicated to predict. We have used remote-sensing techniques to measure the destruction associated with the tsunami in each of the locations in which our respondents were living. Moreover, our interviews covered respondents who did not reside at uniform distances from the beachfront at the time of the tsunami. This means that we capture experiences of physical devastation and loss of life, but also more muted effects of the tsunami, such as infrastructure damage and price changes. People living further inland and in the southern portion of North Sumatra Province noticed few effects.

Data

STAR provides data on Aceh and North Sumatra, the two provinces on the island of Sumatra that sustained damage from the disaster. Aceh, where the tsunami struck with greatest force, is located at the northwestern end of Sumatra (see figure 10.1). As one travels in a southeasterly direction along the coast of Sumatra facing the Indian Ocean (the west coast), the devastation from the tsunami lessens, although, even along short sections of coast, the amount of devastation varies.

In much of coastal Aceh, the intensity with which the tsunami struck and the distance the water wave traveled inland created a true demographic catastrophe of almost unparalleled proportions. Farther from the epicenter of the earthquake, the shock was reflected in reduced food supplies, price increases, job losses, and infrastructure damage. The coastal areas of North Sumatra were relatively unaffected.

The data generated through STAR support an assessment of the disaster's immediate impact. The data include the results of two rounds of a survey conducted among over 10,000 households (in about 600 communities) in Aceh and North Sumatra. The households were first interviewed in early 2004 as part of a much larger survey, Statistics Indonesia's annual cross-sectional socioeconomic survey (see elsewhere above). We refer to the data from the 10,000 households in the baseline survey in 2004 as STAR0. Fieldwork for STAR1, the first post-tsunami follow-up on the STAR0 households, was initiated in May 2005 and completed in June 2006.

FIGURE 10.1 Northern End of Sumatra

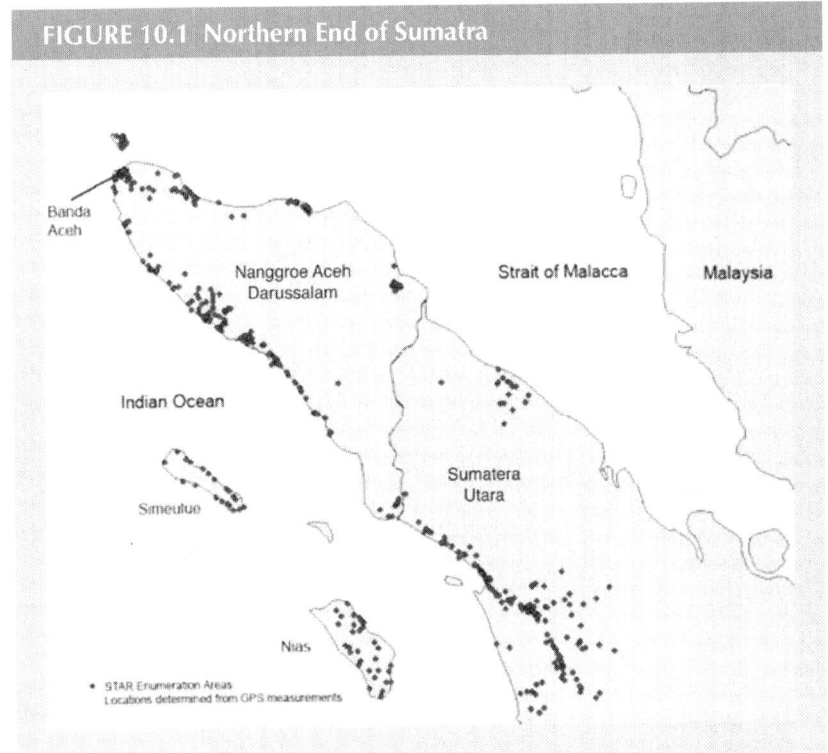

Source: Constructed by the authors.
Note: The dots indicate Study of the Tsunami Aftermath and Recovery (STAR) enumeration areas for which global positioning system (GPS) measurements were available in February 2006.

A central task in describing and analyzing the impact of the tsunami is the development of multiple measures of the physical devastation the tsunami caused. Satellite images provide critically important information on changes in the natural and built-up environments in the immediate aftermath of the tsunami and on the subsequent regeneration and recon-struction of these environments (see Gillespie et al. 2007). As part of the fieldwork, we have collected measures of latitude and longitude based on the global positioning system (GPS) in every enumeration area included in the STAR0 interviews in 2004, in all locations in which people were living at the time of the STAR1 interviews, and on all the schools and health facilities identified as sources of services during these periods. In each subsequent wave of STAR, the locations of people who have moved are recorded through the GPS.

The combination of these GPS-based locations with a geographic information system database of remotely sensed images of the study site spanning the period prior to the tsunami through (ultimately) five years after the tsunami supplies an exceptionally rich resource for the measurement of destruction and reconstruction. With these data, alternative measures of destruction will be explored. These data include the extent of water inundation in each enumeration area immediately after the tsunami, as well as changes between late 2004 and early 2005 in the vegetation cover and the reach of bare earth. We are also constructing estimates of the damage to buildings, roads, bridges, arable land, and rice paddies in the tsunami's immediate wake. A key advantage of the satellite imagery is that it permits the measurement of the pace of vegetation regrowth and of the reconstruction of buildings, roads, bridges, and paddy walls, thus facilitating the creation of a time- and location-specific database of regeneration and reconstruction as the months and years pass since the tsunami.

Measures established from remotely sensed data offer one means of characterizing the destruction caused by the tsunami and the progress of the subsequent recovery. Measures established from data collected through direct observations by our fieldworkers and community informants and at health facilities, schools, and markets represent another source of information.

As a first step in the creation of ground-based measures of community conditions, the supervisors on the household field teams during STAR1 were asked to fill out a short direct observation questionnaire for each enumeration area. These questionnaires surveyed the impressions of the supervisors about the amount of destruction in communities and were associated with brief interviews with community leaders about the impact of the tsunami. The STAR fieldworkers digitally photographed the enumeration areas as additional evidence.

Shortly after the fieldwork for the STAR1 round of the survey began, we also initiated detailed community and facility survey components in each of the 591 villages in which our STAR enumeration areas are located. (The interviews took place 5–18 months after the tsunami.) These components build on the community and facility surveys we designed for the Indonesia Family Life Survey. However, there is an enhanced focus on the reconstruction experience. In each community, we conducted a lengthy interview with the village leader. One of the domains about which we collect information is the changes in the leadership structure of the village since the tsunami, including whether leadership positions have remained unfilled following the deaths of leaders or staff.

Other modules analyze the condition of markets, transport hubs, transportation centers, public phones, post offices, and banks and whether such services have become less accessible in the aftermath of the tsunami either because of destruction or because, for example, public transportation has become less well provided. There are questions about the damage to roads, bridges, docking facilities, farmland, livestock, and fishing enterprises in the community and on the availability of electricity and clean drinking water before the tsunami, immediately after the tsunami, and at the time of the interviews. Comparing these data with estimates of destruction produced through satellite surveys supplies unique opportunities for ground-truthing the satellite-based estimates.

Specially designed sections of the survey focus on changes in population as a result of deaths and in- and out-migration; community needs and the extent to which these needs are being met by basic services; damage to health centers, schools, and credit institutions and changes in the availability of these facilities; and activities geared toward community development and reconstruction, including activities conducted by community residents, nongovernmental organizations, or the government in the aftermath of the disaster.

Many of these modules are repeated with additional informants such as the heads of village women's groups. This second set of responses offers a different perspective on conditions and problems in the community and helps paint a more thorough picture of the extent of destruction and reconstruction and the quality of community life in general.

The STAR facility survey component involves interviews at public health clinics, private health practices, community health posts, and primary and secondary schools. The component focuses on facilities mentioned by household respondents as the service providers the households use. In most communities, it has been possible to carry out interviews at all the facilities mentioned by household respondents. When this process has not been possible, a sample has been chosen based on the number of mentions by household respondents. The interviews at health facilities focus on the availability and prices of key services and drugs, on the barriers the facilities face in improving service provision, and on the health needs of the local population in the aftermath of the tsunami. The interviews at schools assess similar sorts of issues in education. At each school and health facility, a GPS reading of the location is taken so that we may construct measures of distance from the community center to the facility.

As part of the STAR community and facility survey components, interviewers also visit markets and stalls to collect data on the availability and prices of food and other basic goods. These data are essential in adjusting the expenditure data for the inflation that has become more evident since the tsunami.

The Service Environment in the Wake of the Tsunami

An important objective of STAR is to provide information on the service environment in Aceh and North Sumatra in the aftermath of the disaster and, where possible, to contrast the situation before the tsunami and the situation after the tsunami. The community and facility components are tightly linked to the household survey. Ultimately, this information will enable us to describe the service environment from three perspectives: individuals (who are the service end users), communities (the characteristics of which often feed into allocation decisions), and facilities. In this chapter, we focus primarily on the latter two perspectives, but we describe our approach in each case.

To establish a portrait of the population's access to services, we begin, as part of our household survey instrument, by asking individuals to identify the health and school facilities that are of greatest relevance to them. For schools, any individual who has attended school at any time since November 2004 (that is, before the tsunami) is asked to provide precise information on the name and location of the school even if it is no longer functioning. For health facilities, any individual who has used outpatient care during the month before the survey is asked to identify the facility, and individuals who have not used care are asked to supply information on the facilities they would rely on if they needed care. These responses are used to construct community-specific lists of facilities (stratified by school level and by type of health care provider). In most communities in Aceh and North Sumatra, the number of facilities is small enough so that all may be visited. When this is not so, a sample of facilities is drawn. These facilities are visited, and staff members are interviewed.

To show service availability within communities, we use service availability rosters to list every facility identified by the household respondents. These rosters are administered to the community leaders. We ask the leaders to give us information about each relevant facility on the list. This information includes data on the distance, cost, and travel time to reach the facility from the community; on any damage to the facility by the tsunami; and on the status of the facility as a functioning entity in the aftermath of the tsunami. The community leaders are asked to add to the list any additional facilities that may be considered service options by their communities. The enumerators visit each facility on the rosters to obtain GPS information on the facility location.

Apart from the rosters, community leaders and the heads of village women's groups are asked more general questions on service availability and community service needs in the aftermath of the tsunami. To illustrate the kinds of information provided, we have constructed overview tables based on data collected on Aceh Province. We have divided the communities into three groups: those suffering heavy tsunami-related damage (as indicated by clear inundation by floodwaters detected by Landsat satellite), those suffering some or moderate damage (as indicated by potential inundation in satellite imagery, complemented by ground reports of damage), and the remainder, which we classify as indirectly affected or unaffected communities.

In table 10.1, we see that, in 68 percent of the communities most heavily affected by the tsunami, access to primary and lower-secondary schools is reported by community leaders to have worsened in the aftermath of

TABLE 10.1 Disruptions in Service Provision in the Aftermath of the Tsunami, December 26, 2004
percent

Community status	Heavy damage	Some damage	No damage
Service disruptions or less access			
Elementary schools	68	34	5
Lower-secondary schools	68	34	4
Upper-secondary schools	56	31	3
Problems in primary health care (general)			
Community health posts	64	23	2
Village midwives	49	17	0
Public health centers	63	22	2
Private health practices	49	15	3
Emergency services were established			
Primary health care	31	8	2
Elementary schools	34	8	0
Lower-secondary schools	28	5	1
Upper-secondary schools	21	5	1

Source: Compiled by the authors.
Note: The level of damage refers to a classification of communities according to the damage caused by the tsunami (see the text).

the tsunami, whereas this is true of only about one-third of the moderately damaged communities and only 5 percent of the remainder group. A similar gradient in the reduction in access applies to upper-secondary schools: 56 percent of the most heavily damaged communities have reduced access to these schools versus 3 percent in the unaffected areas. Community leaders in over 60 percent of the communities severely affected by the tsunami report that access to primary health care has worsened in the aftermath of the tsunami (either at public health centers or community health posts). More than 20 percent of the leaders in moderate or lightly damaged areas report a reduction in access to primary health care, whereas only 2 percent of the leaders in the indirectly or unaffected communities report a worsening in access.

For health services, community leaders are also asked to report whether disruptions have occurred among particular types of providers. In tsunami-affected areas, the level of the disruptions reported among private health practices is lower than the corresponding levels for government and community sources of care, but it is unclear if the reports are accurate or if the leaders are merely less knowledgeable about services that are not directly connected to their mandates.

Table 10.1 provides information on the establishment of emergency services in the aftermath of the tsunami. Emergency services were far more likely to be provided in tsunami-affected communities, and they were more likely to be provided in primary health care, as well as in elementary education rather than at higher schooling levels.

Table 10.2 presents illustrative descriptive statistics based on aggregations up to the community level of information in the service availability rosters on specific facilities after the tsunami (in this example, public health centers and elementary schools).

The first row in table 10.2 shows the percentage of communities in which facilities were damaged or destroyed during the disaster as a share of all the communities in each group. Among the communities most directly affected by the tsunami, 73 percent experienced damage to or destruction of at least one elementary school, and 63 percent experienced damage to or destruction of at least one public health center. The corresponding shares were 24 and 31 percent among the communities that were moderately affected by the tsunami and 4 and 3 percent among the communities that were relatively unaffected. It is important to recall that, although a community may not have sustained sufficient damage to be included among the communities in groups considered to have been

TABLE 10.2 Communities Experiencing Changes in the Availability of Elementary Schools and Public Health Centers
percent

Community status	Elementary schools			Public health centers		
	Heavy damage	Some damage	No damage	Heavy damage	Some damage	No damage
Facilities were damaged or destroyed	73	24	4	63	31	3
Facility staff were killed	22	2	0	22	2	0
Facilities were closed after the tsunami	82	39	2	60	30	6
All closed facilities are now reopened	18	61	98	40	70	94
New facilities have been established since the tsunami	10	2	1	6	10	10

Source: Compiled by the authors.
Note: The level of damage refers to a classification of communities according to the damage caused by the tsunami (see the text).

directly affected by the tsunami, community members may have used services in areas that were affected. Our approach captures this disruption in nearby facilities.

Staff members killed in the tsunami represent another measure of disruption among facilities. In 22 percent of the heavily damaged communities, the capacity of at least one facility was diminished by the death of staff in the tsunami. The deaths of facility staff members in the tsunami have been reported in only 2 percent of the lightly damaged communities and in none of the communities in unaffected areas.

The third and fourth rows in table 10.2 report on service disruptions because of facility closures. Most communities heavily affected by the tsunami experienced the closure of at least one elementary school, and 60 percent experienced the closure of at least one public health center, but closures were also common in the more lightly damaged areas. The majority of the facilities that had been closed in lightly damaged areas had reopened by the time of the community interviews; however, most of the facilities in heavily damaged areas remained closed, especially the primary schools.

In the fifth row, we explore whether community members had access to facilities that had become newly available since the tsunami. This situation was relatively uncommon at the time of the interviews. Only 10 percent of the communities in heavily damaged areas were using elementary schools that had not been available before the tsunami, for example. Many heavily damaged communities had still not regained full use of key health and education facilities at the time of the survey.

Table 10.3 shows the results of data collection at facilities through interviews with staff. To demonstrate the nature of the data, we present illustrative statistics on public health centers and schools. The table focuses on specific service areas that became somewhat or much worse in the immediate aftermath of the tsunami. Facilities are grouped according to whether they are located in subdistricts that were directly affected by the tsunami or subdistricts that were indirectly affected or unaffected. As an indicator of whether a subdistrict was affected, we have adopted the definitions proposed by Statistics Indonesia for determining the impact of the tsunami based on field reports by local government representatives. We have adopted this official subdistrict measure because we lack a measure constructed from satellite imagery for facilities located outside STAR enumeration areas, and many of the staff interviews were conducted at such facilities.

The top part of table 10.3 records whether various salient aspects of service delivery at public health centers were detrimentally affected by the tsunami. Differences are readily apparent between health facilities in tsunami-affected subdistricts and those in unaffected subdistricts. Among the former, 17 percent reported lower numbers of staff; among the latter, the corresponding share was 1 percent. Other areas in which the differences are notable are the condition of buildings, supplies of pharmaceuticals, and access to adequate water (reflecting at least in part the damage caused by the earthquake that was associated with the tsunami).

The picture of schools in the bottom part of table 10.3 is qualitatively similar. A significant disruption in educational services occurred, and overall educational facility quality worsened in tsunami-affected subdistricts. This contrasts with the situation among schools in the other subdistricts.

TABLE 10.3 Facilities Reporting Worse Conditions after the Tsunami, by Service Area *percent*		
Facilities	Directly affected subdistricts	Indirectly or unaffected subdistricts
Public health centers		
Number of staff	16.7	1.4
Condition of buildings	20.4	8.1
Adequacy of water	18.5	8.1
Adequacy of toilets	18.9	12.2
Adequacy of sterile treatment conditions	18.5	5.4
Supply of pharmaceuticals	20.4	6.8
Supply of equipment	18.5	8.1
Availability of family planning	5.7	2.7
Schools		
Number of teachers and staff	27.9	2.3
Training of teachers	20.2	2.3
Condition of building	34.5	13.1
Availability of books	36.1	8.1
Availability of other supplies	31.3	5.4
Adequacy of extracurricular infrastructure	25.6	5.4
Adequacy of water and hygiene	22.6	8.1
Availability of scholarship funds	10.6	1.8

Source: Compiled by the authors.
Note: The subdistricts have been grouped according to whether they were directly affected or relatively unaffected by the tsunami. The sample includes 54 public health facilities and 208 schools in subdistricts affected by the tsunami; the corresponding numbers in the unaffected subdistricts are 74 and 221.

A substantially higher proportion of schools in tsunami-affected subdistricts lost teachers and staff, suffered building damage, and experienced reductions in the availability of books and other school supplies.

Table 10.4 presents selected dimensions of education and health service delivery at the time of the survey, which may be up to 18 months after the tsunami. It explores student enrollments and school staffing measured in December 2004 (immediately before the tsunami) and at the time of the survey. There was an average increase from 401 to 446 students in the tsunami-affected subdistricts and from 263 to 307 students in the unaffected

TABLE 10.4 Enrollments and Staffing before the Tsunami and at the Time of the Survey						
	Tsunami-affected subdistricts			Unaffected subdistricts		
Indicator	Before	After	Difference[a]	Before	After	Difference[a]
Number of students	400.6	446.3	45.7	263.4	307.3	43.9
Number of teachers	25.1	25.4	0.3	17.1	18.2	1.1
Student–teacher ratio	16.0	17.6	1.6	15.4	16.9	1.5
Number of other staff	3.5	3.3	−0.2	2.2	2.3	0.1
Student–teacher and staff ratio	14.0	15.6	1.5	13.6	15.0	1.3

Source: Compiled by the authors.
Note: The subdistricts have been grouped according to whether they were directly affected (204 schools) or relatively unaffected (213 schools) by the tsunami.
a. Numbers are rounded.

subdistricts. This increase reflects the closure of facilities, as well as the displacement of households to other subdistricts. Meanwhile, the average number of teachers in the schools was largely unchanged, indicating substantially reduced resources per student as measured by the student–teacher ratio. These changes suggest that disaster impacts on service delivery may be felt beyond the immediate disaster area because some households relocate from affected to unaffected places, while total local resources remain limited. Only a postdisaster study design that includes unaffected areas will be able to identify such spillover effects.

Table 10.5 shows simple differences in the condition of electricity and water connections in community health posts across subdistricts that were either affected or unaffected by the tsunami. In general, electricity and water supplies were available to relatively more of the health centers in tsunami-affected subdistricts. Because these subdistricts were among the wealthier areas in Aceh, it is difficult to discern whether the underlying infrastructure in the functioning health centers in tsunami-affected subdistricts is in better condition as a result of the reconstruction process or because these areas had better infrastructure initially. The table demonstrates

TABLE 10.5 Condition of Electricity and Water Connections in Community Health Posts

percent

Facility connections	Tsunami-affected subdistricts	Unaffected subdistricts
Electricity	93	80
Piped water	83	67
Interior water source	91	69
Private toilet with septic tank	78	68
Running waste water system	72	72

Source: Compiled by the authors.
Note: The subdistricts have been grouped according to whether they were directly affected (54 community health posts) or relatively unaffected (75 health posts) by the tsunami.

some of the shortcomings when predisaster baseline information is absent in postdisaster research.

The tables included in this chapter are illustrative. They suggest the types of analyses the STAR data make possible. Clearly, these data will support unparalleled analyses of the immediate and longer-term effects of the tsunami on the people of Indonesia that will inform the design of policies intended to mitigate the impact of a major disaster. These analyses include linking household and individual service utilization patterns and service-related outcomes to community and facility data to measure the lingering effects of disaster on service availability and the efficacy of subsequent reconstruction aid.

Conclusion

This brief snapshot of the service delivery environment in post-tsunami Aceh Province highlights the potential uses of disaster research data in policy making and disaster recovery. There is a clear application of such data in reconstruction and planning. The data help identify gaps in the service delivery environment and anticipate some of the consequences of behavioral responses to disaster. An example of these responses is the movement of people and households from disaster areas to surrounding unaffected areas. Another example is the use of health and education facilities outside the disaster area. Reconstruction aid that does not account for the increased demand in areas neighboring a disaster area may not be entirely effective.

The unique nature of the study, which includes a predisaster baseline of households that is representative of the population before the tsunami, is difficult to replicate in other disaster settings. However, no such baseline was available for the community or facility part of the study. The design lessons are therefore applicable in a wide variety of postdisaster settings in which facility-level data are collected. Sampling the households that remain in a disaster area and tracking the households displaced by the disaster are critical to the proper assessment of the full impact of a disaster on the service provision environment. In addition, any postdisaster study should include contrasting neighboring areas that may be experiencing spillover effects. If a baseline is lacking, the degraded service environment may be assessed through contemporaneous and retrospective information collected among households, communities, and facilities. However, a retrospective study must be carefully planned if it is to provide a meaningful retrospective baseline for comparison; otherwise, it may suffer pitfalls such as the one highlighted by the difficulties encountered in interpreting the results shown in table 10.5.

Following a disaster, policy makers are confronted by the choice of rebuilding what has been ruined or seeking new ways of accomplishing the tasks. The appropriate choice is governed by the specific location and sector. A matched household and facility survey provides crucial information on the demand for health and education services and the supply of such services that is essential in selecting a reconstruction strategy. Analyses of the type carried out in studies such as STAR that trace key outcomes of a disaster among a population over a long period of time and that interact with facility and community measures of service provision will be useful in meeting the unfortunate, but certain, future need for postdisaster aid and reconstruction planning in a variety of settings.

References

Bappenas (National Development Planning Agency) and Consultative Group on Indonesia. 2005. *Indonesia: Preliminary Damage and Loss Assessment, the December 26, 2004 Natural Disaster.* Technical report, document 16324. Jakarta: Consultative Group on Indonesia and National Development Planning Agency.

BBC (British Broadcasting Corporation). 2005. "Overview: Aceh after the Tsunami." *BBC News* (February 18), British Broadcasting Corporation. http://news.bbc.co.uk/go/pr/fr/-/2/asia-pacific/4274747.stm.

Black, Richard. 2005. "Navy Releases Tsunami Images." *BBC News* (February 9), British Broadcasting Corporation. http://news.bbc.co.uk/2/hi/science/nature/4247409.stm.

Doocy, Shannon, Yuri Gorokhovich, Gilbert Burnham, Deborah Balk, and Courtland Robinson. 2007. "Tsunami Mortality Estimates and Vulnerability Mapping in Aceh, Indonesia." *American Journal of Public Health* 97 (Supplement 1): S146–51.

Frankenberg, Elizabeth, Jed Friedman, Thomas Gillespie, Nicholas Ingwersen, Robert Pynoos, Iip Rifai, Bondan Sikoki, Cecep Sumantri, Wayan Suriastini, and Duncan Thomas. 2007. "Mental Health in Sumatra after the Tsunami." Unpublished working paper, World Bank, Washington, DC.

Gillespie, Thomas, Jasmine Chu, Elizabeth Frankenberg, and Duncan Thomas. 2007. "Assessment and Prediction of Natural Hazards from Satellite Imagery." Unpublished working paper, World Bank, Washington, DC.

Kerr, Richard A. 2005. "Model Shows Islands Muted Tsunami after Latest Indonesian Quake." *Science* 308 (5720): 341.

Lay, Thorne, Hiroo Kanamori, Charles Ammon, Meredith Nettles, Steven Ward, Richard Aster, Susan Beck, Susan Bilek, Michael Brudzinski, Rhett Butler, Heather DeShon, Goran Ekstrom, Kenji Satake, and Stuart Sipkin. 2005. "The Great Sumatra-Andaman Earthquake of 26 December 2004." *Science* 308 (5725): 1127–33.

Marris, Emma. 2005. "Inadequate Warning System Left Asia at the Mercy of Tsunami." *Nature* 433 (7021): 3–5.

Ramakrishnan, D., S. K. Ghosh, V. K. M. Raja, R. Vinu Chandran, and A. Jeyram. 2005. "Trails of the Killer Tsunami: A Preliminary Assessment Using Satellite Remote Sensing Techniques." *Current Science* 88 (5): 709–11.

WHO (World Health Organization). 2005. "Epidemic-Prone Disease Surveillance and Response after the Tsunami in Aceh Province, Indonesia." *Weekly Epidemiological Record* 80 (18): 160–64.

Zipperer, Melanie. 2005. "Post-Tsunami Banda Aceh: On the Road to Recovery." *Lancet Infectious Diseases* 5 (3): 134.

11

Ukraine School Survey

Design Challenges, Poverty Links, and Evaluation Opportunities

Olena Bekh, Edmundo Murrugarra, Volodymir Paniotto, Tatyana Petrenko, and Volodymir Sarioglo

This chapter describes the motivations and the implementation process involved in the Ukraine Social Facility Survey of Public Educational Institutions in General Education (hereafter, the school survey), which was conducted in late 2005. The school survey is the first and only such survey designed to be representative nationally and at the oblast (province) level in Ukraine. It was designed in the context of the analytical activities developed under the Programmatic Ukraine Living Standards Exercise, which explored poverty, labor markets, and oblast issues (see World Bank 2005a, 2006a). Given the broad coverage of the education system in

This chapter has been produced through the Programmatic Ukraine Living Standards Exercise with financial support from the World Bank–Belgian Trust Fund Budget for Poverty and Social Impact Analysis. The authors wish to acknowledge the fruitful discussions with the team responsible for the Trends in International Mathematics and Science Study pilot exercise during the design and implementation of the survey that is the subject of this chapter. The authors also wish to thank the Ministry of Education and Science of Ukraine for facilitating the survey fieldwork, as well as all participating school principals and teachers. Special thanks for advice and guidance go to Ana M. Jeria, manager of the Equal Access to Quality Education in Ukraine Project. The authors are grateful to the State Statistics Committee of Ukraine for its generous support in their use of its Household Living Conditions Survey.

Ukraine, the survey was meant to assess the quality of education service delivery. During the design and testing process, the survey accommodated two other possible uses. First, the design may accommodate analyses of decentralization, which is particularly important given the extreme level of fiscal delegation of expenditures in the country. Since 1999, most public expenditures (schools included) have been channeled through more than 600 local administrations rather than through the Ministry of Education and Science. Second, the survey was designed to take advantage of the Equal Access to Quality Education in Ukraine Project—a national education project funded by the World Bank—and, hence, sought to exploit possible synergies with this project. Because of this link, the survey design and the survey instrument became critical elements in the evaluation activities of the project.

The next section discusses the motivations behind the school survey. The subsequent section describes the challenges in designing the survey. The penultimate section examines the survey instrument. The final section highlights the complementarities with other efforts in education and the potential use of the survey in evaluation, including the pilot testing of instruments of student assessment.

The Education System and the Survey Objectives

The structure of the education system in Ukraine includes preschool, elementary (primary), lower-secondary, upper-secondary, and tertiary education. General secondary education consists of three distinct levels: four years of elementary or primary school, five years of lower-secondary school, and three years of upper-secondary school (see http://education.gov.ua/pls/edu/docs/common/secondaryeduc_eng.html). A range of vocational and training institutions is also available to lower-secondary and upper-secondary graduates. School coverage is nearly universal in most parts of Ukraine, and the country has exhibited rapidly rising enrollments in tertiary education. Analyses of household data have shown, however, that there are large disparities in enrollments across oblasts, particularly between large cities and the rest of the country. The gap in enrollment rates has been observed mainly in preschool and tertiary education, while the coverage in general secondary education is nearly universal (World Bank 2006a).

The school survey was designed to capture the characteristics of primary and secondary schools (that is, the general secondary level). During the first part of the country's transition from central planning to the market from 1989 to 1999, the overall enrollment of children 7 to 15 years of age fell from 92.8 percent to 89.9 percent, but then began to increase to almost universal levels (Darvas 2002). In 1999, compulsory general secondary education was extended from 10 to 11 years. A 2000 law raised the number of mandatory school years to 12. While most secondary-school-age children attend regular general education schools, the number of which remained fairly stable in 1990–2000, the range of new alternative options (for example, gymnasiums and lyceums) has been expanding since the early 1990s (see Razumkov Center 2002). Almost all such elite schools are located in urban areas, while about 70 percent of general secondary schools are rural (World Bank 2005b).

Government expenditures on education are sizable (about 6 percent of gross domestic product), but most of these expenditures are exhausted on salaries and utility costs. Ukraine has a student–teacher ratio close to 11 to 1 in primary and secondary education combined because of a severe decline in the total fertility rate (close to 1.1) and a mostly unchanged teaching force. The reduction in the student population and the lack of adjustment in the size of the teaching force and in educational facilities have resulted in a high cost per student. The increasing cost of energy (gas for heating and electricity) has reduced even more the share of other expenditures such as teaching materials, equipment, and training.

The school survey was aimed at systematically documenting differences in the quality of education because of the broad coverage of the education system in Ukraine. As part of a poverty assessment, the differences in the quality of education were examined as a way to measure inequality in household well-being. Given the drastic changes in the education system, the survey had to address numerous issues, from the quality of physical infrastructure to school management and the role of the private sector (households) in schools. Moreover, the survey was to act as a baseline for the Equal Access to Quality Education in Ukraine Project, which would emphasize quality issues in education. The need to document service quality and provide a national picture was accommodated through an appropriate sample and instrument design.

Designing a School Survey: What Are We Looking For?

A key issue in any school survey is the identification of the main objective of the exercise. In the case of Ukraine, the main objective was to capture the quality of the education services received by the student population.

The explicit reference to the student population is critical since it anchors the survey on information gathered on students (and households) and imposes conditions on the weighting used in the sample of schools from various locations to obtain a national picture of the services received by students. The need to capture the quality of the education services being provided to the population was driven by the parallel program of analysis in the Programmatic Ukraine Living Standards Exercise (World Bank 2005a, 2006a).

Anchoring the School Survey

The Ukraine school survey team used the nationally representative Household Living Conditions Survey to anchor the school sample. The living conditions survey is carried out every year. It collects detailed information on household income and expenditures and selected information on housing conditions. However, little information is collected on other topics, including educational status. This household budget survey is representative of a standard model survey in the former Soviet republics. It emphasizes the income and expenditures of households and individuals and assigns much less attention to consumption and other nonincome dimensions of well-being.

Because the school survey thus became part of a broader exercise assessing living conditions, the challenge was to design a sample of schools that would cover the areas also included in the household survey. This way, one may examine the quality of education services through the school survey and compare this information across other living standard measures from the household survey such as consumption and labor market indicators. In principle, one should be able to collect information on students in the household survey, including the name of the educational institution, and then field school questionnaires at these facilities. This is the approach of the Indonesia Family Life Survey, for example. In Ukraine, however, because of logistical and regulatory considerations, the household survey was unable to accommodate such detailed questions.

Matching Schools and Households

To combine the data from the school survey and the living conditions survey, a geographical matching procedure was designed to allow interviews to be conducted at schools in the same localities as the households. A first obstacle emerged when regulatory restrictions on the use of household information impeded access to specific data included in the living conditions survey, such as the name of the locality (for example, the name of a village). Because of this concern about confidentiality, the school survey team asked the State Statistics Committee to select a sample of schools that would be located within or in the immediate proximity of the primary sampling units of the living conditions survey. The confidentiality of the matching information about localities and households was, therefore, maintained. (Additional efforts to strengthen statistical capacity in Ukraine include improving public access to survey data and making some information, including locality names, available to the general user.)

Because of the limitations on identifying localities in the living conditions survey, the team also asked the State Statistics Committee to include welfare indicators on the selected primary sampling units, such as per capita incomes and expenditures. The Ukraine poverty assessment (World Bank 2005a) had created a consumption aggregate according to World Bank best practice, and it found a strong correlation between this indicator and per capita expenditure. Because the selection of schools was thus associated with household welfare information, an association between poverty and the quality of service delivery was sure to emerge. One weakness of this approach is that a single primary sampling unit, especially in urban areas, may contain households at different socioeconomic levels. Moreover, in large cities, households may decide to send their children to more distant schools, thereby loosening the link between school quality and estimated neighborhood welfare (per capita expenditure in the primary sampling unit). One way to solve this problem would be to collect information on schools also at the household level so as to match households and schools. This strategy, however, was not pursued because of time and resource constraints. In any case, the most important gaps in the quality of service delivery are the gaps between large cities, small towns, and rural areas.

Other Survey Requirements

There were several additional requirements in the selection of schools for the sample. First, schools were to be selected from the official roster of public education institutions issued by the Ministry of Education and Science. About 98 percent of students in Ukraine attend public schools. Second, the resulting school sample was to provide a representative picture of the education services available to the student population; the school enrollment numbers needed to determine this were taken from the same ministry source. Third, the survey was to be stratified according to types of population settlement (large cities, small towns, and rural areas). About 850 schools were found either within or close to the sampled primary units of the living conditions survey. The same sources were used to generate the sample weights (see annex 11.1 for a detailed technical discussion of the methods used).

Timing of the Survey

If the aim of a facility survey is to reflect the quality of particular services, the timing of the fieldwork is critical because external conditions may affect the way the services are delivered, and this must be taken into account. In Ukraine, for instance, winter is an especially harsh season that tests the school infrastructure. In contrast, September is the beginning of the school year and the end of whatever renovation efforts have been implemented during the summer. The school survey was fielded during November and December 2005. It thus captured the situation at the beginning of the cold season, but not the situation during the extreme cold weather of January. Ideally, a survey to measure the quality of services in a region or country with large variations in weather (or in budgets or other factors) should consider surveying facilities at different times of the year to identify the way schools cope with the variations. However, because of budget constraints, this survey visited facilities only once.

The final school sample covered 417 schools. Rural schools were relatively overrepresented. The final weights in the analysis, however, accounted for this oversampling of rural schools so as to match the distribution of the student population.

The School Survey Instrument

It was possible to collect information quickly about the coverage of education services by fielding specific education modules along with the living conditions survey, but these household surveys do not gather accurate school-specific information. The preparatory work suggested the need to obtain systematic evidence about the quality of education services and variations in quality and coverage across oblasts. The characteristics of the education system and interviews with teachers and other education experts corroborated some of the concerns about the quality of service delivery that the survey was meant to examine. Because quality is a multidimensional concept, the survey addressed a range of school characteristics that reflect quality (such as quality of infrastructure) or that affect quality outcomes (such as school management).

The Ukraine school survey was designed to provide information about the characteristics of the service delivery process, including physical infrastructure, the teaching force, equipment and materials, and management. The content of the survey questionnaire was the result of a process that involved education experts from Ukraine and the World Bank, as well as survey specialists. The survey was created in both Ukrainian and Russian to accommodate the pilot stage in areas where these languages are spoken. (There are numerous speakers of each language in the country.) Pilot questionnaires in both languages were tested in schools in the large cities of Kyiv and Zhytomyr, in the town of Berezan, and in villages in Zhytomyr Oblast between June 23 and July 4, 2005.

The survey instrument was accompanied by an interviewer's journal, which allowed interviewers to record the locations, dates, and number of interviews conducted and explain the reasons some interviews were not conducted. Also used were a set of flash cards in two languages to help respondents answer the questions in the instrument; an interviewer's manual, which covered specific features of the sample and the questionnaire; an interviewer's routing sheet for adding information about the locations of interviews and other interviewer remarks; and a control questionnaire, which was an additional instrument needed to perform internal survey controls. The internal controls included phone calls to verify that an interview had taken place and the collection of information on survey selection quality.

The following areas were covered in the instrument:

- *Physical infrastructure.* In line with the experience of other facility surveys (the Indonesia Family Life Survey, the Quantitative Service Delivery Surveys, and the Demographic and Health Surveys), the Ukraine survey focused on issues relevant to education services, including the quality and age of buildings, the quality of certain infrastructure elements and other service elements (for example, bathrooms), and the operation and reliability of utilities (gas and electricity). The survey captured only gross measures of utility access such as the existence of utility provision or reported disconnections. Detailed measures of energy and other utility services would require more detailed questions in the survey instrument. Pilot tests of such questions resulted in little gain in information, although the questions might be more significant in other contexts (see Lampietti, Banerjee, and Branczik 2007). Simpler questions on basic services (water and electricity) show little variation across schools. As Lampietti, Banerjee, and Branczik (2007) point out, the quality of services might be more readily measured using indicators of service reliability and actual payments relative to the costs and billings. Variations in these measures were reportedly more acute in the early transition years; they did not show up in the pilot stage.

- *Teaching force.* The teaching force was assessed according to grade, gender, type of training, and seniority; the teaching force has been aging rapidly because of the small inflow of new teachers (World Bank 2005c). One specific concern in the education system has been the seeming overstaffing in schools. The need for information in this area was addressed by asking questions about appointments of full- and part-time teachers according to grade and type of school. The team spent significant time refining the instrument on teachers to capture the details of the teaching force without overburdening respondents, including principals.

- *Equipment and materials.* One of the major issues in a system in which budgets are exhausted on salaries and utilities is the lack of updated teaching aids. Questions on the coverage and age of textbooks, the availability of information technologies, and other, similar issues were included in the survey.

- *Management.* The budgeting process has been altered in Ukraine, and local schools are now funded by local administrations. The relevant budget allocations are disbursed by the Ministry of Finance to each of the 684 local administrations, which are then responsible for distributing the allocations across sectors and rayons (districts). The allocation guidelines are precise and leave little room for discretion, and case studies have shown that, indeed, the allocations have not been significantly affected (World Bank 2006b). Any marginal effect on school quality may thus be expected to arise from private funding sources such as household contributions and business donations. The survey collected information on specific contributions from households and local organizations, as well as decision-making processes in staffing, wages, and renovations.

The questions on management followed some of the ideas used in the school component of the Trends in International Mathematics and Science Study (TIMSS) conducted by the International Association for the Evaluation of Educational Achievement. This study includes the collection of information on key decisions related to schools and the delivery of education and describes the role of various institutions formally or informally associated in the decision-making process. Key decisions might have a direct financial impact, through expenditures on staffing or renovation, for example, but may also affect curricula, extracurricular activities, and the role of parent-teacher associations in a school. The players in school decisions range from school boards to local governments and central government authorities (at the ministerial level, for instance) and may include local business groups, parents, and political organizations. In Ukraine, the preliminary discussion with a consultative group of education experts advising the school survey team and the experience of the pilot stage were essential in refining the instrument and identifying core areas where variations in the data might be found.

Meanwhile, Ukraine has joined the TIMSS effort. The exercise is to test school children in grades 4 and 8 on mathematics and science questions during 2007. The results may be compared with the results in other countries. (See Mullis et al. 2004 for a detailed description of the survey and results from previous exercises in 1995, 1999, and 2003.) A joint initiative by the school survey team and the TIMSS pilot team in Ukraine generated a common sampling frame for both survey activities. This step may be attributed to the consultative group of education experts, which included the director responsible for testing the TIMSS study instrument. Because the TIMSS effort was being prepared at the time, the group sought advice on their own school survey sampling and instrument pilot exercises. Because of the pilot nature of the current TIMSS effort in Ukraine, it covers only 120 schools in six oblasts, compared with the broader coverage of the school survey. Nonetheless, the joint discussions facilitated the enhancement of the TIMSS sampling frame, turning it into a subsample of the school survey. Thus, the test scores may still be useful as a baseline in the six oblasts once proper sampling weights have been calculated.

Uses for the School Survey

The Ukraine school survey fills several needs. First and foremost, it provides detailed information about the quality of the schools that children are attending and the associated measures of well-being such as income or consumption from household surveys. The preliminary results of the school survey are discussed in the poverty assessment volume on the social dimensions of well-being (World Bank 2006a). Since the final report on the survey was released (KIIS and World Bank 2006), other important findings based on the survey have emerged, including the fact that school buildings in large cities are more likely to have leaky water pipes (43 percent) relative to schools in rural areas (27 percent). In contrast, the use of wood or coal for heating is more significant in rural schools (50 percent) relative to schools in large cities (only 1.2 percent). Schools in rural areas are likely to have roofs composed of asbestos slates (81 percent relative to 32 percent in large cities). There may also be differences among oblasts in these areas. These findings suggest the existence of health and environmental problems, particularly since children spend so many hours in class. The policy agenda ought to include these issues.

Second, because the focus of the recently implemented Equal Access to Quality Education in Ukraine Project is enhancing the quality of education, especially in rural areas, the school survey may act as a baseline for measuring improvements in education quality in large cities, towns, and villages (see World Bank 2005b). More than 25 percent of the students in rural areas do not have access to computers, for example, compared with only 5 percent in small towns. Rural schools are more likely to rely on multigrade classes (18 percent), and school principals also tend to be younger and less experienced in rural areas. Measures aimed at improving the availability of equipment (such as computers) may need to be coupled with teacher and management retraining to enhance the complementarity of inputs. A detailed analysis of the school survey should provide the basis for allocating resources across alternative inputs.

The survey evidence on school staff, equipment, funding patterns, and the distribution across oblasts of educational establishments might be used to support analyses of public education expenditures. In a context of fiscal decentralization such as in Ukraine, comparisons across oblasts and types of population settlement are required to identify inequitable patterns. The survey may help generate information on these patterns given the detailed data on human and physical resources. It may also shed light on the role of households and other private sector actors in funding public education services.

The experience summarized in this chapter suggests at least three main lessons about facility surveys and the delivery of services. First, a concerted effort involving a range of players is important. Agreement among those players might be encouraged through the formation of consultative or advisory teams. A strategy that is inclusive among participants will create opportunities to share resources and expertise, such as in the TIMSS case.

Clearly, this requires more time dedicated to planning, which may not always be available.

A second lesson is that substantial attention must be paid to the features of the local environment. The severity of winter, the timing of specific holidays, and local budget cycles may have significant distorting effects on the accuracy of the overall picture one is trying to obtain. Adequate responses by a survey team and the team's ability to accommodate information on these distorting effects are crucial in the implementation of a survey and, indeed, the design of a survey questionnaire.

The third lesson revolves around the restrictive data environment. This is probably the most significant lesson in the case of Ukraine. The limits on access to certain types of data, such as detailed information on the locations of households and the names of individuals, should not be allowed to become an insurmountable hurdle in the design of a good facility survey. Thus, the team in Ukraine exploited other features of the resources available on schools and households so as to create links between welfare and service quality. The long-term objective of producing relevant information on localities was not dropped, but assigned to other ongoing activities such as World Bank projects to strengthen statistical capacity in the country (see World Bank 2004).

ANNEX 11.1

PRINCIPLES OF SAMPLE DESIGN

A stratified multistage probability sample of general educational institutions in all oblasts of Ukraine was constructed for the survey. For this purpose, a subsample of primary sampling units in every oblast was gathered from the sample in the Household Living Conditions Survey (see SSC 2005a). Educational institutions located in or nearby sampled primary units were surveyed.

The steps in the procedure for constructing the territorial sampling units were as follows (see SSC 2005b and figure 11A.1: (a) the exclu-

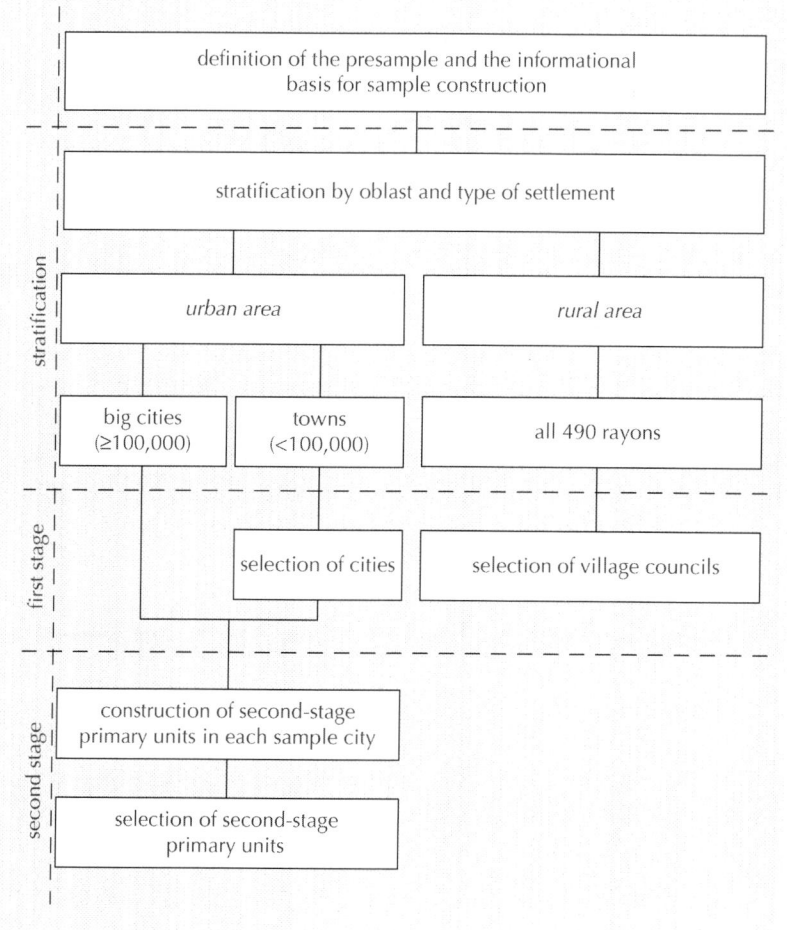

FIGURE 11A.1 Formation of the Territorial Sample for the Household Living Conditions Survey, 2004–08

Source: Sarioglo 2005.
Note: The dashed lines indicate the separate steps in the sampling strategy.

sion of territories that it is not possible to survey, including rural settlements (village councils) located in areas closed or restricted because of radiation contamination resulting from the accident at Chernobyl; likewise, the populations of these areas were excluded from the relevant population counts; (b) the stratification of the general totals; (c) the selection of first-stage sampling units; and (d) the selection of second-stage sampling units.

In the rural area strata, councils were ordered by geographical proximity according to the geographical serpentine principle. The number of village councils selected in each rayon was defined mainly by the area of the rayon, and the number of environmental and climatic zones in the rayon was taken into account as well.

Stratification is carried out so that the sample will adequately reflect the main features of the country's administrative and territorial divisions and guarantee the selection of households that reflect the different characteristics of all households. Thus, in each oblast, the following strata were defined: city councils with a population of 100,000 or more, town and rural councils with a population of less than 100,000, and administrative rayons in rural areas; the urban populations of rayons were excluded from the rural strata.

Selection of First- and Second-Stage Sampling Units

At this point in the sample design, the selection of city and village councils in urban areas and of village councils in rural areas was carried out. A population-size threshold (a self-representation threshold) was calculated to determine self-representative city councils. The threshold of self-representation was equal to 79,241 people. This finding means that city councils with populations of this size or larger were necessarily included in the sample (with probability equal to 1). Taking into account this self-representation threshold, there were no self-representative village councils.

For the councils that are not self-representative, one council was selected to stand in for each group of such councils that accounted for a total population sufficient not to fall below the self-representation threshold.

The selection of city and village councils that are not self-representative was carried out in each strata separately. In the urban area strata, a list of councils was established in descending order according to population. The number of councils that had to be selected in each stratum was obtained by taking the total population of all councils that were not self-representative in the stratum and dividing this by the self-representation threshold.

At this stage, a sample of second-stage territorial units was established for each city or village council sampled in urban areas. Selection was carried out using the same scheme described above for first-stage territorial units in urban areas. All second-stage sampling units in each selected city or village council were ordered according to the geographical serpentine principle.

The self-representation threshold for second-stage units was established separately for each city or village council by taking into account the size of the second-stage primary sampling unit relative to the size of the council.

The Primary Sampling Units for the Survey of General Educational Institutions

The number of educational institutions that was to be surveyed was set at 450. The number of rural and urban schools was determined based on available statistics on the distribution of schools and students by settlement type (see SSC 2005c). Thus, for example, 32 percent of regular general educational institutions, accounting for 65 percent of all students, are located in urban areas, while 68 percent of all institutions, accounting for 35 percent of all students, are located in rural areas. The majority of schools are, therefore, located in rural areas, but the majority of students are concentrated in urban areas. The general educational institutions of the new type (such as gymnasiums and lyceums; see elsewhere above) account for about 11 percent of all educational institutions and about 13 percent of all students. These institutions are located mainly in urban areas.

Given these numbers, it was decided to distribute the sample of institutions according to an intermediate approach, whereby 60 percent were in urban areas, and 40 percent were in rural areas. This distribution is actually closer to the distribution of students.

It was determined that, in each territorial sampling unit, one educational establishment would be surveyed, along with an additional replacement establishment.

The selection of territorial sampling units for the survey of educational institutions was carried out based on a list of second-stage primary sampling units in urban areas and a list of first-stage primary sampling units in rural areas. The primary sampling units on the lists were ordered according to the principles of sample construction used in the Household Living Conditions Survey. The primary sampling units were selected with probability proportional to the number of school-age children living in the households that were sampled for that survey in 2005. The territorial distribution of the educational institutions selected for the research is presented in table 11A.1 by oblast and type of settlement area.

TABLE 11A.1 Distribution of Sampled Institutions, by Oblast and Type of Settlement

Oblast	Urban settlements	Rural settlements	Total
Cherkaska	7	6	12
Chernigivska	7	6	10
Chernivetska	6	7	12
Autonomous Republic of Crimea	8	8	15
Dnipropetrovska	24	6	27
Donetsk	28	5	31
Ivano-Frankivska	6	9	13
Kharkivska	19	7	24
Khersonska	7	7	11
Khmelnytska	8	7	15
Kirovohradska	7	6	12
Kyiv City	25	—	21
Kyivska	5	9	14
Luganska	15	5	19
Lvivska	14	17	24
Mykolaivska	7	7	13
Odeska	15	8	16
Poltavska	9	10	17
Rivnenska	7	9	15
Sevastopol City	3	0	3
Sumska	5	3	8
Ternopilska	6	8	7
Vinnytska	8	8	15
Volynska	8	9	15
Zakarpatska	5	7	4
Zaporizka	13	7	19
Zhytomyrska	7	9	11
Total	279	190	469

Source: Sarioglo 2005.
Note: — = not available.
The *total* column has a combined number of replacement institutions that is not the same number of the replacement institutions in urban and rural areas. A replacement institution is the institution that would be surveyed in case the sampled one refuses or is not available.

To identify the educational institutions located in or nearby sampled primary units, the team examined the territory in which selected sampling units are located. All institutions located within the territory of a sampling unit were included on the list and organized according to their proximity in the unit. In urban settlements, there might be as many as three institutions per sampling unit (see table 11A.1). A total of 604 educational institutions in the 279 urban sampling units was included on the list. In rural areas, only one establishment per sampling unit was usually included on the list. A total of 209 institutions in the 190 rural sampling units was included on the list. One establishment from each sampling unit was selected for the research. Thus, the probability that a particular establishment would be sampled was equal to the general probability that a specific sampling unit would be selected.

Generation of Sample Weights

To generalize the survey results for the total population, a system of statistical weights was constructed with the main aim of taking into account: (a) the general probability of the selection of a particular educational institution and (b) the correlation of the survey results with existing data from other sources, especially statistical data.

The final weight of an educational establishment i was calculated by multiplying the base weight of the educational establishment and a weight coefficient (the reweighting coefficient) according to the following equation:

$$w_i = w_{Bi} \cdot k, \qquad (11A.1)$$

where w_i is the final weight of the educational establishment, w_{Bi} is the base weight of the educational establishment, and k is the weight coefficient. In the probability sample, every educational establishment had a general probability p_i of being selected. Thus, this educational establishment represented $1/p_i$ of all educational institutions. In making inferences about the total population, one must therefore take the establishment into account $1/p_i$ times. The value $1/p_i$ is the base weight of the educational establishment in generalizing the survey results in terms of the universe of establishments so that:

$$w_{Bi} = 1/p_i. \qquad (11A.2)$$

The sample design realized for the survey stipulated that the following components be included in the process of constructing the base weights: (1) P_{1i}, the probability of the inclusion of the first-stage primary sampling units in the living conditions survey (city and village councils); (2) P_{2i}, the probability of the inclusion of second-stage sampling units in urban areas; and (3) P_{3i}, the probability of the selection of primary sampling units in subsamples. The inverse of the number resulting from the multiplication of these probabilities is the base weight of educational establishment i.

Thus, in the organization of the survey sample on the supply of educational materials and other technical inputs for general educational institutions, the value of p_i was defined by the following equation:

$$p_i = \begin{cases} P_{1i} \cdot P_{2i} \cdot P_{3i} & \text{in urban settlements} \\ P_{1i} \cdot P_{3i} & \text{in rural settlements} \end{cases} \quad (11A.3)$$

The probability of the selection of urban and rural settlements, P_{1i}, was determined for each oblast separately according to the following equation:

$$P_{1i} = a \cdot \frac{M_i}{M}, \quad (11A.4)$$

where a is the number of urban settlements or village councils that are being selected in the oblast, M_i is the size of the primary territorial sampling unit where the educational establishment i is located (the population of the urban settlement or the number of households in the village council), and M is the population of the urban settlements in the oblast or the number of total households in rural areas in the oblast.

In the living conditions survey sample, urban settlements with a population slightly greater than 79,000 were self-representative. Thus, for these settlements, $P_{1i} = 1$.

P_{2i}, the probability of the selection of a second-stage primary sampling unit in an urban settlement, was calculated for each selected settlement according to the following equation (analogous to equation 11A.4):

$$P_{2i} = b \cdot \frac{Q_i}{Q}, \quad (11A.5)$$

where b is the number of primary sampling units that is being selected in the settlement, Q_i is the population of the primary sampling unit in which educational establishment i is located, and Q is the population of the urban settlement.

The selection of primary sampling units for the survey among educational institutions was carried out on the basis of the general lists for urban and rural areas separately. The probability of selection, P_{3i}, was determined according to the following equation:

$$P_{3i} = c \cdot \frac{L_i}{L}, \qquad (11A.6)$$

where c is the number of primary sampling units that are being selected, L_i is the number of school-age children who live in the households sampled in the living conditions survey in 2005 in each primary sampling unit, and L is the total number of school-age children living in the households sampled in the living conditions survey in 2005 in all primary sampling units.

To adjust the base weights so as to increase the representativeness of the survey results, a system of cells was constructed according to the following classification variables: economic region (eight discrete numbers; see table 11A.2 for the regions), type of educational establishment (two discrete numbers: regular educational institutions or educational institutions of the new type), and type of settlement (two discrete numbers: urban area or rural area). According to this indicator, there was no variation in the educational institutions of the new type. N_q, the number of students in any cell within the total, was determined using social statistics for the 2005/06 school year.

k_q, the coefficient for the adjustment of the base weights, was calculated for each cell q according to the following equation:

TABLE 11A.2 Composition of the Economic Regions

Economic region	Oblast
East	Kharkivska, Poltavska, Sumska
Donetsk	Donetsk, Luganska
Dniprovskyi	Dnipropetrovska, Kirovohradska, Zaporizka
Black Sea	Autonomous Republic of Crimea, Khersonska, Mykolaivska, Odeska, Sevastopol City
Podillia	Khmelnytska, Ternopilska, Vinnytska
Central	Cherkaska, Kyiv City, Kyivska
Carpathian	Chernivetska, Ivano-Frankivska, Lvivska, Zakarpatska
Polissia	Chernigivska, Rivnenska, Volynska, Zhytomyrska

Source: SSC 2005c.

$$k_q = \frac{N_q}{\sum_{i=1}^{L_q} w_{Bi} \cdot \lambda_{qi}},$$ (11A.7)

where $\lambda_{qi} = \begin{cases} 1, & \text{if } i \in X_q \\ 0, & \text{if } i \notin X_q \end{cases}$, X_q is a set of surveyed students in the cell q,

and N_q is the set of students in cell q according to the external data.

w_i, the final statistical weight of educational establishment i, is calculated according to the following equation:

$$w_i = w_{Bi} \cdot k_q \text{ where } i \in L_q.$$ (11A.8)

To facilitate a more accurate analysis of the survey results, two systems of final weights were calculated: (a) weights that would ensure the correspondence between the survey results and the available external data on the number of institutions and (b) weights that would ensure the correspondence between the survey results and the available external data on the number of students. These weights were determined according to the features of the overall samples (see elsewhere above), the peculiarities of the construction of the subsample of establishments in the territorial sampling units, and the deviation between the actual number of institutions surveyed according to settlement type and a theoretical number. To adjust the system of base weights, the analysis used statistics on the number, location, and structure of the various types of institutions and the number of students as of the beginning of the 2005/06 school year (see SSC 2006).

References

Darvas, Peter. 2002. "Ukraine: Education Reform Policy Note." Policy Note, Human Development Sector Unit, Europe and Central Asia Region, World Bank, Washington, DC.

KIIS (Kiev International Institute of Sociology) and World Bank. 2006. "Ukraine Social Facility Survey of Public Educational Institutions of General Education: Analytical Report." Unpublished report, Kiev International Institute of Sociology and World Bank, Kyiv.

Lampietti, Julian A., Sudeshna Ghosh Banerjee, and Amelia Branczik. 2007. *People and Power: Electricity Sector Reforms and the Poor in Europe and Central Asia.* Directions in Development Series (Energy and Mining). Washington, DC: World Bank.

Mullis, Ina V. S., Michael O. Martin, Eugenio J. Gonzalez, and Steven J. Chrostowski. 2004. *TIMSS 2003 International Mathematics Report: Findings From IEA's Trends in International Mathematics and Science Study at the Fourth and Eighth Grades.* Chestnut

Hill, MA: International Association for the Evaluation of Educational Achievement, TIMSS & PIRLS International Study Center, Lynch School of Education, Boston College.

Razumkov Center (Ukrainian Center for Economic and Political Studies Named after Olexander Razumkov). 2002. "The System of Education in Ukraine: The State and Prospects of Development." *National Security and Defence* 4 (28): 2–35.

Sarioglo, Volodymir. 2005. "Sampling Frame Methodology for Surveying Quality Indicators in Facility Surveys." Background Note, World Bank, Kyiv.

SSC (State Statistics Committee of Ukraine). 2005a. *Household Income and Expenditures in Ukraine in 2004: Statistical Compendium.* Kyiv: State Statistics Committee of Ukraine.

———. 2005b. *Economic Activity of the Population of Ukraine 2004: Statistical Compendium.* Kyiv: State Statistics Committee of Ukraine.

———. 2005c. "General Educational Institutions of the Ukraine as of the Beginning of the 2004/05 School Year." Statistical Bulletin, State Statistics Committee of Ukraine, Kyiv.

———. 2006. "General Educational Institutions of Ukraine as of the Beginning of the 2005/06 School Year." Statistical Bulletin, State Statistics Committee of Ukraine, Kyiv.

World Bank. 2004. "Multicountry Statistical Capacity Building Program." Project Appraisal Document, Report 28026-GLB, Development Economics Data Group, World Bank, Washington, DC.

———. 2005a. *Ukraine Poverty Assessment: Poverty and Inequality in a Growing Economy.* Report 34631-UA. Washington, DC: Human Development Sector Unit, Europe and Central Asia Region, World Bank.

———. 2005b. *Equal Access to Quality Education in Ukraine Project.* Project Appraisal Document, Report 32175-UA. Washington, DC: Human Development Sector Unit, Ukraine, Belarus, and Moldova Country Unit, Europe and Central Asia Region, World Bank.

———. 2005c. *Growth, Poverty, and Inequality: Eastern Europe and the Former Soviet Union.* Washington, DC: World Bank.

———. 2006a. "Ukraine Poverty Assessment: Poverty and Inequality in Social Dimensions." Unpublished report, Human Development Sector Unit, Europe and Central Asia Region, World Bank, Washington, DC.

———. 2006b. *Ukraine, Creating Fiscal Space for Growth: A Public Finance Review.* Report 36671-UA. Washington, DC: Poverty Reduction and Economic Management Unit, Europe and Central Asia Region, World Bank.

12

Qualitative Research to Prepare Quantitative Analysis

Absenteeism among Health Workers in Two African Countries

Pieter Serneels, Magnus Lindelow, and Tomas Lievens

Exploratory data analysis has an important role to play in economics. It may be seen as the first stage in social research, followed by the formulation of theory, testing and estimation, and prediction and policy evaluation (see Banerjee et al. 2005). In practice, exploratory analysis in economics is typically quantitative in nature, adhering to the bias of the economics discipline toward quantitative research.[1] This chapter argues that qualitative analysis is an important complementary tool and that such analysis may help define policy and research questions, fine-tune hypotheses generated from theory, and develop appropriate approaches to measurement and empirical analysis.

The focus of this chapter is absenteeism among health workers in developing countries, a topic that is attracting growing attention. Most of the work on this issue in economics has relied on quantitative analysis. The work has been largely exploratory in nature, and, although it has iden-

The work reflected in this chapter has been funded by the World Bank, the Bill & Melinda Gates Foundation, and the Norwegian government. We would like to thank Agnes Soucat for her support throughout this project. We would also like to thank Abigail Barr and Gavin Roberts for useful comments, Danila Serra for excellent research assistance, and Teigist Lemma, Jean Damascene Butera, and Aline Umubyeyi for their help with project implementation.

tified a number of correlates of absenteeism, it has also raised a number of questions of both a methodological nature and a substantive nature. How should absenteeism in the health sector be conceived and modeled in developing countries? What is the relevance of existing theoretical models in the analysis of absenteeism in these countries? What issues arise in measuring absenteeism and its determinants? These questions are the focus of this chapter, which argues that qualitative research may help provide a more complete understanding of absenteeism, including the role of institutional and psychosocial factors that have not been captured in quantitative work. But the chapter also acknowledges and discusses important limitations of qualitative work: such work is not representative in a statistical sense, the results are sensitive to methodological choices, and the work does not provide any quantitative or otherwise precise information on the relative importance of various factors in explaining outcomes.

The chapter is based on qualitative work carried out in Ethiopia and Rwanda. These two countries are among the poorest in the world, with low per capita consumption and poor human development outcomes. Gross domestic product per capita is US$695 in Ethiopia and US$1,160 in Rwanda (in purchasing-power-parity dollars in 2000), and the infant mortality rate is 110 per 1,000 live births in Ethiopia and 118 per 1,000 in Rwanda (see World Bank 2006). High infant mortality, malnutrition, and other health problems are complex and have multiple determinants, but failings of the health system are undoubtedly part of the explanation. In recent years, the human resource challenges facing Africa's health systems have been receiving more attention (see JLI 2004; Hongoro and Normand 2006; WHO 2006). These challenges include overall workforce shortages, geographical imbalances, and an inappropriate skill mix; absenteeism among health professionals is often held up as a powerful example of the way health services fail poor people (World Bank 2003).

The qualitative work has been designed to explore key human resource challenges in Ethiopia and Rwanda, understand the way policies and institutions operate in practice, and show how these policies and institutions are perceived by health professionals and users. In both countries, the work has been undertaken as the first phase of a broader engagement; the qualitative work represents the foundation for subsequent quantitative analysis. Indeed, the qualitative work on which the chapter is based covers many issues, in addition to absenteeism. The broader set of findings of the study are discussed in detail elsewhere (see Lindelow and Serneels 2006).

The chapter is organized as follows. In the next section, we discuss how current economic theory models absenteeism. In the subsequent section, we examine the methodology and the findings of the qualitative preresearch. In the penultimate section, we look at the way the preresearch helps to prepare for the quantitative research, while the final section describes the lessons we have learned.

Understanding Absenteeism from a Theoretical Perspective

The economic study of absenteeism is fairly recent. Allen (1981) was the first to model worker absenteeism from an economics viewpoint. His approach provided a mold for a first generation of models of absenteeism formed within a standard labor-leisure framework of choice, wherein workers choose to be absent from work when the working hours required by employers exceed the number of hours at which workers maximize their utility (see Allen 1981; Brown and Sessions 1996). Absenteeism is then explained as a function of three factors: wages (w), the flexibility of the contracted number of hours (h_c), and the expected cost of detection (C). The last factor may be thought of as the product of the probability of being detected (π) and the penalty if detected (P). The model includes a penalty function, and later extensions include the presence of a sick-leave plan as an explanatory variable (see Winkler 1980).

A second generation of models was inspired by the Shapiro-Stiglitz version of efficiency wages (see Shapiro and Stiglitz 1984). In these models, absenteeism is interpreted as an extreme case of shirking, and the explanation focuses on unemployment. When unemployment is high, workers are expected to work harder because there is an army of unemployed waiting to take their places. One may think of this as the endogenization of the expected cost of detection, whereby the expected cost is determined by the level of unemployment. Absenteeism is then modeled as a function of wages, the unemployment rate, and the expected cost of detection.

In table 12.1, we summarize the explanatory variables that are highlighted by theory and that point to a corresponding empirical equation with absenteeism as the dependent variable.

Parallel to the theoretical literature, there has also been quantitative empirical analysis. Most of the literature in this area has focused on the private sector in rich countries in attempts to test the above model (for example, see Allen 1981; Kenyon and Dawkins 1989; Winkler 1980; Cloud 2000).

TABLE 12.1 Explanatory Factors of Absenteeism from Theory and Empirical Analysis	
Variable	Expected sign of relationship
Wages (w)	−
Contracted working hours (h_c)	+
Expected cost of detection (C)	−
Sick leave (S)	+
Unemployment (U)	−

Source: Compiled by the authors.

Demographic variables such as gender, marital status, and age are usually included to allow for a shift in the budget constraint (for instance, see Leigh 1983; Paringer 1983).

Studies on absenteeism among health professionals in developing countries are more exploratory. They do not rely on theory, but try to establish whether absenteeism is an issue and to identify the correlates. Results from surveys in five countries show that, on average, 35 percent of health workers are absent at any given time; variations among the countries range between 25 percent and 40 percent (Chaudhury et al. 2006). The research also finds that absenteeism is different among distinct occupational groups. Thus, doctors are absent more often. Moreover, better facility conditions tend to improve attendance. Other research on health workers finds even higher absenteeism (45 percent) in rural Rajastan, India, while absenteeism in Bangladesh is highly correlated with the cost of getting to the workplace (see Banerjee, Deaton, and Duflo 2004; Chaudhury and Hammer 2004). Similar studies among teachers in developing countries find lower absence rates and are able to identify more correlates, such as male (+), union membership (+), the literacy rate of the parents of students (−), and school infrastructure (−), as well as illness (+) (see Chaudhury et al. 2006; Das et al. 2005).

Qualitative Preresearch

Method

Although the use of qualitative methods in economics has been limited, there is a strong tradition in both public health and medical anthropology on which the study supporting this chapter may build.[2] Qualitative research covers a wide range of approaches and techniques. One may, for example, distinguish between individual and group processes, among interview, discussion, and participatory approaches, and among structured, semistructured, and unstructured approaches. Each method has advantages and methodological requirements.

This chapter is based on information from focus group discussions carried out among health professionals and users of health services. Focus group discussions are frequently drawn on in public health (Yach 1992). Successful focus group approaches rely on the composition of the group and on group dynamics to stimulate discussion. At relatively low cost and within a short time, focus group discussions may generate a wealth of information on opinions, perceptions, beliefs, and attitudes about a wide range of issues and may also shed light on the systems and processes that underpin outcomes. Focus group discussions have also been successfully used to elucidate sensitive topics, such as corruption, because group dynamics may facilitate openness (Farquhar 1999).

The work in Ethiopia and Rwanda followed a strict methodology to determine the groups, select the participants, carry out the discussions, and record and analyze the data. In each country, eight focus group discussions structured the study in separate sessions with doctors, nurses, health assistants, and users and covered both urban and rural areas. Each group counted eight participants, who were selected to ensure diversity along a number of dimensions.[3] Individual characteristics that are believed to influence occupational choice or performance levels were also represented in a well-balanced manner among the participants in each focus group. In general, a key to the richness of qualitative data is the fact that only a minimum structure is imposed on the process of collection and analysis, thereby permitting the main messages to emerge freely. We adhered to this practice and held semistructured discussions for which the interview scripts served as checklists only. The discussions lasted approximately two hours and were audio recorded, literally transcribed, and translated. During analysis, we also imposed a bare minimum structure, categorizing the data by theme and comparing the quotes across focus groups using matrices.[4]

As shown in table 12.2, a total of 95 health workers and 46 users of health services participated in the discussions. About half the health workers (52 percent) were women, and about three-quarters (76 percent) had children. Fifty-eight percent were working in the public sector, while 23 percent were working in the private for-profit sector, and 19 percent in the private nonprofit sector. Forty-one percent of the users were women, and 87 percent had children.

Participants	Ethiopia	Rwanda	Total (number)	Total (%)
TABLE 12.2 Focus Groups and Focus Group Participants in Ethiopia and Rwanda				
Focus groups	9	9	18	100
Health assistants	2	2	4	22
Nurses and midwives	2	2	4	22
Doctors and specialists	2	2	4	22
Health users	3	3	6	33
Health workers	47	48	95	100
Health assistants	16	16	32	34
Nurses and midwives	15	16	31	33
Doctors and specialists	16	16	32	34
Women	16	16	32	52
Men	15	16	31	48
With children	35	37	72	76
No children	12	11	23	24
Public	21	34	55	58
Private for-profit	11	11	22	23
Nongovernmental organizations	15	3	18	19
Users	22	24	46	100
Women	8	11	19	41
Men	14	13	27	59
With children	16	24	40	87
No children	6	0	6	13

Source: Compiled by the authors.

Findings

Why are Health Workers Absent from Work?

We find strong evidence that absenteeism is a serious problem in Ethiopia and Rwanda. Health workers and users of health services were keen to discuss absenteeism, and the overall picture is remarkably consistent. Four key messages emerge from the data. First, absenteeism occurs primarily in public sector facilities. Second, absenteeism is more likely to be associated with individuals who have second jobs or who perform other activities in the health sector. The link is sometimes direct (some health workers carry out their other activities while at their first jobs) and sometimes indirect (health workers are absent because they are tired after the long hours at two jobs). Third, the causes of absenteeism vary across occupational categories, and the incidence of absenteeism is greater among higher-level health professionals, especially doctors.[5] Fourth, weak accountability in the public sector, whereby repeated absenteeism may be punished only rarely, facilitates absenteeism (see box 12.1).

Absenteeism in Ethiopia and Rwanda: How Far Does the Theoretical Framework Take Us?

Theory suggests four potential reasons for absenteeism (see elsewhere above): low earnings, the number of contracted working hours, a low expected cost of detection (possibly driven by unemployment), and the type of sick-leave policy. What do the findings from Ethiopia and Rwanda suggest about the relevance of this framework for understanding absenteeism in the health sectors of developing countries?

BOX 12.1 Incidence and Nature of Health Worker Absenteeism

"We observe it; we cannot lie about it. Not respecting working hours is a problem that we have gotten used to, and this has created a problem for the patients."   —*HEALTH ASSISTANT IN URBAN ETHIOPIA*

"Office hours are not respected. It started little by little, and now it has become widespread. None of us are innocent in this. This has really affected the patients."   —*HEALTH ASSISTANT IN RURAL ETHIOPIA*

"Absenteeism is the problem in the public sector."
                                                       —*NURSE IN RURAL ETHIOPIA*

"In the private sector, you can only be absent when you die."
                                                       —*NURSE IN URBAN ETHIOPIA*

"All doctors have a second job and take time off from their principal job to do it."   —*DOCTOR IN RURAL RWANDA*

"Today, representatives of the population control the functioning of health centers. If you're absent, even an ordinary citizen can accuse you by saying he has seen you in that place and you were not working."   —*HEALTH ASSISTANT IN URBAN RWANDA*

Most health workers indicate that their earnings are low relative to expectations. Does this also explain absenteeism? Many health workers in the public sector argue that if they earned more, they would not need to have second jobs and would therefore be less likely to be absent from work. Conversely, absenteeism is not an important problem in the non-profit sector, although salaries tend to be similar to those in the public sector. This analysis suggests that salary level is not the only determinant of absenteeism. Indeed, higher earnings are not the only motive for taking up a second job. Because the attributes of their various jobs may be complementary, some health workers prefer to hold a portfolio of jobs. They may wish, for example, to keep their jobs in the public sector to guarantee income stability, access to training and chances for promotion, while their jobs in the private sector increase their earnings and enable them to gain access to modern equipment.

A second factor put forward by theory is the number of contracted working hours required by the employers of health workers. If this is higher than the number of hours at which a worker maximizes his or her utility, the worker is more likely to be absent. The group discussions during the research confirm that the number of contracted working hours plays a role. Health workers in the public sector in Ethiopia and Rwanda point out that, unlike the private sector, the public sector in Ethiopia and Rwanda provides only one type of contract, which is fixed term and full time and thus prohibits health workers from part-time employment. Moreover, in Ethiopia, public sector health workers are not allowed to work in the private sector concurrently (although this occurs in practice). The disparity between contracted hours and preferred hours at prevailing wages is therefore likely to be one factor in explaining absenteeism.

Theory also suggests that low expected costs of detection contribute to absenteeism. The expected cost of detection depends on the monitoring regime and the potential penalties. The group discussions provide clear evidence of substantial problems in both these areas. In the private sector, managerial monitoring is intensive, and there is a system of rewards and sanctions that is used effectively. In the public sector, sanctions are available, but are more limited than those in the private sector. Moreover, they are not accompanied by effective monitoring and are rarely applied. Indeed, as a rule, misconduct remains unpenalized in the public sector. At least in part, this reflects classic agency problems arising from differences between owners and managers, but it also reflects the greater monitoring challenges in the public sector because of the remoteness of some facilities.[6]

Finally, the theoretical framework set out above points to the potential importance of the unemployment rate (through the rate's impact on the expected cost of detection) and sick-leave policy (see box 12.2). Neither of these factors appear important in Ethiopia and Rwanda. Unemployment is low among health workers (it occurs mainly among school leavers), and

BOX 12.2 Health Worker Employment Conditions

Low earnings

"There's no material compensation. That's what's missing; it's really not enough."   —*DOCTOR IN URBAN RWANDA*

"Health workers are pleased with their jobs, but are far from pleased with their salaries."   —*USER IN RURAL RWANDA*

"If our salary were increased, we would work better and, moreover, be extremely happy while at work."   —*HEALTH ASSISTANT IN RURAL RWANDA*

Number of contracted hours

"In the public sector, we work eight hours per day, five days per week."
                                                                —*NURSE IN URBAN RWANDA*

"There is a government regulation to work for eight hours a day."
                                                                —*NURSE IN URBAN ETHIOPIA*

Monitoring, accountability, and incentives

"There's no system of supervision in the public sector."
                                                                —*DOCTOR IN URBAN RWANDA*

"On disciplinary measures . . . ? There is no such thing in the public sector. If someone is not efficient, there is no punishment or feedback, and there is no encouragement for good and efficient health workers."
                                                                —*NURSE IN RURAL ETHIOPIA*

"At the moment, complaints remain hearsay. There needs to be a legal code to deal with such issues and to hold health workers accountable."
                                                                —*USER IN RURAL ETHIOPIA*

(continued)

"Here in the hospital, a nurse may make a professional mistake, but there's no law to punish him."   —*USER IN URBAN RWANDA*

"I have the impression that the system works as follows: only when it really goes badly and when it is absolutely clear that there is a serious problem is something done, such as the person receiving the blame."
                                                          —*DOCTOR IN URBAN RWANDA*

Unemployment

"There has been a great scarcity of health workers and physicians for many years."   —*DOCTOR IN RURAL ETHIOPIA*

"There is no unemployment among medical doctors. On the contrary, there are not enough of them."   —*DOCTOR IN URBAN RWANDA*

the risk of job loss because of misconduct is low in the public sector. We find no evidence that sick-leave policy plays a major role, mainly because social security regulations are relatively underdeveloped in both countries. This is not to say that illness is not a potentially significant reason for absenteeism, as we see in the next section.

New Perspectives on Absenteeism: Explanations Emerging from the Group Discussions

Apart from the above factors, the group discussions point to four additional variables that may explain absenteeism. A first factor concerns the opportunity cost of time spent on the job from which the health worker is absent. In particular, access to a second job emerges from the group discussions as a major determinant of absenteeism. Many of the participants were involved in outside economic activities in one way or another. Some had formal second jobs in clinics or pharmacies; others were engaged in informal health care provision from their homes or from other establishments. Informal health care seems to be widely practiced by nurses and lower-level health workers in Ethiopia, for instance, while doctors tend to be engaged in formal jobs in the private sector. Implicitly, this all indicates that, even if monitoring is weak, health workers may be absent less frequently if they are unable to access second jobs, for example, in rural areas.[7] The discussions also point out that earnings in the second jobs may be different from wages in the first jobs, suggesting that a segmented model of the labor market may be more appropriate than the standard labor-leisure model underlying the classic approach.

A second factor that consistently emerged is the importance of intrinsic motivation, which may be defined as an individual's desire to perform a task for its own sake because of, for instance, professional ethics or norms (see Deci 1975; Bénabou and Tirole 2003). The significance of intrinsic motivation in the health sector in the form of commitment to professional ethics and norms has long been recognized (see Arrow 1963; Le Grand 2003; Frank 2004).[8] The behavior and performance of health professionals may also be shaped by broader social or moral norms and values. Both these dimensions of intrinsic motivation were apparent among the health workers during the group discussions. Participants emphasized the importance of professional and social commitment. They also made clear that norms and values are not fixed features of organizations or individuals. Indeed, there is considerable heterogeneity in intrinsic motivation; some health workers express a strong commitment to helping people in need or to principles of professional duty or responsibility. Participants also made clear that norms and values evolve over time. Thus, the discussions in Ethiopia suggest that norms have eroded over time, while, in Rwanda, norms seem to have become stronger over time. In any case, although intrinsic motivation is unmistakably a determinant of health worker behavior, the impact of norms and values on absenteeism is not immediately apparent. In principle, one would expect more motivated health workers to be absent less often. However, if working conditions in the public sector are such that health workers are unable to perform their jobs effectively, health workers with a strong commitment to help the poor or sick may actually prefer to engage in dual practice. Hence, although motivation is plainly a potentially important factor in absenteeism, its effect on absenteeism remains ambiguous.

A third explanation for absenteeism that was brought up is the issue of job mismatch and limitations in job mobility. Both are especially important in Ethiopia, where health workers whose studies have been funded by the government—the vast majority—are assigned their jobs by lottery. Beginning health workers are also not allowed to take up jobs in the private sector until they have received a release from the public sector, which they may only receive after having served the required amount of years to pay back the government for their studies. Public authorities in Rwanda have sometimes hindered health workers from leaving the public sector. A poor job match has two consequences: it may affect the motivation of health workers, and it may reduce the value of the penalties in cases in which a worker is discovered to be absent (since losing a job that a worker does not like presumably does not have such a big impact on the worker's happiness). The limited mobility points again to the possible segmentation of the labor market.

A final factor raised during the discussions is the perceived health risk at the workplace. Health workers complain that, because of the spread of HIV/AIDS, not only have their workloads increased significantly, but the health risks have also become more dramatic. The risk is perceived to be greater in the public sector, where health workers report a patient mix that is different from the mix in the private sector, a consistent lack of gloves and other protective items, and weak compliance with biosecurity protocols. Perceived health risks may therefore increase the likelihood of absenteeism (see box 12.3).

BOX 12.3 Limitations and Risks in Employment

Access to a second job

"In rural areas, having a second job in the medical sector is not possible because there are no opportunities."   —DOCTOR IN RURAL RWANDA

"During day time, they work in one place, and, in the evening, they work in another place; this is not possible in rural areas."

—NURSE IN URBAN RWANDA

Intrinsic motivation

"Even though there are many problems, I would advise even my children to join the health profession."   —DOCTOR IN URBAN ETHIOPIA

"Health workers in the faith-based sector are more committed to their work compared with those in the public sector."

—HEALTH ASSISTANT IN RURAL RWANDA

BOX 12.3   *(Continued)*

"The fact of having a vocation makes it impossible to do something else."

—HEALTH ASSISTANT IN RURAL RWANDA

Job mobility and job allocation

"It is almost impossible to get a transfer from an allocated post to a post in another region."   *—NURSE IN URBAN ETHIOPIA*

"One is typically obliged to stay in his first posting for a long time, and this is usually outside the capital."   *—HEALTH ASSISTANT IN URBAN ETHIOPIA*

"You are asking what is an accepted reason to be transferred from rural to urban areas? There is none. It is a miracle."   *—DOCTOR IN URBAN RWANDA*

Perceived health risk

"We are too exposed. We can be contaminated because we are in direct contact with patients and persons living with HIV/AIDS."

—NURSE IN URBAN RWANDA

"The effect of HIV/AIDS on health workers has been totally ignored. In the face of extreme shortages of gloves and other supplies, health workers are exposed to difficult situations; it is like sacrificing your life."

—HEALTH ASSISTANT IN RURAL ETHIOPIA

"One is not secure against contracting the virus during treatment. The present procedure for postexposure to HIV/AIDS is to take prophylaxis treatment if tested positive, and one has to take postexposure prophylaxis for four weeks through ARV [antiretroviral treatment]. But this is only what it says on paper. It is not practiced. Nobody is really working to protect health professionals."   *—DOCTOR IN RURAL ETHIOPIA*

"In the community, there is a stigma, and, if a physician has the virus, all will suggest that he or she is promiscuous. Many students are going to public health rather than clinical practice."   *—DOCTOR IN RURAL ETHIOPIA*

Considerations for Quantitative Analysis

The main purpose of the qualitative work has been to inform the quantitative research on human resource issues, including absenteeism, in the two countries. So, what do the findings from the group discussions imply for a quantitative research strategy?

Enriching the Model

The preresearch indicates that theory falls short of providing a full framework for analyzing absenteeism among health workers in Ethiopia and Rwanda. The discussions confirm that wages, contracted working hours, and the expected cost of detection affect absenteeism as indicated by theory, although their importance may depend on the country context. The discussions also indicate that additional factors such as access to a second job, intrinsic motivation, job mobility, and perceived health risks play a role. This role argues for revisiting theory and empirical estimation to take this broader set of determinants into account.

The recognition of additional factors that determine absenteeism is an important contribution of the qualitative preresearch. However, the identification of the underlying processes may be more challenging, depending on the variable. Especially the role of intrinsic motivation is hard to pin down and needs more work from the theoretical and empirical perspectives.[9] From a theoretical perspective, the most straightforward approach is to continue using the standard labor-leisure model, whereby the additional explanatory variables of intrinsic motivation and perceived health risks are to be viewed as shifting the preferences of health workers as is common practice. (For now, we consider those preferences exogenous.) The variables of access to a second job and job mobility may also be included as indicators of any additional constraints health workers may face in the labor-leisure trade-off. This approach allows us simply to extend the empirical framework implied in table 12.1 through a similar equation; thus, all variables in table 12.3 now serve as right-hand-side variables.[10] In any case, however, even this simplified static theoretical model represents challenges in estimation, as we discuss in the next section.

Estimation Challenges in the Enriched Model

Assume for the moment that we collect cross-sectional data that contain good proxies for each of the above variables. There are two challenges in the

Variable	Expected sign of relationship
TABLE 12.3 An Expanded Model of Absenteeism	
Basic model	
Wages (w)	−
Contracted working hours (h_c)	+
Expected cost of detection (C)	−
Expanded model	
Access to a second job (S)	+
Intrinsic motivation or internalized norms (M)	+ or −
Job mobility (JM)	−
Perceived health risks (R)	+

Source: Compiled by the authors.

estimation of the single equation implied by table 12.3: endogeneity and unobserved heterogeneity.

Endogeneity is a concern when, on conceptual-theoretical grounds, one is unable to exclude that a right-hand-side variable is caused by the left-hand-side variable (reverse causality) or that the right-hand-side variable arises together with the left-hand-side variable, and these both are simultaneously caused by a third variable (simultaneity); the latter is especially a problem if the third variable is unobserved.

We exclude reverse causality, arguing that, in the current context, absenteeism does not *cause* any of the right-hand-side variables.[11] Simultaneity, however, is a potential problem. This is clearest in the case of motivation. Significant absenteeism and low intrinsic motivation may be simultaneously caused by a third factor. As seen elsewhere, intrinsic motivation may be defined as the internalization of external norms. The norms in the direct environment thus have a potential effect on intrinsic motivation even though there is still limited empirical documentation on the way this process works. Indeed, in both countries, discussants implicitly point at the importance of norms, arguing that problems such as absenteeism occur simultaneously with other performance problems such as favoritism, overcharging, embezzlement, and other corrupt practices. They say that where this kind of behavior is viewed as normal and acceptable, thereby leading to deterioration in workplace standards and the erosion of ethics, absenteeism is more likely. Both absenteeism and intrinsic motivation may therefore be caused by workplace norms.

From an econometric perspective, there are two classic ways to address simultaneity: instrumental variable estimation and differencing out unobserved effects. The first solution is to find a variable that is correlated with intrinsic motivation, but not with the unobserved part or the error term. In effect, we are looking for a variable that proxies the part of intrinsic motivation that remains constant over time. Probably, the most convincing candidates are factual variables that proxy norms with which one grew up, for example, the role of religion during childhood. However, as discussed in detail below, measurement remains a challenge.

A second way of addressing simultaneity is to difference out the unobserved part, using data on the same individual at two points in time. This approach would eliminate the part of intrinsic motivation that is constant over time. The coefficient on the difference in intrinsic motivation will then reflect the effect of changes in external norms on changes in absenteeism, and we may compare this change with the effect of intrinsic motivation in the level equations. Provided we have a good proxy for intrinsic motivation and other variables of interest and provided these variables change over time, this approach would generate the insights we seek.

This discussion brings us to the wider issue of unobserved characteristics. We have focused on the simultaneity of absenteeism and motivation and the role of norms. Similar arguments may be raised about other variables because norms may simultaneously affect absenteeism and detection or perceived health risks. The unobserved nature of at least part of the norms (assuming we are able to measure reasonably well the other part) supplies another argument for the collection of panel data.

Measurement Challenges with the Newly Identified Correlates

The focus group discussions highlighted the importance of a number of variables not considered in the basic theoretical framework. But they also revealed the measurement challenges that arise for many of these variables. Of course, measuring absenteeism itself is a challenge, perhaps more so for health workers than other service providers such as teachers because the former have more legitimate reasons for being absent from a facility (for instance, outreach or home visits). This problem may be partially overcome by combining unannounced visits (for example, see Chaudhury et al. 2006) and supplemental data collection on the reasons for absenteeism, although the reliability of information on these reasons is far from certain. One improvement would involve triangulating this information with administrative information, for instance, by asking whether outreach was planned. Thus, Banerjee, Deaton, and Duflo (2004) look at whether health workers were working in branch centers during absenteeism from their main workplaces. One might also carry out a survey among users, asking them whether health workers are absent from facilities when they expect them to be there. Another possibility is to revisit health workers away from their jobs (such as at their homes) to ask about the reasons for the observed absenteeism, which may increase the reliability of this information (see box 12.4).

The measurement of earnings, of the number of contracted hours, and of job mobility is relatively straightforward in considering the determinants of absenteeism.[12] However, difficulties arise in measuring the expected cost of detection, access to a second job, and intrinsic motivation.

BOX 12.4 Challenges to Measuring Absenteeism Quantitatively

"I think the problem is that it is rather difficult to organize the labor schedule of a doctor. If you are, for example, alone in a hospital, you're supposed to be there day and night. This is impossible for a human body. This means that you're in the hospital when you're not tired and that you leave when you're tired. By consequence, you will not necessarily be there during all working hours, while you'll be there outside working hours. The lack of a difference between working hours, nonworking hours, and recovery hours makes it difficult to make a sound judgment."

—*DOCTOR IN RURAL RWANDA*

"Suppose that a doctor goes through a night until daybreak and that he's supposed to be consulting in the morning; because he is tired, it's understandable that he will be late for the consultation. Somebody who's looking for him at eight o'clock will not find him and think he's absent."

—*DOCTOR IN RURAL RWANDA*

"And why are they so often absent? Maybe he went to read his medical books; maybe he has a second job; maybe he's consulting elsewhere, teaching, or administering training somewhere."

—*DOCTOR IN RURAL RWANDA*

Any measure of the monitoring and penalty regime will inevitably be partial. In the Rwandese context, for example, it would be useful to measure whether a health committee is monitoring health workers and determine the powers of this committee. It would also be useful to find out whether there is a performance-payment scheme in place. In Ethiopia and Rwanda, one might seek to capture information on monitoring procedures and monitoring intensity from the administrative unit responsible for the facility in question. Sanctions may be measured in a similar way by asking about experiences with penalties among other workers or in a hypothetical case. In most contexts, however, it is easier to capture how the monitoring and sanctioning system is *supposed* to work rather than how it *actually* works. It is also likely that any variation in monitoring is endogenous; thus, the identification challenge extends well beyond measurement. As discussed next, this extension means that credible estimates of the impact of the features of the monitoring and sanctioning regime on absenteeism would have to be derived from a policy experiment, combined with the collection of baseline and follow-up data.

The group discussions indicated that many health workers combine different jobs. The importance of the second jobs (either formal or informal) can be measured through survey questions. Because second jobs are typically prohibited by the main employers, often the government, these are sensitive questions. It would, therefore, be better to interview health workers away from work. Moreover, given that a second job may be informal, time use models, which typically register all household activities during a reference period (for instance, 24 hours), might capture the labor supply for each job. Another possibility is to introduce a module to capture consumption or permanent income, savings, and other sources of income, which would enable a comparison between income sources. Consumption modules are typically difficult to collect, but the use of assets to predict consumption levels may be feasible (for example, see Grosh and Baker 1995).

Finally, intrinsic motivation is notoriously challenging to measure. One potential approach is to measure attitudes by selecting survey questions from psychological studies on motivation and using these as proxies for latent norms. However, because reported motivation does not necessarily reflect actual motivation, the validity of this measure is far from certain. Nonetheless, this approach has led some to develop expansive questionnaire modules to try to capture different dimensions of motivation (for example, see Bennett et al. 2001; Franco, Bennett, and Kanfer 2002). An alternative approach more grounded in the previously discussed labor economics framework is to allow health workers to rank the importance of a number of criteria when choosing between two jobs and then include a variable that reveals intrinsic motivation in the list.[13] However, reporting bias is likely once again. A safer approach may, therefore, be to observe various types of behavior stemming from different norms in an incentive-compatible environment. In behavioral economics, there is now extensive experience with the use of games or experiments to measure different dimensions of preferences or motivation (for an overview, see Camerer, Loewenstein, and Rabin 2003). Such games are typically played in a controlled environment with real money at stake. This approach has generated major new insights and underlines the importance of factors such as norms and beliefs in the explanation of economic behavior. Following on the first wave of experiments, there is now an emerging tendency to test the external validity of these laboratory games and link them to real data (for example, see Cardenas 2003; Carpenter, Burks, and Verhoogen 2005; Karlan 2003; Barr and Serneels 2004). One way to do this is to play the games with a sample of subjects of interest. The challenge is then to find or design a game that reveals and measures motivation.

Toward Implementation: Possible Survey Approaches

The simplest way to approach new quantitative research is to carry out a cross-sectional survey. However, as argued above, from an econometric perspective, there are strong arguments for collecting panel data. This is useful in differencing away unobserved characteristics (but also in studying actual job mobility and other changes over time). Consider, for example, the question of the size of the effect of wages on absenteeism. Here, policy makers are looking for precise advice about the level at which to set wages. Estimation using survey data is unlikely to yield a precise answer. We have seen that motivation and wages are both potential determinants of absenteeism. However, motivation and wages may depend on each other, and the sign of the relationship is not entirely clear. Experimental work in behavioral economics has shown that, while higher earnings may motivate workers, they may also erode intrinsic motivation (see Gächter and Falk 1998). Because our proxy for intrinsic motivation will be imprecise, the effect of wages on absenteeism will also be imprecise. The coefficient will be unbiased, but its significance may be low.

An alternative approach involves a more controlled setting, wherein identification is based on the random assignment of a policy change, that is, a salary increase, using a treatment and control group.[14] The challenge is to avoid contamination of the control group. Therefore, a randomized program should use only small differences, preferably be implemented in similar subareas, and possibly use variation in attributes other than wages, such as benefits. A concern that is often raised about this approach is the ethical question of whether one should be allowed to experiment so that some health workers are paid more than others. Proponents argue that such different treatments are a fact of life anyway and that the systematization is the only difference and worth the benefit of building insight. Another problem is that politicians and the civil service are often reluctant to implement randomized experiments. An alternative approach may therefore entail the consideration of the intermediate case, whereby panel data are collected before and after a policy change (nonrandom treatment) and subsequently used to evaluate the effect (for details, see Ravallion 2001).

Whatever approach is applied, a questionnaire-based survey may be usefully combined with complementary behavioral games or experiments to measure motivational or preference variables. There are examples of surveys where this has been done successfully, but the technical and logistical challenges are considerable.

Lessons Learned

The qualitative research reported in this chapter has proved a powerful tool to complement quantitative analysis in understanding absenteeism. First, it has been instrumental in clarifying the meaning of classic explanatory variables such as wage levels. For example, health workers in the faith-based sector seem to exhibit far less absenteeism relative to their public sector colleagues, all factors being more or less equal, including wage levels. This observation calls for caution in interpreting the wage coefficient and needs more inquiry. Second, the qualitative research has allowed the identification of correlates that are not put forward in standard theory, such as intrinsic motivation, the perception of job-related health risks, and job mobility. These correlates would potentially permit the construction of an enriched model for the explanation of absenteeism in developing countries. Third, the qualitative approach has shed light on the complexity of the issues involved, revealing how the underlying processes in important relationships greatly contribute to a more accurate insight into the drivers of absenteeism, as well as how little we know at present.

At the same time, qualitative work has shortcomings. It provides information on whether absenteeism occurs and whether there is a relationship with some factors, but it is not capable of providing representative or quantified information about the extent of absenteeism or the determinants of absenteeism. If one is to address these issues, quantitative research is needed. Yet, the group discussions in Ethiopia and Rwanda make clear that, because of measurement and estimation challenges, answering important policy questions through quantitative analysis will often be difficult in practice. The collection of panel data, perhaps combined with explicit policy experiments, may help overcome some of these challenges, and qualitative preresearch may help in identifying key policy levers to consider in such experiments. But even these approaches will have limitations. Qualitative research may also help by providing a model for the first-stage regression for instrumental variable estimation and by pointing toward valid instruments for which quantitative data may be collected to address simultaneity at the stage of estimation.

Hence, while researchers and policy makers must be careful about how they use the results of qualitative research in the design or evaluation of policy, such research does have a function that extends beyond preresearch. For example, in both Ethiopia and Rwanda, health workers expressed frustration about arbitrariness and favoritism in human resource management (deployment, transfers, promotions, performance rewards, and so on). The validity of such perceptions is difficult to verify. (A quantitative survey may shed light on how widespread perceptions are, but is unlikely to demonstrate whether there is, indeed, favoritism in the system.) In this case, detailed case reviews or audits may be called for, and the results of the qualitative research may thus have direct implications for policy. In other areas, such as the case of intrinsic motivation, the measurement challenges may be so difficult or expensive to overcome that qualitative analysis remains an important tool in its own right, not merely in informing quantitative research.

It is also worth asking what methodological lessons were learned in the experiences of qualitative research on human resource issues in the two countries. Some of the lessons have been highlighted in this chapter. Focusing on group discussions, we have underlined the need for a careful, consistent, and well-documented approach to group selection, focus group moderation, data analysis, and write-up. The Ethiopian experience has also revealed how time-consuming the analytical phase may be, and the Rwanda study has introduced the use of software for text analysis, lowering the time needed and improving the possibilities for a richer analysis.[15] But there is clearly scope for improvement. Logistical and budgetary restrictions have prevented us from registering individualized responses from group members during the discussions (for instance, through the use of video recordings) and collecting some individual information through a minisurvey at the end of the session. Although such an approach entails risks, it would also permit an analysis of correlates between opinions and individual characteristics, which we may now only do by inference or by contrasting opinions. If budget and time constraints allow, another step in this direction would involve carrying out individual in-depth interviews. There is also scope for embedding qualitative studies such as those undertaken in Ethiopia and Rwanda more deeply in the policy dialogue with governments and other stakeholders. This would strengthen the interpretation of findings, while also enriching follow-up analytical work.

Notes

1. As an illustration, we have investigated the frequency of the term "qualitative research" in two highly esteemed economic journals that specialize in overview articles: the *Journal of Economic Literature* and the *Journal of Economic Perspectives*. We find that neither of the two journals has published a paper dedicated to qualitative research in the past 20 years (1986–2005 for the first journal and 1987–2005 for the second). The estimated total number of papers during this period is 960 for the *Journal of Economic Literature* and 760 for the *Journal of Economic Perspectives*. This indicates that, although there is good qualitative work (for example, see Bewley 1999), the methodology seems to receive limited recognition. The potential value of qualitative work and the link between quantitative and qualitative research have recently been receiving more attention in economics and, specifically, in poverty analysis and program evaluation (see Harriss 2002; Kanbur 2003; White 2002; Rao and Woolcock 2003). Even though there is agreement about the value of combining qualitative and quantitative research, the combined approach is still rare.
2. For a discussion of the role of qualitative work in public health, see Yach (1992). The disciplines of public health and medical anthropology have contributed to an emerging literature on the behavior of health workers. Jaffré and Olivier de Sardan (2003) carry out, arguably, one of the most thorough anthropological studies of the relationship between health workers and patients in the capitals of five West African countries, but they do not discuss absenteeism in depth. Luck, Fernandes, and Ferrinho (2000) rely on group discussions with African nurses in Lisbon, but focus on international migration. Fehrsen, Ogunbanjo, and Shaw (2000) focus explicitly on absenteeism.
3. In Ethiopia, we combined health officers and doctors because the former have the same function and status as doctors; nurses and midwives have at least two years of formal training after secondary school, while health assistants typically have one year of formal technical training. Because of considerable heterogeneity among users in Addis Ababa, separate focus groups were held with relatively more well

off users (who rely primarily on private clinics) and with relatively poor individuals (who rely mostly on public facilities). In Rwanda, the groups corresponded to doctors (A0 educational certificate), nurses (A1 and A2), auxiliary workers or health assistants (A3 and A4), and users. To guarantee heterogeneity within each group of health workers, we selected participants who were working in different sectors (public, private for-profit, and private nonprofit), participants who were combining work in two sectors, and men and women participants who were living in different household situations because these factors have been empirically shown to affect occupational choice and labor supply. For the users, we allowed for diversity in gender, household welfare, number of children (or lack of children), the sector of the facility visited most frequently, and experience with inpatient treatment (either for themselves or for relatives). We also took technical criteria into account to safeguard group dynamics by ensuring that the participants did not know each other or the discussion leaders in advance and that they were willing to become actively involved in the group discussions. No two health workers from the same facility were allowed to take part. All the users were expected to have visited a facility during the previous year, and no user was allowed to participate who had been working in the health sector.

4. For both countries, quotes were grouped into common themes and subgrouped within each theme. This grouping provided a full matrix for the analysis, wherein themes were organized in rows and focus groups were organized in columns. This procedure was implemented manually in the case of Ethiopia; while, in the case of Rwanda, we used QSR International's NVivo 2.0 qualitative research software.

5. Participants in Rwanda indicated that absenteeism among doctors is mostly an urban issue. Greater social control, leading to decreasing information asymmetries, combined with the lack of occupational alternatives, may explain why absenteeism is less common in rural areas.

6. One way to solve the classic agency problem is to make earnings dependent on performance; this approach induces self-monitoring. The government of Rwanda is testing a system of performance-related pay, whereby funds are paid to a facility conditional upon its performance. Predetermined rules are used to distribute the received premiums among the health professionals in the facility, thereby also stimulating monitoring among health workers. To raise the individual accountability of health workers additionally, local communities have now become involved in deciding the level of payment to health workers. Some of the resulting health committees have made a bonus dependent on a good record regarding absenteeism. Rwandese health workers themselves evaluate the performance-pay approach as positive and feel that it enhances performance. Also, users evaluate the initiative positively and indicate that absenteeism has decreased: An urban user in Rwanda says, "The community now has the power to exclude a health worker from the health center. This is why the health centers function better today."

    Another says, "You know that, when you don't work well, if you're absent, if you're late, if your service is not appreciated, this will decrease the premium that the health center receives; this means that the personnel check on each other. Everybody knows that the one that works badly can be sacked and risks being accused by his colleague; this leads to a certain degree of accountability and better productivity."

7. Doctors in Rwanda, for instance, cite the absence of opportunities for second jobs in the medical sector in rural areas as a major reason to prefer urban postings.
8. In many cases, references to intrinsic incentives may, in fact, reflect the responses of workers to fuzzy extrinsic motivators such as a fear of discharge or concerns about one's career (see Kreps 1997).
9. For the variables of access to a second job and limited job mobility, one may rely on labor theory to understand the underlying process and develop finer models (using simultaneous or segmented labor markets and censoring in labor supply), although the role of the variable of perceived health risk may be more readily understood through the existing literature on risk and economic behavior (for example, see Gollier 2001).
10. Within this framework, one may also test whether the conditions for the classic labor-leisure model are violated, as may be suggested by two of our findings, namely, that access to a second job may be censored and that job mobility is imperfect.
11. Theoretically, absenteeism may induce greater monitoring, but, given the poor state of monitoring in Ethiopia and Rwanda, this seems irrelevant in the current context. We also consider access to a second job exogenous because this will mostly capture the difference between rural and urban areas and has little to do with the search effort of health workers.
12. Mobility may be measured by comparing intended and actual moves between jobs.
13. The list might, for example, contain salary, access to training, chances of promotion, and helping patients, the last a proxy for intrinsic motivation. We explored this approach in a subsequent quantitative survey with health students to study the role of motivation in decisions to work in rural areas (see Serneels et al. 2005).
14. The aim is to select a geographical area where the experiment may be implemented. Within this area, a random sample of health workers is selected, and the sample is divided into two groups: a treatment group and a control group, that is, each health worker is randomly assigned to one of the two groups. Baseline data, including information on absenteeism and payment, are collected for both groups. Then the treatment is implemented, and the treatment group receives a higher payment, while the control group receives the same payment it received previously. Subsequently, a second wave of data is collected. Comparison of the treatment group and the control group before and after permits the identification of the treatment effect.
15. The two main advantages of using text software is that it is more rapid and that it remains extremely flexible; any categorization or structure may be changed or imposed on the text. It also allows for exploration into the relationships among different categories of quotes. For example, one may rather easily verify whether participants refer to performance pay when they talk about absenteeism.

Bibliography

Allen, Steven G. 1981. "An Empirical Model of Work Attendance." *Review of Economics and Statistics* 63 (1): 77–87.
Arrow, Kenneth J. 1963. "Uncertainty and the Welfare Economics of Medical Care." *American Economic Review* 54 (5): 941–73.

Banerjee, Abhijit V., Pranab Bardhan, Kaushik Basu, Ravi Kanbur, and Dilip Mookherjee. 2005. "New Directions in Development Economics: Theory or Empirics?" BREAD Working Paper 106, Bureau for Research and Economic Analysis of Development, Center for International Development at Harvard University, Cambridge, MA.

Banerjee, Abhijit V., Angus S. Deaton, and Esther Duflo. 2004. "Wealth, Health, and Health Services in Rural Rajasthan." *American Economic Review* 94 (2): 326–30.

Barr, Abigail, and Pieter Serneels. 2004. "Wages and Reciprocity in the Workplace." Working Paper 218, Centre for the Study of African Economies, University of Oxford, Oxford.

Bénabou, Roland J. M., and Jean Tirole. 2003. "Intrinsic and Extrinsic Motivation." *Review of Economic Studies* 70 (3): 489–520.

Bennett, Sara, Lynne Miller Franco, Ruth Kanfer, and Patrick Stubblebine. 2001. "The Development of Tools to Measure the Determinants and Consequences of Health Worker Motivation in Developing Countries." Major Applied Research 5, Technical Paper 2, Abt Associates, Bethesda, MD.

Bewley, Truman F. 1999. *Why Wages Don't Fall during a Recession*. Cambridge, MA: Harvard University Press.

Brown, Sarah, and John G. Sessions. 1996. "The Economics of Absence: Theory and Evidence." *Journal of Economic Surveys* 10 (1): 23–53.

Camerer, Colin F., George Loewenstein, and Matthew Rabin, eds. 2003. *Advances in Behavioral Economics*. Roundtable Series in Behavioral Economics. Princeton, NJ: Princeton University Press.

Cardenas, Juan-Camilo. 2003. "Bringing the Lab to the Field: More Than Changing Subjects." Paper presented at the International Meeting of the Economic Science Association, Pittsburgh, June 19–22.

Carpenter, Jeffrey P., Stephen V. Burks, and Eric A. Verhoogen. 2005. "Comparing Students to Workers: The Effects of Social Framing on Behavior in Distribution Games." In *Field Experiments in Economics*, ed. Jeffrey P. Carpenter, Glenn W. Harrison, John A. List, 261–90. Research in Experimental Economics 10. Amsterdam: Elsevier.

Chaudhury, Nazmul, and Jeffrey S. Hammer. 2003. "Ghost Doctors: Absenteeism in Bangladeshi Health Facilities." Policy Research Working Paper 3065, World Bank, Washington, DC.

———. 2004. "Ghost Doctors: Absenteeism in Rural Bangladeshi Health Facilities." *World Bank Economic Review* 18 (3): 423–41.

Chaudhury, Nazmul, Jeffrey S. Hammer, Michael Kremer, Karthik Muralidharan, and F. Halsey Rogers. 2006. "Missing in Action: Teacher and Health Worker Absence in Developing Countries." *Journal of Economic Perspectives* 20 (1): 91–116.

Cloud, Darnell L. 2000. "Absenteeism and Endogenous Preferences." North Carolina A&T State University Working Paper in Economics, School of Business and Economics, North Carolina Agricultural and Technical State University, Greensboro, NC.

Das, Jishnu, Stefan Dercon, James Habyarimana, and Pramila Krishnan. 2005. "Teacher Shocks and Student Learning: Evidence from Zambia." Policy Research Working Paper 3602, World Bank, Washington, DC.

Deci, Edward L. 1975. *Intrinsic Motivation*. New York: Plenum Press.

Farquhar, Clare. 1999. "Are Focus Groups Suitable for 'Sensitive' Topics?" With Rita Das. In *Developing Focus Group Research: Politics, Theory, and Practice,* ed. Rosaline S. Barbour and Jenny Kitzinger, 47–63. London: Sage Publications.

Fehrsen, Sam, Gboyega Ogunbanjo, and Vincent Shaw. 2000. "Coping Strategies of Health Personnel: Experiences from South Africa." In *Providing Health Care under Adverse Conditions: Health Personnel Performance and Individual Coping Strategies,* ed. Paulo Ferrinho and Wim van Lerberghe, 223–30. Studies in Health Services Organization and Policy 16. Antwerp: ITGPress.

Franco, Lynne Miller, Sara Bennett, and Ruth Kanfer. 2002. "Health Sector Reform and Public Sector Health Worker Motivation: A Conceptual Framework." *Social Science and Medicine* 54 (8): 1255–66.

Frank, Richard G. 2004. "Behavioral Economics and Health Economics." NBER Working Paper 10881, National Bureau of Economic Research, Cambridge, MA.

Gächter, Simon, and Armin Falk. 1998. "Work Motivation and Performance: How Can Incomplete Employment Contracts Be Enforced?" Working paper, Institute for Empirical Research in Economics, University of Zurich, Zurich.

Gollier, Christian. 2001. *The Economics of Risk and Time.* Cambridge, MA: MIT Press.

Grosh, Margaret E., and Judy L. Baker. 1995. "Proxy Means Tests for Targeting Social Programs: Simulations and Speculation." Living Standards Measurement Study Working Paper 118, World Bank, Washington, DC.

Harriss, John. 2002. "The Case for Cross-Disciplinary Approaches in International Development." *World Development* 30 (3): 487–96.

Hongoro, Charles, and Charles Normand. 2006. "Health Workers: Building and Motivating the Workforce." In *Disease Control Priorities in Developing Countries,* 2nd ed., ed. Dean T. Jamison, Joel G. Breman, Anthony R. Measham, George Alleyne, Mariam Claeson, David B. Evans, Prabhat Jha, Anne Mills, and Philip Musgrove, 1309–22. Washington, DC: World Bank; New York: Oxford University Press.

Jaffré, Yannick, and Jean-Pierre Olivier de Sardan, eds. 2003. *Une médecine inhospitalière: les difficiles relations entre soignants et soignés dans cinq capitales d'Afrique de l'Ouest.* Series Hommes et sociétés: sciences économiques et politiques. Paris: Karthala.

JLI (Joint Learning Initiative). 2004. *Human Resources for Health: Overcoming the Crisis.* Cambridge, MA: Joint Learning Initiative, Global Equity Initiative, Harvard University.

Kanbur, Ravi, ed. 2003. *Q-Squared: Qualitative and Quantitative Methods of Poverty Appraisal.* Delhi: Permanent Black.

Karlan, Dean S. 2003. "Using Experimental Economics to Measure Social Capital and Predict Financial Decisions." *American Economic Review* 95 (5): 1688–99.

Kenyon, Peter, and Peter Dawkins. 1989. "A Time Series Analysis of Labour Absence in Australia." *Review of Economics and Statistics* 71 (2): 232–39.

Kreps, David M. 1997. "Intrinsic Motivation and Extrinsic Incentives." *American Economic Review* 87 (2): 359–64.

Le Grand, Julian. 2003. *Motivation, Agency, and Public Policy: Of Knights and Knaves, Pawns and Queens.* Oxford: Oxford University Press.

Leigh, J. Paul. 1983. "Sex Differences in Absenteeism." *Industrial Relations* 22 (3): 349–61.

Lindelow, Magnus, and Pieter Serneels. 2006. "The Performance of Health Workers in Ethiopia: Results from Qualitative Research." *Social Science and Medicine* 62 (9): 2225–35.

Luck, Margaret, Maria de Jesus Fernandes, and Paulo Ferrinho. 2000. "At the Other End of the Brain-Drain: African Nurses Living in Lisbon." In *Providing Health Care under Adverse Conditions: Health Personnel Performance and Individual Coping Strategies,* ed. Paulo Ferrinho and Wim van Lerberghe, 157–69. Studies in Health Services Organization and Policy 16. Antwerp: ITGPress.

Paringer, Lynn. 1983. "Women and Absenteeism: Health or Economics." *American Economic Review* 73 (2): 123–27.

Rao, Vijayendra, and Michael Woolcock. 2003. "Integrating Qualitative and Quantitative Approaches in Program Evaluation." In *The Impact of Economic Policies on Poverty and Income Distribution: Evaluation Techniques and Tools,* ed. François Bourguignon and Luiz A. Pereira da Silva, 165–90. Washington, DC: World Bank; New York: Oxford University Press.

Ravallion, Martin. 2001. "The Mystery of the Vanishing Benefits: An Introduction to Impact Evaluation." *World Bank Economic Review* 15 (1): 115–40.

Serneels, Pieter, Magnus Lindelow, José García Montalvo, and Abigail Barr. 2005. "An Honorable Calling?: Findings from the First Wave of a Cohort Study with Final Year Nursing and Medical Students in Ethiopia." Unpublished report, World Bank, Washington, DC.

———. 2007. "For Public Service or Money: Understanding Geographical Imbalances in the Health Workforce." *Health Policy and Planning* 22 (3): 128–38.

Shapiro, Carl, and Joseph E. Stiglitz. 1984. "Equilibrium Unemployment as a Worker Discipline Device." *American Economic Review* 74 (3): 433–44.

White, Howard. 2002. "Combining Quantitative and Qualitative Approaches in Poverty Analysis." *World Development* 30 (3): 511–22.

WHO (World Health Organization). 2006. *The World Health Report 2006: Working Together for Health.* Geneva: World Health Organization.

Winkler, Donald R. 1980. "The Effects of Sick-Leave Policy on Teacher Absenteeism." *Industrial and Labor Relations Review* 33 (2): 232–40.

World Bank. 2003. *World Development Report 2004: Making Services Work for Poor People.* Washington, DC: World Bank; New York: Oxford University Press.

———. 2006. *World Development Indicators 2006.* Washington, DC: World Bank.

Yach, Derek. 1992. "The Use and Value of Qualitative Methods in Health Research in Developing Countries." *Social Science and Medicine* 35 (4): 603–12.

13

Use of Vignettes to Measure the Quality of Health Care

Jishnu Das and Kenneth Leonard

No matter how one looks at it, as differences across nations or as differences within nations, poor people systematically suffer from health outcomes that are worse than those among rich people. What role does medical care play?

This chapter outlines a research project that seeks to measure the quality of care, understand how quality of care varies according to geographical location and sectors (private, nongovernmental, or public organization), and how (and whether) quality of care has an impact on health choices and outcomes. We discuss an instrument—vignettes—and a measure of the quality of care—competence—that focus on what doctors *know* or the maximum quality of medical advice that doctors might provide if they did all they know how to do. Vignettes involve the presentation of simulated patients to doctors that is paired with an instrument that evaluates the quality of care provided by the doctor. Performance on the vignette is an indicator of the competence, skill, or ability of the doctors. We show how competence may be validated and what may be learned by looking at correlations between competence and various attributes of the health care provider. We propose ways in which this measure may be widely collected, while, at the same time, arguing for (some) uniformity in cross-country studies to enable more extensive comparisons.

The chapter is structured as follows. The next section presents a prima facie case for (a) incorporating the quality of care in studies on the demand for health care and on outcomes and (b) measuring the quality of care through the quality of medical advice that doctors give to patients, rather than, for instance, the infrastructure in a facility. The subsequent section introduces vignettes as a measurement tool and describes how the data are collected and validated. The penultimate section outlines the relevant results of recent studies. The final section concludes by summarizing some lessons learned, caveats, and proposals for additional research.

Why and How Should We Measure the Quality of Care?

Numerous studies have documented the role of households in producing good health outcomes: children are healthier when mothers are more educated; rich households are better able to insure against health shocks; rich households live in areas with better sanitation and enjoy better nutrition. According to such studies, the explanations for health outcomes among poor people have centered almost exclusively on household choices: either poor people do not use the health system as much as they should or, if they do go to doctors, it is usually too late. However, recent work shows that, even when the poor do visit health facilities frequently and more frequently than do the rich, the health outcomes among these poor people remain dismal; the quality of the medical system must, therefore, also play a large role in health outcomes.

Earlier studies sought to measure the quality of care through the presence or absence of a primary health care center; they found little or no relationship between the existence of a health care center and health outcomes. The lack of a relationship left many questions about providers unanswered: Was there a lack of relationship because the doctor was never there? Was the doctor qualified (holding a degree) and competent (knowledgeable)? The data to answer these crucial questions simply did not exist.

The next wave of studies tried to address those questions by using structural measures of quality, that is, quality alternatively defined by physical infrastructure, the stock of medical supplies, the total number of assigned personnel, the availability of refrigeration units, the availability of electricity, or a combination of some of these. Thus, Collier, Dercon, and Mackinnon (2002) and Lavy and Germain (1994) found that health care demand responded to structural quality: more people visited health clinics when the structural quality was higher.

A remarkable omission from the indicators examined in these studies is a measure of process quality, particularly the quality of medical personnel. If structural quality were well correlated with process quality, this omission might be explained by the fact that it is easier to collect data on structural quality. However, the two are not well correlated, and there is good reason to believe that process quality is more significant than structural quality. First, structural measures such as drug availability are largely determined by the level of subsidies and the cost of transportation, making structural quality a predictable feature of ownership (private versus public, for example) and location, whereas process quality is more likely to vary within these parameters. To the degree that one facility is more likely to experience pharmacy stock-outs than another, similar facility, the explanation may be differences in demand, which may cause misclassification. Second, medicines and consultation are both important in a patient's health, but, whereas households are able to mitigate problems in drug supplies by purchasing on other markets, they are unable to do this with medical care.

We propose to measure the (maximum) quality of medical advice patients are likely to receive when they consult doctors, and we propose to measure the correlates of this quality. Information such as this is more difficult to collect than information on structural quality because it typically involves either detailed interviews with doctors or clinical observation of interactions between individual doctors and a number of patients. Together with information on structural quality, this research presents a more complete picture of the quality of medical advice.

Process Quality Evaluation Methods

Why Use Vignettes?

There are many ways to measure process quality, and the instruments—both actual and theoretical—vary according to realism, relevance, and comparability. A *realistic* quality measurement instrument is one that collects data on the activities of doctors in a setting that closely resembles the setting in which most care is delivered. A *relevant* instrument collects data on processes that are significant in the sense that the observed activities are important to outcomes among a large segment of the potential population. A *comparable* instrument is one that collects data that may be compared across a broad spectrum of health care providers and settings.

In practice, some compromise across these goals is inevitable. For example, the fake patient (an actor posing as a patient and visiting a large number of providers) is both comparable (the same patient visits all providers) and realistic (the doctor is unaware of the fact that the actor is not a regular patient). However, the fake patient is unlikely to be relevant because an actor is only able to pretend to have a limited set of illnesses (a headache or sore muscle, for example), and these illnesses are rarely the subject of our research. A fake patient is unable convincingly to pretend to have tuberculosis, for instance. Direct clinician observation (observing the activities of doctors with their regular patients) is realistic and relevant, but is not generally comparable because strong assumptions are necessary to compare the activities of doctors who see different types of illnesses and patients.[1] Vignettes—the subject of this chapter—are specifically designed to be both comparable and relevant because the same case is presented to every doctor, and the researcher may choose to present almost any relevant illness. However, vignettes are not as realistic as other instruments because doctors know that the patient is an actor pretending to be sick, not a regular patient. We argue that this shortcoming may be mitigated through the proper design of the instruments and the proper interpretation of the results.

Vignettes will play an important role in investigations where relevance and comparability are overriding concerns. Research focused on the distribution and the determinants of the distribution of quality on a regional, national, or international scale must be both relevant and comparable and will probably benefit from the inclusion of data generated by the use of vignettes. Meanwhile, an empirical investigation of health-seeking behavior in a particular population or a particular setting will put a higher premium on realism than on relevance or comparability and would find vignettes less well suited to the problem than other instruments might be.

What Are Vignettes?

Many different types of vignettes are used in health care research today. The underlying element that connects these different instruments is the presentation of a case to the doctor that is paired with an instrument for the evaluation of the activities of the doctor. In some versions of vignettes, the case is a fixed narrative read from a script; in others, someone pretending to be the patient acts out the case. In some types of vignettes, doctors are asked to list the activities that they would undertake; in other types of vignettes, the doctor interacts with the (fake) patient by asking questions to which the patient responds. Finally, in some types of vignettes, the doctor is prompted by the examiner with questions such as "Would you prescribe treatment X?"

The vignettes represented in Das and Hammer (2005) and Leonard and Masatu (2005) rely on an enumerator who is trained to act as a sick person rather than an enumerator who reads from a script. The characteristics of the illness and the patient are predetermined, but unknown to the doctor. Except for the first complaints described by the patient, the practitioner must ask questions to discover the characteristics of the illness. Because the patient is not actually sick, the physical examination is presented in a question–answer format, whereby the doctor explains what he is looking for, and the patient tells him what he would find. The measured quality of the consultation is based on the doctor's activities during the consultation. Because doctors know that the patient is simulated and that the physical examination is carried out through questions and answers, some realism is sacrificed. However, unlike some other types of instruments, the process by which the doctor examines and diagnoses the patient resembles the actual process a doctor would normally undertake. Thus, even though the doctor knows that the simulated patient is not real, the doctor is sitting at his or her desk and gathering information about a case to reach a diagnosis and prescribe a treatment. Our version of vignettes is as realistic as we are able to make it without sacrificing comparability or relevance.

How Easy or Hard Is It to Use Vignettes?

It is impossible to measure process quality accurately without visiting all facilities in a sample, and vignettes require that doctors be present at the time of the visits. However, once a doctor has been located, vignettes are relatively inexpensive to administer. Nonetheless, the increased realism of our vignettes does have an important cost: enumerators must completely memorize a case presentation and be sufficiently well trained to adapt to the different questions posed by practitioners, while still maintaining the same characteristics across all practitioners. This approach is much more challenging than training someone to read a list of questions from an instrument.

Validating Vignettes

Do vignettes measure competence, and is competence—as measured through vignettes—correlated with the important underlying aspects of quality? To answer those questions, the validity of vignettes may be checked for internal consistency, and the results obtained using vignettes may be compared with the results obtained using more realistic instruments, in this case, direct observation.

Internal Validity and Item Response Theory

The researcher simultaneously designs the case study patient and the diagnostic and treatment protocol. In some cases (Tanzania, for example), the protocol for certain types of illnesses already exists in the form of national diagnostic guidelines. Thus, rather than measuring competence according to the number of actions a doctor takes, the researcher measures the percentage of the required or rational items that are actually implemented by the doctor. Those data may be translated into a series of correct and incorrect responses, whereby correct implies that a doctor used an item required by protocol, while incorrect implies that the doctor did not use an item required by protocol. Any questions that are not part of the protocol are not used in this process. This list of correct and incorrect responses lends itself to internal validation through item response analysis or item response theory. Item response analysis simultaneously solves for a single overall score for each doctor, a standard error for the score, and the relative contribution of each individual item to that score (see Das and Hammer 2005). An internally valid vignette has a number of testable features. First, for every item in the vignette, good doctors (those with a high overall score) should be at least as likely to implement the item as are bad doctors (those with a low overall score). Second, the standard errors associated with overall scores should be small enough that significant differences exist in the scores of doctors across the sample. Such tests are possible because a vignette measures multiple aspects of the same underlying characteristic. The vignettes discussed in Das and Hammer (2005) and Leonard and Masatu (2005) are internally valid by these standards. Although the design of the vignettes used in Indonesia (see Barber, Gertler, and Harimurti 2006a, 2006b) is slightly different, they also lend themselves to item response analysis and are internally valid according to these standards.[2]

Comparing Vignettes and Direct Observation

We have been careful to cast vignettes as a measure of competence, not as a measure of actual practice quality. Leonard and Masatu (2005) compare the performance of doctors on vignettes and their performance in practice with their regular patients. This comparison suggests that performance on the vignette is a measure of maximum performance in practice, but not a measure of actual performance. However, the vignette score and the practice quality score are significantly correlated over the sample; a doctor's actual performance is closely tied to his potential or maximum performance. Despite their lack of realism, vignettes are a good first order measure of practice quality. Still, the differences between competence and practice quality are potentially important; Leonard, Masatu, and Vialou (2007) suggest that the gap between ability and practice is partially determined by the organizational form of the health facility. Comparing quality within organizational type (public, nongovernmental, or private) and vignettes is probably more valid than comparing quality across organizational types.

Additional Sources of Validation

In Tanzania, doctors who were examined through the vignette were asked to provide a diagnosis at the end of each case. Because all practitioners who were examined were trained in the same medical system, their diagnoses may be compared with the true diagnosis for that case. Practitioners who scored better on the vignette were significantly more likely to give the correct diagnosis (Leonard and Masatu 2007). In addition, Barber, Gertler, and Harimurti (2006a) find that, in Indonesia, health outcomes are worse in facilities with lower vignette scores. Those results provide additional evidence that the measurement of competence does, in fact, produce some information about quality.

Some Results

Now that we have a measure of quality based on competence, what do we do with it? As a first pass, we may try to benchmark the quality of care and provide some information about whether the quality of care is high or not. Next, we may try to look at differences in the quality of care, perhaps across geographical or income groups.

Results on the Baseline Quality of Care

Despite the evidence that performance on vignettes is likely to be an upper bound, the overall quality of care is low. However, there is considerable variation across countries and even within countries over time. In India, doctors completed only 26 percent of the tasks that were medically required for a patient presenting tuberculosis, and only 18 percent of the tasks required for a child with diarrhea (see Das and Hammer 2006). Similarly, doctors in Tanzania completed less than one-quarter (24 percent) of the essential checklist when faced with a patient with malaria and 38 percent in the case of a child with diarrhea (Leonard and Masatu 2007). Indonesian providers perform better than those in India for patients presenting tuberculosis and for patients presenting diarrhea, but there is a disturbing time trend. As Barber, Gertler, and Harimurti (2006b) document, a virtual hiring freeze in the public sector led to a decline in the quality of care between 1993 and 1997 and a 7 percent drop in the percentage of checklist items completed in the vignettes.

Results on Correlates of the Quality of Care across Countries

Though the quality of care is generally low, it is not evenly distributed. In Delhi, high-quality doctors appear to be self-sorting into locations where they serve richer clients even within the public health system. In Indonesia, quality is much higher in relatively wealthier Java and Bali than in other areas (Barber, Gertler, and Harimurti 2006a). In Tanzania, the quality of care available in rural areas is much lower than that available in urban areas (Leonard and Masatu 2007). In addition, in Tanzania, the nongovernmental sector delivers marginally better health care overall and also manages to provide relatively constant quality across the rural and urban divide, but accounts for a small share of the services provided (Leonard and Masatu 2007).

Meanwhile, there is little evidence to suggest that purely private health care is better than public health care. Although the private care available in urban areas and the wealthy areas of towns is generally superior to that available in rural or poor neighborhoods, this is no different than the pattern among public health facilities. Private providers in rural and poor areas are not superior to public providers in those same areas (Das and Hammer 2006; Leonard and Masatu 2007).

Discussion

Do Vignettes Measure Aspects of Medical Quality that Matter?

Clearly, vignettes do not measure everything that is important in health care. A measure of practice quality that is more realistic, while retaining the relevance and comparability of vignettes would be desirable. Nonetheless, vignettes make an important contribution to knowledge because they allow some understanding of the distribution of competence, which, in turn, is correlated with the distribution of practice quality. In addition, competence, as measured by vignettes, is not a function of location. The exact same case is presented to urban and rural doctors, doctors accustomed to treating poor patients, and doctors accustomed to treating rich patients. The differences in competence across doctors may be highly correlated with location, but they are not *caused* by location.

Other measures of process quality are more susceptible to endogenous determination according to location. For example, educated patients are more likely to argue with doctors or insist on providing information that might be of use to doctors. Thus, doctors who see mostly educated patients are more likely to follow protocol simply because their patients either encourage this or make this easier. Allowing the education level of the patient to influence quality may or may not be a good approach, but the influence is clearly caused by the patient mix rather than the skills of the doctor. The vignette may avoid this problem because it controls for illness and patient characteristics. The research may choose to implement the vignette with an informative or an uninformative patient, but the same patient will be presented to all doctors.

The distinction between quality that is poor *because of* the location and quality that is poor *at* a location is important to policy. The results that we have found through vignettes suggest that lower-quality doctors locate near poor patients. This is true even within the public sector. It suggests that poor-quality doctors are sent to work with poorer patients. From the perspective of the patient, it does not matter whether a doctor learned to be good from his experience with other patients or whether he was good when he was sent there, but, for the administration of a public health care system, this difference is important and may only be uncovered through the use of an instrument such as vignettes.

Importance of Quality Measures with Standard Errors

Any type of process quality measure will probably suffer from measurement error, and vignettes are no exception. Unlike many other measures of process quality, however, we may approximate the error in our measure of competence using item response analysis. Item response analysis on the vignettes collected in India, Indonesia, and Tanzania shows that measurement error is not constant across the sample within each country. In particular, the standard errors are much lower in the middle of the competence distribution and higher at the tails. Figure 13.1 shows the distribution of

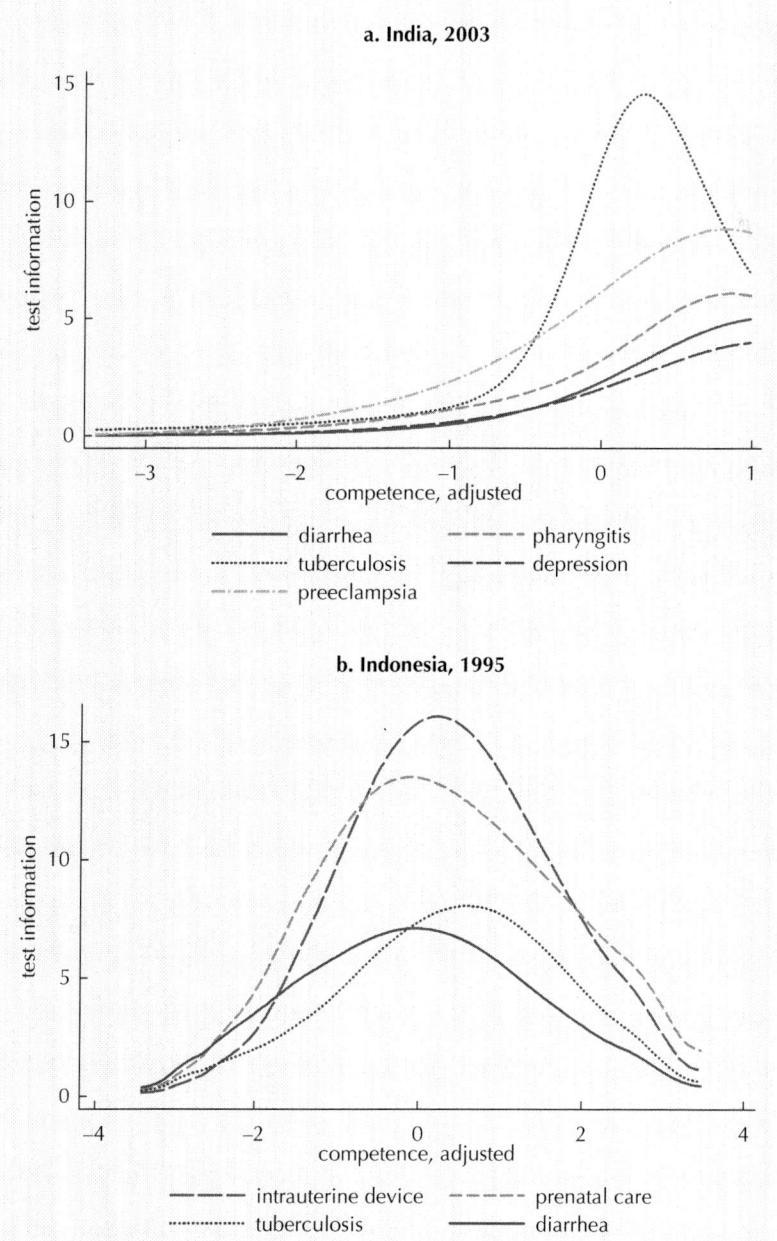

FIGURE 13.1 Information by Vignette and Country

FIGURE 13.1 *(Continued)*

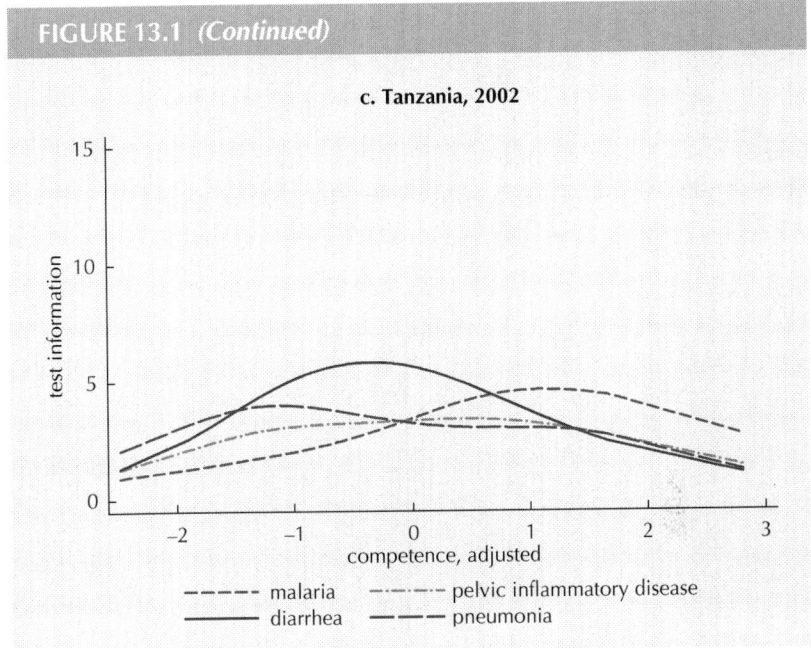

c. Tanzania, 2002

- - - - - malaria   - - · - - - pelvic inflammatory disease
———— diarrhea   - - - - pneumonia

Sources: Calculations of the authors based on a study carried out in India by the World Bank and the Institute of Socio-Economic Research on Democracy and Development (see Das and Sánchez-Páramo 2003; Das and Hammer 2005); the Indonesia Family Life Survey; and outpatient facility evaluations in Arusha Municipality, Arumeru and Monduli Districts in the Arusha Region, Tanzania.

the information score across competence for each vignette in each of these countries. The information score is a function of the inverse of the standard error; therefore, high information scores indicate low standard errors. In India, the vignettes are not good at distinguishing among low-competence providers, although they are good at distinguishing among high-competence providers and between high- and low-competence providers. Although this result appears to be specific to India, the survey there included informal sector providers who dominate the lower tail, and the results shown for India would likely be obtained in any survey that encompasses such providers. It is easy to identify poorly trained providers, but much more difficult to measure the differences among such providers. In Indonesia and Tanzania, vignettes are less useful at the tails of the distribution and better in the middle. In general, it is difficult to distinguish the differences among doctors with low competence and among doctors with high competence, although it is not difficult to distinguish the difference between low- and high-competence providers. From a policy perspective, not being able to classify correctly the best doctors is much less important than trying to classify the worst doctors. Any policy that publishes information gathered from vignettes would have to be careful to interpret findings in light of what we know about the standard errors. In addition, if policy makers believe that the differences among low-quality providers are economically important, we recommend that they use a different instrument to differentiate among these providers.

It is tempting to look at the results obtained through vignettes and draw the conclusion that standard errors are too high. However, it is not true that other instruments show lower standard errors; it is only true that many of these instruments have unmeasured or unmeasurable standard errors.

Lessons for the Design of Vignettes

The information scores in figure 13.1 give a picture of the accuracy of the different case studies and their contributions to the overall assessment of competence. The patterns suggest that, even for illnesses that are relevant and comparable, some cases are more useful than others. The tuberculosis vignette in India and the intrauterine device and prenatal care vignettes in Indonesia stand out relative to the other vignettes in those countries. Information is additive; so, even a vignette with a low total contribution to overall competence scores (such as the depression vignette in India) does contribute something. However, given the cost to develop vignettes and train the personnel, it is clear that the value of the preeclampsia and tuberculosis vignettes in India and the intrauterine device and prenatal care vignettes in Indonesia is greater than the value of other vignettes in those countries. Meanwhile, in Tanzania, with the exception of the vignette on pelvic inflammatory disease, each vignette is useful for a different segment of the distribution of competence. Information about the usefulness of vignettes may be gathered in a pretesting stage and used to choose among vignettes, trading off the contribution to total information and the cost of data collection.

Issues for the Implementation of Vignettes on an International Scale

As we allude earlier, implementing vignettes requires extensive training and some degree of adaptation to the local setting. The questions that an actor should be prepared to answer will generally differ from one country to another, particularly for questions that are not medically relevant, but for which answers must be standardized. Thus, it is unlikely to be true that an entire vignette manual might be designed for use anywhere in the world. In addition, illnesses such as malaria are different across different regions and would be difficult to standardize. However, there are potentially important benefits to using the same cases across countries. Tuberculosis is the same in India or Indonesia, and doctors are only graded on whether or not they ask medically relevant questions. The fact that a doctor in Indonesia may ask questions about religious practices and a doctor in India may ask questions about the food eaten for dinner the previous evening should not prevent us from comparing competence across doctors, albeit with less confidence than in our comparison across doctors within countries. Because there is greater variance in training, placement, and incentives across countries than within countries, these studies may only improve our understanding of how competence is delivered.

Notes

1. Leonard and Masatu (2006) show that the presence of the researcher may affect the activities of a doctor in a way that will call into question the realism of the process, but one may control for such effects.
2. The vignettes used in Indonesia followed a script rather than relying on an actor. In addition, vignettes were administered at the facility level, not the doctor level. In this manner, one doctor at a facility may have participated in one vignette, and another doctor on the other vignette, but only facilities are identified.

References

Barber, Sarah L., Paul J. Gertler, and Pandu Harimurti. 2006a. "Promoting High-Quality Care in Indonesia: Roles for Public and Private Ambulatory Care Providers." Unpublished working paper, Institute of Business and Economic Research, University of California at Berkeley, Berkeley, CA.

———. 2006b. "The Effect of the Zero Growth Policy in Civil Service Recruitment on the Quality of Care in Indonesia." Unpublished working paper, Institute of Business and Economic Research, University of California at Berkeley, Berkeley, CA.

Collier, Paul, Stefan Dercon, and John Mackinnon. 2002. "Density Versus Quality in Health Care Provision: Using Household Data to Make Budgetary Choices in Ethiopia." *World Bank Economic Review* 16 (3): 425–48.

Das, Jishnu, and Jeffrey S. Hammer. 2005. "Which Doctor?: Combining Vignettes and Item Response to Measure Clinical Competence." *Journal of Development Economics* 78 (2): 348–83.

————. 2006. "Location, Location, Location: Residence, Wealth, and the Quality of Medical Care in Delhi, India." Unpublished working paper, World Bank, Washington, DC.

Das, Jishnu and Carolina Sánchez-Páramo. 2003. "Short But Not Sweet: New Evidence on Short Duration Morbidities from India." Policy Research Working Paper 2971, World Bank, Washington, DC.

Lavy, Victor Chaim, and Jean-Marc Germain. 1994. "Quality and Cost in Health Care Choice in Developing Countries." Living Standards Measurement Study Working Paper 105, World Bank, Washington, DC.

Leonard, Kenneth L., and Melkiory C. Masatu. 2005. "The Use of Direct Clinician Observation and Vignettes for Health Services Quality Evaluation in Developing Countries." *Social Science and Medicine* 61 (9): 1944–51.

————. 2006. "Outpatient Process Quality Evaluation and the Hawthorne Effect." *Social Science and Medicine* 63 (9): 2330–40.

————. 2007. "Variation in the Quality of Care Accessible to Rural Communities in Tanzania." *Health Affairs* 26 (3): w380–92.

Leonard, Kenneth L., Melkiory C. Masatu, and Alexandre Vialou. 2007. "Getting Doctors to Do Their Best: The Roles of Ability and Motivation in Health Care." *Journal of Human Resources* 42 (3): 682–700.

14

Client Satisfaction and the Perceived Quality of Primary Health Care in Uganda

Mattias Lundberg

I n recent years, there has been increasing emphasis on quality in health care in both developing and developed countries. This attention partly reflects the implicit acknowledgment that many health services do not meet minimum standards for clinical effectiveness or client satisfaction. In addition, *The World Health Report 2000* (WHO 2000) and *The World Development Report 2004* (World Bank 2003) have emphasized the importance of client power and the responsiveness of public services to public needs. According to the World Health Organization, responsiveness is an intrinsic goal of national health care systems (WHO 2000). Client power and health system responsiveness are largely a function of the ability of patients to make their wishes heard.

This chapter represents part of a larger research project on performance-based contracting for the delivery of primary health services in Uganda that is being conducted by the World Bank in collaboration with the Makerere University Institute of Public Health and the Ministry of Health in Uganda. Funding for the research project has been provided by the Canadian International Development Agency, and the U.S. Agency for International Development has supplied supplemental funding. The author would like to thank Tonia Marek, Peter Okwero, Mead Over, George Pariyo, Alex Preker, Robert Taylor, and the team of researchers at Makerere University for their contributions.

313

Patients value good quality in health care. In principle, they evaluate the evidence on the relative quality of alternative providers and on the prices they charge and choose the provider who satisfies their preferences and their budgets. They exercise their rights to exit (to move to a different provider) or to voice (to influence the quality of the services provided). But, in practice, patients do not have adequate information to make choices; they may not have the capacity to evaluate the evidence that is presented; and there may be only a small number of alternative providers in the local neighborhood, effectively preventing exit and obviating the need for providers to compete over quality.

Those factors have led to significant public sector intervention in health care. In many countries, a large share of services are provided publicly. In most countries, even private providers are at least partly publicly funded and regulated. Regulating agencies, as well as patients, are eager to measure and improve the quality of health care services, even those provided by the private sector.

But quality is difficult to define and measure, and, even though the regulating agencies and patients both want higher-quality services, they may have different perceptions on what constitutes good quality. Although patient satisfaction is important in its own right, what the patient wants from health care may not be the factors that are valued by the public health bureaucracy, nor the attributes that actually lead to improved health. Conversely, the attributes that lead to improved health may not enhance the patient's experience of health services.

Providers may be thought of as agents who must satisfy the demands of two principals—the health care bureaucracy and the patients—who have differing and possibly conflicting definitions of quality. The patients and the public health establishment both value technical quality in health care, but the patients also appreciate being treated well by providers.[1]

Numerous tools have been developed to assess the quality of health care. Most of these have focused on the technical side, examining inputs, processes, and outcomes. Even the relatively straightforward measures are complicated because they must weigh outcomes according to the complexity or severity of the conditions of patients and establish a standard against which providers may be evaluated.

The measurement of quality according to the perceptions of patients is even more difficult. The interpretation of responses to opinion surveys is complicated because opinions are functions of expectations and knowledge, and these opinions vary enormously across patients, even those with comparable needs and requirements in levels of care. Considerable effort has gone into developing questionnaires that elicit more rigorous and accurate information from patients, as well as separate opinions about the technical quality of health services and the quality of amenities such as food in hospitals and the politeness of providers.

The use of patient satisfaction surveys is now widespread. Most of the published research using exit polls has been primarily descriptive or carried out to understand the correlates of patient satisfaction. Mendoza Aldana, Piechulek, and Al-Sabir (2001), for example, interview nearly 2,000 users of public health facilities in rural Bangladesh. They find that patients are concerned much more about the respect and politeness of their providers than about technical measures of the quality of care or provider competence and that reducing waiting time is much more important to clients than increasing the duration of the consultation. In Burundi, Cetinoglu et al. (2004) compare client satisfaction with services across groups of facilities with different price regimes. They find that clients are less likely to be satisfied with care in facilities that set fees high enough to recover costs completely than with care in facilities that charge a flat fee, even if there are no significant differences in the content of the services. Williams, Schutt-Aine, and Cuca (2000) have conducted exit interviews in eight Latin American and Caribbean countries to measure levels of satisfaction with various aspects of family planning services.

Other studies have attempted to evaluate facility performance to enhance governance or to provide greater information to patients. Among the more well known of these studies are the report cards used to assess client satisfaction with a wide range of publicly and privately provided services, including water, electricity, transport, and housing, as well as health (for instance, see Paul 1995).

Exit polls may be used to evaluate specific interventions among health care workers or innovations in service provision if interviews are conducted among clients of both treated and untreated facilities. DiPrete Brown et al. (2000) evaluate the impact of a training program designed to enhance the interpersonal communication skills of doctors in Honduras. Patients of doctors who have received the training are more likely to report more positive and less negative talk from providers and more medical counseling and are more likely to be satisfied with the care. Peters, Rao, and Ramana (2004) examine the distribution of benefits from reforms to health services in India and find that there has been a significantly positive impact on patient satisfaction, especially at lower-level facilities, but not among patients in the poorest 40 percent of the population.

Some studies use exit polls to understand the determinants of demand or the constraints on use. Newman et al. (1998), for instance, have conducted exit interviews at 34 health clinics to identify the obstacles to care in rural Mozambique. They find that the most commonly mentioned impediments to the increased use of health services are distance to a facility, long waiting times, and lack of medications.

These studies elicit the opinions of people who are already consuming health services. They tell us what attributes of health services clients value and may suggest improvements that might enhance the experience of consumers or encourage those who are already clients to consume even more services. But they do not necessarily provide information on the barriers to health care facing the general population or the changes that would be needed to encourage more people to seek care. Nor do these surveys necessarily reflect the opinions of the general population concerning health services. Clients interviewed within or close to facilities may provide overly generous assessments of the care they have now received (the courtesy bias).[2] Finally, the people who seek care are not necessarily representative of the general population. They may be more ill, or more able to afford services, or more convinced than the general population that health services may actually help to alleviate their problems.

This chapter presents the results of a series of exit surveys conducted in Uganda as part of an experiment to encourage the delivery of primary health services to the poor. It also compares the results of the exit surveys to household surveys that were carried out in the catchment areas surrounding the participating health facilities. What might we learn from these exit surveys? Might those lessons be extrapolated to the general population?

Examination of the exit polls permits the analysis of a number of different questions regarding health services in Uganda. First, how do clients regard health services in Uganda? Much has been made of differences in the services offered by public providers and nongovernmental organizations (Reinikka and Svensson 2003). Are these differences apparent in the opinions of users? Second, if there are systematic differences across institutional types, may it be that the different types of providers (public, private, and nongovernmental organizations) serve different populations of clients? Third, the data used for this analysis have been collected as part of an experiment to introduce performance-based bonuses for nongovernmental health services. Has the introduction of those incentives had any effect on the perceived quality of services? Finally, the Uganda Ministry of Health has recently introduced a quality assurance program whereby facilities that meet certain criteria are awarded yellow stars. Some of the yellow star facilities are included in the current sample. Do these facilities differ from others in terms of perceived quality of services?

Uganda Contracting Experiment

Uganda has experienced several social, political, and economic reforms in the past decade, most notably the decentralization that started in 1993 and was given a more sound legal basis through the new constitution in 1995. The major thrust of the reforms has been to promote participatory democratic governance at the subnational and community levels through the devolution of power over local governance, resource allocations, and service delivery. Through local governments, the Ministry of Health pays base grants to private not-for-profit (PNFP) facilities to provide basic health services under the terms of memorandums of understanding. The grants are assigned for the provision of specific services and the delivery of defined outputs, and the use of the grants is restricted to the purchase of specific inputs, such as medicines and medical consumables. Since 1997, the government has increased public subsidies to PNFP providers with the aim of expanding access to health care through public-private partnerships, especially in underserved parts of the country. In 2000, a basic minimum package of health services was instituted in an attempt to reduce morbidity and death from the most common preventable diseases.

The PNFP health services were mostly founded initially by the various religious missions that came to Uganda in the late 19th century. They are now coordinated and supported by medical bureaus set up by the respective religious denominations, that is, the Uganda Catholic Medical Bureau, the Uganda Protestant Medical Bureau, and the Uganda Muslim Medical Bureau. PNFP providers play a significant part in Uganda's health care system. At present, 44 hospitals and 525 lower-level health units—about one-third of all health facilities in the country—are operated by PNFPs. These health units account for as much as half of all the health services provided in the country and an even larger share of certain services, such as childhood immunizations (see Reinikka and Svensson 2003; Lindelow, Reinikka, and Svensson 2003). PNFP units had a key role in providing health service access to the poor, who are

318 ARE YOU BEING SERVED?

often located in rural areas where there are no other providers. There have been ongoing discussions between the Ministry of Health and the PNFPs on ways to balance the needs of citizens for health services and the mechanisms to fund the services (for example, user fees) against the ever-precarious financial situation and the sustainability concerns of the PNFP units.

The data presented here were collected during a study examining the introduction of performance-based contracts between purchasers (the district governments) and the PNFPs and the impact of these on health service targeting. In five districts, Arua, Bushenyi, Jinja, Kyenjojo, and Mukono, additional contract terms were specified in an addendum to the memorandums of understanding between district governments and PNFP health facilities. All 68 PNFP facilities in the five districts were enrolled in the study. The study had a prospective, quasi-experimental design, with three arms (two intervention groups [study groups A and B] and one control group [C]). PNFP facilities were randomly assigned to each of the three arms of the study. Only PNFP facilities were included in the two experimental arms; the control group was a mixture of public, private for-profit, and PNFP facilities.

During the study, the control group (C) was subject to the financial arrangements that existed as of the onset of the study. Facilities in the second study arm (B) continued to receive the existing base grants, but were permitted the freedom to spend the grants without restriction. PNFP facilities in the main experimental arm (A) were also allowed the freedom to spend the base grants and, in addition, were to be awarded bonus payments if certain self-selected output targets were achieved. A version of the relevant memorandum of understanding was developed and used to expand coverage among public facilities and private for-profit health practitioners.

Repeated surveys were conducted at the 118 health facilities selected (68 PNFPs, 24 private for-profit facilities, and 26 public facilities). The study also collected staff surveys and exit polls at each facility and conducted repeated interviews with a sample of households in the catchment areas of each facility. The household sample was obtained after a primary enumeration of households in randomly selected clusters defined by the Uganda Bureau of Statistics. The enumeration clusters were selected according to probability proportional to size. In each selected enumeration area, the household list of the Uganda Bureau of Statistics was updated, as necessary, in collaboration with local council leaders.

Interviews were conducted every six to eight months by teams from the Makerere University Institute of Public Health. The teams worked closely with the Uganda Bureau of Statistics, the Ministry of Finance, Planning and Economic Development, and participating religious medical bureaus and district health and administrative authorities. Each wave of the study required between 19 and 26 days to complete. Whenever necessary, the teams made callbacks to complete survey questionnaires or trace missing respondents. The questionnaires were translated into local languages, field tested, and back-translated for accuracy. Table 14.1 shows the sample sizes for wave 1 of the study. The first row indicates regions (central and so on), while the second row indicates districts (Mukono and so on).

Over the course of the study, two facilities dropped out, and the number of staff and exit surveys collected at each facility declined. In total, 1,399 exit interviews were conducted over the three waves: 622 in wave 1, 447 in wave 2, and 330 in wave 3. This drop-off may affect the results of the analysis, but there is no obvious counterfactual against which to compare.[3] Wave-specific and pooled analysis is presented below.

For the contracting experiment, a set of six performance targets was chosen in consultation with the directors of all participating PNFP facilities.

TABLE 14.1 Sample Size of Wave 1 of the Uganda Primary Health Contracting Study

Element	Central Mukono	Eastern Jinja	Northern Arua	Western Bushenyi	Western Kyenjojo	Total
Local language	Luganda	Lusoga	Lugbara	Runyankore	Rutoro	
PNFP units	15	14	14	16	9	68
Public units	5	5	5	6	5	26
Private for-profit units	5	5	5	5	4	24
Facility surveys	25	24	24	27	18	118
Staff surveys	54	64	92	123	53	386
Exit polls	102	152	177	84	107	622
Household interviews	249	238	239	280	177	1,183

Source: Compiled by the author.
Note: PNFP = private not-for-profit.

The targets were (a) a 10 percent increase in total outpatient visits, (b) a 5 percent increase in the number of births attended by skilled personnel, (c) a 10 percent increase in the number of children immunized, (d) a 5 percent increase in the acceptance of modern family planning methods, (e) a 10 percent increase in the number of antenatal visits, and (f) a 10 percent increase in the number of cases of malaria treated among children. Each participating PNFP facility assigned to the bonus group (A) was asked to choose three of the six performance targets. For each target achieved during each six-month period, the facility would receive an extra 1 percent of its base grant. Extra bonuses might be obtained by meeting two or three targets and by meeting targets in two consecutive six-month periods. The maximum bonus a facility might achieve during a single year was 11 percent of the base grant. Because the base grant makes up the majority of funding for most PNFP facilities, the maximum obtainable bonus amounted to roughly 5–10 percent of the total operating revenue, on average.

Over the course of the three waves of the study, 22 of the 24 facilities in the experimental group (A) received bonuses. The amount received increased over the course of the study, suggesting that facilities faced a learning curve with the bonus scheme.[4] In total, the median bonus group facility received about US$500, or about 11 percent of the base grant, over the 18-month study period. This funding ranged from as little as US$150 to more than US$10,000 in the case of two hospitals, Nyenga in Mukono District and Kuluva in Arua.

Although most of the facilities in the bonus scheme achieved their performance goals and were awarded bonuses, the comparison with the other facilities reveals that the performance-bonus facilities did not outperform others during this period. Double-difference comparisons suggest that, if anything, facilities in the bonus group performed slightly worse than the facilities receiving only the untied base grant and about as well as the facilities in the control group.

Results of the Exit Polls

Here, we present the results of the exit polls to provide insights on the questions posed above. How do clients regard the quality of services provided? Do opinions vary across providers? Do the clients differ systematically across type of provider? Has the introduction of performance-based incentives had an impact on perceived quality? In the opinion of clients, do facilities that qualify for the yellow star program of the Ministry of Health rank higher relative to other facilities?

Nearly 1,400 exit interviews were conducted over the three waves. Outright refusal was extremely low, but missing and incomplete answers plagued a number of the individual interviews. To maintain a consistent sample size for the questions included here, we reduced the sample to 1,208. Three-quarters of the respondents were women, and the mean age was 32. About half were attending a facility to obtain treatment for themselves, about 40 percent to obtain treatment for another family member (usually a child), and the remaining 10 percent for other reasons. The vast majority had visited a facility previously. The interviews were spread fairly evenly across the days of the week, although relatively fewer were conducted on the weekends.

Perceptions of Heath Services

Clients judge facilities based on their impressions of the technical quality of care and on the attributes that make their experience pleasant or, at least, reduce their costs both financially and in terms of time and suffering. Figure 14.1 shows the relative amounts of time that clients spent traveling to or from a facility (one way), waiting at a facility, and in consultation with a provider. On average, respondents spent an hour traveling and an hour waiting to see the provider for about 15 minutes. The median consultation time in all facilities was 5 minutes. The mean waiting times and travel times were significantly longer for clients at public facilities, but so was the mean consultation time. These times compare favorably to those in Bangladesh (Mendoza Aldana, Piechulek, and Al-Sabir 2001) and Trinidad and Tobago (Singh, Haqq, and Mustapha 1999), which report mean consultation times of 2.3 and 3 minutes, respectively.

Previous studies have shown that the time and expense of getting to a facility are a significant burden (for example, see Newman et al. 1998). But it is not clear that clients will choose to visit the closest facility. Respondents were asked how long it would take them to travel to up to three alternative facilities to receive the same service they received at the facility where they were interviewed. The mean difference in travel time between the current and alternative facilities was about 15 minutes, and the median was zero. This time supports the findings of Collier, Dercon, and Mackinnon (2002) in Ethiopia that patients are more responsive to the quality of services than to distance.

About half the respondents reported that the waiting times were too long, although clients at PNFP facilities were less likely to report this issue

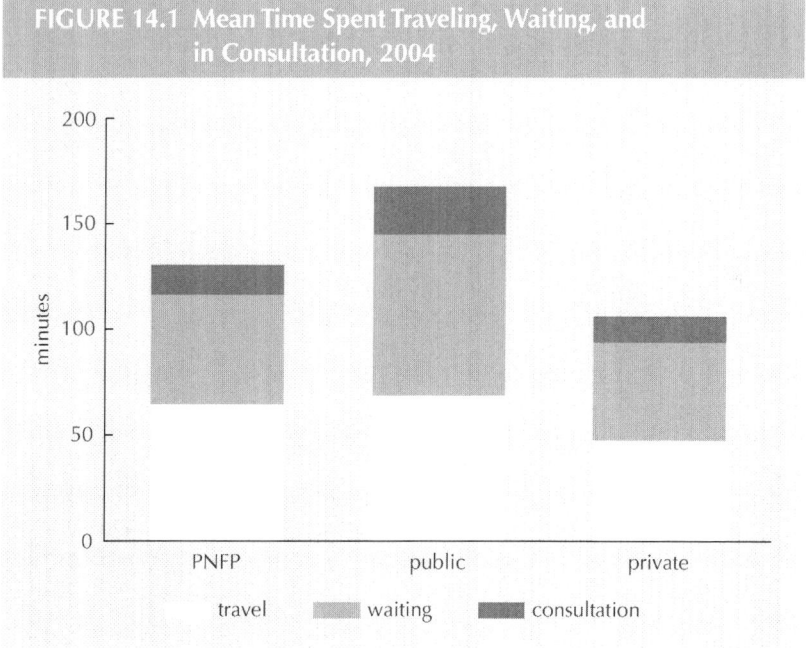

FIGURE 14.1 Mean Time Spent Traveling, Waiting, and in Consultation, 2004

Source: Compiled by the author.

than respondents at other facilities. There was no notable difference on this issue between clients at public facilities and clients at private-for-profit facilities. The results most likely reflect differences in expectations, as well as differences in actual waiting times. Surprisingly, nearly 90 percent of the respondents felt that they had enough time for their consultations. There was no difference in satisfaction across facility types. More than 90 percent of patients at all facilities reported that they had been treated politely while waiting and during consultation.

Clients do sort across facility types according to their willingness to queue and their willingness to pay. Patients at public facilities put up with longer travel and waiting times in return for lower prices. Respondents were asked to give the main reason they chose to come to that facility rather than another. About 40 percent of the clients at public facilities mentioned price. In contrast, those attending PNFP facilities were more likely to cite quality as the reason for their choice, and clients at private facilities cited distance as the motivating factor. The responses differ somewhat from those reported by Lindelöw, Reinikka, and Svensson (2003), who find that proximity is the most important factor among all respondents, particularly those using government facilities. Good treatment and staff are more important among clients at private for-profit and PNFP facilities.

When respondents were asked to estimate whether they would pay the same amount, more, or less for the care they received if they were to seek care at a different facility, those attending public facilities were significantly more likely to estimate that the price for care would be higher at a different facility. Respondents were generally correct in their assessments of relative prices. Fees are highest at private facilities, where respondents are also more likely to report giving gifts, in addition to official fees (see table 14.2). Note that, although user fees were introduced in public facilities in the early 1990s and were abolished by presidential directive in 2001, mean fees are not zero at public facilities (although the median fee is zero).

This finding is not likely to represent evidence of a slow trickling down of information to the local level. The first round of surveys for this study was conducted in the spring of 2004, nearly three years after the official elimination of fees in public facilities. The trends reveal that the proportion of clients who reported paying fees in public facilities increased from 8 percent during the first wave to 18 percent during the third wave.

Figure 14.2 shows the content of consultations as reported by patients during exit interviews. Most, though not all providers asked questions of the patients. The content of the consultations was similar among PNFP and for-profit providers; the consultations with public providers were less likely to involve activities generally considered routine features of a medical consultation. More than 60 percent of private and PNFP caregivers conducted

TABLE 14.2 What Did You Pay for the Care You Received Here Today?
in U Sh

Facility type	Fees	Gifts	Medicines
PNFP	2,611.11	6.27	376.79
Public	300.68	5.33	59.95
Private	3,315.00	99.02	330.71
Total	1,949.12	13.89	274.22

Source: Compiled by the author.
Note: U Sh = Uganda shilling.

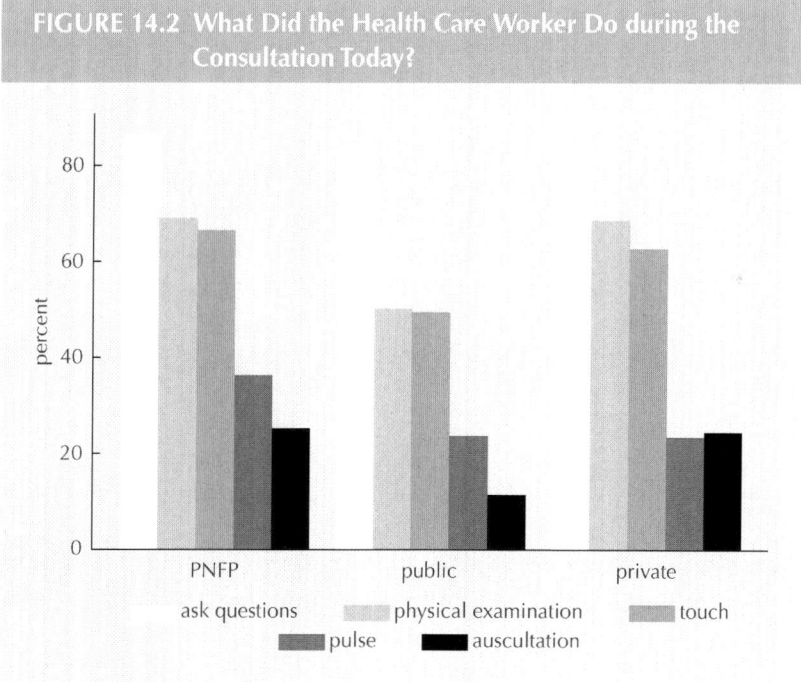

FIGURE 14.2 What Did the Health Care Worker Do during the Consultation Today?

Source: Compiled by the author from pooled data from three survey rounds, 2004-06.

examinations of patients; nearly all of these involved physical manipulations. In contrast, only half the public providers conducted physical examinations. PNFP providers are more likely to take the pulse of the patient and to listen to the patient's chest with a stethoscope (auscultation). There is more variation in these two specific components of the examination, although in neither case do public providers outperform the other two groups.[5]

Table 14.3 shows the opinions of patients concerning different aspects of care at facilities. The opinions are represented by the share of respondents who believe that the care they received was good or very good. In general, clients at private and PNFP facilities have a better opinion of the care they have received than do clients at public facilities, with one substantial exception: the price of care.

Table 14.3 begs the question: what goes into the client's opinion about the overall quality of care? Without a structural model, one may merely try to find correlates of satisfaction in, one hopes, more objectively measured aspects of care. Table 14.4 presents the results of two probit regressions on

TABLE 14.3 Share of Respondents Expressing a Positive Opinion of Care at a Facility

Aspect of care	PNFP	Public	Private	Total
Availability of medicines	0.74	0.38	0.69	0.62
Attitude of staff	0.87	0.73	0.94	0.83
Prices	0.57	0.77	0.65	0.64
I was treated well	0.83	0.72	0.85	0.80
Provider listened to me	0.87	0.77	0.90	0.84
Overall	0.78	0.61	0.86	0.74

Source: Compiled by the author.

overall satisfaction (from Table 14.3) against a number of characteristics of the care experience. Again in support of the findings of Collier, Dercon, and Mackinnon (2002), travel time is insignificant. Waiting time matters, but the most significant correlates of a satisfactory experience are the indicators that the patient has been treated kindly. Were you treated politely? Did the health care worker actually talk to you?

Although the patient values these aspects of care, they may have nothing to do with the technical quality of the care or the impact of the care on health outcomes. Conversely, none of the indicators of the technical quality of consultations (the characteristics of the physical examination) are valued by the patient. Finally, there is the unexpectedly negative (though barely significant) correlation between the patient's satisfaction with the experience and the length of time for the consultation. This result disappears if the top single outlier in consulting time is dropped from the sample; the other correlations are unchanged. This analysis confirms the findings of other studies that consulting time is relatively unimportant and that patients are satisfied with the limited consulting time they receive. One recent study on five developed countries has found, in fact, that the country in which consultation time was longest reported the lowest rates of consumer satisfaction (Donelan et al. 1999).

Do Clients Vary Systematically Across Facility Type?

Client satisfaction certainly varies with previous experience, with the expectation of care, and with the client's own health. The results presented earlier show that clients sort themselves among PNFPs (higher quality at higher

TABLE 14.4 Correlates of Overall Satisfaction with the Care Experience

probit, marginal effects

Correlate	dF/dx	Z-statistic	dF/dx	Z-statistic
Travel time (minutes)	−0.009	(0.71)	−0.009	(0.71)
Waiting time (minutes)	−0.050	(5.52)**	−0.049	(5.47)**
Consultation time (minutes)	−0.025	(1.76)+	−0.025	(1.80)+
Treated politely while waiting	0.169	(2.64)**	0.171	(2.66)**
Treated politely during the consultation	0.152	(2.11)*	0.152	(2.09)*
Asked questions	0.144	(3.67)**	0.149	(3.75)**
Given physical examination	0.059	(1.39)	0.060	(1.43)
Touched during examination	0.014	(0.33)	0.019	(0.45)
Pulse taken	0.059	(1.53)	0.053	(1.37)
Auscultation	−0.050	(1.16)	−0.044	(1.02)
My own health is good	0.086	(3.20)**	0.094	(3.44)**
PNFP facility	0.097	(3.38)**	0.107	(3.69)**
Private facility	0.162	(3.62)**	0.172	(3.86)**
Controls for other client characteristics[a]	no		yes	
Joint significance test for client characteristics				(8.04)
Log-likelihood		(617.09)		(613.01)
Likelihood ratio X^2 (marginal effect)		(162.55)**		(170.72)**
Pseudo-R^2		(0.12)		(0.12)
Total sample		1,208		1,208

Source: Compiled by the author from pooled data from three survey rounds, 2004-06.
Note: + Significant at <0.1. * Significant at <0.05. ** Significant at <0.01.
a. Controls do not include days ill or children's vaccination. See Table 14.5 for a list of the controls.

cost), private facilities (shorter distance at higher cost), and public facilities (lower quality at lower cost). Are there other dimensions or individual characteristics that might influence the expectations that people have and, thus, the level of satisfaction people express?

Note that, if different types of clients systematically seek care at different types of facilities, opinions derived from exit interviews would not be directly comparable across facility types. Table 14.5 presents a comparison of descriptive statistics on clients across the three types of facilities. The table reveals that the sample interviewed at each type of facility differs significantly in many respects. The clients at PNFP and private facilities were more knowledgeable than the clients at public facilities about the causes of disease, and PNFP clients were more likely than clients at private facilities to answer these questions correctly.[6] The clients at public facilities were more likely to have had a death in the family in the past year. Those clients with more severe illnesses—measured crudely by the number of days that the respondent had been ill—were less likely to seek care at private facilities. There was no significant distinction in household size, nor (among clients who had children under 10) in whether the youngest child had been vaccinated. The clients at PNFP and private clinics were likely to have more education.

TABLE 14.5 Characteristics of Clients, by Facility Type

Characteristic	PNFP	Public	Private
Know the cause of malaria[a, b, c]	92.05	87.77	79.41
Know at least one cause of diarrhea[a]	86.85	79.52	83.33
Know the cause of HIV/AIDS[a, c]	89.04	85.37	81.37
Severity of illness (days ill)[c, d]	11.22	9.43	5.99
Had a death in the family in the past year[a, b]	28.9	37.23	23.53
Youngest child has been vaccinated[d]	35.59	28.57	41.67
Household size	6.70	6.39	7.20
Have primary education[a, b, e]	56.16	60.11	61.76
Have secondary or higher education[a, b, e]	26.99	17.55	24.51
Wealth index[a, b]	0.22	−0.52	0.35

Source: Compiled by the author from pooled data from three survey rounds, 2004-06.
Note:
a. The difference between PNFP and public facilities is significant at <0.05.
b. The difference between private and public facilities is significant at <0.05.
c. The difference between PNFP and private facilities is significant at <0.05.
d. Days ill are represented by 1,184 observations; children's vaccinations, by 598 observations.
e. The differences in education are estimated as ordered probit.

Partly to facilitate comparisons with the household survey (see later), we have constructed a principal components index on a comprehensive set of physical and human capital variables (ownership of various animals and items, household size, education, dwelling size and amenities, and so on). According to this index, respondents at public facilities are significantly poorer than those at PNFP and private facilities.

The results suggest that simple comparisons of exit interviews across classes of health facility may be biased. However, the second pair of columns in Table 14.4 shows that the inclusion of client characteristics—beyond the indicator of own health—has no effect on the service-specific correlates of client satisfaction. (The individual parameter estimates are not presented, but are available.) The only client characteristic that affects satisfaction directly is whether the household has experienced a recent death. The household's relative wealth, its knowledge of diseases, and other characteristics are unimportant to the client's assessment of the quality of care.

Have the Performance-Based Incentives Had Any Impact on Perceived Quality?

The exit polls were collected as part of the experiment to introduce performance-based incentives to PNFP facilities. The data on the measurement of facility performance and on the calculation of performance bonuses come from output data collected at the facilities. The team collected household data and exit interviews partly to corroborate the information coming from the facility surveys and to understand the perceptions and behavior of the population in the participating facility catchment areas.

We know that the performance bonus has had little effect so far on the volume of facility output. But one of the implicit goals of the experiment was to encourage greater consumption of health services and improved health-seeking behavior on the part of the traditionally underserved target population, especially poor households. Even though the total volume of services produced has not changed, it may be that the composition of clients has changed such that facilities are now providing more services to the poor.

Table 14.6 presents the results of double-difference regressions of perceived quality in performance-scheme PNFP facilities (A) and PNFP facilities in the second experimental group with freedom to allocate the base grant (B). The individual t-statistics are for significant differences with respect to the PNFP control group. The table shows that the perceived availability of the medicines, the attitude of staff, and the prices charged by the facility worsened

TABLE 14.6 Changes in Perceived Quality after the Introduction of the Bonus Scheme

Characteristic	Facilities in bonus scheme (A)		Facilities able to allocate grant (B)		F-test that the two groups are the same
	Estimate	T-statistic	Estimate	T-statistic	
Ln (consultation time, minutes)[a]	-0.004	(0.02)	-0.199	(1.21)	(1.39)
Ln (waiting time, minutes)[a]	0.405	(1.41)	0.321	(1.18)	(0.09)
Waiting time was too long	0.062	(0.57)	-0.192	(1.98)*	(6.32)*
Consultation time was adequate	0.039	(0.67)	-0.028	(0.43)	(1.21)
Overall quality of care	-0.155	(1.59)	0.020	(0.26)	(3.49)+
Availability of medicines	-0.174	(1.74)+	0.006	(0.06)	(3.43)+
Attitude of staff	-0.161	(1.74)+	-0.096	(1.26)	(0.43)
Prices	0.175	(2.17)*	0.091	(1.12)	(1.32)
Provider treated me well	-0.015	(0.19)	0.026	(0.36)	(0.30)
Provider listened to me	-0.019	(0.27)	-0.043	(0.61)	(0.10)
Ln (total amount paid)[a]	0.684	(0.57)	1.284	(1.13)	(0.27)
Wealth index[a]	0.838	(1.95)+	-0.531	(1.30)	(10.96)**

Source: Compiled by the author from pooled data from three survey rounds, 2004-06.
Note: Parameter estimates are taken from separate probit regressions unless otherwise noted.
a. Continuous variables; parameter estimates from ordinary least squares regressions. Ln refers to the Natural log.
+ Significant at <0.1. * Significant at <0.05. ** Significant at <0.01.

(in the view of the respondents) more among the bonus group than among the PNFP control group following the implementation of the bonus scheme.

Conversely, the wealth index of clients treated by the PNFP bonus group increased relative to that of the clients treated by the PNFP control group. Sadly, the mean wealth index in the exit sample actually declined over the survey period. This suggests that, rather than increasing their service to the poorer segments of the population, the PNFP facilities in the bonus group were caring for clients who were wealthier relative both to the clients served by the PNFP control group and to the population.

Among PNFP facilities in the second experimental arm (B), with freedom to allocate the base grant, but without the bonus scheme, the only significant change following the introduction of the experiment was that clients complained less about waiting times. Interestingly, there was no corresponding change in actual waiting times; it was simply that the clients were less likely to report that they had waited too long.

The final column in table 14.6 shows the results of tests of the equivalence of perceptions of quality in the two PNFP experimental arms. Waiting times have become more acceptable and the availability of medicines and the overall quality of care have improved more (or rather have not worsened) among the freedom-to-allocate facilities relative to those in the bonus group. In contrast to clients in the PNFP bonus group, the wealth composition of the clients in the PNFP freedom-to-allocate group has not changed.

These difference-in-difference results should be treated with some caution because they are the result of comparisons of one single preintervention wave to two postintervention waves. Thus, they may not avoid the problem of separate trends. It may be that the care being offered was already declining among the PNFP bonus group, but increasing among the other PNFP facilities in the sample. Although this change is possible, it is unlikely given that facilities were assigned to experimental arms randomly.

Do Yellow Star Facilities Rank Higher Than Others?

In 2000, the Ministry of Health implemented a program to improve the quality of health services. Participating facilities are evaluated quarterly on the basis of a set of 35 indicators of technical and interpersonal quality, including factors such as recordkeeping, the disposal of medical waste, waiting times, privacy, and respect. Facilities that score 100 percent in two consecutive quarters are awarded a yellow star, which is prominently displayed outside the facility. This program has garnered a good deal of attention in the popular press in Uganda and among researchers studying health care quality. It has been cited as best practice (DISH and Measure Evaluation 2003; WHO 2006), and it was one of a few programs highlighted in the chapter on health care quality in the recent volume *Disease Control Priorities in Developing Countries* (see Peabody et al. 2006). The program has been credited with increasing the quality of health services. Thus, McNamara (2006) reports that the average score of participating facilities rose from 47 percent to 65 percent between the first two evaluations.

A number of the facilities in the current sample carry a yellow star, and, although the exit interviews collected information on only a small subset of yellow star variables, we may compare perceptions of quality in certified and uncertified facilities. Table 14.7 presents the means on specific characteristics of facilities with and without yellow star certification.

TABLE 14.7 Differences between Facilities with and without Yellow Star Certification

Characteristic	No star	With star	T-statistic of equality of means
Travel time (minutes)	65.74	60.09	(1.30)
Waiting time (minutes)	60.13	54.78	(1.00)
Consultation time (minutes)	17.21	14.67	(0.53)
Waiting time was too long	0.46	0.38	(2.46)*
Consultation time was adequate	0.88	0.86	(0.77)
Treated politely while waiting	0.95	0.95	(0.16)
Treated politely in consultation	0.97	0.94	(1.64)
Asked questions	0.86	0.84	(0.72)
Given physical examination	0.64	0.60	(1.32)
Touched during examination	0.61	0.60	(0.17)
Pulse taken	0.32	0.28	(1.49)
Auscultation	0.22	0.17	(2.06)*
Overall quality of care	0.73	0.76	(1.01)
Availability of medicines	0.63	0.58	(1.56)
Attitude of staff	0.83	0.85	(0.87)
Prices	0.61	0.75	(4.66)**
Provider treated me well	0.80	0.80	(0.04)
Provider listened to me	0.84	0.85	(0.65)

Source: Compiled by the author.
Note: * Significant at <0.05. ** Significant at <0.01. Author used proportion of respondents indicating "yes" or "satisfactory" in answer to the question.

The most obvious point is that the facilities are generally alike. Few of the characteristics measured in the exit poll differ by yellow star certification, and only one of these—satisfaction with waiting times—is in favor of facilities with the certificate. Surprisingly, providers in facilities without a yellow star are more likely than providers in facilities with a star to listen to a patient's chest with a stethoscope. And patients are more likely to be happy with the price of care in facilities without a yellow star. This data set does not include prices for specific services, but it may be that the yellow star allows facilities to charge prices higher than those they would be able to charge in the absence of the star.

Do Exit Polls Differ Significantly from Household Surveys?

Now we come to the last question concerning the use of exit polls. To what extent are exit polls valid? May the information gathered in exit polls be used to make inferences about the behavior of households, about the constraints facing potential clients, or about the impact of different policy interventions? How different are the clients from the general population?

We know that exit polls are more likely to yield positive opinions about the quality of care than alternative sources of information. Community-based focus group discussions in South Africa have provided a picture of health care providers and services that is more negative than the picture derived from exit polls (Schneider and Palmer 2002).

Exit polls may also yield information about individual respondents that differs from the information supplied through household surveys. This difference may be caused by deliberate obfuscation on the part of respondents in exit polls, but it may also be caused because the two sets of respondents are distinct populations. Meekers and Adhiambo Ogada (2001) have found that respondents in exit surveys and household surveys in Rwanda report different rates of sexual risk behavior, including condom use and the incidence of multiple sexual partners. They have found that these differences are largely caused by differences in the populations and that respondents interviewed at places where condoms may be obtained (shops, nightclubs, pharmacies) are not representative of the general population. Controlling for these observable differences in respondent characteristics reduces the discrepancy in reported behavior between the two groups of respondents.

Bessinger and Bertrand (2001) have compared the results of exit polls and direct observations of family planning services in Ecuador, Uganda, and

Zimbabwe. The results are consistent across methods for some indicators, less so for others. According to both the direct observations and the exit interviews, clients were treated with respect and accorded sufficient privacy. There was greater disagreement between the two methods on more specific aspects of the consultation, such as whether the provider discussed HIV/ AIDS and whether the provider explained that family planning methods other than condoms (such as the intrauterine device and the pill) do not prevent HIV infection.

The exit polls and household surveys both collected information on an inventory of physical and human capital such as ownership of animals and land, dwelling unit characteristics, consumer durables, education, household size, and so on. This collection made it possible to construct a wealth index from the pooled data of both samples. The analysis below presents the respondents' opinions on a variety of aspects of care on which identical questions appeared in both the household survey and exit poll questionnaires. This grouping is a subset of the questions in the exit polls. The sample is the exit polls and those households that report seeking care in the past month. This information is about 5 percent of the total household population.

Table 14.8 shows the differences between exit polls and household surveys in perceived quality. The table presents a comparison of the raw data and a comparison of a propensity-score–matched sample, wherein the treatment is the selection into the exit poll sample as a function of the wealth index. This comparision represents an attempt to reduce the differences in responses that are caused by differences in observable respondent characteristics between the two samples. The z-statistics are from bootstrapped tests of differences between the means of the matched data set.

The table shows some interesting differences between the two samples. First, households report travel and waiting times that are much lower than those for the exit sample at the facilities. One reason is that the household sample is drawn from the catchment area around each facility, and, although the catchment areas are defined broadly, facilities draw their clientele from even a much wider area than that. But this does not explain the differences in waiting times. There is no reason, a priori, that patients who travel a greater distance should wait any longer than patients who live nearby. Respondents in the exit sample feel their need for medical care is great enough to outweigh the cost of travel and waiting. They are willing to travel and wait, while the household sample may have a higher opportunity cost of time, or it may place a lower value on the benefits of care. The finding that there is no difference in consultation time reinforces the sug-

TABLE 14.8 Differences in Perceived Quality and Treatment Characteristics between Household Surveys and Exit Polls

Characteristic	Differences in raw data set		T-statistic of equality of means	Differences in ps-matched sample		Bootstrapped z-statistic on difference
	Household	Exit		Household	Exit	
Travel time (minutes)	42.35	64.42	(7.09)**	44.38	65.21	(4.51)**
Waiting time (minutes)	28.90	58.88	(8.28)**	24.59	59.15	(4.28)**
Consultation time (minutes)	12.72	16.62	(1.92)+	16.28	16.81	(0.15)
Fee paid (U Sh)	5,621.45	1,923.31	(3.84)**	7,423.30	1,840.41	(1.93)+
Cost of medicines (U Sh)	3,822.81	267.63	(9.21)**	3,497.38	255.85	(2.82)**
Gift to provider (U Sh)	380.06	13.74	(2.01)*	426.85	14.29	(2.17)*
Waiting time was too long (proportion)	0.33	0.44	(4.70)**	0.39	0.45	(1.16)
Consultation time was adequate (proportion)	0.61	0.88	(11.69)**	0.68	0.87	(3.61)**
Treated politely in consultation (proportion)	0.71	0.96	(12.65)**	0.75	0.96	(5.55)**
Given physical examination (proportion)	0.56	0.63	(2.66)**	0.60	0.63	(0.55)
Touched during examination (proportion)	0.54	0.61	(2.77)**	0.59	0.60	(0.23)
Pulse taken (proportion)	0.35	0.31	(1.51)	0.46	0.31	(2.46)*
Auscultation (proportion)	0.29	0.21	(3.41)**	0.34	0.21	(2.18)*
Overall quality of care (proportion)	0.50	0.74	(9.44)**	0.61	0.73	(1.89)+

Source: Compiled by the author.
Note: + Significant at <0.10. * Significant at <0.05. ** Significant at <0.01.

gestion that this is relatively unimportant to clients, but the clients in the exit sample are more likely to agree that the time for consultation is sufficient. This finding again suggests that the actual content of the treatment and a client's opinions about it may not be closely related.

The clients in the exit poll are more likely to report that they were treated politely. Surprisingly, clients in the household survey are more likely to report that the health care worker took their pulse and listened to their chest. The findings reinforce the results presented in table 14.4 that clients care more about being treated kindly than about the technical quality of care. Among the clients in the exit poll, 73 percent reported that the overall quality of care was good or very good compared to 61 percent of the clients in the matched household sample.

The most disturbing part of table 14.8 is the enormous difference in the amount respondents report paying for care. Respondents in the household survey report paying 4 times more in fees, greater than 10 times more in medicines, and 20 times more in informal gifts to providers. This difference might be partly explained by differences in the severity of illness. It might be that the clients in the exit poll are more likely than the clients in the household survey to seek care for minor ailments, for which the fees and related expenses are lower. In this case, the differences would be exaggerated by the differences in the intensity of the required treatments. However, this is probably not the case. The clients in the exit poll report that they had been ill for 10 days, on average, whereas those in the household survey who had sought care had been ill for 3 days. Although it is still possible that the illnesses suffered by the clients in the household survey have been more acute (that is, more severe, but of shorter duration), it is also possible that the payments are substantially different for comparable services.

Equally disturbing is the distribution of these payments across facility types. Because a large number of households report paying no fees, comparisons of the means is misleading, partly because the means are fraught with large standard errors. Table 14.9 shows the share of respondents who report paying a positive amount for services, medicines, and gifts to providers. It appears that the respondents in the exit poll underreport paying fees relative to respondents in the household survey. Or it may be that the respondents in the household survey misremember and overreport. The household survey asks about payments for care sought in the past month, whereas the exit interview asks only about payments that same day. In any event, between 10 and 40 percent of patients report paying fees for services in public facilities. This finding is, again, in contrast to the official

TABLE 14.9 Proportion of Respondents Reporting Paying Non-Zero Amounts, Matched Sample

Facilities	Exit poll	Household survey	Bootstrapped z-statistics of differences
PNFP facilities			
Paying fees	0.65	0.71	(0.95)
Purchasing medicines	0.20	0.59	(7.32)**
Giving gifts to providers	0.00	0.07	(1.47)
Total	0.66	0.88	(5.00)**
Public facilities			
Paying fees	0.10	0.39	(3.42)**
Purchasing medicines	0.04	0.41	(5.18)**
Giving gifts to providers	0.00	0.08	(2.47)*
Total	0.10	0.62	(6.22)**
Private for-profit facilities			
Paying fees	0.55	0.84	(3.47)**
Purchasing medicines	0.08	0.81	(7.80)**
Giving gifts to providers	0.01	0.02	(0.21)
Total	0.58	0.93	(4.80)**

Source: Compiled by the author from pooled data from three survey rounds, 2004-06.
Note: + Significant at <0.10. * Significant at <0.05. ** Significant at <0.01.

claim that fees were abolished in public facilities in 2001. In addition to the fees, 8 percent of households report giving gifts to providers, whereas none of the interviewees in the exit polls acknowledge doing so.

Conclusions

Client satisfaction and the responsiveness of providers to the needs of clients are now among the primary concerns of public health systems. Exit surveys provide a rich source of information on the expressed needs, experiences, and perceptions of clients. This source may be used to measure consumer satisfaction and its correlates and to evaluate the impact of facility-level interventions.

In general, three-quarters of the clients responding to exit polls in Uganda are happy with the quality of care they receive. This finding compares favorably with Bangladesh (68 percent), Mozambique (55 percent), and others, although it is lower than the levels obtained in developed countries.[7] The levels of satisfaction are significantly lower among respondents interviewed at public facilities, with the exception that the patients prefer the prices at the public facility to those charged by other providers. A number of patients and households report paying for care received in public sector health facilities even though those services are supposed to be free.

Clients seem to value the *qualité d'accueil* over the technical quality of the service. In neither the household survey nor the exit polls do respondents value the factors that most closely represent technical quality: the physical examination, having the pulse read, and auscultation. This finding confirms the results of many other studies around the world. It also implies that the results of exit polls may not provide good guidance for the design of policies to improve the quality of health care services if quality is taken to mean clinical efficacy.

Finally, the analysis also suggests that the sample of facility clients is not randomly drawn from the population. It is possible to minimize the impact of the observable exogenous differences in respondent characteristics between the two samples. But, even if we control for the differences in the observed characteristics of the respondents in the two samples, the answers of the two groups of respondents still differ. This difference may be because the two groups genuinely differ in their experiences and opinions or because there are unobserved characteristics that influence both a client's decision to seek treatment and a client's opinion of that treatment. In either case, it is a good idea not to rely exclusively on the results of exit polls.

ANNEX 14.1

SUMMARY STATISTICS FOR OBSERVATIONS INCLUDED IN AND EXCLUDED FROM THE FINAL SAMPLE

TABLE 14A.1 Summary Statistics for Observations Included in and Excluded from the Final Sample			
	In sample	Out of sample	t-statistic
Number of children (average)	3.55	3.07	(2.18)*
Age of respondent (average years)	31.90	30.23	(1.41)
Sex of respondent	0.74	0.78	(0.97)
Days ill	10.22	11.12	(0.55)
Fee paid (U Sh)	1,949.12	1,452.84	(1.55)
Gift to providers (U Sh)	13.89	54.32	(0.91)
Payment for medication (U Sh)	274.22	314.85	(0.43)
Total payment (U Sh)	2,204.68	1,062.47	(4.56)**
Paid for services	0.48	0.23	(8.39)**
Travel time (minutes)	64.42	58.55	(1.13)
Waiting time (minutes)	58.88	66.24	(1.07)
Consultation time (minutes)	16.62	17.32	(0.17)
Waited too long	0.44	0.51	(1.48)
Treated politely while waiting	0.95	0.94	(0.80)
Consultation time was long enough	0.88	0.87	(0.08)
Treated politely during consultation	0.96	0.96	(0.36)
Given physical examination	0.63	0.59	(1.09)
Touched during examination	0.61	0.58	(0.78)
Pulse taken	0.31	0.30	(0.25)

(continued)

TABLE 14A.1 *(Continued)*

	In sample	Out of sample	t-statistic
Auscultation	0.21	0.13	(2.70)**
Provider asked questions	0.85	0.84	(0.41)
Own health is good	0.38	0.39	(0.17)
Overall opinion of care is good	0.74	0.70	(0.82)
Availability of medicines is good	0.62	0.64	(0.45)
Attitude of staff is good	0.83	0.84	(0.30)
Prices are good	0.64	0.34	(9.47)**
Treated well by provider	0.80	0.72	(2.10)*
Provider listened to me	0.84	0.81	(1.07)
Children vaccinated	0.34	0.25	(1.64)
Death in family	0.31	0.30	(0.33)
Household size	6.64	6.45	(0.61)
Know cause of malaria	0.90	0.47	(13.45)**
Know cause of diarrhea	0.84	0.45	(12.28)**
Know cause of HIV/AIDS	0.87	0.40	(15.30)**
Have primary education	0.58	0.32	(8.36)**
Have secondary, higher education	0.24	0.12	(5.05)**
Wealth index	0.00	0.27	(0.97)

Source: Compiled by the author.
Note: + Significant at <0.10. * Significant at <0.05. ** Significant at <0.01.
Proportion of response unless otherwise indicated.

Notes

1. A term in French, *qualité d'accueil,* is appropriate for this treatment. There is no precise English equivalent. The term might be translated as the quality of the consideration and attention.
2. For example, see Bitran Dicowsky (1995, cited in Lindelöw and Wagstaff 2003), who finds that patients report being satisfied, regardless of the technical quality of the services provided.
3. Table 14A.1 presents summary statistics comparing the interviews retained with those dropped. Most significantly, those retained indicate that the interviewees were more likely to feel that they had been treated well by providers, but were not more likely to be satisfied overall; that they had more education; that they were more likely to identify the causes of diseases correctly and pay more for their treatment; that they were less likely to be unhappy over prices; and that they were not wealthier than the interviewees dropped from the sample.
4. This finding has been confirmed by the analysis of facility output data (see Lundberg, Marek, and Pariyo 2007).

5. All the differences between PNFPs and public providers and between private and public providers are significant at <0.01, with the exception of "ask questions," which is the same across all groups, and "pulse," which is the same among public and for-profit providers.
6. Knowing the cause of HIV/AIDS includes correctly rejecting false causes such as contaminated food or casual contact.
7. See Newman et al. (1998) for Mozambique; Mendoza Aldana, Piechulek, and Al-Sabir (2001) for Bangladesh; Donelan et al. (1999) for developed countries.

References

Bessinger, Ruth E., and Jane T. Bertrand. 2001. "Monitoring Quality of Care in Family Planning Programs: A Comparison of Observations and Client Exit Interviews." *International Family Planning Perspectives* 27 (2): 63–70.

Bitran Dicowsky, Ricardo. 1995. "Efficiency and Quality in the Public and Private Sectors in Senegal." *Health Policy and Planning* 10 (3): 271–83.

Cetinoglu, Dalita, Pascale Delchevalerie, Veronique Parqué, Mit Philips, and Michel van Herp. 2004. "Access to Health Care in Burundi: Results of Three Epidemiological Surveys." Report, April, Médecins Sans Frontières, Brussels.

Collier, Paul, Stefan Dercon, and John Mackinnon. 2002. "Density Versus Quality in Health Care Provision: Using Household Data to Make Budgetary Choices in Ethiopia." *World Bank Economic Review* 16 (3): 425–48.

DiPrete Brown, Lori, Bérengér De Negri, Orlando Hernandez, Lilian Dominguez, Julie H. Sanchak, and Debra Roter. 2000. "An Evaluation of the Impact of Training Honduran Health Care Providers in Interpersonal Communication." *International Journal for Quality in Health Care* 12 (6): 495–501.

DISH (Delivery of Improved Services for Health) and Measure Evaluation. 2003. "Uganda Delivery of Improved Services for Health (DISH) Facility Survey 2002." Measure Evaluation Technical Report 14, Delivery of Improved Services for Health, Kampala, Uganda; Carolina Population Center, University of North Carolina at Chapel Hill, Chapel Hill, NC.

Donelan, Karen, Robert J. Blendon, Cathy Schoen, Karen Davis, and Katherine Binns. 1999. "The Cost of Health System Change: Public Discontent in Five Countries." *Health Affairs* 18 (3): 206–16.

Lindelow, Magnus, and Adam Wagstaff. 2003. "Health Facility Surveys: An Introduction." Policy Research Working Paper 2953, World Bank, Washington, DC.

Lindelow, Magnus, Ritva Reinikka, and Jakob Svensson. 2003. "Health Care on the Front Lines: Survey Evidence on Public and Private Providers in Uganda." Africa Region Human Development Working Paper 38, Human Development Sector, Africa Region, World Bank, Washington, DC.

Lundberg, Mattias, Tonia Marek, and George Pariyo. 2007. "Contracting for Primary Health Care in Uganda." Unpublished report, World Bank, Washington, DC.

McNamara, Peggy. 2006. "Provider-Specific Report Cards: A Tool for Health Sector Accountability in Developing Countries." *Health Policy and Planning* 21 (2): 101–09.

Meekers, Dominique, and Edna Adhiambo Ogada. 2001. "Explaining Discrepancies in Reproductive Health Indicators from Population-Based Surveys and Exit Surveys: A Case from Rwanda." *Health Policy and Planning* 16 (2): 137–43.

Mendoza Aldana, Jorge, Helga Piechulek, and Ahmed Al-Sabir. 2001. "Client Satisfaction and Quality of Health Care in Rural Bangladesh." *Bulletin of the World Health Organization* 79 (6): 512–17.

Newman, Robert D., Stephen Gloyd, Julio M. Nyangezi, Francisco Machobo, and Jorine Muiser. 1998. "Satisfaction with Outpatient Health Care Services in Manica Province, Mozambique." *Health Policy and Planning* 13 (2): 174–80.

Paul, Samuel. 1995. "A Report Card on Public Services in Indian Cities: A View from Below." Research Paper 1, Public Affairs Center, Bangalore.

Peabody, John W., Mario M. Taguiwalo, David A. Robalino, and Julio Frenk. 2006. "Improving the Quality of Care in Developing Countries." In *Disease Control Priorities in Developing Countries*, 2nd ed., ed. Dean T. Jamison, Joel G. Breman, Anthony R. Measham, George Alleyne, Mariam Claeson, David B. Evans, Prabhat Jha, Anne Mills, and Philip Musgrove, 1293–1308. Washington, DC: World Bank; New York: Oxford University Press.

Peters, David, Krishna Rao, and G. N. V. Ramana. 2004. "India: Equity Effects of Quality Improvements on Health Service Utilization and Patient Satisfaction in Uttar Pradesh State." HNP Discussion Paper, Reaching the Poor Program Paper 5, Health, Nutrition, and Population, Human Development Network, World Bank, Washington, DC.

Reinikka, Ritva, and Jakob Svensson. 2003. "Working for God?: Evaluating Service Delivery of Religious Not-for-Profit Health Care Providers in Uganda." Policy Research Working Paper 3058, Development Research Group, World Bank, Washington, DC.

Schneider, Helen, and Natasha Palmer. 2002. "Getting to the Truth?: Researching User Views of Primary Health Care." *Health Policy and Planning* 17 (1): 32–41.

Singh, H., E. D. Haqq, and N. Mustapha. 1999. "Patients' Perception and Satisfaction with Health Care Professionals at Primary Care Facilities in Trinidad and Tobago." *Bulletin of the World Health Organization* 77 (4): 356–60.

WHO (World Health Organization). 2000. *The World Health Report 2000: Health Systems, Improving Performance.* Geneva: World Health Organization.

———. 2006. *The World Health Report 2006: Working Together for Health.* Geneva: World Health Organization.

Williams, Timothy, Jessie Schutt-Aine, and Yvette Cuca. 2000. "Measuring Family Planning Service Quality through Client Satisfaction Exit Interviews." *International Family Planning Perspectives* 26 (2): 63–71.

World Bank. 2003. *World Development Report 2004: Making Services Work for Poor People.* Washington, DC: World Bank; New York: Oxford University Press.

15

Health Facility and School Surveys in the Indonesia Family Life Survey

Kathleen Beegle

The Indonesia Family Life Survey (IFLS) is a continuing longitudinal socioeconomic and health survey of households, communities, and service providers in Indonesia. The IFLS data are unique in several ways, including the panel nature of the data, the depth of the questionnaires, and the collection of data from the communities in which the households are located. The facility data among the information collected in communities are the focus of this chapter.

The IFLS is based on a random sample of households in 13 of the nation's 26 provinces in 1993. The 13 provinces included about 83 percent of the population of Indonesia as of that year. The survey collects data on individual respondents, their families, their households, the communities in which they live, and the health and education facilities they use. The first wave (IFLS1, in 1993) was conducted on individuals living in 7,224 households (Frankenberg and Karoly 1995).[1] IFLS2, the second wave, sought to reinterview the same respondents four years later, including respondents who had migrated from their 1993 (IFLS1) dwellings. This approach included efforts to follow individuals who had left their previous households, such as young adult children moving away from parents. In IFLS2,

The author thanks Sumeet Bhatti for excellent research assistance.

about 7,500 households were interviewed (Frankenberg and Thomas 2000).[2] The third wave, IFLS3, was fielded in 2000 and resulted in a sample of over 10,000 households, again reflecting the protocol of tracking respondents who had split from the original households and formed new households (Strauss et al. 2004b).

The IFLS contains a wealth of information collected at the individual and household levels, including multiple indicators of economic well-being (consumption, income, and assets); education, migration, and labor market outcomes; marriage, fertility, and contraceptive use; health status, use of health care, and health insurance; relationships among coresident and non-coresident family members; processes underlying household decision making; transfers among family members and intergenerational mobility; and participation in community activities. By simultaneously collecting data on a wide range of topics (as in the Living Standards Measurement Study surveys), the IFLS favors analyses of interrelated issues not possible in single-purpose surveys. The data allow researchers to study the effects of changes in government programs and household decisions over time during a period of rapid demographic and economic transformation. More interestingly, because the waves of the IFLS span the period from several years before the economic crisis in Indonesia to three years after the crisis, extensive research may be carried out on the living conditions and coping mechanisms of Indonesian households during this tumultuous time. The fourth full round of the IFLS is planned for 2007; it will extend the scope of potential analyses that may be undertaken with this rich data set.

In addition to individual- and household-level information, the IFLS provides detailed information on the communities in which IFLS households are located and the health and education facilities that serve residents of these communities. (The term *community* refers here to the enumeration area, a geographical area defined by Statistics Indonesia. Such a community may be part of a village or a neighborhood in an urban setting.) The data cover various aspects of the physical and social environment, ranging from infrastructure, employment opportunities, and food prices to access to health and educational facilities and the quality and prices of services available at these facilities. In addition, the health facility surveys in IFLS1 and IFLS2 include five hypothetical patient scenarios or vignettes that probe the knowledge of facility respondents about the process for patient care at the facilities. The vignettes cover information on the provision of intrauterine devices and oral contraceptives, prenatal care, treatment of children with vomiting and diarrhea problems, and treatment of adults with respiratory illnesses. In IFLS3, the facility surveys introduced new questions on budget issues to capture features of the decentralization of services in Indonesia. The school survey contains some information on schooling outcomes as measured according to test scores in a random sample of student scores on a nationally administered achievement test (*Evaluasi Belajar Tahap Akhir Nasional*).

By linking data from IFLS households and data from the communities in which the households are located, the analyst may address many important questions regarding the impact of policies on the lives of the household respondents. The analyst may also document the effects of social, economic, and environmental changes on the population. The facility data contribute insights and information on the supply of health and educational services in 321 communities.

The focus of this chapter is the IFLS interviews among health care providers and schools. The discussion that follows describes the approach used in the IFLS so as to include surveys of health care providers and schools and the substantial ways these surveys differ from traditional large-scale household surveys. Thereafter is an analysis of the advantages and problems of these data relative to alternative data sources. The final section reviews studies that have used the data set and ways in which the data set may be explored.

Health Facility and School Surveys in the IFLS

It is often hypothesized that the characteristics of communities affect individual behavior, but rarely are multitopic household survey data accompanied by detailed data about the communities in which households are sampled. For instance, many of the more than 60 Living Standards Measurement Study surveys are accompanied by community surveys wherein community informants report on the physical, economic, and social infrastructure of communities. However, few of the measurement study surveys are accompanied by facility surveys.[3] The Demographic and Health Surveys rarely include community surveys or facility interviews. Fifty-two of the 217 Demographic and Health Surveys have included either community or facility surveys, but mostly community surveys. The three other Family Life Surveys (the Guatemalan Survey of Family Health, the Malaysian Family Life Survey, and the Matlab [Bangladesh] Health and Socio-Economic Survey) include only community surveys. In this respect, the IFLS is an exception. In each IFLS community in which households are interviewed, extensive information is collected from community leaders and staff at education and health care facilities that provide services to community residents.

Collecting a facility survey in conjunction with a household survey is not the only way to link household data to information on service providers.

An alternative method would use existing data on facilities and link these data to the household survey data. To accomplish this requires that the alternative facility data: (a) cover the same communities; (b) include unique facility identification codes, such as names or official statistical identification numbers; and (c) are collected during the same period as the household survey data. It is rare that all three conditions are met. Thus, to explore household behavior through data on service providers, one usually needs to collect the facility data as part of the household survey effort.

The IFLS community and facility surveys have sought information about the communities in which the household respondents live. Most of the information has been obtained in three ways. First, official village or township leaders and staff members have been interviewed about various aspects of community life, and supplementary information has been obtained by interviewing the heads of community women's groups. Second, during survey visits to local health care facilities and schools, staff representatives have been interviewed about staffing, operations, and usage at their facilities. Third, statistical data have also been extracted from community records, and data on local prices have been collected through interviews with two to four informants in each village.[4]

All three rounds of the IFLS use the same protocol for selecting health service providers and schools for the survey. For IFLS2 and IFLS3, it was decided not to go back to the same facilities that were visited in previous rounds. It was judged to be important to refresh the sample in 1997 and 2000 to allow for shifts in the patterns of service supply and use. Refreshing the sample was consistent with the goal of the community and facility surveys, which is to portray the current nature of the communities in which the IFLS households are located and the facilities available to the households. Because facility identification codes are maintained over time, it has been possible to identify sample facilities across rounds if these are interviewed more than once. In any case, as described in the section on the service availability roster (SAR), some information is known about the status of facilities interviewed in previous rounds even if these facilities have not been selected for reinterviews.

Health Care Facilities

The health care facilities surveyed in the IFLS are selected according to a probability sample among the facilities that serve households in the community. The sample is drawn from a list of facilities known by the household respondents. Some facilities serve more than one IFLS community. The sampling frame is different for each of the 312 IFLS communities and for each of the three strata of health care facilities: public health centers and branch centers (*puskesmas* and *puskesmas pembantu* or *pustu*); community health posts (*posyandu*); and private facilities, including private clinics, doctors, nurses, paramedics, village health workers, midwives, and village midwives (*kliniks, praktek umum, perawats, paramedis, mantra, bidans,* and *bidans desa*).

At the end of the household survey within each of the 312 communities, the facilities in each strata that have been reported as known in the responses to the household questionnaire by the household heads or most knowledgeable respondents are ranked according to the number of times they are mentioned. Health care facilities are then chosen randomly up to a set quota for each stratum. The quotas are as follows:[5]

- public health centers and branch centers = 3
- private facilities = 6
- community health posts = 2

The single most frequently reported facility is always chosen for the sample. Thereafter, two to four more facilities (depending on the quota) are selected at random from the entire listing.

There are two exceptions to this random selection process. First, not all the facilities identified are eligible for interview. Facilities were *excluded* from the sample frame if (a) they had been interviewed in connection with a previous community (this would occur among bordering IFLS communities), (b) the facility was more than a 45-minute motorcycle trip (in practice, this is rare), or (c) the facility was located in another province in which the survey team did not have permission to conduct fieldwork. Second, in a small number of communities, the list of facilities derived from the household survey was not sufficient to fill the quota. In this case, the information supplied by community leaders was used to supplement the sample.

Table 15.1 shows the distribution of sampled health care facilities and schools in the three rounds of the IFLS. Annex 15.1 shows a more detailed breakdown by type. The share of public health centers went up slightly in IFLS3 relative to branch centers. Among private facilities, the share of private physicians and nurses dropped slightly from 1997 (IFLS2) to 2000 (IFLS3), while the share of midwives increased.

TABLE 15.1 IFLS Health Care Facility and School Samples

Sample	IFLS1 1993	IFLS2 1997	IFLS3 2000
Health care facilities			
Public health center or branch center	993	919	943
Private facility, practitioner (doctor, clinic, nurse, midwife, paramedic)	2,065	1,832	1,904
Community health post	899	619	630
Schools			
Primary	944	964	960
Lower secondary	900	945	951
Upper secondary	584	618	618

Source: Strauss et al. 2004b.

Schools

Schools are sampled in basically the same way except that the list of schools contains only those schools in which survey household members under age 25 are currently enrolled. Thus, the sample frame for schools is limited to those schools that are actually used by IFLS households. The school sample is divided into three strata: primary, lower-secondary, and upper-secondary levels. For schools, there are very few compositional changes across IFLS waves by school strata (see table 15.1 and annex 15.1).

The Service Availability Roster

The SAR was added for IFLS2 and maintained for IFLS3. It was added after an analysis of the IFLS1 data showed that community informants provided incomplete lists of the health care facilities and schools to which household respondents had access (relative to the knowledge and use of facilities reported by households in the IFLS household survey). The SAR was a compilation of the information on all the schools and health care facilities available to residents of the IFLS communities as reported in three sources. These sources are (a) the facilities identified by household respondents; (b) facilities interviewed in IFLS1, but not mentioned in IFLS2 by community leaders and households; and (c) any other facilities mentioned by village or township heads or women's group leaders during the IFLS2 community surveys.

Once the SAR had been compiled, the village or township heads or the women's group leaders were asked to estimate the distance, travel time, and cost of travel for each facility listed. In addition, interviewers visited the facilities to obtain a global positioning system reading of latitude and longitude. The readings were used to construct measures of distance to each facility from the center of the respective IFLS cluster and from the respective office of the village or township head.

Key Features of the IFLS Health Facility and School Surveys

The IFLS offers unique data on health care facilities and schools. In this section, we highlight some of the key features that make the IFLS facility survey advantageous relative to alternative approaches. We also discuss some of the shortcomings or caveats of the IFLS facility survey data.

Sample Frame

By sampling facilities that are known or used by households as reported in the preceding household survey, the survey avoids designating arbitrary boundaries (with the exceptions noted elsewhere above, such as facilities more than 45 minutes by motorbike, which are few in practice). In most communities in Indonesia and other countries, the characteristics of the catchment areas for facilities that serve households vary. A priori, there is no clear way to establish boundaries for the definition of the enumeration areas for facilities, such as boundaries defined by distance (for example, 30 kilometers from the community center) or time (such as one hour by a major means of transportation). There may be an exception for rural areas that have poor infrastructure. For instance, villages in rural areas might only be served by one well-defined primary school. The sample frame for the selection of the facilities to be surveyed is therefore not constrained by a requirement to include only facilities within the administrative boundary of a village.

The IFLS encompasses information on facilities of relevance to household survey respondents rather than depending on a small number of selected community informants who may or may not be reliable sources of information on accessible facilities. Moreover, because the facilities are picked based on a tally of the respondents mentioning them, the IFLS allows for the creation of weights to reflect the importance of the interviewed facilities within the constellation of all available facilities. Facility weights have so far been constructed only for IFLS1. Annex 15.2 describes the facility weights.

Service Environment

The facility surveys are, by definition, a subsample of all service providers available to the communities. However, because the entire list of reported facilities is recorded in the SAR, one may describe the general service delivery environment of households in terms of the number of and distance to existing facilities. In addition, there is information on turnover because the SARs for IFLS2 and IFLS3 contain information on all providers reported in the previous IFLS, including those that have been closed (with dates of closure) or are otherwise no longer in operation.

Matching Facilities to Users

The IFLS also allows one-to-one matching of respondents and the facilities they actually use. For both health care utilization and school enrollment, the household questionnaire records the identification codes for the relevant facilities. These identification codes allow the analyst to match the respondent and the facility (for example, if an adult is receiving treatment from a private physician or a child is attending a private primary school). For all facilities reported by households, we have at least some basic information in the SARs. For those facilities that have been selected and interviewed, detailed information has been collected through the facility questionnaire. Table 15.2 shows the matching rates for the facilities reported by households in IFLS1 either as a known facility or a facility actually used, depending on the questionnaire section. The proportion of matches varies by strata according to the number of unique facilities identified by household respondents, the proportion of identified facilities eligible for interview, and the quota of facilities per strata. Among health care facilities, matching rates were highest for health centers. Among schools, primary and lower-secondary schools were more likely to be matched than upper-secondary schools. We expect the matching rates to decline with subsequent rounds of the IFLS because a greater portion of the households interviewed are located in communities outside the baseline 321 communities in which the facility surveys have been implemented.

Completeness of the Sample Frame and Sample

The sample frame for the facility surveys has been designed to reflect all facilities that serve the households in a community. The selected and interviewed

TABLE 15.2 IFLS1 Matching Rates: Health Facility and School Surveys and the Household Questionnaire

Health care facilities	Facility knowledge, book I, section PPO	Facility use, book III, section RJ	Facility use, book V, section RJ	Facility use, book IV, section CX	Facility use, book IV, calendar and prenatal care
Medical Facilities					
Public health center or branch	92 (6,283)	89 (1,052)	92 (630)	90 (2,787)	92 (470)
Doctor, clinic	40 (4,656)	39 (746)	62 (506)	33 (482)	38 (89)
Nurse, paramedic, midwife	65 (4,607)	57 (508)	64 (239)	65 (1,118)	78 (309)
Schools	*School use, book I, section AR*	*School use, book V, section DLA*			
Primary	83 (5,160)	79 (4,657)	n.a.	n.a.	n.a.
Lower secondary	72 (1,619)	71 (810)	n.a.	n.a.	n.a.
Upper secondary	48 (1,137)	n.a.	n.a.	n.a.	n.a.

Source: Frankenberg and Karoly 1995.
Note: The first numbers in each cell are the percentage rates. The numbers in parentheses are the denominators to which the rates apply. The denominators reflect the frequency of mention in the responses to the household questionnaire according to eligibility for the particular section and the question about facility knowledge or use. n.a. = not applicable.

facilities are not necessarily representative of the facilities in an area unless weights are applied that reflect the sampling probability. Moreover, the sample frame is incomplete to the extent that the survey of IFLS household respondents fails to identify all facilities of relevance to the population in a community. The reasons the sample frame may be incomplete differ for health care facilities and schools. Recall that the sample frame for health care facilities has been developed on the basis of the identification of known facilities by the IFLS households, while schools are listed based on actual enrollments among school-age children in the IFLS households. It is possible that older, more well-established health care facilities are included in the sample frame since they are more well known than the clinics that have opened recently. Similarly, poorer low-quality schools may be excluded from the sample frame if households switch to better schools.

The quotas for facilities may likewise result in an insufficient number of matches between the facilities identified in the household survey (service users) and the services actually utilized. For example, the matching rates in table 15.2 would become smaller as the types of users (such as poorer households within a given province) or of facilities used (such as private primary schools) become more specific. This result depends on the precise questions that are addressed. For more narrow topics, it might be advantageous to interview people at more facilities, although, because of the fixed budget, this understanding implies a shorter questionnaire.

Weighting

If the data are to be used to describe the service delivery environment, the facility data must be appropriately weighted. We know of no studies that have used the weights constructed for IFLS1 or that have created new weights for the IFLS2 and IFLS3 facility interviews.

Representativeness over Time

As a longitudinal survey, the IFLS follows households that, since the baseline survey was run, have moved from the 321 communities of that survey. This finding includes households that have moved together as one household and individuals who have left their original households and moved to new locations. However, for households outside the baseline 321 communities in IFLS2 or IFLS3, no facility interviews have been conducted, and no SARs have been established. Because the sample frame is compiled from the reports of households on the knowledge of household members on health service providers and the use of schools, there is generally only one or two migrant IFLS households from which to construct the sample frame in the new communities. There is no facility sample frame from which to draw a facility sample for these migrant IFLS households in new communities. Even if there were an alternative sample frame, interviewing facilities serving only one or two households would be relatively costly. This approach raises two issues. First, the extent to which the original 321 communities and the facilities associated with the nonmigrant IFLS households in these communities are representative of the overall service delivery environment after 1993 is not clear. This finding presumably depends on the patterns of migration of households and other demographic and economic shifts in population and policies. Second, in linking individuals to the data on service providers, the facility information pertains *only* to nonmigrant households and nonmigrant respondents in the second and third rounds of the IFLS.

Indirect Costs

Implementing the facility survey requires coordination with the household survey team.[6] The data collected by the household survey team through the household questionnaire are handed over to the community and facility survey team. (Appropriate pages in the paper questionnaire are printed in triplicate to keep the actual household questionnaire intact.) The community and facility survey team then compiles the sample frame for the selection and the interviews among facilities and for the SAR. The process thus refers back to the household questionnaire. After the SAR has been compiled, the community and facility survey team attaches the identification codes for the individual facilities. These codes are based on previous IFLS rounds or are created anew for facilities that have never been interviewed. To link the respondent knowledge and use of specific facilities to the SAR and facility surveys, the household survey team looks back at completed questionnaires to enter the relevant identification codes.

Role of the community questionnaire

As an alternative to a complete facility survey, the use of a community questionnaire for the collection of facility information may be feasible (to question community informants about the availability of doctors at the nearest health clinics and so on). For example, Frankenberg, Suriastini, and Thomas (2005) evaluate the impact of the expansion of a health program on health outcomes among Indonesians. Specifically, they study the Midwife in the Village program, through which the share of IFLS communities with access to a midwife rose from 9.4 percent to 45.6 percent between 1993 and 1997.

The data about community health care provision were collected through the community questionnaire rather than through a direct facility questionnaire. The community questionnaire complements the IFLS household data with information on community health services.

Panel of Facilities

The facilities surveyed in the IFLS2 and IFLS3 are not, by design, a panel of facilities interviewed in the previous IFLS. As shown in table 15.3, a large portion of the facilities in IFLS1 were not reinterviewed in IFLS2.[7]

Analysis of the IFLS Facility Surveys

Several studies use summary statistics on the survey of health care providers and schools to document changes in the prices, quality, and availability of health and education services at public and private facilities. Examples include Frankenberg, Thomas, and Beegle (1999), Frankenberg et al. (1999), and Strauss et al. (2004a). The studies highlight the changes in the quality of services provided to households, but also indicate the ways in which these services are most amenable to policy interventions. However, they do not directly assess the impact of the services covered in the facility survey on the outcomes measured in the IFLS household survey.[8]

Some studies look solely at the facility survey data to understand the determinants of the availability and quality of specific services at health care facilities. Barber, Gertler, and Harimurti (2006a) examine the determinants of technical quality as measured through the vignettes mentioned elsewhere above and focus on the role that qualified facility staff play in improving the related outcomes. Barber, Gertler, and Harimurti (2006b) also use the vignette data. They investigate the availability of health care treatments and the proportion of correct procedures mentioned during the vignettes (according to scores of quality through the completed vignettes) in relation to facility type (public or private), gross domestic product of the district in which the facility is located, and facility infrastructure.

An analytically more complex use of the facility survey involves linking the survey data to household- or individual-level outcomes. For example, one might use the facility data to analyze the effect on outcomes of the characteristics of the health or educational services available to households.[9] Only a few studies have used the data in this way, and the ones we have found

TABLE 15.3 IFLS Cross-Wave Facility Interviews, by Facility Type

Facility type	IFLS1, 1993 Total	IFLS2, 1997 IFLS1 facilities %	Total	New facilities	IFLS3, 2003 IFLS1 facilities %	Total	IFLS2 facilities	New facilities	IFLS1–2 facilities	Total	IFLS1–3 facilities
Health care facilities											
Public health centers	993	66.6	662	259	63.1	627	634	211	732	943	529
Private clinics, practitioners	1,439	40.4	582	1,249	32.8	472	712	1,045	859	1,904	325
Schools											
Primary	944	64.8	612	351	53.4	504	555	319	641	960	418
Lower secondary	900	55.3	498	447	50.3	453	537	304	647	951	343
Upper secondary	584	44.2	258	360	33.0	193	217	334	284	618	126

Sources: Frankenberg and Karoly 1995; Frankenberg and Thomas 2000; Strauss et al. 2004a.

all focus on the health facility data. Frankenberg, Sikoki, and Suriastini (2003) and Frankenberg, McKelvey, and Thomas (2004) rely on information on family planning services, including prices and other characteristics, to assess the impact of the supply of services on women's contraceptive use as reported in the household survey. Using data from the household survey, Frankenberg (2004) evaluates preventive care among children as a function of the provision of supplementary feeding at community health posts. She finds a strong correlation between supplementary feeding and the use of health posts by children. Frankenberg controls for the quality of public health centers by constructing an index of quality from the health center surveys and averaging across the community health centers interviewed.[10] Barber and Gertler (2002) link child growth outcomes (height and weight) to the quality of community health care facilities; they conclude that children in communities with high-quality services are healthier than their counterparts in areas with lower-quality services.

However, depending on the questions being addressed, the facility data are not necessarily appropriate for describing the supply of services related to particular outcomes as measured through the IFLS household survey. This analysis would be the case if the outcomes in the household survey also reflect a past facility or service environment or past service utilization decisions. In such a situation, only the responses of household interviewees who have recently used the facilities would be helpful in understanding the impact of current service quality. For example, Newhouse and Beegle (2006) examine the effects of school type on student test scores by relying on IFLS household survey data on test scores and school types. They could measure the supply of public schools within 25 miles using the IFLS. However, the measure of school access from the IFLS is applicable only to the subsample of students who were interviewed in the same subdistricts where they attended lower-secondary school and at which they had test scores. This finding reduced the total sample by about 40 percent. Limiting the sample to students who had not moved since graduation created a selection bias; thus, in the final version of their paper, Newhouse and Beegle use measures of access derived from the school census.

Conclusion

The IFLS is a rich source of longitudinal data on households and communities in Indonesia. The data represent a unique opportunity to study many dimensions of living standards over time. Furthermore, unlike most multi-topic household surveys, the IFLS includes additional surveys of facilities that provide health and educational services to the baseline communities. In this review, three major points arise.

First, the use of the IFLS facility data has been limited. All studies relying on these data that we have been able to find are listed in this review. They make up only a small portion of the studies that have been produced based on the IFLS.[11]

Second, only a portion of the studies using IFLS facility data explicitly link the facilities to households. Most of the other studies describe the characteristics of the surveyed service providers in general. The studies that link facility data to households cover only health facilities. The data on education facilities have been used solely to describe the supply of schools. They have never been directly linked to households, and they have not been used to examine the relationship between school attributes and outcomes such as attendance. Among the studies using health facility data, two explore the effects of the supply of family planning advisory services on contraceptive use; one examines preventive health care use as a function of supplementary feeding schemes at community health posts, and one links measures of child growth to an index of health facility quality. It is unclear why the data have apparently been the subject of such little analysis. It is also unclear how the application of the data in analysis might be increased. Nonetheless, for descriptions of the service delivery environment in communities, it may still be worthwhile to collect facility data in conjunction with the larger IFLS household survey, particularly because the survey provides an appropriate facility sample frame.

Finally, the relevance of the facility data to the household survey becomes more limited as the households and household members in the panel sample migrate to new communities where the collection of data would be too costly. Therefore, the first wave (the only wave covering a truly representative sample of households) may have been well suited for the approach to facility surveys that has been adopted. For the later rounds of the panel survey, information on service delivery may be more readily obtained by linking administrative data and household survey data. This conclusion is partly so because of the lack of analytical work using the facility data. However, linking administrative data and household survey data is a nontrivial task that requires both (a) access to administrative data and (b) geographical links to the IFLS households.

ANNEX 15.1

THE IFLS2–3 SAMPLES

TABLE 15A.1 IFLS2–3 Health Care and School Facility Samples *percent, except for number of observations*		
Sample characteristics	IFLS2, 1997	IFLS3, 2000
Public health care facilities		
Public health centers	61.4	65.9
Branch public health centers	37.9	34.1
Unknown type	0.7	0.0
Number of observations	920	944
Private practitioners		
Private physicians	28.5	25.4
Clinics	8.0	11.3
Midwives	28.6	29.4
Paramedics, nurses	25.5	24.4
Village midwives	7.3	9.5
Unknown type	2.1	0.1
Number of observations	1,832	1,904
Schools		
Primary, public	33.0	32.2
Primary, private	5.1	5.8
Lower-secondary, public	23.1	23.5
Lower-secondary, private	14.3	14.1
Upper-secondary, public	12.0	11.6
Upper-secondary, private	12.4	12.8
Number of observations	2,525	2,530

Source: Strauss et al. 2004a.

ANNEX 15.2

IFLS1 FACILITY WEIGHTS

No facility weights have been constructed for IFLS2 or IFLS3. The discussion below is drawn from the IFLS1 user's guide (Frankenberg and Karoly 1995).[12]

Ideally, a facility should receive a weight equal to the facility's sampling probability. The sampling probability is a function of the sampling scheme and the sampling frame. The sampling frame of the facility surveys is incomplete in that the sample of household respondents fails to identify all facilities of relevance to the populations in the enumeration areas. The sampling scheme specifies that sampling probability must be proportional to the market share of the facility, that is, the share of overall service provision accounted for by the individual facility. The construction of weights based on sampling probabilities is complicated by the fact that we do not know the true market share of each facility. Instead, we know the market share that a particular facility captures among the sample of household respondents in the relevant enumeration area. We use a model of market shares to simulate the observed market shares by assuming a fixed number of household respondents and a multinomial sampling method. A comparison of the simulated outcomes and the observed outcomes yields an estimate of the true number of facilities in each enumeration area. The estimated number of facilities in each area determines the estimated market share and, thus, the rank of each facility in the area.

The next step is to identify the position of each observed facility within the estimated distribution of all facilities and the associated market shares. We do not know the true market share (or even the rank) of an observed facility among all facilities. Instead, we observe a facility's rank (as determined by the number of respondents mentioning that facility) among those facilities identified by our sample of enumeration area residents. This observed rank may or may or not be the true rank. For example, the most frequently mentioned facility among sampled enumeration area residents might be only the second or third most frequently mentioned facility if we were to interview all enumeration area residents. Although the observed rank does not necessarily equal the true rank, it provides information about the true rank. Using the observed rank, we make a determination of the probability of each facility's true rank. We then determine the facility's sampling probability using this model. Our final weight may be described as an estimate of the probability that we would sample the observed facility if we were to conduct another survey relying on the same sample design.

Notes

1. The time between the collection of the data and the public release of data sets varies with each round. The fieldwork for IFLS1 was completed at the end of 1993 and was placed in the public domain in December 1995. The fieldwork for IFLS2 was completed in December 1997 and was placed in the public domain in March 2000 (with the exception of the modules on employment and health measures). The fieldwork for IFLS3 was completed in December 2000 and was placed in the public domain in February 2004.

2. A follow-up survey (IFLS2+) was conducted in 1998 with 25 percent of the sample to measure the immediate impact of the economic and political crisis in Indonesia. This survey is not discussed in detail here in part because it covered one-quarter of the total sample and because it deviated from the existing procedures for surveying facilities. Specifically, in IFLS2+, the facilities are a panel (that is, the sample of facilities interviewed in IFLS2) rather than a redrawn sample such as in IFLS2 and IFLS3. For details, see Frankenberg, Thomas, and Beegle (1999).

3. See http://www.worldbank.org/lsms. The following Living Standards Measurement Study surveys included a facility survey: Côte d'Ivoire (1997), health care facilities; Guyana (1992–93), service availability listing; Jamaica (1993), schools; Morocco (1992), health care facilities; Kagera, Tanzania (1991–94), health care facilities, (1991–94, 2004), primary schools; and Vietnam (1992–93, 1997–98), health care facilities and schools.

4. IFLS2 and IFLS3 expanded the scope of the information on communities. IFLS2 included two sets of interviews. One set was conducted with community members considered expert in the *adat,* the traditional or customary law code that influences behavior in a community. The second set was conducted with community social activists and examined the projects in which those activists were involved. IFLS2 and the IFLS3 also included visits to three markets in each community to obtain additional information on prices.

5. Because of time and money constraints, IFLS2 and IFLS3 did not interview traditional practitioners, as did IFLS1. Moreover, whereas IFLS1 grouped doctors and clinics within a separate stratum from midwives, nurses, and paramedics, these strata were combined in IFLS2 and IFLS3 because of the difficulty of categorizing practitioners correctly. An advantage of grouping all private practitioners in one stratum is that the mix of provider types interviewed within the stratum reflects the facility availability in the community more accurately. For example, in communities where paramedics are more plentiful than doctors, the mix of providers interviewed reflects this fact. Hospitals are excluded for three reasons: (a) they are an uncommon source of outpatient care, (b) there are few of them in rural areas, and (c) an effective hospital questionnaire would probably be quite different from the questionnaires for other health care providers.

6. The IFLS fieldwork has been organized around two sets of field teams: the household survey team and the community and facility survey team. The latter followed the household survey team to the 321 enumeration areas during the fieldwork after a lag of about two weeks.

7. Table 15.3 excludes community health posts because no health post interviewed during IFLS3 had the same identification code as in previous IFLS waves. This

exclusion is because both the locations and the volunteer staff changed, making it difficult to identify the same health posts from one wave to the next.

8. Although Frankenberg, Thomas, and Beegle (1999) do not explicitly link the facility survey data to the household survey data, they do draw conclusions based on the two separate analyses of changes in facility characteristics and household health care utilization. Among their conclusions are (a) high private sector prices in 1997 discouraged the use of private sector facilities in 1998 by the youngest children, and (b) increases in public sector drug stock-outs encouraged the use of private sector facilities among older children and adults in 1998.

9. One caveat to the use of health facility data in describing the service environment available to households is the lack of hospital coverage in the data.

10. In a slightly different study, Frankenberg, Thomas, and Beegle (1999) find that, in 1998, visits to health posts by young children were more likely if supplementary feeding was available.

11. The IFLS Web site maintains a list of studies using the facility data (see http://www.rand.org/FLS/IFLS). The list is incomplete because many researchers do not notify the IFLS of their papers despite explicit requests to data users to help update the Web site.

12. An alternative approach would involve constructing facility weights on the basis of a list of all facilities. This approach would require that a government—through the ministry of education, the ministry of health, or the bureau of statistics—supply an accurate list of all facilities by type and public or private status.

References

Barber, Sarah L., and Paul J. Gertler. 2002. "Child Health and the Quality of Medical Care." Working paper, Institute of Business and Economic Research, University of California at Berkeley, Berkeley, CA.

Barber, Sarah L., Paul J. Gertler, and Pandu Harimurti. 2006a. "The Effect of the Zero Growth Policy in Civil Service Recruitment on the Quality of Care in Indonesia." Unpublished working paper, Institute of Business and Economic Research, University of California at Berkeley, Berkeley, CA.

———. 2006b. "Promoting High-Quality Care in Indonesia: Roles for Public and Private Ambulatory Care Providers." Unpublished working paper, Institute of Business and Economic Research, University of California at Berkeley, Berkeley, CA.

Frankenberg, Elizabeth. 2004. "Sometimes It Takes a Village: Collective Efficacy and Children's Use of Preventive Health Care." California Center for Population Research Working Paper CCPR-028-04, California Center for Population Research, University of California, Los Angeles.

Frankenberg, Elizabeth, Kathleen Beegle, Bondan Sikoki, and Duncan Thomas. 1999. "Health, Family Planning, and Well-Being in Indonesia during an Economic Crisis." Working paper DRU-2013-FGI/NICHD/UNFPA, RAND Corporation, Santa Monica, CA.

Frankenberg, Elizabeth, and Lynn Karoly. 1995. "The 1993 Indonesian Family Life Survey: Overview and Field Report." Working paper DRU-1195/1-NICHD/AID, RAND Corporation, Santa Monica, CA.

Frankenberg, Elizabeth, Christopher McKelvey, and Duncan Thomas. 2004. "Fertility Regulation and Economic Shocks." California Center for Population Research Working Paper CCPR-022-05, California Center for Population Research, University of California, Los Angeles.

Frankenberg, Elizabeth, Bondan Sikoki, and Wayan Suriastini. 2003. "Contraceptive Use in a Changing Service Environment: Evidence from Indonesia during the Economic Crisis." *Studies in Family Planning* 34 (2): 103–16.

Frankenberg, Elizabeth, Wayan Suriastini, and Duncan Thomas. 2005. "Can Expanding Access to Basic Health Care Improve Children's Health Status?: Lessons from Indonesia's 'Midwife in the Village' Program." *Population Studies* 59 (1): 5–19.

Frankenberg, Elizabeth, and Duncan Thomas. 2000. "The Indonesia Family Life Survey (IFLS): Study Design and Results from Waves 1 and 2." Working paper DRU-2238/1-NIA/NICHD, RAND Corporation, Santa Monica, CA.

Frankenberg, Elizabeth, Duncan Thomas, and Kathleen Beegle. 1999. "The Real Costs of Indonesia's Economic Crisis: Preliminary Findings from the Indonesia Family Life Surveys." Labor and Population Working Paper DRU-2064-NIA/NICHD, RAND Corporation, Santa Monica, CA.

Newhouse, David, and Kathleen Beegle. 2006. "The Effect of School Type on Academic Achievement: Evidence from Indonesia." *Journal of Human Resources* 41 (3): 529–57.

Strauss, John, Kathleen Beegle, Agus Dwiyanto, Yulia Herawati, Daan Pattinasarany, Elan Satriawan, Bondan Sikoki, Sukamdi, and Firman Witoelar. 2004a. *Indonesian Living Standards Before and After the Financial Crisis: Evidence from the Indonesia Family Life Survey.* Rand Labor and Population. Santa Monica, CA: Center for the Study of the Family in Economic Development, RAND Corporation.

Strauss, John, Kathleen Beegle, Bondan Sikoki, Agus Dwiyanto, Yulia Herawati, and Firman Witoelar. 2004b. "The Third Wave of the Indonesia Family Life Survey (IFLS): Overview and Field Report." Report WR-144/1-NIA/NICHD, RAND Corporation, Santa Monica, CA.

16

Collection of Data from Service Providers within the Living Standards Measurement Study

Kinnon Scott

The surveys of the Living Standards Measurement Study (LSMS) are an important source of data on household welfare and the interaction between households and government programs and services in developing countries. Of the 60-plus LSMS surveys that have been implemented since 1985, a handful have been expanded to collect more information directly on the supply of services. This contribution is important because there are significant synergies to be gained from linking data on service providers or facilities to data on households. Such data collection efforts, however, are not the norm in LSMS surveys. The purpose of this chapter is to identify reasons for the scarcity of such efforts and, it is hoped, provide information that might promote the inclusion of data collection on facilities in future surveys.

The first part of the chapter provides a brief description and history of the LSMS program and its goals, as well as the surveys that have been developed and implemented through the program. Tracing the evolution of the program provides insights on why facility surveys are not a mainstay of LSMS surveys. The second section outlines what has been done in regard to the collection of facility-level data in the LSMS surveys. The third section contains a discussion of the key issues that arise when planning a facility survey and considerations that should be taken into account. A summary of the work that might be needed to encourage more facility surveys in conjunction with the LSMS surveys is found in the final section.

The LSMS Surveys

Over a period of several years in the late 1970s and early 1980s, a team at the World Bank, in consultation with academics, policy analysts, and survey practitioners, developed the LSMS program. The objective of the program was to improve the type and quality of the household data collected by national governments with specific attention to meeting the demand for data on poverty and inequality and for data relevant to policy formulation. The LSMS surveys were born of this effort. The first surveys were implemented in Côte d'Ivoire and Peru in 1985. Three LSMS surveys are ongoing as this chapter is being written. More than 40 countries have implemented the surveys since the first two experimental ones were conducted.[1]

In practice, LSMS surveys provide data for a wide range of analyses. Of fundamental importance is the ability to measure welfare in both monetary and nonmonetary terms. The identification of the causes and correlates of observed outcomes is also given precedence over the simple construction of indicators. The benefits of government spending may be tracked because the data identify who receives services and transfers from governments and how these affect welfare levels. Of course, the data collected in the LSMS surveys allow ex ante evaluations of various policy tools, as well as ex post evaluations of the impact of programs.

Two key decisions about the LSMS surveys were reached in the early phases that have had important implications for the way the surveys have evolved and been implemented. First, the LSMS surveys are demand driven, that is, they are implemented in a country as needed and as requested by the country.[2] Second, when a new survey is developed in a country, priority is given to meeting the policy needs of that country. Generating comparable data across countries has been relegated to a secondary order of importance. In practical terms, this arrangement has two implications. First, there is no single standard set of LSMS questionnaires; the content, length, and complexity vary by country and, often, over time within a given country. Second, the development of the questionnaires frequently entails a lengthy design phase in which data users, stakeholders, and data producers negotiate the final content of the survey (usually a compromise because the number of questions requested far exceeds the number that may feasibly be included in a questionnaire). The nonstandard questionnaire and the negotiation process that is involved are among the elements influencing the implementation of facility surveys within a given LSMS survey.

LSMS Survey Instruments

The form in which the LSMS surveys exist today is quite different from the original concept. As one might expect, much of the early thinking about the form the LSMS surveys would take was heavily influenced and constrained by the survey practices and knowledge of the time. However, three key ideas found in the original thinking on the LSMS surveys—as outlined in Chandar, Grootaert, and Pyatt (1980) and Saunders and Grootaert (1980)—have led to substantial innovations in the surveys. First, as the name of the program implies, the emphasis of the LSMS was to be on living standards, poverty, inequality, and the correlates and determinants of these. Second, the unit of analysis was to be the household seen as both a consuming unit and a producing unit. Third was the notion that one survey involving the collection of data on a range of topics would be a more powerful tool for policy formulation than a series of single-purpose surveys; the sum would be greater than the parts. Arising from these three ideas, the concept of the multitopic household questionnaire gained ground as the *core* survey instrument of the LSMS.

Although the list of topics that was originally considered for inclusion in the survey was fairly limited, the household questionnaire was truly multitopic by the time the first surveys were fielded (see table 16.1). It collected data from and about individuals, households, and household businesses and farms or plots. The multitopic approach to collecting data at the household level has facilitated analyses of the determinants of observed outcomes and the study of specific facets of households, individuals, and their activities. Because welfare measurement was the fundamental goal, a substantial share of the questionnaire addresses monetary measures of welfare, including income and the more frequently used measure, consumption.[3]

The emphasis on a money-metric measure of welfare raised the issue of the best way to make appropriate price adjustments for differences across time and geographical area. National data collection exercises on consumer price indexes are an inadequate foundation for these adjustments. Data are often collected only in the capital or major urban areas and may not be disaggregated to the geographical areas in which the interviewed households are located. It was clear from the start that additional data would be

TABLE 16.1 Topics Covered in a Typical LSMS Household Questionnaire	
Sectors	**Consumption**
Demographics	Food expenditures
Education	Home production
Health, fertility	Nonfood expenditures
Migration	Housing
Labor	Durable goods
Housing	
Savings and credit	
Income	
Nonfarm self-employment	Wage and salary
Agriculture and livestock	Other income (transfers, rents)

Source: Compiled by the author.
Note: To meet pertinent data needs, many countries have incorporated completely different modules in their questionnaires. For a list, see Scott, Steele, and Temesgen (2005).

required. It was originally posited that such data would be gathered through retail outlets in the areas where households were interviewed or by forming focus groups of housewives to gauge prices (see Chandar, Grootaert, and Pyatt 1980). A more detailed study of the issue by Wood and Knight (1985) resulted in the recommendation that a second questionnaire be added to the LSMS survey. The additional questionnaire would be used to collect data on prices at retail establishments in the areas where sampled households are located. This auxiliary questionnaire—auxiliary in the sense that the data would be of use only in the context of the household survey—was to be administered in parallel with the household questionnaire. Such an instrument is now administered in almost all LSMS surveys to permit intertemporal and spatial cost-of-living adjustments.[4]

When the price questionnaire and the content of the household questionnaires were being discussed, the idea of implementing a third, parallel questionnaire at the community level was raised. The initial reasoning for developing such an instrument was threefold. First, there was a great deal of interest in collecting longitudinal data, though it had been determined that the incorporation of this panel component into the household survey would be too complicated because households are difficult to track over time. Communities, in contrast, have fixed locations, which facilitates the collection of longitudinal data.[5] Second, communities are interesting units of study in their own right. Third, a parallel community questionnaire might be used to relieve some of the pressure on the already overburdened household survey instrument (see Chandar, Grootaert, and Pyatt 1980).

Thus, an additional community survey instrument was incorporated into the basic package of instruments that make up an LSMS survey. In the end, the emphasis in the community questionnaire reflected more the desire to relieve pressure on the household survey and less a consideration of the first two points mentioned above. This emphasis resulted from the multistage sampling strategy that was adopted for the LSMS surveys. Because households are selected in clusters (multiple households within small census enumeration areas, for example), a community questionnaire becomes an efficient tool for gathering information on the environment in which households function. Instead of a survey asking each of the 12–16 households in a cluster for the same information, the questions are put to a single (or a few) community informant(s) only once, and the data can then be linked to the relevant households.

What this approach means, however, is that the notion of community used in LSMS surveys is quite idiosyncratic. It relies on a definition that is based on a geographical area, which is the census enumeration area or cluster in which the household is located. This approach does not necessarily map to any particular concept of community found in sociology, anthropology, or political science. The data collected are complementary to the household data and are not designed to describe the universe of communities within a country or region. In many LSMS surveys, these community data are gathered only in rural areas because urban areas are considered to have all services and not lack infrastructure. More recent surveys in Latin America (Ecuador, Guatemala, and Panama, for example) have expanded the data collection to urban areas. They have recognized that service provision, social capital, and public infrastructure are not uniformly distributed within a given urban area or across urban areas. In recent years, recommendations have been circulated to improve the definition of community in the LSMS surveys, but, for the most part, the original geographical notion of community continues to be used (see Frankenberg 2000).

The community instrument is fairly short and is administered to community leaders, key informants, or focus groups of community members. The first topic covered usually concerns the main economic characteristics of the area, such as the share of the population engaged in various activities, the main crops and sources of income, the seasonal migration, the markets, and the like. Transportation links, electricity, and sanitation are the most common areas of investigation on infrastructure. A large section of the questionnaire is usually devoted to cataloging the presence of or distance to available service providers; the list of service providers covered includes a wide range, running from education and health service providers through post offices. In some cases, additional data are collected about the use of the services (the share of school-age children attending the primary school, for example) and the basic quality measures that are based on the presence of inputs (health personnel in the clinic or textbooks in the schools, for instance). In more recent years, community questionnaires have also been used to gather data on social capital.

Facility Surveys

Evolution

The use of additional survey instruments to collect data directly from service providers was not contemplated when the LSMS surveys were being developed. The only attention paid to service providers was through the questions on the community survey about the physical locations of service providers. The assumption was that this was a useful proxy for household access to services. Even the paper commissioned to identify the key areas of health that should be covered in the LSMS surveys (Ho 1982) makes no attempt to discuss the analytic benefits of separate health facility surveys. Data on the quality of health services, while mentioned as potentially important in countries where the quality of health care might vary among facilities, were not identified as data that needed to be collected under the LSMS umbrella. Neither of the first full LSMS survey experiments included facility questionnaires of any kind.

However, limiting the survey information to data on access to facilities was felt to be a constraint fairly quickly. In the third year of the Côte d'Ivoire survey, complementary data on health and education facilities were collected not as a facility survey per se, but by mining administrative data from the Ministry of Health and the Ministry of Education. In this case, the expanded demand for data was the result of a World Bank research project on the determinants of fertility (the Economic and Policy Determinants of Fertility in Sub-Saharan Africa project). The project required more detail on the actual services provided rather than simply on the locations of the services. A year later, in Ghana, the first authentic facility survey within an LSMS survey was introduced. Over the years since, an additional dozen such questionnaires have been administered as part of LSMS surveys (see table 16.2 for a complete list).

TABLE 16.2 Facility Surveys in the LSMS by Country and Year

Health	Education
Côte d'Ivoire, 1987-88[a]	Côte d'Ivoire, 1987-88[a]
Ghana, 1988–89	Ghana, 1988–89
Jamaica, 1989 (2)	Jamaica, 1990
Morocco, 1991	Morocco, 1991
Kagera Region, Tanzania 1991–94	Kagera Region, Tanzania, 1991–94
Nicaragua, 1998	Nicaragua, 1998
Vietnam, 1998	Vietnam, 1998
Tajikistan, 2003-04	Tajikistan, 2003-04
	Kagera Region, Tanzania, 2004

Sources: World Bank 1999a, 1999b, 2000, 2001, 2002a, 2002b, 2004, 2006; World Bank and Institut National de la Statistique 1996; Stone and Webster Consultants and CSR Zerkalo 2005.
a. The Côte d'Ivoire survey collected data on facilities from administrative records, not from the facilities themselves.

Because the facility survey was developed in the context of the LSMS program, it is no surprise that the facility questionnaires were treated in much the same fashion as the price and community questionnaires, that is, as auxiliary instruments designed to collect data to supplement household information. No effort was made to collect data to describe or understand the universe of service providers or to supply nationwide data on services. Instead, the intent was to collect information on those service providers most likely to be used by households. Such service providers were usually understood to be those located physically within the cluster or enumeration area of the sampled households or, in the absence of a provider within the cluster, the nearest provider outside the cluster. Table 16.3 offers a brief summary of the universe and sample of facilities used. In one case, a national census of health providers was actually conducted. Otherwise, however, the facility questionnaires in LSMS surveys have mimicked the notion of community and the sampling strategy used in the other two auxiliary questionnaires.

Content

The primary areas of focus in facility questionnaires have been education and health. Only in the 1998 Nicaragua LSMS survey, which involved an impact evaluation of the Emergency Social Investment Fund, were any

TABLE 16.3 Features of the Facility Surveys in the LSMS

Country, year	Sector	Sample	Purpose	Topics covered	Special notes
Côte d'Ivoire 1987–88	Health	Frame, universe: names of dispensaries and maternity clinics that are nearest to the cluster; these are taken from the previous year's community questionnaire Not a random sample; not useful for national statistics on health care provision	Analyze household demand for medical care as a function of the service characteristics	Public or private, number of beds, number of personnel (doctors, paramedics, nurses, other staff), services offered	Administrative data only
Côte d'Ivoire 1987–88	Education	Frame, universe: all primary and secondary schools located within the cluster or, if none is in the cluster, the one nearest the cluster; only urban	Economic and policy determinants of fertility in Sub-Saharan Africa; research project; no information on why school data were collected except as part of the research project	Level, public or private, library, housing for teachers, number of grades, number of classrooms, number of students enrolled, number of girls	No rural data were collected; it was assumed these would be obtained from rural surveys
Ghana 1988–89	Health	Health facilities: health facility nearest to each cluster; the nearest public health facility (if the nearest health facility is private) and the nearest source of family planning (if not available at the nearest health facility or the nearest public health facility); in rural areas, community questionnaires were used to determine the nearest facility; in urban areas included the facilities nearest the center of the cluster; the result is not a random	Examine the effect of the quality and availability of health and family planning services near the households	Type of facility, infrastructure, fees, services offered, including schedules and costs, availability of immunization, personnel, beds, equipment, drug supply, family planning services, type, hours,	Carried out after the household survey

		sample; may not be used for national or regional statistics (facilities in rural areas and in less populated areas are overrepresented); 231 health facilities interviewed Pharmacies: nearest source of drugs other than a health facility; 169 drugstores, pharmacies, and drug vendors		electricity and refrigeration, qualified pharmacists, drugs available
Ghana 1988–89	Education	Each primary and secondary school in the clusters where cognitive testing was conducted were surveyed (half of all clusters in the survey); if no primary (secondary) school is in the cluster, the nearest one to the cluster was interviewed; may have missed some schools in urban areas Not a national survey of schools; provides a measure of the quality of schooling available to households in the survey, but not necessarily national averages	Quality of education available to households in the sample	School characteristics: infrastructure, supplies, enrollment and passing criteria, staffing, fees
Jamaica 1989 (2)	Health	The sample frame was a Ministry of Health census of health facilities; all public health facilities were surveyed; all private tertiary facilities (hospitals) were surveyed From the sample frame compiled by the Jamaican Medical Association and community health workers, a random sample of up to 15 primary facilities in each parish was identified and surveyed	To complement the expanded health module in the 1989 (2) round of the Jamaica Survey of Living Conditions	Four questionnaires were used (by type of facility): catchment areas, services offered, supplies, equipment, personnel, transportation, drug supply, laboratory (where relevant); for the private sector:	Carried out in September 1990, that is, after the household survey; in the household questionnaire, the name of the health facility used by the household was collected and used to

(continued)

TABLE 16.3 (Continued)

Country, year	Sector	Sample	Purpose	Topics covered	Special notes
Jamaica 1989 (2) (continued)	Health	Nationally representative, full census on public health facilities and tertiary-level private facilities; probability sample among other private providers		information on wages, revenues, and expenditures	link household and facility data
Jamaica 1990	Education	Schools attended by any household member surveyed in the Jamaica Labor Force Survey or the Jamaica Survey of Living Conditions Not a probability sample of schools	Effects of schooling quality and access on achievement; focus of the 1990 living conditions survey was education; expanded module for individuals; achievement tests and scores for all primary and secondary students who were members of households in the labor force survey and the living conditions survey		Survey of school administrators, plus a random selection of teachers
Morocco 1991	Health	Sample of dispensaries: only those closest to the households surveyed Not a probability sample of health facilities or dispensaries	No set purpose indicated	Health services offered, costs, type of trained personnel, equipment, types of vaccines offered, drug supply	Does not link individual households to specific dispensaries

Country/Region/Year	Sector	Sample/coverage	Survey	Characteristics	Notes
Tanzania (Kagera Region) 1991–94	Health	Health facility nearest to the community as indicated in the community questionnaire (dispensary, health center, hospitals); where more than one facility is within a cluster, all were interviewed; traditional healers were listed, and two were randomly selected within each cluster. Not a national survey; data were only to be linked to the household data	Special survey on the effect of adult deaths (due to HIV/AIDS, primarily) on households	Characteristics of facilities, trained personnel, equipment, services provided, immunizations offered, family planning services, inpatient services, fee policies, availability of drugs	Specific research project (Economic Impact of Fatal Adult Illness from AIDS and Other Causes in Sub-Saharan Africa); not a national survey; four-wave panel survey
Tanzania (Kagera Region) 1991–94	Education	Primary school nearest the cluster; if more than one facility is within a cluster, all were interviewed. Not a national survey; data were only linked to household data	Special survey of the impact of adult death (due to HIV/AIDS primarily) on households; the school data were collected to respond to the demand for education analysis	Characteristics of schools, total and female enrollment, fees, textbooks, attendance, presence of two-parent orphans	As above
Nicaragua 1998	Health	Sample of health posts benefiting from an Emergency Social Investment Fund project and health posts without such a project (for comparison); the sample was designed to measure the impact of fund projects only; 44 health posts	Evaluation of Emergency Social Investment Fund	Schedule, catchment area, services offered, infrastructure, equipment, financing, sanitation, personnel	Specific evaluation project; project also collected data on water and sanitation projects and latrine projects

(continued)

TABLE 16.3 *(Continued)*

Country, year	Sector	Sample	Purpose	Topics covered	Special notes
Nicaragua 1998	Education	As above; sample of preschools and primary schools (48)	As earlier	Type, grades offered, enrollment, main problems, parental involvement, supplies, infrastructure, personnel, funding, maintenance	Specific evaluation project
Vietnam 1998	Health	Commune health stations in communes with sampled households Not a nationally representative sample	Nothing specific stated in the basic information document	Distance to health center, staffing, schedules, beds, services provided, equipment, drugs, costs, fees	This survey forms a panel with the 1993–94 Vietnam Living Standards Survey; no facility survey was administered in the 1993–94 survey, but some data on health facilities were collected through the community questionnaire

Country/Year	Sector	Sample	Objective	Data collected	Notes
Vietnam 1998	Education	All schools within the cluster. Not a national probability sample	Nothing specific stated in the basic information document	Type, level, schedule, classes, enrollment, personnel, infrastructure, supplies, examination results, school fees	This survey forms a panel with the 1993–94 Vietnam Living Standards Survey; no facility survey was administered in the 1993–94 survey, but some data on schools were collected through the community questionnaire
Tanzania (Kagera Region) 2004	Education	Primary schools located in the cluster where households were sampled or, if none was within the cluster, the primary school nearest the cluster. Not a national probability sample; the list of schools was identified through the community questionnaire	School data were collected to respond to the demand for education analysis	Characteristics, enrollment, fees, textbooks available, grades and number of classes, graduation rates, number of teachers	This forms a panel with the 1994 Kagera, Tanzania Health and Development Survey
Tajikistan 2003–04	Health	Urban: all polyclinics located within city limits, all types of medical institutions that provide services to the population of a primary sampling unit, health facilities and nongovernmental organizations providing services within 1 km of the primary sampling unit. Rural: all health facilities within the primary sampling unit; if the bulk of the unit popula-	Overall state of health service provision, reliance on international support for inputs, and variation in the quality of the services available to households, by poverty status	Type of facility, services, inputs, personnel, financing, governance (auditing, decision making), sanitation, infrastructure	An LSMS survey was conducted in 2003; in 2004, a household energy survey was conducted that used a partial panel of households from

(continued)

TABLE 16.3 *(Continued)*

Country, year	Sector	Sample	Purpose	Topics covered	Special notes
Tajikistan 2003–04 *(continued)*		tion used a facility slightly outside the unit, this was also included A nonrandom sample			the 2003 LSMS survey; data were collected for the facilities in 2004
Tajikistan 2003–04	Education	Urban: all basic, primary, and secondary schools were surveyed if they were within the primary sampling unit where the panel households were located or within a 1 km radius Rural: all basic, primary, and secondary schools were surveyed if they were within the primary sampling unit where panel households were located; if no school was within the unit, the schools in which the most children from the unit were enrolled or that were, at least, within a 5 km radius, were surveyed	Physical infrastructure issues, school boards, teacher attendance, list of all teachers, characteristics, equipment, textbooks, computers, community participation, funds, renovations in the last five years	State of the system, how it functions, links to household poverty	As above

Sources: World Bank 1999a, 1999b, 2000, 2001, 2002a, 2002b, 2004, 2006; World Bank and Institut National de la Statistique 1996; Stone and Webster Consultants and CSR Zerkalo 2005.

other facilities included.[6] The purpose of these facility surveys has been to examine the ways the characteristics of service providers may affect household demand for services, as well as tracking variations in household service availability according to household welfare levels. Questions have focused on the specific services offered, the personnel available and their qualifications, the equipment and supplies on hand, and infrastructure. In some surveys, questions have been included on the autonomy of service providers (in budgets, fee setting, and decision making). Although the principal intent has been to capture differences in the quality of services, this finding has been measured largely through inputs. In two cases, students were actually tested to assess outcomes associated with school facilities. However, no efforts have been made to measure the proficiency or skills of medical personnel, although there have been recommendations to experiment with vignettes in the health care setting (see Gertler, Rose, and Glewwe 2000).

Lessons for the Future

What does this analysis tell us about why facility surveys have or have not been implemented as part of LSMS surveys? What can be done to facilitate the incorporation of such surveys in the future? Clearly, there is no single answer. The actual form that each LSMS takes is the result of protracted negotiations among national and international data users and producers. Each survey reflects the priority needs of the country at a given point in time and takes into account the capacity, time, and other constraints that always exist. There are, however, some lessons that may be drawn.

Timing

The facility questionnaires were not part of the original design of the LSMS surveys. This means that, to a large extent, the process of thought, review, consultation, and development applied to the rest of the LSMS and the other three survey instruments (the household, price, and community questionnaires) has not been applied to the facility questionnaire. Thus, little attention has been paid to the potential analytic advantages that the availability of these data might confer, nor has demand been built up for such data. To some extent, it is likely that this approach has limited the ease with which new facility surveys may be incorporated. Information is scarce about what may be done, why it is important, and what issues need to be addressed for such data collection to be successful. It was not until the appearance of the 2000 book *Designing Household Survey Questionnaires for Developing Countries* (Grosh and Glewwe 2000) that specific recommendations were forthcoming on the design of facility surveys and the types of policy analyses that might benefit from these data.[7] Before this survey, to incorporate the facility survey into a new LSMS essentially required reinventing the wheel, a somewhat daunting prospect. It is important to note, however, that even this more recent advice does not provide guidance on all facets of data collection at the facility level.

The inclusion of facility questionnaires during a later period in the evolution of the LSMS surveys has had other implications as well. The facility questionnaire emerged after decisions had already been taken on the relevant sample and universe for the price and community questionnaires. Following a similar logic, the facility questionnaires were developed to collect data that were complementary to the household data. Important new analytic areas thus opened up because it had become possible to link the household data with detailed information about the supply of facilities available to the households. However, one wonders if the decision to collect only facility data that were complementary to the household data has served to limit demand for new facility surveys. One obvious source of demand for facility data and the potential users of the data are the line ministries that provide the services. Yet, because the facility data collected do not allow an understanding or even an overview of health or education service provision in a country, the utility of the data is perceived to be narrow. Service demand analysis aside, policy makers may see limited relevance in the data. The result is low demand for facility surveys and difficulty in demonstrating the value of the data to users. Without strong champions, the facility survey within an LSMS project may, therefore, fall by the wayside during the negotiations that form the core of the project design phase within a given country. Indeed, much of the demand for the facility questionnaires that have been administered appears to have stemmed from specific research projects with facility components: in Ghana, to address a research question on fertility; in Nicaragua, to evaluate the impact of the Emergency Social Investment Fund; and, in Tajikistan, to determine the extent of the reliance of the health system on external funding.[8]

Definitions and Sampling Issues

Another potential barrier to the inclusion of facility surveys as part of the LSMS survey is the unresolved problem concerning the relevant unit of observation in facility surveys and the definition of the universe of these facilities. The LSMS surveys have focused on facilities as fixed locations at which services are provided. But not all facilities are fixed. Many countries have mobile health posts or other mobile services. In some countries, the service providers themselves are mobile, such as health workers in rural and indigenous areas in Panama and teachers in the Falkland Islands, for example. Finally, for certain policy questions, one may imagine that the more relevant unit is the actual service that is being provided, not merely the provider.[9] In short, the determination of the unit of analysis calls for a decision about the policy and research questions to be answered. Do the answers require data on the service, the service provider, or the physical infrastructure supporting the service? One may imagine a situation in which the infrastructure matters substantially less than the service provider. In Afghanistan, for example, health care use among women is considered to depend not only on the proximity of a health post, but also, in part, on the presence of medical staff who are women.[10] In contrast, in a country with difficult transportation infrastructure, the location of the facility may be the driving factor. Guidance on this issue appears scarce.

Even once the unit of observation for a facility survey has been determined, identifying the relevant universe of such facilities or service providers and determining how to sample this universe correctly are not straightforward. Although a census of facilities may supply a broad overview of service provision, many policy questions relating to household behavior are concerned with household choices relative to services. Determining the relevant universe for an analysis of household behavior with regard to interactions with service provision is tricky, and a variety of methods have been used, each with its own costs and benefits.

The simplest approach would seem to involve identifying the facilities to which households have access by listing the facilities within the census enumeration areas where the households are located. But those areas are constructed on the basis of the workload of census takers and are, therefore, a function of the number of households, not of the geographical area. In urban settings, an enumeration area may be a city block or even a large, single apartment complex. In rural settings, in contrast, an enumeration area may cover more than one settlement. Thus, the presence of a service in the enumeration area in which a household is located may have little to do with physical proximity or access. In Panama, for instance, the *corregimientos* (the smallest administrative unit) with no health care facilities actually show health outcomes that are better than the outcomes among corregimientos with primary health care facilities (see table 16.4). One reason is simply the fact that the corregimientos with no direct services tend

TABLE 16.4 Health Facilities and Health Outcomes in Panama, by Corregimiento

Indicator	No facilities	Primary facilities only	Primary, plus secondary or tertiary
Distribution			
Corregimientos (total)	116	201	276
Corregimientos (%)	19.6	33.9	46.5
% of population	8.5	75.1	16.4
Health outcomes			
Mortality	20.8	30.6	18.7
Chronic malnutrition	13.6	32.6	12.5
Unattended births	6.8	25.6	3.2

Sources: Data from the Ministry of Economics and Finance, Panama, 2006; Scott and Bendini 2006.
Note: Corregimientos in the smallest administrative unit.

to be in densely populated locations in which services always exist nearby (see Scott and Bendini 2006).[11] In contrast, those corregimientos with only primary care facilities tend to be isolated, and households have no access to higher levels of care and difficult access even to the primary care facilities that do exist.

To avoid this problem, most of the LSMS facility surveys also identify and survey facilities that are used by households even if these are outside the enumeration area or cluster. Generating the list of these facilities is a bit more complex, however. Community leaders have provided such lists (through the community survey), but it has been found that the lists may omit important sources of services; community elites may not know about all the services used (Frankenberg 2000). In other surveys, the households themselves are asked to list the names of all service providers used. Of course, this approach has the obvious drawback of providing a sample of the facilities used and sheds no light on those services that exist, but which households eschew for whatever reason. A combination of the two sources of data is probably needed, as Frankenberg (2000) suggests.

The availability of a combination of sources for listing the services that are used and the services that exist is important. However, political issues and cultural norms will also confound the ability to sample facilities or service providers appropriately for the analysis of household behavior. To obtain health care in Bosnia and Herzegovina after the conflict in the 1990s, some individuals living in an entity where they were part of an ethnic minority would travel to the other entity of the country where they would be part of the ethnic majority. For at least some of this period, physical proximity to a care facility was, therefore, not a useful proxy for access. Additionally, because of cultural norms, the ability of an individual to make use of a service may be affected by the individual's health status so that a person who is generally physically healthy may be unable to access a service located nearby for reasons that have nothing to do with the distance, costs, or quality of the service. The only truly accessible service may be quite distant. The relevant pool of services is thus not easy to define or identify.

Logistics and Complexity

Carrying out a facility survey is a substantial additional effort at all stages of the development, implementation, and analysis of an LSMS survey. During questionnaire design, the facility survey represents an extra task requiring consultation with data users on content, implementation, and ways to link effectively to the household data that will be collected. Mechanisms need to be developed to identify and select the facilities to be included, and there must be additional supervision mechanisms and resources to ensure that the selection is respected in the field. Formal permission from line ministries will be needed because, without their approval of the questionnaire and the overall task, it will not be possible to collect the facility data in most countries. (Sometimes even with permission of the ministries, it has been difficult to obtain entry to all facilities.) The questionnaire itself has to be tested.

Once the instrument has been developed, administering it may generate the biggest struggle. Typically, an LSMS survey relies on mobile teams of two or three interviewers, a supervisor, a data entry person, and a driver. The supervisor, in addition to assisting the interviewers, is also usually responsible for administering the price questionnaire and the community questionnaire. It is not at all clear that the supervisor will have time to administer the facility survey, especially in areas with multiple facilities. Hiring an additional person to perform this task is difficult because the team usually already fills a vehicle. How is this additional person to be integrated? Obviously, one option would involve defining the facility survey as a separate activity to be carried out either by a different team in parallel, or by the same team after the household survey has been completed. Both steps would have a serious impact on costs and would increase the logistic complexity of the LSMS. Then, of course, to be useful, the data must be analyzed.

None of these activities are beyond the scope or capacity of a statistical office or survey firm that is undertaking an LSMS. Clearly, successful facility surveys have been implemented, and useful analyses have been carried out. The problem is simply that the LSMS survey is already a complex activity in which compromise and negotiation are the order of the day. To the extent that there is no vocal champion for the data that emanate from a facility survey, it is more likely that the survey will not be conducted. In many cases, statistical offices already believe the collection of some of the household data is outside their areas of interest. Many are focused only on income and expenditure surveys or, perhaps, labor force surveys. A survey of service providers may be considered by the statistical office to be even more beyond its areas of expertise.

Conclusions and Recommendations

Although the facility surveys were not designed as a core element of the LSMS program from the outset, there is no reason why facility surveys may not be incorporated into LSMS surveys. The analytic advantages of the ability to link data on facilities to data on households may often warrant the extra work involved in developing and administering the facility surveys along with the price, community, and household questionnaires of the LSMS surveys. Such efforts have been carried out successfully in several countries. However, despite the successes, these efforts are not usual. If facility surveys are to be incorporated into new LSMS surveys, a method needs to be found to make the cost-benefit analysis more favorable.

One way to accomplish this goal is to increase the benefits by providing more (higher-quality) data to more users. This change might be done by adopting a full probability sample of facilities, as well as a sample of facilities near the households in the survey. Generating a nationally representative data set of facilities would expand the range and type of analyses that might be realized and help foster the support of the often powerful line ministries. A more accurate understanding of the demand for data would also be useful. More work is needed in reviewing, collating, and demonstrating the benefits of detailed facility data. Finding examples of useful applications of the data in policy making is key.

The costs of developing and implementing a facility survey may be lowered by developing and propagating guidance on procedures to address the various issues in definitions and sampling that are involved. There will be clear links between the way these issues are settled and the policy questions of interest. By clearly identifying these links, survey designers, be they data users or data producers, will be able to determine more easily the design that is required. Not all policy or research questions will be of equal interest or importance in a given country. The availability of a means to discriminate among competing interests lowers the costs of design substantially.

Finally, the LSMS "Implementation Manual" (Grosh and Muñoz 1996, 1999) needs to be updated with a new chapter on designing and implementing a facility survey. This chapter would provide information on the list of activities that should be carried out; the order in which these activities should be undertaken; the methods to ensure proper links between the household and community questionnaires; the way implementation will affect the fieldwork for the rest of the LSMS survey; and the alterations that will be needed in the recruiting, training, data entry, and data set preparation phases. Some estimate of the actual costs involved is critical, be these costs in time, personnel, budgets, or other resources.

Notes

1. To ensure the continued relevance of LSMS surveys and to promote the use of LSMS data, a series of other support and review activities has been carried out under the LSMS program. These activities encompass, for example, investments in data archiving and dissemination (see Grosh and Glewwe 1995), the major stocktaking exercise to evaluate the policy relevance of LSMS surveys (see Grosh and Glewwe 2000), and ongoing activities under phase IV of the LSMS program, including methodological experiments aimed at improving the measurement of key concepts and topics and determining ways to take advantage of new technologies to enhance data quality (see World Bank 2006). See also Scott, Steele, and Temesgen (2005).
2. Unlike other international survey efforts such as the Multiple Indicator Cluster Surveys of the United Nations Children's Fund or the Demographic and Health Surveys funded by the U.S. Agency for International Development, there is no institutional mandate in the World Bank to carry out a fixed number of LSMS surveys in a specific group of countries in any given time period.
3. See Deaton and Zaidi (2002) for a discussion of the issues involved in using consumption as a measure of welfare.
4. The notable exception is the Jamaica Survey of Living Conditions. For this survey, it was decided early on that the size of the country and the uniformity of prices throughout the country rendered the need for additional price adjustments unnecessary (see World Bank 2002a).

5. The feasibility and analytic benefits of carrying out panel surveys on households was revisited in 2000 with a slightly more positive focus (see Glewwe and Jacoby 2000). By then, several successful panel surveys had been carried out as part of LSMS surveys.
6. Data on sanitation provision were collected because the Emergency Social Investment Fund supported sewerage and latrine projects, as well as more general health and education projects (see World Bank 2000).
7. See, for example, the chapters on health (Gertler, Rose, and Glewwe 2000) and education (Glewwe 2000) in Grosh and Glewwe (2000).
8. A bibliography including many papers that use facility survey data may be found on the LSMS Web site, at http://www.worldbank.org/lsms.
9. Early surveys, for example, focused on collecting information specifically about family planning programs, not only the presence of health workers.
10. The Afghanistan National Risk and Vulnerability Survey 2007 includes such options for questions on the use of health care services by women.
11. Other reasons for this finding include problems in the measurement of health outcome variables and the exclusion of private care and public mobile care.

References

Chandar, Ramesh, Christiaan Grootaert, and Graham Pyatt. 1980. "Living Standards Surveys in Developing Countries." Living Standards Measurement Study Working Paper 1, World Bank, Washington, DC.

Deaton, Angus S., and Salman Zaidi. 2002 "Guidelines for Constructing Consumption Aggregates for Welfare Analysis." Living Standards Measurement Study Working Paper 135, World Bank, Washington, DC.

Frankenberg, Elizabeth. 2000. "Community and Price Data in the Living Standards Measurement Surveys." In *Designing Household Survey Questionnaires for Developing Countries: Lessons from 15 Years of the Living Standards Measurement Study*, ed. Margaret E. Grosh and Paul W. Glewwe, 1: 315–38. Washington, DC: World Bank; New York: Oxford University Press.

Gertler, Paul J., Elaina Rose, and Paul W. Glewwe. 2000. "Health." In *Designing Household Survey Questionnaires for Developing Countries: Lessons from 15 Years of the Living Standards Measurement Study*, ed. Margaret E. Grosh and Paul W. Glewwe, 1: 177–216. Washington, DC: World Bank; New York: Oxford University Press.

Glewwe, Paul W. 2000. "Education." In *Designing Household Survey Questionnaires for Developing Countries: Lessons from 15 Years of the Living Standards Measurement Study*, ed. Margaret E. Grosh and Paul W. Glewwe, 1: 143–75. Washington, DC: World Bank; New York: Oxford University Press.

Glewwe, Paul W., and Hanan G. Jacoby. 2000. "Recommendations for Collecting Panel Data." In *Designing Household Survey Questionnaires for Developing Countries: Lessons from 15 Years of the Living Standards Measurement Study*, ed. Margaret E. Grosh and Paul W. Glewwe, 2: 275–314. Washington, DC: World Bank; New York: Oxford University Press.

Grosh, Margaret E., and Paul W. Glewwe. 1995. "A Guide to Living Standards Measurement Study Surveys and Their Data Sets." Living Standards Measurement Study Working Paper 120, World Bank, Washington, DC.

————, eds. 2000. *Designing Household Survey Questionnaires for Developing Countries: Lessons from 15 Years of the Living Standards Measurement Study.* 3 vols. Washington, DC: World Bank; New York: Oxford University Press.

Grosh, Margaret E., and Juan Muñoz. 1996. "A Manual for Planning and Implementing the Living Standards Measurement Study Survey." Living Standards Measurement Study Working Paper 126, World Bank, Washington, DC.

————. 1999. "Manual de diseño y ejecución de encuestas sobre condiciones de vida (LSMS)." Documento de trabajo del estudio LSMS 126S, World Bank, Washington, DC.

Ho, Teresa J. 1982. "Measuring Health as a Component of Living Standards." Living Standards Measurement Study Working Paper 15, World Bank, Washington, DC.

Saunders, Christopher, and Christiaan Grootaert. 1980. "Reflections on the LSMS Group Meeting." Living Standards Measurement Study Working Paper 10, World Bank, Washington, DC.

Scott, Kinnon, and Magdalena Bendini. 2006. "Panamá: Educación y Salud, Resultados Preliminares 1997–2003." Paper presented at the United Nations Development Programme Workshop, "Poverty Assessment for 2003," Panama City, February 8.

Scott, Kinnon, Diane Steele, and Tilahun Temesgen. 2005. "Living Standards Measurement Study Surveys." In *Household Sample Surveys in Developing and Transition Countries,* ed. United Nations, 523–56. Studies in Methods ST/ESA/STAT/SER.F/96. New York: Statistics Division, Department of Economic and Social Affairs, United Nations.

Stone and Webster Consultants and CSR Zerkalo. 2005. "Tajik Facility Surveys Technical Report." Consultant report for the World Bank, Stone and Webster Consultants, London.

Wood, G. Donald, Jr., and Jane A. Knight. 1985. "The Collection of Price Data for the Measurement of Living Standards." Living Standards Measurement Study Working Paper 21, World Bank, Washington, DC.

World Bank. 1999a. "Ghana Living Standards Survey (GLSS) 1987–88 and 1988–99: Basic Information." Basic information document, Development Research Group, World Bank, Washington, DC.

————. 1999b. "Morocco Living Standards Survey (MLSS) 1990/91: Basic Information." Basic information document, Development Research Group, World Bank, Washington, DC.

————. 2000. "Nicaragua: Ex-Post Impact Evaluation of the Emergency Social Investment Fund (FISE)." Report 20400-NI, Human Development Sector Management Unit, Latin America and the Caribbean Region, World Bank, Washington. DC.

————. 2001. "Vietnam Living Standards Survey (VLSS) 1997–98: Basic Information." Basic information document, Development Research Group, World Bank, Washington, DC.

————. 2002a. "Jamaica Survey of Living Conditions (JSLC) 1988–2000: Basic Information." Basic information document, Development Research Group, World Bank, Washington, DC.

————. 2002b. "Basic Information Document: Nicaragua Living Standards Measurement Study Survey, 1998." Basic information document, Development Research Group, World Bank, Washington, DC.

————. 2004. "User's Guide to the Kagera Health and Development Survey Datasets." Basic information document, Development Research Group, World Bank, Washington, DC.

————. 2006. "LSMS IV: Research for Improving Survey Data." Unpublished research paper, Development Economics Research Group, World Bank, Washington, DC.

World Bank and Institut National de la Statistique, Côte d'Ivoire. 1996. "Côte D'Ivoire Living Standards Survey (CILSS) 1985–88: Basic Information for Users of the Data." Basic information document, Development Research Group, World Bank, Washington, DC.

17

Sharing the Gain

Some Common Lessons on Measuring Service Delivery

Markus Goldstein

One clear message that emerged in the workshop we held to discuss the papers that form the chapters in this volume is that measuring service delivery data is a messy and sometimes painful process. This chapter pulls together some relevant general lessons from this volume and the authors' workshop.

The ultimate question to keep in mind as you proceed in the design of your service delivery exercise is: is it worth it? As we have seen in the preceding chapters, much may go wrong, and many factors will complicate the exercise (see later). Against these factors and the obvious costs of collecting the data, one must weigh the benefits. The benefits arise from the uses to which the collected data are put. This analysis includes both the purpose for collecting the data and the probability that the results will have an impact. We have seen a range of purposes throughout the book: strengthening monitoring systems, building more accountability into systems, answering research questions, and rigorously evaluating programs. We have also seen that these data may yield powerful results. However, the general introduction titled "Why Measure Service Delivery?" notes that

The author wishes to thank Samia Amin, Jishnu Das, Kenneth Leonard, and Maureen Lewis for useful comments and discussions.

the cases here do not include abject failures. Hence, in considering the usefulness of an exercise, one must balance the feasibility of the exercise and the ultimate policy impact that the data will have. Although the effort will not always be worth carrying out, the lessons described below are meant to aid in increasing the feasibility and impact of the exercise. The lessons are loosely organized as follows: the bigger picture, which considers lessons regarding the conceptualization and definition of the exercise; how to get started, which discusses issues involved in the design of the exercise; and how to implement.

The Bigger Picture

- *Carefully consider scope versus depth in your service delivery measurement exercise.* The first step is to identify clearly the central question the exercise is designed to answer. Once this has been done, the next step is to consider the trade-offs between depth and breadth. A broader survey might provide more information of use to a range of actors or cover a larger geographical area. Furthermore, by providing a bit of information on numerous areas of service, particularly in an environment where monitoring systems are weak, a broad survey may become quite useful to policy makers. However, for a given set of supervisory resources (or constrained finances), the broader a survey becomes, the greater the risk that the quality of the underlying questions will be compromised. In addition, a broad survey or a broad question may miss important parts of the picture. Indeed, as we saw in the chapters on the Public Expenditure Tracking Survey (PETS), for example, even surveys that intend to capture only one slice of the broader service delivery picture require careful attention to definitions and measurement issues. Indeed, as Filmer notes in his chapter, in the collection of financial data, it is best to use a survey instrument that is more specific such as one that explicitly asks about various sources of funds by name. Asking about facility income in general in a situation where there are many funding sources increases the odds that some of the resources will be left out by the respondents.

- *Weigh the trade-offs between relevance and comparability.* Borrowing from the discussion of Das and Leonard in chapter 13, on important characteristics of vignettes, we may define two critical features of all service delivery measurement exercises: relevance and comparability. First, relevance means that the activities covered by the exercise are fairly accurately measured and cover a significant swath of the population of concern and that the exercise will be useful for local decision making. Second, comparability refers to the ability to compare results across providers and settings, including across countries. There will be a trade-off between these two features: the more specific and, hence, the more accurate an instrument is (for example, in capturing various sources of facility income by source), the less likely it is that the results will be comparable given the variations in specific areas across systems.

Make sure the data will be used. As Lindelow and Wagstaff note in their chapter, service delivery data have been underutilized in many cases. Their concern was echoed during the authors' workshop, where participants indicated that the issue was a particular area of concern in multi-topic surveys. To avoid the problem, one may find that it is helpful to identify concrete uses and applications for the data and, ideally, the persons responsible for realizing these uses and applications before undertaking data collection. One obvious application for the data is analytical work, but one should also consider how the data may be used to feedback into the design of policy measures to address any problems identified during data collection and the subsequent analytical work. A well-designed dissemination and consultation plan is critical to ensuring that the impact of the work is significant. Finally, it is important to be open, particularly during the early pilot stages of a survey, to other potential uses of the survey. As Bekh and others point out in chapter 11, two other uses became evident during the testing of their school survey in the Ukraine: the analysis of decentralization and project evaluation. Ultimately, the use to which data will be put and the central question to be addressed will define the sampling strategy.

Getting Started

Understand that administrative data are the starting point for any exercise. As we can see from the chapters in this volume, administrative data may suffice as a source of information on service delivery. Indeed, as chapter 5 by Galasso shows, administrative data may help get us farther along the way than we might initially think. As she points out, administrative data tend to be collected more frequently and over a longer period of time relative to survey data. Nonetheless, as she and others in this volume indicate, we will need data on nonparticipants in some cases, and, for this, administrative data are unlikely to be useful.

Ultimately, if administrative data were of better quality, then we would need fewer facility surveys and PETSs. Thus, we should: (a) Examine the available administrative data before undertaking a purposive survey. For example, Wane argues in chapter 8 for a rapid data assessment using a simple questionnaire administered to a few facilities. (b) If possible, use the service delivery data exercise to strengthen administrative data. For instance, as part of a PETS, point out why expenditures have been so hard to track. (c) Make sure that improving administrative data is on the overall national agenda. For example, as part of building a poverty reduction monitoring system or national statistical capacity. Finally, it is important to note that, whatever tool is chosen to measure service delivery, administrative data will be a critical first step. For instance, a facility survey of schools will require a school census, which may (or may not) exist within the records of the education ministry. This census means that assessing the quality and scope of existing administrative data is an important early step. If these data are inaccessible or of poor quality, this problem will delay any planned service delivery measurement exercise, even one that does not rely on administrative data, such as a school facility survey.

* *Know that administrative data that are actively used are more likely to be of higher quality.* As Galasso points out in chapter 5, the data that program managers use tend to be updated more regularly and of higher quality (given that manipulation would more likely be detected).

* *When looking at the effects of a program, administrative data may provide critical information.* Even if the ultimate analysis involves a facility survey, administrative data may supply important information on certain aspects of program operation, including implementation lags (see below). This concern is addressed by Behrman and King in chapter 6, where they also advocate complementing administrative data through discussions with program field staff so as to enhance understanding of the service delivery environment.

* *Understand that the exercise of carrying out many of these data collection efforts may change the underlying processes that produce the data.* One may imagine that the execution of a community report card initiative, for

example, will change the expectations individuals might have regarding their service providers. In the case of a PETS exercise, the chapters in this volume show how these surveys have raised questions about the differences between leakages and legitimate changes in flows. This information will have an effect on a system either by teaching some people how to be less obvious in diverting funds or by teaching others how to improve the controls and management of the system to reduce leakage.

Be sure to tread lightly. The cooperation of providers is critical in many service delivery measurement exercises. As Lindelow points out in chapter 7, unannounced visits by a survey team are essential in measuring absenteeism. However, for the collection of most other sorts of data, the cooperation of facility staff is crucial, and unannounced visits risk alienating the facility staff and may result in additional costs (because staff are not prepared or are, indeed, absent). Lindelow also provides another lesson in this regard: broadening the scope of a survey may sometimes be useful in making the survey less threatening. In the case he considers, broadening the questionnaire to serve the needs of a wide group of stakeholders reduced the focus on leakage.

Build cooperation around the service delivery measurement exercise. The start of a service delivery measurement exercise may offer the opportunity to build cooperation among interested ministries, donors, and research organizations. For example, Bekh and others in chapter 11 suggest creating consultative or advisory teams. This change has obvious costs in terms of the time needed to coordinate the various actors and build a service measurement tool that can be linked to a broad range of data and includes the risk of creating an unmanageably broad measurement tool. However, this can have several benefits. First, the participation of numerous actors may facilitate access and linkage to diverse sources of useful data. Second, broadening the scope of ownership increases the probability that the service delivery data will be put to good use.

Use the service delivery measurement exercise to strengthen institutions. The service delivery measurement exercise, which involves a hard look at existing data and data collection systems, as well as possible new endeavors, provides an opening for building institutional capacity and commitment to the collection and use of monitoring data. For example, Filmer, in chapter 9, argues that housing a survey within the ministry of education helped build capacity. And, as Lindelow points out in chapter 7, even low-quality administrative data may be informative. He points out that the attempt to understand leakages in the health sector in Mozambique highlighted weaknesses in the management and control system.

Be sure to triangulate to improve accuracy. Trying to measure the same feature with more than one measurement tool will improve the accuracy of the results and will help compensate for faulty memories and records. For example, Frankenberg and others in chapter 10 discuss the usefulness of comparing damage estimates generated through facility and community surveys and the corresponding estimates produced on the basis of satellite imagery. In another striking example, in chapter 14, Lundberg shows how household surveys and exit surveys elicit different numbers on informal payments. In addition to using multiple sources of data, triangulation may also involve comparing the same source at different levels (for example, central and facility records) or different modes of reporting (asking the same question to different individuals in a given facility). One example of the usefulness of this approach is illustrated by Lindelow, who argues that, to identify ghost workers accurately, records at many levels (such as at the central and local levels) need to be checked and compared.

Keep the broader picture in mind in designing the measurement tool. In chapter 9, Filmer makes the point that, by collecting detailed information on a range of sources of school income, the school survey in Indonesia was able not only to track a central government grant program for schools, but also to show that local governments were reducing their allocations in response to these central grants. Another example is provided by Frankenberg and others in chapter 10, who, in capturing spillover effects, show the importance of surveying surrounding areas, as well as those directly hit by a disaster. Awareness of the possibility that general equilibrium effects may exist may help yield useful policy conclusions.

Do qualitative work. As chapter 12 by Serneels, Lindelow, and Lievens makes clear, qualitative work—interviews, discussions, or participatory approaches—not only is valuable in refining the quantitative tool, but also may prove critical in deciding which quantitative tool to use. This work may seem like an extravagance, but the cost of performing the wrong quantitative exercise altogether means that the work is worthwhile if you have not identified the best tool for obtaining the information you need. In addition, once the quantitative data have been collected, qualitative work may help guide the analysis and explain the results, for example, by providing a detailed understanding of the underlying processes.

- *Do pilot testing.* Pilot testing helps in choosing a better measurement tool. Thus, you may discover that a facility survey is not producing the data you need, as we saw with some of the public expenditure tracking experiences. After you have chosen the appropriate tool, of course, pilot testing will assist you in improving the quality of the tool. In the end, though, the scope of pilot testing is likely to be constrained by the time and financial resources available. Nonetheless, pilot testing is particularly critical for surveys in the measurement of service delivery because, at least relative to household surveys, the experience with what works and what does not work is less well developed.

- *Think carefully about the unit of observation and the sampling strategy.* Determining the appropriate unit of observation and the proper sampling strategy is more tricky in the effort to measure service delivery than in, say, the measurement of household welfare. If you wish to measure the delivery of health care, the facility will likely be the focus. But if you want to include health-seeking behavior (the demand side), then you will want another unit of analysis, such as individuals, the village, or the catchment area. The main question to be answered through the analysis will guide the sampling strategy. Indeed, given the range of perspectives from which one may try to measure service delivery, there is no common approach to sampling (relative to, for example, the case of household welfare surveys). The chapters by Beegle (15), by Bekh and others (11), by Lundberg (14), and by Scott (16) provide some food for thought on how one might approach this issue, but you should bear in mind the different perspectives from which they are approaching service delivery measurement.

- *Think about the level of disaggregation.* In tandem with the considerations on sampling and the unit of observation, it is important to examine the level at which data are aggregated for reporting purposes. This is likely to be a particular problem in using administrative data. As

Galasso notes in chapter 5, "it is common in most monitoring data systems that only a subset of the extensive information recorded at the unit level of intervention is transmitted upward to higher administrative entities." Indeed, this problem bedeviled the work described by Lanjouw and Özler in chapter 4; the administrative data system they were using aggregated data at a level that was higher than the level relevant to some of the projects they wanted to analyze. As a result, in communities with more than one project, data for multiple projects was combined, which complicated the analysis. Although there may be cases where you are constrained by the structure of an existing management information system, if it is possible (and affordable) to alter the structure and keep the data disaggregated, this may turn out to be useful. In other cases, it may be possible to rely on the administrative system as a guide and return to the lower levels of the system to collect data at greater disaggregation.

Examine potential ways to apply geographical information. Geographical information provides a powerful way to integrate, link, and display different types of data. For example, in chapter 10, Frankenberg and others show how these types of data may supply valuable measurements of infrastructure reconstruction and vegetation regrowth over time. However, in the application of geographic information system data, a number of issues are important. First, proper training (which will not necessarily take much time) is key in avoiding problems such as schools that are mysteriously located in the middle of the ocean. Second, geo-referenced data also need to be time referenced, a fact that is often overlooked. This approach facilitates the process of updating the data and is useful if the data are applied in reaching policy decisions. Third, it is helpful to have some central coordination so that various government ministries have access to the same level of information. Such an approach not only prevents the duplication of data collection efforts, but also avoids potential discrepancies. Such coordination is not a trivial undertaking, and there is relatively little experience with this sort of coordination in developing countries, although Kenya is currently making the attempt. Fourth, while privacy issues are not likely to be a concern with geographical information on facilities, they will be with geographical information on households. This issue will have to be addressed during any effort to release household data so as to merge them with facility and other geographical data.

● *Do not forget mobile service providers.* As Scott points out in chapter 16, many countries have mobile service providers or mobile facilities (for example, health workers in the rural and indigenous parts of Panama and teachers in the Falkland Islands).

● *In looking at policy changes or program effects, keep in mind potential implementation lags, as well as the amount of time for the information to filter through the system.* As we see in the Behrman and King chapter (6), for example, implementation lags may provide powerful information for analysis. Indeed, this lag is so for most analyses; if the program or the policy has not yet started to have an effect, you may want to delay the data collection effort. Another issue of concern, particularly in the use of administrative data, is the amount of time it takes information to be entered into the system and to move through the system to a point where it is accessible. This consideration calls for work to assess the timeliness of records in the system under consideration.

Implementation

● *Listen to the survey and data collection teams.* This approach is always good practice in any type of survey, but it is especially important in service delivery surveys. The following issues are among those that might be missed during preliminary qualitative work and pilot testing, but that will become obvious to enumerators visiting facilities: certain important factors that are not currently included in the instrument for measurement, the effectiveness of questions in eliciting useful information, and program implementation lags. Thus, debriefings among field teams, particularly early on in the survey effort, may lead to valuable adjustments in the survey.

● *Time the data collection carefully.* There are four main ways in which timing may be important. First, in some cases, the quality of administrative data may decay quite rapidly as records are destroyed or lost. As Wane argues in chapter 8, the best time to do a PETS is after the records on all transactions have been entered for the previous fiscal year, but before the records are placed in storage. Second, timing may be important if service use varies over the year. For example, malaria may peak during certain seasons. Third, the environmental conditions faced by facilities may change during the year. As Bekh and others in chapter 11 indicate, winter tests school infrastructure, and this fact had to be taken into account in scheduling their survey. Fourth, the flow of resources between the center and facilities may also vary during the course of the year. For example, delays in approving the national budget or cost overruns at the end of the fiscal year may cause significant changes in the amount of resources that the central government provides to facilities. This problem will affect the measured level of services, as well as measures of resource flows and leakages. Figure 9.3 offers a graphic example of the variations in resource flows over time.

Be specific about definitions. Definitions will be driven by the data the service delivery measurement exercise is trying to capture. Although this concern may be obvious in a general way, it may not be a simple task to reach this goal. As the chapters by Lindelow (7) and Wane (8) make clear, if the goal is to measure leakage, a fair amount of time will have to be spent defining what is meant by leakage in the context of the country being examined. These definitions may also need to be adapted as the survey progresses; as Lindelow explains in chapter 7, the definition of leakage was refined during the attempt to deal with allocation rules for drugs.

Understand that linking different types of data increases the power of the analysis, but is messy. Matching different types of data allows for powerful analysis because data on households, facilities, geographical conditions, and the like may be merged to answer a host of questions. Many of the chapters in this book use more than one source of data, and one issue that arose repeatedly during our authors workshop was the difficulty of linking these different data sources.

The issues involved in linking data sets may become manifest in a number of ways. First, finding common identifiers that can facilitate creating links among data sets may be difficult because (a) a ministry may rely on administrative units that only partially overlap with the units used by other ministries or in household surveys within a single country (in this case, geo-referencing would be a helpful tool); (b) each ministry within a single country may have its own unique set of codes for regions or facilities; (c) within a given ministry, different departments may use unique identifiers for each task or project (such as one set of codes for a national examination and another for funding), or, even worse, they may use the same names, but spell them differently, shorten place names in different ways, or use different languages; and (d) administrative changes, such as the splitting or combining of districts, may lead to changes in codes, and the old codes may not be kept for later use. In addition to these problems in using identifiers, there may be regulatory issues that hinder matching. An example is found in chapter 11 by Bekh and others, which discusses a case in which confidentiality restrictions hampered the creation of links between facility survey data and household survey data. A final issue to consider, as highlighted by Beegle in chapter 15, is whether the linked sets of data will cover the same period of time (as well as the same communities).

A number of options might make the task of addressing those issues easier. The central message is: the earlier you start, the better. A little bit of foresight can have significant long-run payoffs. For example, if the sampling for your exercise is being carried out on the basis of census records, keep records that will allow your survey to be linked to the census, not only to take advantage of small area estimation techniques (see later), but also because the census is likely to serve as the basis of sampling in most household surveys. In addition to the census, it is worth investing in an exploration of current classifications and codes before the exercise so as to be able to link your data more rapidly to other relevant sources after the exercise. At the very least, this addition will allow the matching effort (which may become quite time consuming) to proceed in tandem with the data collection. Finally, it may be worth exploring the potential for using geographical information to match various surveys. This technique may be particularly helpful in matching data sources that rely on different units for measurement (for example, school catchment areas and census tracts).

● *Set up your data so that they may be used by others.* The way in which you organize your data will help determine whether or not others may use the data to measure the same aspect or other aspects of service delivery. Hence, following the principles for effectively linking data discussed above (for instance, by using the most common reference codes or keeping lists to match units) will form part of your legacy for the next generation of activities.

● *Consider the potential for applications of census data, including small area estimation.* In addition to administrative data, one of the other types of data that is likely to be accessible in many countries is census data. Through the application of small area estimation techniques (discussed in chapter 4 by Lanjouw and Özler), census data may become a source of detailed information on the socioeconomic characteristics of communities for use in any analysis (for example, in conjunction with administrative data, as outlined in chapter 5 by Galasso).

- *Use a data-entry program and process that permit the rapid detection and correction of mistakes.* This basic principle is good practice in all surveys, but is particularly important in measuring service delivery because the results may be needed quickly to guide policy decisions. Setting up a good data-entry process at the outset will help avoid a great deal of data cleaning after the exercise has been completed.

- *Make copies of all records discovered or used.* This source will allow the analysis, interpretation, and verification of data to continue after data collection and facilitates the prevention and correction of recording errors. This approach is obviously relevant to work using only administrative data, but is also likely to be of use if the survey relies on facility records and other records, such as in the case of a PETS or facility surveys.

Index

use of administrative data to study, 132, 144*n*2

outmigrant surveys, 49

outputs

in education systems, 70

heterogeneity of, 29, 53*n*5

measurement of, 28–30, 53*nn*5–7

output index, 29–30, 53*n*6

Özler, Berk, xx-xxi, 5, 16, 111–30, 396

P

Palanpur, India, 116–20

Panama, 381–82

panel surveys, 54*n*13, 354, 355*t*13.2, 368, 386*n*5

Paniotto, Volodymyr, xxi, 251–70

Papua New Guinea school-focused survey

background, 222

conclusions concerning, 231

conducting the survey, 222–24

difficulty of, 228–30

justification for, 230–31

results of, 224–28

parent interviews, 230–31

parroquias, 113

multiple projects in, 125

other control variables used to determine FISE project choice, 120–22

population of, 120

poverty and inequality estimates for, 115–20, 128*n*3

as recipients of FISE project, 115

sample of data for, 122–23

as units of analysis, 123

patients

characteristics of by facility type, 325, 327–28

fake patients, 301–2

patient-provider interactions, 32

patient satisfaction surveys, 314–17, 339*nn*1–2

review of records of, 53*n*9

satisfaction of, 32–34, 54*n*11

simulated, 31–32, 53–54*nn*9–10

See also clients; physical examinations

per capita consumption, 119

perceptions

as complement to quantitative data, 224–25

of health services, 32–34, 54*n*11, 321–25, 326*t*14.4, 340*n*5

performance of service providers, 22–25

health care workers, 34–35

link to decentralization, 54*n*13

measure of, 35, 54*n*13

link to salary, 278, 293*n*6

monitoring of, 7–9

performance-based contracts, 13, 317–20

performance-based incentives, 328–30

See also patients; physicians

Peru, 80–81, 84

Petrenko, Tatyana, xxi, 251–70

PETS. *See* Public Expenditure Tracking Survey (PETS)

petty-value items, 198

Philippines, early childhood development program, 160–67, 170*nn*5–8

physical examinations, 323–25, 326*t*14.4, 334*t*14.8, 335, 340*n*5

physicians

absenteeism of, 277, 293*n*5, 294*n*7

communication skills, 315

comparing vignettes with direct observations of, 304–5

competence of, 303–6, 307–11

evaluation of activities of, 302

quality of, 10

and validity of vignettes, 303–5, 311*n*2

pilot testing, 187, 223, 391, 395

PNFP. *See* private not-for-profit (PNFP) facilities

policies

addressed through a PETS or QSDS, 202–5, 220*nn*7–8

based on evaluations, 88

and educational research, 101

policy-relevant research, 15–16, 101

role of EMIS in, 78

targeting of, 9–11

school-focused surveys
  IFLS
    analysis of, 354, 356, 362nn8–10
    conclusions concerning, 262n11,
      356–57
    key features of, 349–54,
      361–62nn6–7
    overview, 345–49, 361nn4–5
  Indonesia and Papua New Guinea
    background, 221–22
    conclusions concerning, 231
    conducting the survey, 222–24
    difficulty of obtaining reliable infor-
      mation for, 228–30
    justification for, 230–31
    results of survey, 224–28
  school grants, 225–26
school quality, impact of government
  policies on, 89
schools
  buildings, 114
  enrollment, 37–38, 68, 156
    accuracy of enrollment data, 103
    post-tsunami period, 245–46
    trends in, 224–25
    Ukraine, 252–53
  equipment and supplies for, 114, 258
  fees for, 226–27
  information on total school incomes,
    228–29
  physical infrastructure of, 257–58
  school-age children, 87
  school questionnaires, 90–91
  school surveys as complement to
    household data, 21–22
  usage of, 92
school vouchers, 144n2, 154
scorecard schemes, 33, 38, 95–97
Scott, Kinnon, xxii, 9, 17, 365–88, 395,
  397
second-stage sampling units, 263–64,
  266–67
Seecaline program, 133
  and use of administrative and moni-
    toring data, 134–40, 145nn5–6

using data to make inferences about,
  140–41, 142t5.1, 143f5.2, 145n7
selection bias, 132, 139, 356
Serneels, Pieter, xxii, 8, 17, 271–97, 394
service availability roster (SAR), 346,
  348–49, 350, 353
service delivery
  in aftermath of tsunami, 240–48
  agents of, 136
  and budget allocations for, 80
  and citizen report cards, 94–95
  and community scorecards, 95–97
  constraints for in Madagascar, 145n7
  environment of, 9–10, 240–47, 392
  impacts of, 151
  lessons concerning, 260–61
  making use of data for, 5–9
  overview of measures of, 1–5
  service environment, 240–47, 350
  targeting policy response to, 10–11
  using data about to capture effects of
    treatment variations, 13–15
  See also education service delivery;
    health care service delivery
service delivery measures
  consideration of relevance vs.
    comparability of, 390–91
  considerations in development of,
    391–92
  scope vs. depth of, 390
  utilization of data, 391
service delivery units, 38, 47
service providers
  Indonesia, 48–49
  monitoring of, 7–9
  See also health care providers; Living
    Standards Measurement Study
    (LSMS) surveys
service provider surveys, 49–50
Service Provision Assessments, 22, 92
services
  demand for, 11, 15
  poverty and the service environment,
    9–10
  range of, 29–30
  units of, 30

wealth index, 92, 333
weather, as a concern in school surveys, 256
weighting, 266–69, 352
  of facilities in IFLS survey, 349, 350, 359–60, 362*n*12
welfare indicators, 255
welfare measurements, 367
women as users of health care services, 381, 386*n*10
women's questionnaires, 91, 93
workfare programs, Argentina, 132, 144*n*1
World Bank, 78, 223, 385*n*2
World Development Indicators, 73

World Development Report 2004, 68, 71, 96, 313
World Fertility Survey, 21, 44–45, 55*n*21
World Health Organization, 313
The World Health Report 2000, 313

Y

Yellow star facilities, 330–32
Yellow Star Program, Uganda, 33, 330–32

Z

Zimbabwe, 155, 157